# PHILOSOPHY OF MIND SERIES

*Series Editor*
David J. Chalmers, University of Arizona

*Self Expressions*
Minds, Morals, and the Meaning of Life
Owen Flanagan

*The Conscious Mind*
In Search of a Fundamental Theory
David J. Chalmers

*Deconstructing the Mind*
Stephen P. Stich

*The Human Animal*
Personal Identity without Psychology
Eric Olson

*Minds and Bodies*
Philosophers and Their Ideas
Colin McGinn

*What's Within?*
Nativism Reconsidered
Fiona Cowie

*Purple Haze*
The Puzzle of Consciousness
Joseph Levine

*Consciousness and Cognition*
A Unified Account
Michael Thau

*Thinking without Words*
José Luis Bermúdez

*Identifying the Mind*
Selected Papers of U. T. Place
Edited by George Graham and
Elizabeth R. Valentine

*A Place for Consciousness*
Probing the Deep Structure of the Natural World
Gregg Rosenberg

*Three Faces of Desire*
Timothy Schroeder

*Gut Reactions*
A Perceptual Theory of Emotion
Jesse J. Prinz

# Gut Reactions

## A Perceptual Theory of Emotion

Jesse J. Prinz

OXFORD
UNIVERSITY PRESS
2004

# OXFORD
## UNIVERSITY PRESS

Oxford   New York
Auckland   Bangkok   Buenos Aires   Cape Town   Chennai
Dar es Salaam   Delhi   Hong Kong   Istanbul   Karachi   Kolkata
Kuala Lumpur   Madrid   Melbourne   Mexico City   Mumbai   Nairobi
São Paulo   Shanghai   Taipei   Tokyo   Toronto

Copyright © 2004 by Oxford University Press, Inc.

Published by Oxford University Press, Inc.
198 Madison Avenue, New York, New York 10016

www.oup.usa.org

Library of Congress Cataloging-in-Publication Data
Prinz, Jesse J.
Gut reactions : a perceptual theory of emotion / by Jesse J. Prinz.
p. cm.—(Philosophy of mind series)
Includes bibliographical references and index.
ISBN 0-19-515145-3
1. Emotions. 2. Perception. 3. Psychophysiology.
I. Title. II. Series.
BF531.P75      2004
152.4—dc22       2004050073

1 3 5 7 9 8 6 4 2

Printed in the United States of America
on acid-free paper

*For Rachel*

# Preface

## Gut Reactions

*It is now known that the sentiments and emotions reside in the stomach.*

—Ambrose Beirce

Emotions play on central stage in our lives. They are what we live for, and what we live to avoid. The thrill of a victory, and the torment of defeat. The satisfaction of an afternoon with an old friend, the painful nag of regret. Without emotion, there is nothing but dull movement, reflex, and routine. Despite their obvious importance, emotions have not always been a prominent topic of research within cognitive science. Cognitive science purports to be an encompassing, interdisciplinary study of the mind. A standard textbook in cognitive science is likely to have chapters on perception, attention, memory, categorization, language, and even consciousness but, oddly, no chapter on the emotions. One reason for such neglect is that cognitive scientists have a longstanding investment in the view that the mind is some kind of computer, and they have had difficulty understanding emotion in computational terms. Another reason for the neglect is that the emotions have been extensively investigated by clinical psychologists, including psychoanalysts. Cognitive scientists have tried to distance themselves from those who study disordered minds.

Emotion research flourished during these decades of neglect. It just failed to capture the attention of many card-carrying cognitive scientists. That is now changing. Recent advances, especially advances in neuroscience, have brought emotions back into center stage. As interest in emotion research grows, new investigators are discovering some of the deep divisions that veteran investigators have long known. There is little consensus on what emotions are. The number of theories trails just behind the number of theorists.

In this book, I add to that growing list. One might wonder whether such an exercise is advisable. With so many theories already out there, do we really need another one? Obviously, I would not have written the book if I didn't think the answer was yes. We need another theory precisely because there are so many theories out there. Some existing theories have emphasized different aspects of

the emotions at the expense of others. Other existing theories have tried to accommodate too many aspects by cobbling together components that belong apart.
The theory I defend is an attempt, in part, at a synthesis. I try to provide a simple, uniform account with ample explanatory power. The theory is an attempt to
reconcile a number of debates in the emotion literature. It bridges the gap between cognitive and noncogntive theories and between biological reductionism
and social constructionism. It is also a Procrustean theory, severing off limbs that
should not weigh down accounts of what the emotions are.

   The theory that I defend is not entirely new. It is a variation of an account that
was pioneered by William James and Karl Lange and has recently been resusci-
tated by Antonio Damasio. According to this tradition, emotions are perceptions
of patterned changes in the body. More informally, emotions are gut reactions.
Theories of this kind have never been popular in philosophy or psychology. They
seem ill equipped to explain many of the things that a theory of emotions should
account for. Most notably, they fail to explain the significance of emotions. Emotions contribute to reasoning, action, and the election of ends. They are triggered
by judgments and amenable to cultural influence. They are central to our comprehension of morality and other lofty domains (as I shall argue in the sequel
to this book). How do palpitations, pangs, and twinges in the gut play these
kinds of roles? This book is an attempt to answer that question. I defend a Jamesian theory with smarts. So, rather than adding to the proliferation of theories, I
hope to show that an old theory can be modified to do the work of many of its
competitors.

I was fortunate to receive considerable feedback and support while writing this
book. Robert Miller of Oxford University Press and Dave Chalmers have been
patient, kind, and understanding. I was lucky to receive detailed and hugely helpful comments on the manuscript from Paul Griffiths, Aaron Ben-Ze'ev, and
anonymous referees from OUP. Many more imperfections could have been
avoided if I had followed all of their excellent advice. Jonathan Prinz helped me
locate dozens of typos. Paul Griffiths deserves further thanks for many useful discussions and for his gracious support. His work on the emotions has been a great
source of inspiration for me and for other newcomers to the field. Bob Solomon
also deserves thanks for support and inspiration and for his years of dedication to
emotion research.

   I have also benefited from valuable discussions with numerous people, including Kathy Bradfield, Louis Charland, Andy Clark, Tim Crane, Joe Cruz,
Bob Gordon, Pat Greenspan, Matteo Mamelli, Batya Mesquita, Simon Moore,
Dominic Murphy, David Papineau, Hannah Pickard, Jessica Phelan, Richard
Samuels, Laura Sizer, Barry Smith, Chandra Sripada, Steve Stich, members of
the Washington University emotion journal club, students in the Griffiths emotion
seminar, and students in my own emotion seminars at Washington University and
the California Institute of Technology. I am grateful to my wonderful colleagues

at Washington University, California Institute of Technology, the University of London, and the University of North Carolina at Chapel Hill for their support.

I have presented material from this book at various campuses, including Caltech, Chapel Hill, Mt. Holyoke, Stirling, Sussex, the University of Missouri at St. Louis, the University of York, University College London, Williams College, and Yale. I also presented material at conferences, including those of the American Philosophical Association, the Association for the Scientific Study of Consciousness, the International Society for Research on Emotions, the King's College conference on Emotion, Evolution, and Rationality, and the Royal Institute of Philosophy conference on Philosophy and the Emotions. I am grateful to audiences in all of these places.

Thanks are due, finally, to my family. My parents and my older brother were my emotional tutors growing up, and they had to endure every one of my tantrums. Rachel Bernstein was the sine qua non while writing this book, and the object of my fondest emotions.

# Contents

# Gut Reactions

# 1

## *Introduction*
## Piecing Passions Apart

### *Elements of Emotion*

Emotions are typically elicited by external events. You might have an emotional response to winning a contest, for example. And you might have a very different emotional response when you fail to win. Consider all the internal changes that take place when such events occur. First, there is a thought. Perhaps it is the realization that you have been awarded a coveted prize. Perhaps it is the realization that the prize you so desperately wanted has gone to someone else. Then comes a tide of physiological changes. If you realize you won the prize, your mouth may stretch into an irrepressible grin. Your face may flush red. Your eyes may glisten. Your heart may bound with excitement. If the news is bad, your head may drop. A lump may swell in your throat as tears well in your eyes. These two possible events may also have disparate effects on attention and memory. Winning may illuminate the scene around you with an electrical current of new possibilities. Memories of past achievements and self-congratulatory thoughts may flood your head. Losing may cast your surround into a drab gray. You may dredge up memories of past disappointments. You may suffocate under the oppressive weight of your piteous self-image. The events will also prompt a compulsion to act. Victory may infuse you with the urge to leap. A loss may send you searching for a hole to crawl in. Of course, all of these changes will also be occasioned by conscious feelings: a heavenly tingle or an insufferable pang.

Typical emotion episodes, like the two scenarios just considered, contain a number of components. There are thoughts, bodily changes, action tendencies, modulations of mental processes such as attention, and conscious feelings. But which of these things *is* the emotion? Suppose we decide that winning a coveted prize induces "elation." What part of the episode does that label designate? Does one single component in the cascade of changes stand out as the emotion? Is elation a feeling? Is it a thought or an action tendency? Might the emotion term refer to more than one component? Might it refer to the episode as a whole? If we were to subtract a part of the cascade of changes, would the emotion remain? Can any given part be subtracted without losing the emotion, or are some parts essential? Call this the Problem of Parts.

### Theories of Emotion

#### From Parts to Theories

Different theories of emotions offer different response to the Problem of Parts. Some have privileged a single component of our emotion episodes, and others have included them all. Folk psychology, our commonsense conception of the mind, tends to privilege conscious feelings. We ordinarily regard feelings as the essence of emotions. If a state did not feel like anything, it could not be a state of elation. To test folk conceptions, Jaak Panksepp (2000) asked people from different walks of life to rank various emotion components in order of importance (including feelings, thoughts, and changes in the autonomic nervous system). Almost all groups of subjects rated feelings most important. The only subjects who did not were a group of college philosophy majors, who claimed that thoughts were more important!

Philosophical biases not withstanding, our ordinary intuitions make it tempting to say that emotions are simply feelings. Being elated is feeling a certain way. This is called the *feeling theory*.

One might wonder where emotional feelings come from. One answer is that they come from the body. Common sense tends to assume that the bodily changes occur only after an emotion is experienced. We feel elated and our hearts race; we feel embarrassed and we blush. At the end of the nineteenth century, William James (1884) and Karl Lange (1885)[1] independently arrived at the conclusion that common sense gets things backward. Bodily changes precede our emotional experiences. Our hearts race, and we feel elated. If James and Lange are right, then emotional experiences are experiences of various changes in the body. We feel our hearts race, our faces smile, our lungs contract, our muscles tense, our palms sweat, and so on. At the start of this chapter, I suggested that emotions are often felt as pangs and tingles. These feelings may derive from changes in the body as well. A tingling feeling can come from erection of the papillae in the skin; a pang can come from a spasm in the digestive track.

In support of his view, James and Lange ask their readers to imagine feeling an emotion and then to imagine systematically subtracting away the feelings of corresponding bodily states. Imagine feeling elated without feeling your heart racing. James and Lange think that this exercise in mental subtraction musters

---

[1]Lang was a Danish physiologist. James, of course, was a pioneer in psychology and a central contributor to the pragmatist movement in American philosophy.

strong support for their theory: once bodily feelings are gone, there seems to be nothing left to the emotional experience.

One can combine the James-Lange proposal about the source of emotional feelings with the feeling theory of emotions. If emotions are feelings, and emotional feelings are feelings of bodily changes, then emotions are feelings of bodily state changes. As James says, "our feeling of the [bodily] changes as they occur *is* the emotion," (1884 p. 190).[2] Call this the *somatic feeling theory* (depicted in fig. 1.1).

Emotion researchers tend to use the term "somatic" broadly. On a narrow use, the "somatic system" refers to the part of the nervous system that receives information about the muscles of the body. In this context, however, the term "somatic" encompasses any part of the body. Somatic states include states of the respiratory system, circulatory system, digestive system, musculoskeletal system, and endocrine system. A somatic change can be a change of facial expression, an increase in heart rate, a secretion of hormones, and so on. Lange focuses his attention on the vasomotor system, which regulates blood flow, but James thought that the range of bodily states underlying emotional experience is much more inclusive. James talks of changes in the viscera, facial expressions, and instrumental actions—everything from tremors and tears to striking out in rage.

The somatic feeling theory has enjoyed a recent revival under the influence of the neuroscientist Antonio Damasio (1994). With James, Damasio argues that emotional experiences are experiences of changes in the body. But his theory differs from James's in several respects. First, Damasio expands the range of bodily states underlying our emotions to include states of the "internal milieu." Emotions can register changes in the levels of chemicals in the brain, such as changes in hormone levels caused by the endocrine system.

Second, Damasio emphasizes the possibility that emotional response can occur in the absence of bodily changes when brain centers ordinarily associated with bodily change are active. The brain can enter the kind of state it would be in if various bodily changes had taken place, in the absence of those changes. This is

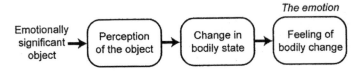

*Figure 1.1.*    The somatic feeling theory.

[2]Ellsworth (1994) has argued that James's considered view may have been a bit different. In a later article, James suggests that emotions often require thoughts (see James, 1894). This suggests a reading according to which emotional *feelings* are sensations of the body but emotions themselves include the judgments that precede those feelings. Reisenzein, Meyer, and Schützwohl (1995) have criticized this interpretation on the grounds that James explicitly identifies emotions with bodily sensations in both his 1884 article and again in *The Principles of Psychology* (James, 1890). I side with Reisenzein. Thoughts may regularly precede emotions, but they are not constituent parts.

analogous to the supposition that we can form a visual image of a red apple when our retinae are not being stimulated. Sensory areas of the brain can be activated endogenously. Damasio calls the pathway that leads to endogenous stimulation of somatic brain areas the "as-if loop": when this pathway is used, the brain functions as if the body had been perturbed in an emotionally relevant way. In a footnote, James anticipates Damasio's as-if loop proposal, saying:

> it is of course possible that the cortical centres normally percipient of . . . organic sensations due to real bodily change, should become *primarily* excited in brain-disease, and give rise to an hallucination of the changes being there . . . Trance, ecstasy, &c., offer analogous examples,—not to speak of ordinary dreaming. (1884, n.4), p. 199n.4

James does not consider the possibility that everyday emotional experiences also bypass the body. Damasio goes a step beyond James in this regard. He suspects that emotions may bypass the body quite regularly. Just as visual brain centers become active when we form visual images of objects, somatic brain centers become active when we imagine undergoing an emotion. Neither case requires an actual stimulus (i.e., a visually perceived object or a bodily change).

The third contrast between Damasio and James is the most important. Like James, Damasio argues that emotional feelings are feelings of bodily changes. But Damasio (1994) does not imply that emotions are exhausted by feelings. The brain can register changes in bodily states without conscious awareness. Those unconscious neural responses to changes in bodily states count as emotions for Damasio. Emotions *can* be conscious, but they need not be. Thus, Damasio holds a *somatic theory* of emotion, and a somatic theory of emotional feelings, but not a somatic feeling theory of emotion (fig. 1.2).

The link between emotions and bodily response is no accident. As I remarked earlier, many of the bodily changes that cooccur with emotions prepare us for behavioral response. Changes in our muscles prepare us for movement, and a racing heart supplies the body with blood. No one observed the connection between body changes and emotion better than Darwin (1872/1998). For example, Darwin surmised that our hair stands on end when we are afraid because in earlier, hairier mammals this would have increase apparent body size, scaring off predators.

Both James and Damasio have called on Darwin for inspiration. But Darwin's

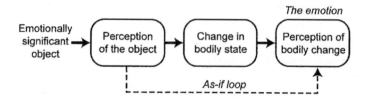

*Figure 1.2.* Damasio's somatic theory.

observations about the link between emotion and overt physical responses have also inspired another kind of account. Rather than identifying emotions with neuronal responses to bodily changes or bodily feelings, one might identify emotions with the behaviors to which bodily changes dispose us.

This view appealed to Gilbert Ryle. Ryle (1949, chap. 4) argues that, while emotion terms can be used in a variety of ways, they usually do not refer to inner feelings or episodes. Most are "liabilities" or dispositions to behave in various ways. Ryle (1949, p. 97) says that to be "in a panic is, for that moment, to be liable to do some such things as stiffen or shriek, or to be unable to finish one's sentence, or remember where the fire escape is to be found." Similar views can be found in the pages of the behaviorist B. F. Skinner, who says: "the names of the so-called emotions serve to classify behaviors with respect to various circumstances which affect its probability" (1953, p. 162). In the same passage Skinner offers an example: "The 'angry' man shows an increased probability of striking, insulting, or otherwise inflicting injury and a lowered probability of aiding, favoring, comforting, or making love." Call this a *behavioral theory*.

J. B. Watson, the founder of behaviorism, defends a somewhat different behavioral theory. Watson (1919) claims that there are innate behavioral dispositions associated with certain emotions. Babies express distress when constrained and joy when gently stroked. They cry when hampered and coo when pampered. Watson is more radical than Ryle. Rather than identifying emotions with dispositions to cry and coo, as Ryle might, Watson observes that crying and cooing are responses to reinforcing stimuli. Emotions are not behavioral dispositions but rather are behavioral responses to rewards and punishments. This could be described as a *behavioral conditioning theory*.

Some researchers find the appeal to behavioral responses overly restrictive. Emotions modulate responses, but not all of those responses are overt behaviors. In recent years, there has been increasing interest in the effects that emotions have on operations inside the mind. Behaviorists abhor appeals to inner states and processes. Modern cognitive scientists believe that such appeals are necessary for explaining how we work. The behavioral conditioning theory has been adapted by some recent authors who are more partial to talk of inner states. Rolls (1999) is one example. Like Watson, Rolls defines emotions as responses to rewards and punishments, but, unlike Watson, he regards emotions as internal states. As responses to rewards and punishments, emotions are still closely linked to behavior on Rolls's view.

Other researchers have dropped the link to behavior. Cognitive scientists have developed detailed accounts of internal systems of categorization, memory, attention, and reasoning. These faculties interact with emotions in systematic ways. In studies of memory, it is easier to recall events when we are in emotional states that are congruent with the events that we are recalling (Bower, 1981). In categorization studies, positive emotions tend to promote the use of stereotypes (Bless, Schwarz, & Kemmelmeier, 1996). Positive emotions also help us to reason in ways that are open-minded, optimistic, and creative. We have an easier time solving problems that require novel applications of familiar materials (Isen, Daubman, & Nowicki, 1987). Negative emotions tend to promote more narrow attentional focus. Anxiety makes us attend to threatening objects (MacLeod & Mathews, 1991; Öhman, Flykt, & Esteves, 2001). Sadness makes us more pessimistic and sensitive to our flaws. This actually leads to a more accurate self-conception—a depressing phenomenon known as "depressive realism" (Alloy & Abrahamson, 1988). For example, people with depression are less likely than nondepressives to have illusions of control when performing tasks that involve a considerable element of chance. Some researches have concluded that emotions can be identified with such systematic changes in faculties of attention, memory, and reasoning. Call this the *processing mode theory*. Oatley and Johnson-Laird (1987) argue that the processing mode theory applies to an important set of emotions, including anger, anxiety, happiness, and sadness (also see Sizer [2000] for a processing mode theory of moods).

So far, I have considered theories that identify emotions with feelings, neural responses to bodily states, behavioral responses, and modulations in cognitive operations. Conspicuously absent from this list are theories that implicate the thoughts associated with emotional response. Thinking often figures prominently in emotion episodes. If someone asks you out on a date, you will almost certainly form beliefs and desires pertaining to that request. Some of those beliefs and desires can have a major impact on the resulting emotion. If you believe your suitor is a dangerous stalker, you will become afraid. If you have reason to think the invitation is a joke, you will be angered. If the request accords with your desires, you will be elated. These observations suggest that emotions are often contingent on having certain thoughts. Some researchers have generalized the conclusion. They claim that thoughts, or "cognitions," are essential to our emotions. This is called a *cognitive theory* of the emotions.

A *pure cognitive theory* claims that emotions are identical to thoughts. A pure cognitive theorist might define fear as a belief that there is a danger present and a desire to avoid danger. Earlier I noted that philosophy students are prone to think that thoughts are especially integral to emotions. It is no surprise, then, that cognitive theories have been ardently defended by philosophers.

The earliest known pure cognitive theories owe a debt to the Stoics. In the third century B.C.E., Chrysippus defended the view that emotions are hasty beliefs. Elation in winning a prize would be a judgment that the prize is a good thing (see Diogenes Laertius, 1925). Pure cognitive theories continue to garner support. Bedford (1957) argues against the equation of emotions with feelings, saying that mere feelings, unlike emotions, are not amenable to rational assessment (see also Pitcher, 1965). Bedford thinks that emotions must be cognitive. Solomon (1976) also defends a cognitive view. He says that emotions are evaluative judgments that provide the structure of our world. Anger consists of an intense judgment that one has been wronged. This judgment presents (Solomon might say "constructs") the world as being a certain way.

Nussbaum (2001), drawing on the Stoic tradition, defines emotions as judgments assenting to "value-laden appearances." A value-laden appearance is something like an evaluative construal of an event. I might regard a death in the family as a grave loss that will make it harder to flourish. So far, this is just a standard cognitive view. But, as I understand her view, it demands something further. To assent to a value-laden appearance, one must form another judgment to the effect that this appearance is justified. This makes her account not just cognitive but metacognitive. Emotions require judgments about judgments.

Some cognitive theorists argue that judgments (or beliefs) are not sufficient for emotions. Desires or wishes also come into play. Gordon (1987) says emotions involve wish-frustration or wish-satisfaction (see also Wollheim, 1999). Warner (1980) appeals to desires. Adapting a bit, he offers the following analysis of enjoyment.

X enjoys experience or activity $\phi$ if and only if:

1. X $\phi$s
2. X's $\phi$ing causes her to:
   Believe that $\phi$ing has certain properties
   Desire that her $\phi$ing occur with those properties
3. X has that desire for its own sake

Like many attempts at philosophical analysis, this one is potentially vulnerable to counterexamples. The suggestion that we can enjoy something only if we believe it has certain desired properties seems to make the cognitive demands on enjoyment too great. Intuitively a person (or animal) can enjoy something without having any beliefs about it, and one's belief that something has desirable properties can be a consequence of that enjoyment rather that the other way around.

Some cognitive theorists look beyond beliefs and desires. Armon-Jones (1989) defines emotions as "imagination-based thoughts." To have an emotion is not to form a judgment about something but to imagine something as if it had certain properties. In a word, having an emotion is forming a construal. Being afraid of something is construing it as dangerous. Robinson (1983) and Roberts (1988) defend theories that combine construal with a desire component. For Roberts, emotions are construals that are based on serious concerns, where concerns include desires, interests, attachments, and aversions. Robinson says emotions are construals caused and colored by desires.

Philosophers sometimes restrict the word "cognitive" to beliefs or judgments (e.g., Nash, 1989). On that use of the term, construal and desire theories do not qualify as pure cognitive theories of emotion, unless, of course, desires are reducible to beliefs. Perhaps a desire is just a belief that something is good. There are philosophers who defend versions of this reduction (e.g., Hájek & Petit, 2004, responding to the critique in Lewis, 1988). Even those philosophers who deny that desires are reducible to beliefs tend to regard them as cognitive states in a broad sense (to be analyzed in chapter 2). Stampe (1987), for example, says a person desires something if it seems that the thing in question would be good,

Table 1.1  Theories that identify emotions with distinct components of an emotion episode

| Emotion episode component | Emotion theory |
| --- | --- |
| Conscious experience | Feeling theories |
| Changes in body and face | Somatic theories |
| Action tendencies | Behavioral theories |
| Modulations of cognitive processes | Processing mode theories |
| Thoughts | Pure cognitive theories |

where seeming is distinguished from believing. If we use the term "cognitive" broadly, then accounts that implicate desires or construals can qualify as purely cognitive. Like the accounts that reduce emotions to beliefs or judgments, most of these accounts distinguish emotions from bodily changes, feelings, and action tendencies.

As this brief survey shows, every obvious part of a typical emotion episode is identified as the essential part of an emotion by some theory. This is summarized in table 1.1.

### Hybrid Theories

Most of the theories considered so far identify emotions with one particular component of an emotion episode. There was at least one exception, however. The somatic feeling theory is, as the name suggests, a feeling theory. It says emotions are conscious experiences. But it also says that emotions are responses to bodily states. That makes it fall into the same class as somatic theories that do not identify emotions with feelings. It would be equally at home in the first or second row of table 1.1.[3] The somatic feeling theory is a hybrid.

Hybrids have been the rule, rather than the exception, in the history of emotion research. Arisitole can be credited with having developed one of the first and most subtle examples. In the *Rhetoric*, Aristotle says that emotions involve both affective feelings, such as distress or pleasure, and desires for action. He suggests that anger, for example, is a distressing desire for revenge. If desires qualify as cognitive, broadly construed, and distress is a feeling, then Aristotle has both a feeling theory and a cognitive theory.[4] Moreover, the desire in question is a desire for action, which makes Aristotle's theory qualify as behavioral as well.

---

[3] Somatic theories in general are also closely related to behavioral theories, insofar as bodily changes prepare us for behavioral response. They do not qualify as behavioral theories, however, because there is a difference between the neural responses to bodily states and the behavioral dispositions afforded by bodily states.

[4] Aristotle may also be interpreted as saying that anger reguires a belief to the effect that one has been slighted. This belief may be separable from the desire component of an emotion.

There is even some evidence that Aristotle identified a role for the body in his theory of the emotions. In the *De Anima*, Aristotle says that mental states, including emotions, have both matter and form. The matter is question is the body, and the form can be understood as the role or function a mental state plays. Aristotle speculates that anger is realized by boiling blood in the heart. Emotions are, thus, felt, action-directed, cognitive states of the body.

Another hybrid is defended by Descartes (1649/1988). Descartes believed that emotions arise when the senses (located in the brain) detect something good or bad and then cause the body to prepare a response. The transition from sensing to acting is enacted by the animal spirits, which are minute particles that relay messages between the body and brain. Descartes believed that the animal spirits were also the messengers between the brain and the soul, by way of the pineal gland. Emotions (or "passions") arise when the soul perceives the movements of the animal spirits that mediate between senses and action. Experiencing an emotion is, thus, experiencing our bodies preparing for action. In this respect, Descartes is a forerunner to James and Lange. But his is not a pure somatic theory. He says many emotions also involve a will to action and a thought. For example, he defines fear as a desire for something coupled with the belief that that thing is unlikely to be attained, and hatred involves the will to be separated from something deemed hurtful. Here Descartes sounds more like Aristotle than like James.

David Hume's (1739/1978) theory of emotion also qualifies as a hybrid. He defines emotions as "impressions," which is his term for conscious feelings. More accurately, Hume defines emotions as second-order impressions. They are impressions caused by other impressions or by ideas. For example, when one encounters a charging boar, one forms a conscious visual image of the boar, which is an impression, and that image causes a feeling of fear, which is another impression. Hume says that emotions represent neither the impressions that cause them nor any external conditions (such as a charging boar). Emotions do not represent anything at all: "A passion . . . contains not any representative quality" (1739/1988, II.iii.3). They are feelings. But it would be misleading to say that emotions are *merely* feelings for Hume. He also thinks that emotions have motivational force. They contain desires, which are a special class of feelings that compel us to act. Fear may contain the felt desire to flee. A desire to flee is, for Hume, an action tendency. It has, all else being equal, the force to make us act. It would be accurate to describe Hume as holding both a feeling theory and a behavioral theory. In addition, Hume says that emotions are the effects and causes of various impressions and ideas. In some cases, the ideas that cause or issue from an emotion are indispensable, insofar as they are needed to distinguish that emotion from other feelings. For example, Hume defines pride as a feeling that causes one to think about one's self. The self is understood by an idea or a collection of ideas. An emotion qualifies as pride only if these ideas come to mind when it occurs. In this respect, Hume can be said to be groping toward a cognitive theory. His theory implicates feeling, action, and thought.

Aristotle, Descartes, and possibly Hume can be regarded as defending *impure cognitive theories* of emotion. They afford a central role to cognition, but they also implicate other kinds of states. Another impure cognitive theory is defended by Spinoza (1677/1994). For him, emotions are thoughts accompanied by pleasures and pains. Emotions combine cognitive states with feelings. Some philosophers continue to defend views of this kind. For example, Greenspan (1988) argues that emotions are compounds of evaluative judgments and "affective states," which she defines as feelings of comfort or discomfort. Fear is discomfort at the thought that danger looms. Nash (1989) argues that emotions involve evaluative judgments and attentional focus. The angry person believes that she has been wronged, and focuses, often obsessively, on the offending situation. Nash calls this a pure cognitive theory, but on my taxonomy it actually combines a cognitive theory with a processing mode theory.

Psychologists have also defended impure cognitive theories. Some of these psychologists make specific assumptions about the order in which the cognitive and noncognitive components of an emotion occur. Consider the theory of Schachter and Singer (1962). They argue that emotions involve both bodily changes ("physiological states") and cognitive interpretations of those states. This requires that the bodily change occur before the cognitive interpretation. Under ordinary circumstances, a perceived event causes arousal and then the arousal is interpreted as deriving from that perceived event. The state of arousal is "labeled" as having some emotional significance. For example, elation arises when my heart begins to palpitate, and I attribute those palpitations to elation. If I were to label my racing heart differently, say as fear or anger, it would comprise a different emotion. If I fail to assign emotional significance to my racing heart, it doesn't qualify as an emotion at all. Call this a *cognitive labeling theory* (fig. 1.3).

The cognitive labeling theory makes an interesting prediction. A state of arousal may be interpreted as resulting from some emotionally significant event even when it really results from another source. If emotions are states of arousal that have been labeled as owing to some external event, it should be possible for emotions to arise through misattribution. This possibility is represented by a dotted line in figure 1.3. In a famous experiment, Schachter and Singer attempted to support the cognitive labeling theory by showing that emotions can arise in just this way.

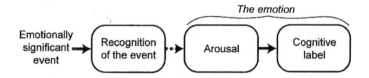

*Figure 1.3.*    Schachter and Singer's cognitive labeling theory. The dotted line indicates that the arousal need not result from the perception of the event that is interpreted as causing it.

In the experiment, subjects were injected with a substance that they were told was a special vitamin that was being tested for its ability to improve eyesight. They were then asked to sit in a waiting room for twenty minutes before an eye exam, so the injection could begin working. In reality, the substance was adrenalin, which causes heightened autonomic responses, such as a racing heart and heavy breathing. Some subjects were told to expect these side effects and others were not. All subjects were then placed in one of two conditions.

Some subjects were asked to fill out a questionnaire in the waiting room. The questions start out fairly innocuously and get progressively more offensive. The offense culminates with a question that asks: "With how many men (other than your father) has your mother had extramarital relationships?" The multiple choice options for answering the question are "(a) 4 and under; (b) 5–9; (c) 10 and over." A stooge who has been placed in the waiting room expresses increasing aggravation with the questionnaire and finally tears it up and storms out. This is the anger condition. The other subjects have a very different experience in the waiting room. They receive no questionnaire and are accompanied by a stooge who makes paper airplanes, stands on a table, and plays with hula hoops. This is the euphoria condition.

All subjects were observed during these conditions. Those who had been informed about the effects of the injection exhibit little emotional response in either condition. Those who had not been informed that the drug would have bodily effects react differently in the two conditions. Uninformed subjects in the anger condition show negative emotional response, agreeing with the stooge's complaints and expressing outrage. Uninformed subjects in the euphoria condition exhibit signs of amusement and participate in the stooge's antics. Schachter and Singer use these results to argue that emotion depends on interpretation of bodily states. They say that the bodily states produced by the injection are the same for all subjects, but they are interpreted as signs of anger by some, as signs of euphoria by others, and as mere drug side effects by others. Context and background knowledge are used to label bodily states, and the labeling process is presumed to be cognitive. I return to Schachter and Singer's theory in chapter 3.

Schachter and Singer imply that autonomic response often proceeds cognitive labeling. Other impure cognitive theories argue for the reverse order. According to these accounts, emotions arise when we form a thought about a situation and that thought gives rise to some other state, which may be a feeling, a bodily change, an action tendency, or some combination of these. Call these *cognitive cause theories* (fig. 1.4).

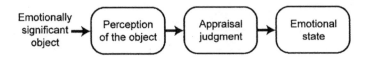

*Figure 1.4.*   The basic structure of a cognitive cause theory.

Cognitive cause theories have been extremely popular among psychologists (and among some philosophers; see Lyons, 1980). The prevailing cognitive cause theories in psychology can be called *dimensional appraisal theories*. They deserve special attention.

## Dimensional Appraisal Theories

The term "appraisal" became popular in emotion research under the influence of Magda Arnold (1960). As Arnold uses the term, to appraise something is to see it as affecting oneself in some way that matters (1960, p. 171). According to dimensional appraisal theory, all emotions include appraisal judgments—judgments to the effect that one is facing a predicament that matters. Dimensional appraisal theorists also claim that those appraisal judgments are drawn from a common set of appraisal dimensions. On Arnold's account, three dimensions are involved. We assess whether the predicament we are in is beneficial or harmful, whether it involves objects that are present or absent, and whether those objects are difficult or easy to attain or avoid. Different answers to these appraisal questions yield different emotions. For example, elation or "joy" involves objects that are beneficial, present, and easy to attain. The general structure of a dimensional appraisal theory is given in figure 1.5.

Critics of Arnold have worried that three simple dimensions may not offer enough detail to distinguish all emotions. For example, anger and disgust are different emotions, but they may involve objects that are harmful, present, and difficult to avoid. This is not a fatal objection to dimensional appraisal theories. It shows only that Arnold's appraisal dimensions are insufficient. To rectify the problem, some researchers have proposed new appraisal dimensions that allow us to make more fine-grained distinctions between emotions.

One of the most fully elaborated appraisal theories owes to Richard Lazarus. Lazarus (1991) defines appraisals as evaluations of what one's relationship to the environment implies for one's well-being. His list of appraisal dimensions is twice as long as Arnold's. The first three appraisals (called primary appraisals) establish that something is emotionally significant, and the second three (called secondary appraisals) pertain to the resources one has available for coping.

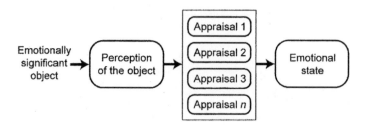

*Figure 1.5.*    The structure of a dimensional appraisal theory.

Lazarus's first dimension is *goal relevance*, which asks whether a given transaction with an object, situation, or event is relevant to one's goals. If it is not, no emotion will ensue. Next there is the dimension of *goal congruence*. We assess whether the transaction thwarts or facilitates our goals. If the former, a negative emotion ensues; if the latter, a positive emotion ensues. Third, we assess the *type of ego-involvement*. This dimension identifies what is at stake during a transaction. Possibilities include one's identity, moral values, life goals, and the well-being of other people. The fourth dimension establishes *blame or credit*. We determine who (or what) is accountable in a transaction and whether the credit or blame should be assigned. We also estimate our *coping potential*, the extent to which we will be able to deal with the results of the transaction. Finally, there is *future expectancy*, which is an estimation of the likelihood that things will change to become more or less congruent with our goals.

To illustrate these appraisal dimensions, consider the case of anger. According to Lazarus, anger occurs when one makes the following appraisals.

*Appraisals that Generate Anger*

*Goal relevance:* relevant
*Goal congruence:* incongruent
*Type of ego-involvement:* self-esteem, social-esteem, or identity
*Blame or credit:* someone is to blame
*Coping potential:* attack is viable
*Future expectancy:* goal congruence predicted to increase by attack

Different combinations of values along the same appraisal dimensions constitute different emotions. With more appraisal dimensions, and a wide range of values available for filling out those dimensions, Lazarus's theory allows for many more combinations than Arnold's theory.

Lazarus refers to products of his six appraisal dimensions as "molecular appraisals." They correspond to the actual judgments that he thinks people make before arriving at an emotion. These judgments can be summarized. The molecular appraisals associated with anger, for example, amount to the recognition that one has been the target of a demeaning offense. Lazarus calls this kind of summary a "molar appraisal." Molar appraisals are not the actual judgments we make; they are the gist of those judgments. Molar appraisals capture what Lazarus calls "core relational themes." A core relational theme is a relation that pertains to well-being. Lazarus's list of core relational themes is reproduced in table 1.2.

The distinction between molar and molecular appraisals may be understood in terms of Marr's (1982) levels of analysis. Marr says we can identify the task that a mental system is designed to perform (the "computational level"), the rules and representations by which it performs that task (the "algorithmic level"), and the physical stuff that implements those rules and representations (the "implementation level"). The molar level may be situated at Marr's computational level. Core

Table 1.2 Lazarus's core relational themes, reprinted from Lazarus (1991, Table 3.4, p. 122) with permission from Oxford University Press.

| Emotion | Core relational theme |
|---|---|
| Anger | A demeaning offense against me and mine |
| Anxiety | Facing uncertain, existential threat |
| Fright | Facing an immediate, concrete, and overwhelming physical danger |
| Guilt | Having transgressed a moral imperative |
| Shame | Having failed to live up to an ego-ideal |
| Sadness | Having experienced an irrevocable loss |
| Envy | Wanting what someone else has |
| Jealousy | Resenting a third party for loss or threat to another's affection |
| Disgust | Taking in or being too close to an indigestible object or idea (metaphorically speaking) |
| Happiness | Making reasonable progress toward the realization of a goal |
| Pride | Enhancement of one's ego-identity by taking credit for a valued object or achievement, either one's own or that of some group with whom we identify |
| Relief | A distressing goal-incongruent condition that has changed for the better or gone away |
| Hope | Fearing the worst but yearning for better |
| Love | Desiring or participating in affection, usually but not necessarily reciprocated |
| Compassion | Being moved by another's suffering and wanting to help |

relational themes are not explicitly represented attitudes. Instead they capture the basic situations that emotions are designed to discriminate. Core relational themes encapsulate collections of more specific appraisals that are explicitly represented. These molecular appraisals correspond to Marr's algorithms. They are the actual representations used in arriving at an emotion state.

Studying Lazarus's list of core themes is instructive, because it helps us understand why appraisal theories have appealed to so many researchers. There is a deep intuition that emotions are meaningful. They are not simply arbitrary feelings. Instead they inform us about our relationship to the world, they embody our convictions, and they factor intelligibly into our decisions in life. The actual appraisals used in arriving at an emotion are, according to most appraisal theorists, more complex than the formulas on Lazarus's list of themes, but the themes compellingly portray the essence of each emotion.

Dimensional appraisal theories constitute one of the dominant forces in contemporary emotion research. Similar theories have been developed by de Rivera (1984), Weiner (1985), Scherer (1984), Roseman (1984), Smith and Ellsworth (1985), Frijda (1986), and others. These authors disagree about the specific dimensions of appraisal, but there is considerable convergence. Roseman, Spindel, and Jose (1990) show that the appraisal dimensions in any one theory often map onto dimensions in other theories. The details of these dimensions are not essential for present purposes. What matters are the underlying theoretical commitments. These authors believe that emotions follow on the heels of appraisals, they view appraisals as cognitive states, and they partition appraisals into a number of distinct dimensions. These theoretical commitments will all be challenged in the next chapter.

### *From Parts to Plenty*

### The Problem of Plenty

Both Arnold and Lazarus can be described as subscribing to cognitive cause theories. They say that emotions are caused by appraisals. Something would not count as an emotion if it were not the result of a dimensional appraisal process. But that does not mean that emotions *are* appraisals. Unlike pure cognitive theorists, Arnold and Lazarus do not say that emotions should be identified with the cognitive appraisals that they postulate. They imply that those appraisals are causes, not components, of emotions. At the same time, they regard appraisals as necessary *preconditions* for emotions. Gordon (1987) has a useful analogy. He says that emotions are like sunburns on some cognitive theories. A sunburn does not contain the sun as a constituent part, but it can qualify as a sunburn only if it was caused by the sun. The sun is a causal precondition. Likewise, appraisals are causal preconditions for emotions, according to Lazarus and Arnold. Something counts as an emotion only if it was triggered by an appraisal, and it counts as the particular emotion that it is in virtue of the particular appraisal that caused it.

If appraisals are just necessary preconditions for emotions, what are the emotions themselves? Lazarus and Arnold give slightly different answers. Lazarus (1991, p. 38) says that emotions are "psychophysiological reactions to . . . cognitive appraisals." This makes his account a hybrid between a somatic theory and a cognitive theory. But Lazarus does not stop there. He also says (p. 40) that emotions include action tendencies. His hybrid encompasses a behavioral theory as well.

Arnold defines emotions as felt tendencies toward something judged beneficial or away from something judged harmful. She goes on to say that emotions are accompanied by physiological changes (Arnold, 1960, p. 182). Thus, her theory combines thoughts, feelings, action tendencies, and somatic states.

Other hybrids are equally ambitious. They allege that emotions involve all of the emotion episode components I have been considering. Nico Frijda (1986) offers such an account. Frijda thinks that emotions are, above all else, action tendencies, but he argues that action tendencies can consist of thoughts, feelings, and bodily changes. A similar view can be attributed to Paul Ekman (2003). Ekman identifies emotions with "affect programs," which are complex, evolutionarily determined responses to various environmental conditions. These responses can include facial expressions, physiological changes, evaluations, and action dispositions. I call hybrids of this kind *encompassing theories*.[5]

Encompassing theories are perhaps the ultimate aspiration of most emotion theorists. Researchers want to afford a place to every aspect of an emotional response. There is a preference for inclusion. This is perfectly reasonable. Emotion episodes are complex, and singling out one component as the emotion may obscure that complexity. We can honor complexity by defining emotions as complex states.

Encompassing theories also come at a price. By including everything, one can lose sight of what emotions are all about. One can also lose sight of how the different components hang together. Privileging a single part is a way of drawing attention to the feature that is most fundamental for understanding emotions. An encompassing account that fails to do this suffers from what can be termed the Problem of Plenty.

The Problem of Plenty is the counterpoint to the Problem of Parts. The Problem of Parts asks: What components of an emotion episode are really essential to its being an instance of some particular emotion? The tempting answer is that all parts are essential. The Problem of Plenty then asks: If all parts are essential, how do they hang together into a coherent whole? Put differently, the Problem of Parts asks for essential components, and the Problem of Plenty asks for an essential function of emotions in virtue of which they may have several essential components.

Some hybrids do a better job of facing the Problem of Plenty. To see this, it is useful to divide hybrids into three categories. The first identifies emotions with a single kind of state but argues that sates of that kind correspond to two or more different items on the list of emotional components. Call this a *multifunction hybrid*. The somatic feeling theory is an example. It combines somatic responses and feelings into unified wholes: feelings of somatic responses. Aristotle's theory is a much more encompassing multifunction hybrid. For him, each emotion integrates a feeling, desire, action tendency, and bodily changes. These are not separate parts but separate aspects of a single state.

Other defenders of hybrid theories opt for a different strategy. They define emotions as structured entities, built of several different kinds of states. Call this a *multicomponent* hybrid. Schachter and Singer's account falls into this category. For them, emotions combine bodily states and cognitive labels. These are not sides of a single coin but dissociable elements, which can occur in isolation. Ekman's affect program theory is a more encompassing example of a multicompo-

[5]Defenders of encompassing theories come in two varieties. They either claim that every instance of an emotion contains all of the kinds of components I have been discussing, or they claim that each emotion must contain at least some of these. The latter option allows that different kinds of components can realize emotions on different occasions. For a philosophical example of this kind, see Pitcher (1965). For him, emotions can contain beliefs, behavioral dispositions, and feelings, but none of these components are necessary. Elster (1999) gestures in a similar direction, pointing to many features associated with emotions but resisting the claim that these features are all necessary. He, like Griffiths (1997), suspects that emotions may not be a natural kind.

nent hybrid. For him, emotions can have many parts. Another multicomponent hybrid is defended by Ben Ze'ev (2000). He says that emotions have four parts. There is a feeling, which is a conscious quality of experience; a motivation or action tendency; a cognition, which is a judgment describing the object of the emotion; and finally an evaluation, which is the appraisal that distinguished one emotion from another.

A third kind of hybrid identifies each emotion with a subset of these components but insists that others are necessary preconditions. Call this a *precondition hybrid*. Theories of this kind can be attributed to Lazarus and Arnold. They both insist that emotions *require* cognitions while denying that emotions *are* cognitions. Cognitive appraisals are causal precondition for the occurrence of an emotion. Moreover, Arnold and Lazarus assume that the identity conditions of an emotion cannot be specified without mentioning the appraisals that cause it. Appraisals are individuating preconditions. Hume's view, which defines emotions as feelings with certain ideas as causes and effects, may also fall into this category.

Multifunction hybrids offer the most elegant solution to the Problem of Plenty. The Problem of Plenty asks how the many parts that make up an emotion hang together. A multifunction theory says these parts are not really separable at all; they are really different aspects of coherent, selfsame states. Multicomponent and precondition hybrids are less elegant in this respect. By associating emotions with dissociable parts, they beg the question of coherence. There is no reason to think the Problem of Plenty is insuperable for the defender of such a hybrid, but it does demand attention.

Some defenders of encompassing hybrid theories have attempted to answer the Problem of Plenty by stipulating that some feature of our emotions is a central pivot around which the other features turn. Lazarus says that emotions necessarily involve a number of components, but appraisals are chief among these. Emotions are in the business of identifying things that relate to well-being. Frijda, as I remarked, makes action tendencies especially important in his encompassing theory. The Problem of Plenty asks how emotion components hang together, and the answer may be that one particular component is the key to coherence. The challenge of identifying that component is an aspect of the Problem of Parts. The Problem of Parts leads to the Problem of Plenty, which leads back to the Problem of Parts.

## Coming Attractions

In the chapters that follow, I argue that leading attempts to address these interlocked problems are inadequate. But my primary goal is constructive, not critical. I will propose a positive theory of the emotions. I develop that theory through ten questions, taken up sequentially.

1. Do emotions necessarily involve cognition?
2. What, if anything, do emotions represent?
3. Are emotions a natural kind?

4. Are certain emotions universal and biologically based?
5. Can emotions be culturally determined?
6. How are emotions related to other affective constructs?
7. What distinguishes positive and negative emotions?
8. What is the basis of emotional consciousness?
9. Is emotion a form of perception?
10. Do emotions have many component parts?

In response to the first question, I will argue that emotions are not cognitive. Prevailing cognitive theories of emotion are fundamentally mistaken (chapter 2). In chapter 3, however, I argue that emotions nevertheless represent core relational themes, just as prevailing cognitive theories maintain. Then I take up the question of whether emotions form a coherent class (chapter 4). I argue that they do, rejecting influential arguments to the contrary. Chapters 5 and 6 address the nature/nurture debate. I think all emotions that we care about involve both dimensions. My view is a form of social constructivism, but it builds on a core of biologically basic emotions. I also reject leading constructivist theories, which are overly cognitive in orientation. In chapter 7, I relate emotions to other affective constructs, such as motivations and moods. Moods, I argue, are a special subset of emotions. Motivations are a separate class of mental states, but emotions do have a motivating component. I give an account of that component in my discussion of emotional valence (chapter 8). I reject the view that positive and negative emotions can be distinguished by their conscious feelings. Emotional consciousness is taken up, in more detail, in chapter 9. I present a unified theory that can explain emotional consciousness in the same way as other forms of consciousness.

My answer to the ninth question holds all of the other pieces of the account together. I believe that emotion is quite literally a form of perception. This is consistent with the view of James, Lange, Damasio, and others who relate emotions to the body. Like them, I defend a somatic theory. At the same time, I think existing somatic theories tend to leave too many questions unanswered. In particular, somatic theories do not explain why emotions seem so meaningful, intelligible, and rational. To rectify this deficit, it is important to show that emotions are not merely perceptions of the body but also perceptions of our relations to the world. This book is an attempt to patch a major hole in somatic theories. It is an attempt to bring body, mind, and world together.

I end by briefly returning to the Problem of Parts and the Problem of Plenty. My answer to the final question, elaborated though the following chapters, is that emotions are relatively simple entities, rather than assemblies of multiple parts. But they are simple entities with complex effects and information-processing roles. They can do plenty without a plurality of parts.

# 2

## *Feeling Without Thinking*

### *Emotion and Cognition*

#### A Tale of Two Fears

A friend has convinced you to go on a hike. You are not much for the outdoors because you suffer from a terrible snake phobia. Reluctantly, you go along. As you set out, all concerns quickly drift away. You are having a good time. But then, out of the corner of your eye, you glimpse a long coiled object nestled in the shadows. You freeze, your heart pounds, your breathing becomes strained, your eyes widen.

Now consider another case. You are a student about to take a final exam. Your grade on the exam will determine your grade for the semester and a low grade will prevent you from making the cutoff for a special honor's program that you desperately want to join. The professor begins to distribute the exams. As she approaches your desk with her stack of blue exam books, you freeze, your heart pounds, your breathing becomes strained, your eyes widen.

Both of these cases seem very much alike, but there is an important difference. In the first case, the fear response is triggered by something visual. You may have beliefs that snakes are dangerous, but explicit deliberation to that effect does not necessarily come into play at the moment of your reaction. The very sight of a snake sets you off. It might not even have been a snake. Perhaps it was a coiled rope, or a vine, or a shadow. Perhaps you are quite sure that the snakes in this region are harmless. Still, you react.

In the second case, seeing the exam books may trigger your fear, but the exam books are not terrifying in and of themselves. Seeing blue books in another context would leave you cold. In this context, they are terrifying, and they would certainly be terrifying even if they were not blue. Their actual appearance does not matter. In this situation your response is directly linked to your beliefs about what is riding on the exam. If you did not have those beliefs, if you did not care about the consequences, you might not be afraid.

In short, the second example of fear seems to be more cognitive than the first.

It seems more cognitive in two respects. First, the object of the fear, an exam, is not obviously something that can be recognized or comprehended without cognition. Snakes can be easily recognized by their appearances; exam recognition requires cultural knowledge, verbal skills, and contextual information. Second, the *link* between the object and the fear response seems more cognitive in the second example. Once a snake-phobic person has identified something as a snake, the fear response may follow automatically. Once the exam has been recognized as such, fear may depend on possession of a further belief that the exam poses a threat in some way.

Intuitions about such cases suggest that emotions can differ in their degree of cognitive involvement. Following this insight, one might be tempted to place emotions on a continuum spanning from minimally cognitive to highly cognitive. Some emotion researchers have claimed that emotions can occur without any cognitive involvement at all. Others have criticized this view, arguing that emotions are always essentially cognitive. In chapter 1, I called these noncognitive and cognitive theories, respectively. The divide between these two camps is one of the major fault lines within emotion research. In this chapter and the next I will try to broker a reconciliation.

### Cognitive Theories in Philosophy and Psychology

I introduced cognitive theories in some detail in chapter 1, but it will help to say a little more about what such theories claim and what they have in common. Cognitive theories that have been developed by philosophers differ from those that have been developed by psychologists, but they have much in common.

The majority of philosophers who embrace cognitive theories assume that the cognitions involved in our emotions are propositional attitudes. A propositional attitude is a mental state consisting of a representation of a proposition and an attitude toward that proposition. A proposition is a state of affairs—something that might be described using a declarative sentence such as "It is raining," "Nixon is president," or "Jones will travel to Rome." Attitudes toward these propositions include believing, supposing, desiring, and so on. If one directs an attitude of believing (or supposing or desiring) toward a proposition, the result is a belief (or a supposition or a desire). All these propositional attitudes can be ascribed using a sentence following the word "that," known as a that-clause. Jones believes *that* she will travel to Rome, desires *that* she will travel to Rome, wants it to be the case *that* she will travel to Rome, and so on. In each instance, the that-clause, "that she will travel to Rome," expresses the same state of affairs. This state of affairs is the "propositional object" of Jones's mental state.

The hypothesis that emotions are propositional attitudes is ambiguous. On the one hand, it could mean that emotions can be *directed toward* propositional objects. This is relatively uncontroversial. Most parties agree that a person can be afraid that the sea is shark infested, or angry that the education budget was cut,

or delighted that the circus is coming to town. All of these are propositional attitudes. The emotion is an attitude directed at a propositional object.

The hypothesis that emotions are propositional attitudes can also be interpreted
in another way, which will be my primary concern here. One might say that emotions are *constituted by* propositional attitudes. When one says that Jones is afraid
that the sea is shark infested, one implies that she has mentally represented the
proposition that the sea is shark infested *and* that she has an emotion, fear, directed toward that proposition. Fear can be considered independent of the propositional object it happens to attach to. The hypothesis that emotions are constituted by propositional attitudes entails that fear, considered on its own, is
constituted by a mental state that can be expressed using one or more that-clause.
For example, one might hold the view that emotions are reducible to beliefs. On
a simple version of this approach, fear might be a belief that danger looms. Ac-
cordingly, Jones's fear that the sea is shark infested would be composed of two
propositional attitudes. There is a belief (or suspicion) that the sea is shark infested, and there is a belief that danger looms. The anger is constituted by the
second of these propositional attitudes.

Philosophers who identify emotions with propositional attitudes, in the sense
just described, disagree about what those attitudes are. Some philosophers think
emotions are reducible to beliefs (e.g., the belief that danger looms), and some
think they also involve desires (e.g., the desire to flee). Some philosophers think
that having an emotion is like entertaining a thought rather than like having a belief or desire. One can entertain the thought that danger looms without believing
it (Greenspan, 1988). Likewise, it seems, one can fear something without believing or desiring that it is dangerous.

When one ascribes a propositional attitude, one generally assumes that the person to whom it is ascribed possesses the concepts that correspond to the words in
the that-clause of the ascription. If I say that Jones believes that she will go to
Rome, I assume that Jones has a concept of Rome, a concept of traveling, and a
concept of herself (the "she" in the that-clause). If emotions are constituted, at
least in part, by propositional attitudes, then having an emotion requires possession of the concepts that would be used to ascribe those propositional attitudes.
If fear is a belief that danger looms, then being afraid requires possession of the
concept of danger and the concept of looming. Thus, defenders of cognitive theories make an implicit commitment to the claim that emotions require concepts.
Call this the *conceptualization hypothesis*.

Philosophers who defend cognitive theories tend to say very little about the nature of the concepts used in cognitive states that constitute our emotions. If fear
contains a danger concept, is it the very same danger concept that we deploy
when we have impassionate thoughts about danger? Suppose Jones believes that
traveling alone in the Amazon is dangerous but has no intentions to do so. She
has no fear of traveling in the Amazon. Is the danger concept she deploys when
thinking about dangers that she does not fear the same as the danger concept she
deploys when feeling mortal terror? And, if so, what is the nature of this con-

cept? The prevailing view in philosophy and psychology is that most concepts are complex: they are built up from other concepts (Prinz, 2002; see Fodor, 1998, for a lonely exception). The concept of danger, for example, may "decompose" into the concepts of potentiality and harm. That is to say, one cannot grasp what danger is without understanding what harm is. In saying that fear involves a belief or construal about danger, philosophers tacitly imply that it involves a danger concept that is built up from other concepts. The conceptualization hypothesis tacitly implies that emotions have rich conceptual structure.

On the face of it, the cognitive theories that psychologists defend differ from the theories of philosophers in at least three respects. First, they usually talk of appraisals rather than propositional attitudes. This difference in vocabulary may be superficial. Appraisals, according to most psychologists, take the form of judgments. For example, Lazarus (1991) says the appraisal that anger comprises can be summarized by the judgment that there has been a demeaning offense against me and mine. Judgments are propositional attitudes *par excellence*. Forming the judgment that there has been a demeaning offense, it would seem, requires possession of the concept of being demeaning and being offensive.

The second apparent difference between philosophical and psychological theories is that psychologists tend to regard judgments as preconditions for emotions, rather than constituent parts (recall the precondition hybrids of chapter 1). For example, Lazarus (1991) says that emotions are *caused by* appraisal judgments rather than saying emotions are *identical with* appraisal judgments. But he thinks that such cognitive causes are necessary for emotions and for emotion individuation. In this regard, his theory is comparable to propositional attitude theories in philosophy. No emotion can occur without some corresponding propositional attitude. Using a neutral term, one might say that cognitive theorists in both disciplines assume that emotions are *bound* to propositional attitudes, rather than saying that emotions have propositional attitudes as component parts.

The third apparent difference between psychological and philosophical theories is that psychologists tend to presume that the cognitive aspects of our emotions are highly structured. For Lazarus, anger involves more than a judgment that there has been a demeaning offense. This is a perfectly good summary approximation, but the anger judgment actually decomposes into six different "molecular" appraisals, which I presented in chapter 1. These include appraisals about coping potential, goals, and blame. Each of Lazarus's appraisal dimensions (discussed in chapter 1) can be regarded as a judgment in its own right. When a person has an emotion, she is really forming a group of judgments, and each of these requires possession of the concepts corresponding to the words that would be used to ascribe them.

Lazarus and other psychologists assume that the very same appraisal dimensions underlie all emotions. Philosophers do not usually make this assumption (though see Ben-Ze'ev, 2000). But philosophers and psychologists who defend cognitive theories make similar assumptions about the conceptual prerequisites of emotions. If emotions depend on a collection of highly structured appraisal, emotions require the possession of the concepts that would be named by a description of those appraisals. Like philosophers, psychologists are implicitly committed to the conceptualization hypothesis. The differences between theories in these two disciplines are overshadowed by similarities.

Philosophical and psychological cognitive theories are also united by two other claims. First, according to all cognitive theories, the cognitive components bound to our emotions are not identical to bodily changes or internal states that register bodily changes. Some cognitive theorists maintain that emotions can occur without any somatic component (e.g., Nussbaum, 2001; Solomon, 1976; I discuss this claim in chapter 4). Other cognitive theorists admit that somatic components are necessary parts of emotions, while insisting that nonsomatic cognitive states are necessary as well (e.g., Lazarus, 1991; Lyons, 1980). According to all cognitive theories, the somatic concomitants of emotions must be distinguished from the concomitant propositional attitudes or appraisals. The cognitive components bound to our emotions are something above and beyond the bodily changes or inner states that register bodily changes. In a word, cognitive theorists are united in holding that the cognitive components bound to our emotions are disembodied. Call this the *disembodiment hypothesis.*

A further unifying factor can be termed the *appraisal hypothesis.* As I have shown, cognitive theories in psychology typically identify emotions with appraisals. Appraisals are representations of an organism-environment relationship that bears on well-being. On this definition, the cognitive theories that philosophers defend qualify as appraisal theories as well. Philosophers who identify emotions with propositional attitudes generally assume that those attitudes represent relations that bear on well-being. Philosophers do not decompose emotional cognitions into separate appraisal dimensions that recur in every emotion, but the propositional attitudes that they identify are generally quite similar to the appraisal summaries provided by Lazarus in his table of core relational themes (see table 1.2). Cognitively oriented philosophers and psychologists both think that the cognitive state bound to fear represents danger, for example (e.g., compare Greenspan with Lazarus). Moreover, both parties tend to assume that such appraisals can be used to individuate emotions. What distinguishes two emotions is largely a matter of the themes that they designate: danger, offense, infidelity, self-achievement, and so on.

The three hypotheses just adduced (conceptualization, disembodiment, and appraisal) unify propositional attitude theories and dimensional appraisal theories of emotion. But what about other cognitive theories? Consider, in particular, cognitive labeling theories, in psychology, and construal theories, in philosophy (see chapter 1). According to labeling theories, having an emotion is a matter of assigning an emotional label to a general state of arousal. According to construal theories, having an emotion is seeing something as manifesting certain properties (e.g., fearing snakes is seeing snakes as dangerous). Can these theories be said to embrace the conceptualization, disembodiment, and appraisal hypotheses?

Defenders of labeling theories and construal theories certainly seem to endorse the conceptualization hypothesis. Construing and labeling both involve placing something under a concept. Defenders of these theories also seem to endorse the disembodiment hypothesis. Schachter and Singer's labeling theory explicitly assume that the cognitive component of an emotion is not a bodily state in its own right; it is a label of a bodily state. Defenders of construal theories often argue that bodily states are only contingently associated with our emotions (e.g., Armon-Jones, 1989). Construals are disembodied.

Things are a bit more complicated when we come to the appraisal hypothesis. Construals arguably qualify as appraisals. If Jones construes snakes as dangerous, she is representing snakes as bearing a relation to her that bears on well-being. It is a bit more difficult to fit the cognitive labeling theory into this mold. Labels do not seem to be appraisals in any obvious sense. When we label a bodily state as anger, the label seems to be a representation of that state, not a representation of our relationship to the environment. On closer examination, however, labels may qualify as appraisals. Schachter and Singer regard labels not as unstructured tags but as causal attributions. When we label a state of arousal as anger, we are not simply adding the word "anger" to it, like a caption on a picture. We are forming the judgment that the state of arousal is a consequence of our relationship to the environment. Anger arises, on the cognitive labeling theory, when one interprets a pounding heart as evidence that one is facing a danger. If this interpretation is right, Schachter and Singer regard labels as evaluative judgments. The labeling theory is consistent with the appraisal hypothesis.

I will say little more about construal and appraisal theories in this chapter, because they share many core assumptions with other prevailing cognitive theories. Construal theories may share all three of the core hypotheses that I have adduced, and labeling theories share at least two of these hypotheses, and possibly all three. I will mostly be concerned with propositional attitude theories and dimensional appraisal theories in the sections that follow. These theories are unequivocally united by the conviction that emotions require conceptualized, disembodied appraisals. This should not be taken as a definition of what it means to be "cognitive." I will have much more to say about the nature of cognition hereafter. The point is that many theories that go under the "cognitive" epithet share a similar vision of what emotions involve. In the sections that follow I will ask, first, whether this vision is supported by the evidence, and second, whether there can be cognitive theories that reject its constituent hypotheses.

## Does Evidence Support Cognitive Theories?

Philosophers and psychologists tend to support their cognitive theories using distinct methodologies. Philosophers traditionally argue by reflection. They do not rely on experiments or quantitative data analysis. In it often said that philosophers do not rely on "empirical" observations. Reflection is sometimes identified with conceptual analysis—analyzing the concepts that we use to think about a particular topic of interest. Thought experiments, involving hypothetical cases, can be used to test intuitions about the application of concepts without the use of experimental methods. It is a bit misleading to describe this as nonempirical, however. The philosopher examines her own mental states, monitors patterns of behavior, and pays close attention to how language is used.

Philosophical arguments for cognitive theories take a variety of forms. One argument begins with the observation that we often assess emotions using the vocabulary of rationality (Bedford, 1957; Pitcher, 1965). We speak of anger being justified, or contempt being warranted, or sympathy being morally correct. Emotions can also be irrational. Fear of benign things is inappropriate or unreasonable. These categories of assessment (reasonability, rationality, warrant, etc.) are generally restricted to propositional attitudes and comparable cognitive states. We do not say of an itch, or a tickle, or an afterimage, or a pang, that it is rational or irrational. Mere bodily sensations do not belong to what Wilfrid Sellars and John McDowell would call the space of reasons.

This argument is not decisive. The fact that we ordinarily use such categories of assessment for emotions does not show that they are truly applicable. Perhaps we are wrong to hold people rationally accountable for their emotions. There is, after all, a conflicting tradition that sees emotions as senseless, passive irruptions that interfere with reasoning. Alternatively, we may be wrong to restrict rational accountability to propositional attitudes and construals. A response of this form will be taken up in chapter 10.

A second philosophical argument for cognitive theories begins with the observation that emotions are generally about something (Pitcher, 1965). To use examples from earlier, one can be afraid that the sea is shark infested or delighted that the circus is coming to town. How, one might wonder, can a feeling or bodily sensation be about something? How can a pang or an itch take on a propositional object? If emotions are beliefs, desires, construals, or something comparable, aboutness is easier to explain. Beliefs, construals, and their ilk are intentional states. The belief that one is in danger can be directed at the fact that the waters are shark infested.

This argument will also be taken up in later chapters. For the moment, a counterexample will suffice. Consider the case of being sickened by something. For example, one can be sickened that many sex offenders get light punishments. This is more than a figure of speech. Thinking about this fact can literally make one feel ill. And the connection here is not merely causal. In this case, one is sickened *over* the offending situation. One's ill-feeling is about something, not just triggered by something. But it would be perverse to conclude that feeling ill is a propositional attitude. The fact that illness can be directed at a propositional object does not show that illness, considered in itself, is propositional in form. Likewise, the fact that emotions take propositional objects does not show that they must be constituted by propositional attitudes or comparable cognitive states.

Following a different course, one might try to defend cognitive theories by appealing to the fact that emotions can be grouped together in orderly ways. For example, anger and love are directed at other people, guilt and pride are directed at the self, and fear and joy can be directed at animals or inanimate objects. Hope and fear are directed at the future, whereas regret and relief are about the past. It is tempting to explain these grouping by saying that emotions are built up from propositional attitudes and then stipulate that some of those attitudes contain overlapping concepts.[1] Perhaps regret and relief contain a concept of the past. Perhaps pride and guide contain concepts of the self.

The problem with this strategy is that the groupings do not always hold up. We can get angry at inanimate objects. (Did you ever smack a computer?). We can be proud and guilty about the actions of others. ("I am so proud of you," "I feel guilty about having survived the attack when so many others did not.") We can regret future events. ("I regret that I will have to cancel the party.") We can have fears about the past. ("I fear that I left the burner on.") Gordon (1987) tries to handle such cases of fear and regret by suggesting that these emotions involve uncertainty and certainty, respectively, rather than past and future. One can resist this proposal. It seems possible to regret things about which one is uncertain (I regret that I might cancel a party), and fear can be especially intense when we are quite certain that we will be harmed. In any case, conceptual truths about when emotions apply do not prove that emotions contain concepts. Suppose a warm pleasant feeling comes over me when I accomplish a difficult goal, and suppose I feel an uncomfortable pang when I violate a moral norm. Would we say these feelings could not qualify as pride and guilt if I do not deploy a concept of the self when they arise? Let's assume that dogs lack a concept of the self. Now imagine a dog who hangs its head down low after making a mess of the carpet. Is it *conceptually* impossible that the dog is ashamed? I don't think so. The most we can infer from the fact that emotions are organized into different classes is that emotions arise under different classes of situations. Some emotions arise under circumstances having to do with the self; but it doesn't follow that they require or contain a self-concept.

Philosophical arguments for cognitive theories often rely on modal intuitions. A philosopher will insist that guilt just cannot occur without thinking about the self and anger cannot occur without judging that someone has delivered an insult. These assertions are based on intuitions. The philosopher will first try to imagine cases of an emotion occurring without a particular concept or propositional attitude. If no case comes to mind, she will stipulate that the link between the emotion and that concept or propositional attitude is analytic. It is a conceptual truth that guilt involves a concept of the self.

Such appeals to intuition are risky (see Griffiths, 1997, for an extended critique). First, intuitions can be idiosyncratic and theoretically biased. Different people, with different theoretical commitments, may use the same emotion terms in different ways. Some philosophers have the intuition that one cannot be angry

---

[1]Psychologists have been known to argue along these lines as well (e.g., Ortony, Clore, & Collins, 1988).

at someone without believing that someone acted wrongfully. I do not share this intuition. If someone said there is a drug that makes one feel furious without adopting any beliefs about the wrongs of others, I would find this perfectly intelligible. Another philosopher might say it is unintelligible, insisting that a there could only be a drug that makes one feel as if one were angry without actually being angry. In response, I would say that, if there is some feeling that feels as if it were anger, it should be regarded as anger. It is hard to know which intuition is right. If intuitions can clash, as they almost always do, theories of emotions should also avail themselves of other kinds of evidence.

Appeals to intuition face another problem. Intuitions derive from reflecting on our concepts (hence "conceptual analysis"), and concepts may contain information that is false or misleading. Analyzing an emotion concept is accessing our beliefs about an emotion. Those beliefs may be based on direct experience, on instruction, or on contemplation. In each case, there is room for error. The things I've learned about emotions from others' testimony or from my own musings may be inaccurate. If I draw conclusions about emotions when I engage in conceptual analysis, there is no guarantee that I will arrive at a correct theory of what emotions are. I may end up regurgitating some folk psychological "platitude" that turns out to be false. If I am going to rely on conceptual analysis, I am better off bracketing everything I have learned from others and restricting myself to beliefs that I have acquired by carefully observing my own emotions. If this bracketing were possible, I would still be seriously constrained by my powers of observation. Suppose I experience myself getting angry whenever I believe that I have been insulted. Does this mean that anger always involves such a belief? I may have failed to observe other sources of anger or I may have misidentified the belief that gave rise to my anger. Suppose I am an exquisitely careful introspector, and I notice that I believe I have been insulted every time I am angry. Still, there is no guarantee that the belief is part of my anger. It may be a reliable consequence of anger fostered by habit and association, or it may be a confabulation. Perhaps the human desire for explanation is so strong that when I introspect on episodes of anger that are not accompanied by beliefs, I unwittingly invent a belief to make sense of the episode. I may have altered my psychology by reflecting on it (a Heisenberg effect). Reflecting on emotion concepts is vulnerable to introspective mistakes.

These concerns threaten traditional philosophical methods quite broadly. Anyone who hopes to make progress by reflection alone should be wary. Reflection may reveal more about the person reflecting than about the phenomenon on which she is reflecting. If one wants to explain something other than one's own personal beliefs, one should exploit more objective methods. In particular, one should make use of scientific experiments. Science cannot achieve perfect objectivity, but in many cases it is an improvement over isolated acts of reflection. Science has long been in the business of using careful controls, replicating results, and diminishing bias by keeping experimental subjects and those administering experiments blind to the hypothesis under investigation. Statistical analyses are designed to filter out anomalous responses and to capture general trends that may be invisible to a casual observer. Psychologists use such techniques in defending their theories. In this regard, they may have a methodological advantage over philosophers.

Before considering the psychological evidence for cognitive theories, I must issue two caveats. First, these quick remarks about science are not intended as a wholesale rejection of philosophical methods. Science always has a philosophical dimension. Whenever a scientist makes the move from data to theory, she must use reason to systematize the data into a coherent set of explanatory principles. Moreover, psychological experiments often ask subjects to reflect on their intuitions in much the way philosophers do. Thus, experiments themselves can use philosophical methods. We cannot and should not do away with the process of philosophical reflection. The key point is that philosophical methods are most powerful when used in conjunction with empirical data. Second, scientific methodology does not guarantee truth. We certainly should not accept every experimentally backed claim made by a psychologist. Experiments can have flaws, and experiments can be used to back theories they simply do not support. Rather than preferring one approach over the other, we should demand that both philosophical and psychological methods be used and that they be used with care and caution.

With these caveats in mind, let us consider the experimental evidence for cognitive theories. I will focus on the evidence for dimensional appraisal theories; the labeling theory is taken up in chapter 3. Early experiments by appraisal theorists sought to establish that thoughts can influence emotional response. In the 1960s, Lazarus and his colleagues performed a series of studies in which subjects viewed a graphic film showing genital surgery ("subincision") performed on adolescent males in the Arunta tribe during a ritual. In a study by Lazarus and Alfert (1964), subjects were divided into different groups, and each group read a different verbal description of the film before viewing it. One description emphasized the trauma of the ritual, while another described the ritual from a detached, anthropological perspective. Self-report and physiological responses suggested that subjects who viewed the film after reading the former description experienced more emotional stress than those who viewed the film after the latter description. The experimenters conclude that emotions are not driven by perceptual stimuli alone. They are influenced by the thoughts we form in viewing perceptual stimuli.

This conclusion is surely correct, and one hardly needs an experiment to show it. A thousand everyday experiences teach us that thoughts can effect emotions. If you see a man approaching you from the far end of a street and you form the belief that he is an old friend, you will feel happy, but if you form the belief that the man is a stranger and a possible assailant, you will feel fear. Positive thoughts lead to positive affect, and negative thoughts lead to negative affect. The Lazarus and Alfert experiment does not transcend this truism. It fails to establish two things that are essential to the appraisal theorist. First, it does not reveal the exact nature of the thoughts that are influencing the emotion. (Are they appraisals? Are they divided into different recurring dimensions?) Second, it does not show that thoughts are necessary for emotions. The appraisal theorists claim that emotions involve appraisals necessarily. The experiment shows, at best, that appraisals can influence emotions should appraisals happen to occur. For all the experiment shows, thoughtless viewing of genital surgery would be sufficient to elicit an emotional response.

More recent experiments have directly probed the role and structure of appraisals. In a typical example, Smith and Lazarus (1993) asked subjects to imagine being in different scenarios described by a series of short vignettes (see also Roseman, 1984; Smith & Ellsworth, 1985). For example, one vignette described a situation in which a relative is dying from cancer. Each vignette had several versions designed to influence judgments. In the cancer scenario, one version emphasized other-blame (you begged your relative to stop smoking); another version emphasized self-blame (you didn't try hard enough to get your relative to quit smoking); a third version emphasized threat (there is a great danger that your relative will die); and a final version emphasized loss (you realize you will never be able to see your relative again). After reading the vignettes, subjects were asked to fill out a questionnaire in which they rated the applicability of various molecular appraisal judgments, molar appraisal judgments, and emotion terms. The experimenters predicted that these questions would be answered in accordance with their dimensional appraisal theory. In the threat version of the cancer scenario, for example, they predicted that subjects would select the word "fear" and report thoughts of physical danger (a molar appraisal) and thoughts of high motivational incongruence and low coping potential (molecular appraisals).

Results tended to favor the predictions. There were positive correlations between the scenarios and the predicted questionnaire responses. But the correlations were not overwhelmingly high. The highest correlation between a scenario and a predicted set of molecular appraisals was 0.32, and the highest correlation between a scenario and a molar appraisal was 0.42. In general correlations were better for molar appraisals than for molecular appraisals. This suggests that the molecular appraisals on Smith and Lazarus's questionnaire do not correspond especially well to the actual judgments that go through a person's head when arriving at an emotion. The underwhelming correlations were surprising because many of the vignettes included leading phrases that should have pointed subjects toward the predicted responses. In the threat version of the cancer scenario, for example, subjects read that there is "great danger" (molar appraisal) that the relative will die, but no one knows for sure (a molecular appraisal). Smith and Lazarus seem to stack the deck in favor of their predictions and still only end up with modest results.

This last problem is avoided in an innovative study by Scherer (1993). Rather than supplying subjects with prefabricated vignettes, Scherer asked subjects to recall an emotional event from their own memories. A computer program then presents subjects with a series of questions about that event. The questions correspond to the appraisal dimensions in Scherer's dimensional appraisal theory. The computer program uses the subjects' responses to guess the emotion that the subjects experienced during the recalled event. If it does not correctly guess the emotion the first time, it tries a second guess.

This method has an advantage over the method used by Smith and Lazarus. By allowing subjects to generate their own scenarios, it does not stack the deck in favor of cases that conform to the dimensional appraisal theory. The fact that subjects associate appraisal judgments with emotional events from their own memories suggests that those judgments correspond to episodes that are arbitrarily chosen rather than carefully constructed.

The results of Scherer's experiment were impressive. Overall, the computer program was correct 77.9 percent of the time in guessing the emotion within two tries. The program was always correct, within two tries, when the subjects' scenarios involved joy, contempt, or grief. But these results may be inflated. Subjects were instructed to consider the possibility that the emotion proposed by the computer reflects some part of what was felt—possibly without the subject having realized it. Some subjects may have counted guesses as correct even when those guesses did not correspond to the dominant emotion in the episodes that they recalled. For example, the perfect success for joy may derive from the fact that every positive emotion episode can be said to contain some degree of joy. The program needed to determine only that an episode was positive to arrive at a correct guess.

Another problem with Scherer's experiment is that it relies on memory. Subjects are asked to recall whether certain appraisals are consistent with an emotion they experienced in the past. Memory is notoriously inaccurate (e.g., Moscovitch, 1995). Rather than recalling the actual judgments that they made when the emotion occurred, subjects may be constructing false memories on the basis of their beliefs about which appraisals go with certain emotions. In other words, people may choose responses to the appraisal questions the basis of their *concepts* of the emotions under consideration rather than on the basis of the emotions themselves.

This raises some general concerns about the methods used to test dimensional appraisal theories (Parkinson, 1995). Subjects in such experiments are always relying on introspection. They respond by reflecting on their emotions. The experiments do not directly probe automatic or unconscious responses that occur while an emotion is taking place. This was a major shortcoming of the philosophical method. Psychological experiments of the kind just described may be equivalent to getting a bunch of novice philosophers together to vote on the best conceptual analysis. Moreover, the introspective reports that subjects produce in psychological experiments are guided by very specific, leading questions. These questions may correspond to widely shared beliefs about the emotions (e.g., "Is sadness consistent with your goals?") rather than judgments that actually occur whenever an emotion is experienced.

A further problem is that the psychological experiments just described cannot distinguish *inner judgments* that cause our emotions, as the dimensional appraisal theory requires, from the *external conditions* that cause our emotions, with or without corresponding judgments. Suppose I ask you to imagine a pain scenario in which someone steps on your foot. You are asked, "Was the feeling you experienced caused by you or by another person?" Of course, you reply that it was caused by another person. You are asked, "Was the feeling consistent with your goals and interests?" Of course, you say no. But that does not mean that pain always occurs after one has gone through an appraisal process. One does ask oneself "Is this event caused by someone else?" before arriving at pain. One does not reflect on goals before arriving at pain. The fact that we can correctly make such assessments about pains does not show that the assessments factor into pain response. Likewise for emotions. The appraisal dimensions postulated by Smith, Lazarus, Scherer, and others may correspond to the conditions that cause emotions without corresponding to judgments we actually make when emotions are caused.

None of these considerations show that dimensional appraisal theories or other prevailing cognitive theories are false. They only show that it is extremely hard to find an adequate way to prove that they are true. The existing experimental results are consistent with prevailing cognitive theories; they just fail to provide evidence that is close to decisive. Rather than trying to provide direct evidence in favor of prevailing cognitive theories, one could try to search for evidence against them. If no such evidence can be found, we might simply accept one of the prevailing cognitive theories as a plausible working hypothesis. If evidence against the prevailing cognitive theories can be found, the existing experiments in their favor will have little mitigating effect. The fate of prevailing cognitive theories currently lies in the hands of their opponents.

### *The Zajonc/Lazarus Debate*

#### Evidence Against Cognitive Theories

In 1980, Robert Zajonc published an article with the provocative subtitle "preferences need no inferences." In it he claimed that emotion could occur without cognitive accompaniments. The thesis was challenged by Lazarus in a 1983 article. In 1984 things came to head when both authors summarized their views in back-to-back articles.

Zajonc (1984) defends the "primacy of affect." By that phrase he means that an emotion can occur prior to and independent of related cognitive states. Emotions do not have obligatory cognitive concomitants. Zajonc offers five lines of evidence is support of this thesis.

First, he claims that emotions are phylogenetically and ontogenetically prior to cognitions. To support this claim, he notes that emotion-indicative facial expressions and behavior can be observed in human infants and nonhuman animals without any reason for thinking there are concomitant cognitions.

Second, Zajonc claims that emotion and cognition involve separate neuroanatomical structures. He was impressed, at the time of writing his 1983 and 1984 articles, with work showing emotional processing localized in the right hemisphere of the brain. There is now evidence that emotional responses are mediated by both hemispheres. Davidson and Irvin (1999) argue that approach-inducing emotions are based in the left hemisphere, while withdrawal-inducing emotions are based in the right. Zajonc also cites evidence for a direct pathway from the retina to the hippocampus. He speculates that this subcortical pathway might mediate between visual perceptions of looming objects and a fear response with no mediation of the neocortex, which is thought to be the seat of cognition. That pathway is no longer thought to play a role in emotion, however. Instead it may help synchronize circadian rhythms with daylight and darkness (Ralph, 1996).

Zajonc's position finds better support in recent studies of the amygdala, a subcortical structure known to play a role in certain emotions, especially fear. It turns out that there is a subcortical pathway from the retina to the amygdala. This pathway probably mediates the fear response to coiled, snake-like objects described earlier. According to LeDoux (1996), the response works as follows. First, we see a snake-like object. It reflects an image on the retinae of our eyes. The retinal images send a signal through the optic nerve into the thalamus, which is the major subcortical hub for the senses before they send signals to the neocortex. The thalamus can register coarse visual features, but it cannot recognize objects. The thalamus sends information onto visual areas of the neocortex, which ultimately achieve recognition, but it also sends a signal directly to the amygdala. The amygdala itself is a complex structure, composed of several nuclei (Amaral, Price, Pitkanen, & Carmichael, 1992; Amorapanth, LeDoux, & Nader, 2000; Davis, 1998; Emery & Amaral, 2000; Lang, Bradley, & Cuthbert, 1998). The lateral nucleus receives the visual signal from the thalamus and sends a signal to the central nucleus. The central nucleus sends a signal to various structures that modulate bodily response. It sends a signal to the dorsal part of a structure called the central grey, which triggers a fight or flight response, and a signal to the ventral dorsal grey, which modulates freezing. The central nucleus of the amygdala is also connected to the medulla and pons, which control heart rate and breathing, and to trigeminal nuclei in the brainstem, which are implicated in the production of facial expression. The amygdala can initiate changes in hormone levels via connections to the hypothalamus, which is linked to the pituitary. And the basal nucleus of the amygdala sends outputs to the basal ganglia, which control motor responses. Through these connections, the amygdala can orchestrate the full suite of bodily and behavioral responses that are associated with fear. The amygdala can set all of these responses in motion without engaging the neocortex, and it does not need any neocortical inputs to get started. The gross shape of a snake-like object, registered by the thalamus, is sufficient to initiate a full-fledged fear response (see fig. 2.1). And there's the rub. If fear can occur without mediation of the neocortex, then perhaps fear can occur without cognition.

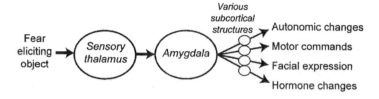

***Figure 2.1.***    A highly schematic diagram of the subcortical fear pathway.

As a third line of evidence, Zajonc argues that appraisal and affect are sometimes uncorrelated. For example, our judgments about persons can come apart from our emotional responses to them. Similarly, a change in appraisal does not always lead to a change in affect. This is all too familiar in everyday life. Suppose Sally gets angry at her husband because he arrived late to an important reception with her colleagues. Subsequently, Sally discovers that her husband's tardiness was due to an utterly unexpected accident on the highway. She may continue to feel angry even after letting him off the hook. She may try to find something else to be angry about, or she may try to channel the anger into another emotion.

Fourth, Zajonc contends that emotional reactions can be established without appraisal. He gives the example of taste aversion. Studies show that an animal can develop an aversion to a food if it is injected with a nausea-inducing substance after that food is ingested. An aversion can be established in this way even if the nausea-inducing substance is administered while the animal is unconscious. Zajonc takes such unconscious learning as evidence for emotion without cognition. He also tries to demonstrate this possibility by appealing to "exposure effects." In humans, merely seeing a stimulus on one occasion can generate a preference for that stimulus on future occasions even if one has no recollection of the first encounter. For example, people may prefer one Chinese ideograph over another just because, unbeknownst to them, they have seen it, and not the other, on a prior occasion (Kunst-Wilson & Zajonc, 1980).

Zajonc's final body of evidence is the most direct. He argues that emotional states can be induced without any prior mental states. Exposure effects and taste aversion involve something like conditioning, but emotions can also be induced by more direct physical means. They can be induced by drugs, hormones, and electrical stimulation. Emotions can even be induced by changing our facial expressions. If you smile, your level of happiness can increase. Zajonc himself has provided some of the most provocative evidence for this "facial feedback" phenomenon. In one striking demonstration, subjects are asked to evaluate stories with many "ü" sounds, which happen to cause facial configurations associated with negative emotions, and stories with vowel sounds that happen to cause facial configurations associated with positive emotions. For example, one story has a protagonist named Jürgen, while another has a protagonist named Peter. Despite no significant differences in content, 81 percent of the subjects said the "ü" stories were less pleasant (Zajonc, Murphy, & Inglehart, 1989). In another study, Strack, Martin, and Stepper (1988) asked participants to fill out a questionnaire, holding a pen in their mouths. Some subjects were asked to hold the pen with their puckered lips, forming an inadvertent grimace, while others were instructed to hold the pen between their teeth, forcing a subtle grin. Among items in the questionnaire, subjects were asked to rate cartoons. Subjects in the teeth condition rated the cartoons as more amusing than subjects in the lips condition, suggesting that their emotional response was being elevated by their unintended facial expressions.

In sum, there seem to be a variety of conditions under which emotions and cognitions come apart. If Zajonc's interpretation of these results is correct, emotions are not cognitive essentially.

## Assessing the Evidence

As noted earlier, Lazarus (1984) responds to Zajonc's arguments. Unsurprisingly, he is not convinced. I will briefly review and assess these replies.

Lazarus offers two avenues of response to the allegation that emotions are ontogenetically and phylogenetically prior to cognitions. First, he says, we cannot be sure that the expressions made by infants and nonhuman animals correspond to emotions. This response is not very satisfying. The continuity between adult human emotional response and behaviors found in infants and animals is considerable. There may be important differences between our emotions and those of simpler creatures, but there is little reason to deny that simpler creatures have emotions.

Lazarus's second response is more convincing. He says that, for all we know, infants and animals are making cognitive appraisals whenever they exhibit emotional responses. Just as continuity in nature demands that simpler creatures have emotions, continuity in nature demands that simpler creatures have cognitions. Admittedly, some cognitive theories postulate cognitions that are too sophisticated to attribute to simple creatures. Recall, for example, Nussbaum's (2001) metacognitive theory. She says that emotions are judgments that our evaluative judgments are justified. Fear might be the judgment that I am justified in believing that something poses a threat to my well-being. I think this theory is too demanding. There is evidence from developmental psychology that we do not develop the capacity for metacognition until some time between the third and fourth birthday (Wimmer & Perner, 1983). Young children and animals could not form the requisite judgment. Nussbaum must either deny they have emotions or amend her theory. She does not want to deny that young children and animals have emotions, so she is left with the second option. Any theory that defines emotions in terms of highly sophisticated cognitions must be rejected. But Zajonc implies that infants and animals are completely incapable of cognizing. Lazarus is quite right to dismiss that claim as unwarranted.

In response to Zajonc's third body of evidence (I will come back to the second), Lazarus challenges the evidence that emotions can be unaffected by appraisals. Consider the case of Sally, who remains angry after letting her husband off the hook. Zajonc would say that Sally's emotion has endured an appraisal change. Lazarus would reply by saying that Sally's appraisal has not really changed. Once she has formed a belief that she has been wronged by her husband, she may be loath to give it up. Lazarus could bolster his reply by citing the ample psychological evidence that people have difficulty relinquishing beliefs. In an experiment by Ross, Lepper, and Hubbard (1975), subjects are given false feedback about how well they perform a task and then told that the feedback was erroneous. If subsequently asked to estimate their performance, they will make estimates in line with the initial false feedback, even after they have been told it was erroneous. The appraisals that give rise to emotions may be like this. Alternatively, Lazarus could propose that emotions that are generated by cognitive appraisals, linger for a while after being generated, and remain temporarily invulnerable to subsequent appraisal changes.

In his fourth line of argument, Zajonc's alleges that emotions can be induced by simple forms of conditioning or exposure. Lazarus handles different cases in different ways. He acknowledges that unconscious nausea induction can lead to food aversion, but he denies that the resulting aversion is established noncognitively. It is perfectly possible, he maintains, that cognitive mediation takes place unconsciously. Zajonc has erroneously conflated cognition and consciousness (more on this later).

Lazarus follows a different route when considering exposure effects. Preferences are certainly influenced by prior exposure, but, he argues, preferences are not necessarily emotions. This response is sanctioned by ordinary language usage. One can prefer something without having one's emotions stirred by it. Lazarus could also argue that exposure effects are cognitively mediated. He could say, for example, that we unconsciously judge previously experienced stimuli to be familiar, we judge familiar things that have not harmed us in the past to be safe, and we judge safe things to be congruent with our goals. This sequence of judgments could lie behind any emotional component in our preferences.

Lazarus has reasonable replies to the evidence considered thus far. His replies to Zajonc's second and fifth lines of evidence are more problematic.

In response to Zajonc's second line of evidence (alleged anatomical dissociations), Lazarus asserts that the debate cannot be resolved by pointing to neural correlates. If we identify a neural structure that correlates with some aspect of an affective response there is still a question about whether activity in that structure qualifies as noncognitive. This question cannot be ajudicated by brain science. To decide whether a brain area underwrites cognition, we must first settle on a definition of what cognition is. That definition may be informed by neuroscience, but it must also respect psychology and pretheoretical use of terms.

This reply leaves Lazarus's account vulnerable to refutation. Let us follow

LeDoux in supposing that phobic responses to snake-like objects are mediated by phylogenetically primitive, subcortical structures. The same may be true of facial feedback (Zajonc, Murphy, & McIntosh, 1993). Lazarus's theory of the emotions identifies each emotion with a response to six appraisal dimensions. As noted earlier, he seems to regard appraisals as propositional attitudes. Propositional attitudes are comprised of the concepts used to ascribe them. It is quite unlikely that appraisals, so construed, are represented at the subcortical level. Lazarus's dimension of ego-involvement, for example, invokes concepts of self-identity, and the dimension of credit or blame requires an assessment of accountability. It is hard to imagine that a primitive structure such as the amygdala harbors such a sophisticated conceptual repertoire. Destruction of the amygdalae can lead to a major deficit in fear, but there is no impairment in one's ability to think about credit, blame, identity, and so on. There is absolutely no reason to think that activity in the amygdala can be characterized in the terms demanded by Lazarus's dimensional appraisal theory.

Perhaps Lazarus could concede this point and say that when emotional responses are triggered by subcortical structures, simpler appraisals are involved. This has three shortcomings. First, to make this reply plausible, Lazarus would have to give some reason for thinking that the amygdala harbors appraisals, even of a very simple nature. The amygdala seems to be a body control center, not an appraiser. As I have noted, the cells in its nuclei send messages to structures such as the hypothalamus and the central gray, which alter bodily states. Second, because the amygdala is a body control center, it is difficult to maintain that appraisals reside in the amygdala while maintaining that the cognitive components of emotions are disembodied, as Lazarus assumes. Third, if Lazarus were to say that cortically induced emotions and subcortically induced emotions rely on different kinds of appraisals, he would not be able to explain why such emotions can seem so similar. We readily recognize both cortically induced fear episodes and subcortically induced fear episodes as fear. They must have something in common, which explains their coclassification. If subcortically induced fear does not include complex dimensional appraisals, such appraisals cannot explain this commonality. Something else must unite fear episodes. Whatever this something else is, it is evidently sufficient for classifying a state as fear. Consequently, there is no reason to regard complex dimensional appraisals as essential to fear. They can be regarded as one of several possible causes of fear, rather than being regarded as necessary components or prerequisites.

Lazarus may try to get out of this corner by questioning the anatomical evidence. He could deny that subcortical structures are the true correlates of our emotions. Perhaps the amygdala is just a hub that mediates between perceptions and emotions. Just as perceptions occur elsewhere in the brain (the thalamus and sensory cortical areas), emotions may occur elsewhere in the brain. On this alternative interpretation of LeDoux's data, one might explain snake-induced fear responses as follows. First, one sees a snake; then the perceptual image of the snake sends a message to the amygdala; the amygdala causes higher cognitive centers of the brain to form complex appraisal judgments; and, finally, these judgments set a variety of bodily changes into motion. The emotion arises only when the higher cognitive centers are engaged.

This reply does not do justice to the anatomical evidence. Even if amygdala activation ultimately leads to the formation of disembodied, concept-laden appraisals, there is no reason to think that such states are needed to initiate bodily changes. The amygdala directly outputs to centers that control the body, without the mediation of the neocortex. Bodily response can be set in motion before the neocortical mantle gets involved. This is inconsistent with Lazarus's theory. He maintains that bodily changes *follow* cognitive appraisals. If bodily changes arise beforehand, then appraisals seem to be superfluous. Suppose that the amygdala sets off bodily changes before explicit judgments in higher cognitive centers occur. Imagine further that those changes are registered by somatosensory areas of the brain and consciously experienced before any explicit judgments in higher cognitive centers occur. Should we say that the experienced bodily change is not yet an emotion? Should we say that its status as an emotion must await subsequent judgments? This would be an odd requirement. After all, the felt bodily change would feel just like ordinary instances of fear (Levenson, Ekman, & Friesen, 1990). If bodily changes can occur without the mediation of complex judgments and if those changes can be felt without such judgments (as they presumably can), there is no theory-independent reason for claiming that such judgments are necessary parts of emotions.

Lazarus is also vulnerable to Zajonc's fifth set of examples. These are the cases of emotions brought on by direct physical means, including drugs, hormones, electrical stimulations, and facial feedback. There is no reason to think that emotions induced in these ways are mediated by complex judgments, propositional attitudes, or construals. Surprisingly, Lazarus (1984) offers no response to these cases. The oversight is especially unfortunate because these cases provide the most direct and compelling evidence for emotion without cognition.

Gerald Clore (1994b) has tried to make up for Lazarus's reticence on this issue. He considers cases of facial feedback and argues that the feelings and physiological changes brought on by making a facial expression do not constitute an emotion. Facial feedback produces a feeling of the kind one would have if one were having an emotion, but that feeling does not count as an emotion in its own right. Perhaps the same can be said about emotion-like states induced by drugs, hormones, and electrodes. To repeat Gordon's (1987) analogy, cited in chapter 1, emotions may be like sunburns. If you get a burn from something other than the sun, it is not a sunburn, even if it is mistaken for one. If you get a feeling from something other than an appraisal, it is not an emotion even if it is mistaken for one.

I am reluctant to follow Clore down this path. Consider an example of how facial feedback works in situations outside of psychologists' laboratories. From the earliest hours of life, all of us are biologically disposed to mimic the facial expressions of the people we encounter (e.g., Melzoff & Moore, 1983). If I see you smile, I will smile back. Because facial feedback occurs, my smile may cause me to enter a state that feels internally like happiness. Thus, your smile causes happiness in me. Clore would say this is not a bona fide instance of happiness. But why say that? In cases where happiness is mediated by appraisal, it occurs after one determines that something that one values has occurred. We certainly value the affection of other people. If someone smiles at me affectionately, and I become happy, my happiness occurs in response to something I value. Happiness is playing a role very much like the role it plays in cognitively mediated cases.

Clore's strategy for dealing with cases of noncognitively induced emotions is rather desperate, but other avenues of response are available as well. One possibility is to say that cases of physical induction involve cognitions after all. Perhaps smiling actually causes one to judge that things are going in accordance with one's plans. Perhaps anxiety-inducing drugs actually causes one to judge that danger looms. This, of course, is sheer speculation. There is little evidence that such physical means of emotion induction have any direct impact on our appraisals. And, even if they did, there would be little reason to think that those appraisals were necessary for the ensuing emotion. Drugs and smiling seem to have a more direct impact on emotional state. They seem to stimulate activity in structures that modulate our autonomic nervous systems. Those modulations lead to bodily states that are recognized as emotional feelings regardless of what judgments arise. Lazarus's theory, which situates judgment before such changes, is once again called into question.

At this point, the best strategy for a cognitive theorist might be to abandon the cognitive cause theory in favor of some other cognitive theory. Some cognitive theorists would say cognitions follow bodily changes, and some would say they can come in any order. Perhaps smiling causes bodily states first, and these cause us to form judgments, and the resulting complex of bodily states and judgments constitutes happiness.

One wonders why this response should be taken seriously. In this context, it is entirely ad hoc. I can think of only one good reason why one might think that judgments must be involved in cases of emotions produced by physical means, such as facial feedback. One might assume, with Schachter and Singer (1962), that bodily states are not sufficient for distinguishing between the emotions produced in this way. If bodily states cannot distinguish between physically induced emotions, judgments may be doing some work. I present evidence against this assumption in chapter 3. If bodily states can distinguish between emotions induced by physical means, there is no reason to suppose that such emotions must be accompanied by judgments.

I conclude that Zajonc's arguments, properly elaborated, are effective against Lazarus. The hypothesis that emotions are set off by complex dimensional appraisals has difficulty explaining cases of physical induction and lacks neuroanatomical support. The conclusion generalizes to any theory that postulates emotional constituents above and beyond bodily changes or internal states that register bodily changes. Bodily changes can be caused without any prior state that deserves to be called a constituent of an emotion. Once these changes take place and get registered by the brain, there is every reason to say that an emotion has occurred. In cases of direct physical induction, there is no reason to postulate anything above or beyond somatic states when saying that an emotion has occurred.

This may look like a solid victory for Zajonc. Standard cognitive theories assume that all emotions are constituted, at least in part, by concept-laden, disembodied states. That seems to be wrong. But this conclusion shows that emotions are not cognitive only if cognitions are necessarily concept-laden, disembodied states. If the term "cognition" subsumes other kinds of states, emotions may be cognitive after all. Such a conclusion would not vindicate prevailing cognitive theories, but it might cast doubt on the kind of theory Zajonc wants to defend. After all, he categorically denies that emotions are cognitive. To determine whether he is right, we must determine what cognitions are. The debate between defenders of cognitive and noncognitive theories comes down to a matter of definition. That is not to say that the debate is merely verbal. By inquiring into the essence of the cognitive, we may discover something about the nature of emotions.

### *What Is Cognition?*

#### Some Definitions

It is scandalous that cognitive science has not settled on a definition of cognition. I would venture to guess that most practitioners have scarcely paused to ask themselves the question. This may be an indication that the question is not worth asking. If cognitive science can get along without a definition of cognition, then perhaps it does not need one. Cognitive scientists can fully describe all mental states and processes without saying which ones count as cognitive.

On the other hand, asking for a definition of cognition can have heuristic value. First, it may help us map the insights of science onto our ordinary conception of the world. Since we pursue science to understand the world, we have great interest in being able to translate science into ordinary talk (Sellars, 1963). "Cognition" is not a common word in ordinary talk, but the closely related word "thinking" certainly is. It is interesting to ask how well folk categories map onto the scientific image of mind. If no mapping can be made, our ordinary understanding of mental life and our ordinary explanatory practices may be called into question. Second, arriving at a definition can advance research by posing interesting questions. For any definition of the term "cognition," there is some interesting question about how emotion relates to the things that fall under that definition. Asking how one thing relates to another can lead to discoveries that we would not make if the question had not been asked.

In defending their respective views, Lazarus and Zajonc have pursued very different and equally valuable research programs. Lazarus's has tended to investigate the connection between emotion and judgment, whereas Zajonc has explored such things as exposure effects and facial feedback. Arriving at a definition of cognition and asking how it is related to emotion may point toward other avenues of research. Definitions help formulate questions whose investigation deepens insight.

These observations place two pragmatic constraints on the search for a definition of cognition. The definition should coincide closely with ordinary and scientific uses of such terms as "cognitive" and "thinking," and it should be sufficiently precise and narrow to guide research.

Let us now turn to some candidate definitions. One possibility is that cognition involves consciousness. Many states that are accessible to consciousness seem paradigmatically cognitive, as when one reflects on a philosophical question or deliberates about what presidential candidate has better policies. Notice that the term "consciousness" is not being used here to designate what philosophers call phenomenology, the felt qualities experience. The fact that certain states feel like something, such as the feeling of butterflies in one's stomach, does not render those states cognitive on any intuitive sense of the term. Instead, the operative notion is closer to what Block (1995) calls access consciousness: being poised for verbal report and deliberate, rational control of action.

The equation of cognition with access consciousness tacitly drives the intuitions behind some of Zajonc's examples. As noted earlier, it may lie behind his intuition that taste aversion is noncognitive when it is induced by the administration of drugs during an *unconscious* state. It may also lie behind his intuition that preferences for things induced by prior exposure count as noncognitive when we cannot *consciously* recall having seen those things before.

Despite his tacit reliance on this definition, Zajonc explicitly rejects the equation of cognition with access consciousness—and with good reason. Modern theories of the mind postulate very complex information processing that cannot be consciously accessed. Consider the incubation effect. After consciously thinking about a problem for some time, one sometimes gives up trying, and then suddenly the answer pops into one's head. This can happen in any domain, from math to macramé. The processing that gives rise to the solution is not reportable or controllable, but it answers to an ordinary notion of being cognitive.

A second proposal defines cognition as the class of mental processes governed by rational state transitions. Unconscious problem solving may satisfy this requirement, for example, while pains do not. The paper cut on my finger is not a rational ground for feeling pain.

One problem with this idea is that it is not clear what should count as rational. On one definition, a "rational" process is one that is truth preserving—that is, highly likely to produce true outputs given true inputs. Psychologists have shown that we are not very rational in this sense. We often draw bad conclusions from good evidence (see Stich, 1990, for a review). In fact, mental activity seems to get increasingly less rational as we move from the sensory periphery to the highest levels of the nervous system. For example, the visual system may be described as using a rule that says: when two adjacent luminance discontinuities are detected, infer that they belong to a common edge (Marr, 1982). This is a highly truth-preserving process. Compare that to the kinds of decision procedures that govern choosing elected officials or estimating probabilities. If the latter processes are presumed to be more typical examples of what is meant by cognition, the proposed account of rationality won't do.

One might escape the problem by defining "rational" more liberally. An alternative definition defines a "rational" process as one that is sensitive to content but not necessarily truth preserving. By content-sensitive I mean the information carried by the input is systematically related to the information carried by the output. This definition makes high-level reasoning qualify as perfectly rational, but it also subsumes most activity in the nervous system. The information carried by cells in the retina are systematically related to the information they send though the optic nerve. Calling these processes cognitive violates the pragmatic requirement for narrowness in seeking a definition of cognition.

The intuition that pain and problem solving differ may stem from the fact that problem solving involves deliberation. Deliberation does not depend on consciousness or rationality, so it escapes problems with the first two definitions. It also matches intuitions about the noncognitive status of pain. We do not deliberate about whether to be in pain when we get cut; we just experience pain. So far, so good. The problem is that "deliberation" may be a near synonym for "cognition." "To deliberate" means "to think about" and "thinking" is a vernacular term for "cognitive processing." We have gone from cognitive to deliberative, to thinking, back to cognition. To escape the circle, one must define deliberation without appeal to thinking.

A natural proposal is to define deliberation as the process of entertaining choices and deciding between them. This definition may be acceptable, but, if so, deliberation is too narrow to define cognition. When we solve a math problem using a familiar technique such as long division, we do not necessarily entertain alternate solutions, yet this is a paradigmatically cognitive task. Cognition must be defined in some other way.

Zajonc offers a definition of his own. He says cognition occurs whenever there is a transformation of present or past sensory inputs. More succinctly, cognition involves "mental work." On the face of it, this cannot be sufficient. Transformations of inputs cannot be sufficient for cognition, because transformations of inputs occur all the way through the nervous system. When the reflection on the retina sends a signal through the optic nerve, that is a transformation of inputs.

Perhaps the emphasis in Zajonc's definition should be on transformations of *sensory* inputs. Zajonc may mean to suggest that cognition begins where sensory processing stops. But where is that? What counts as a nonsensory transformation? One is tempted to say that nonsensory transformations are those that count as cognitive. But this makes his definition circular. Moreover, it would be a mistake to say that the senses cannot participate in cognition. If Einstein has an insight about physics using mental imagery, do we say he was not cognizing? Do we say it was an impurely cognitive process? I think not. Moreover, it would beg the question against Lazarus to stipulate that cognition cannot occur in the senses.

Lazarus (1999) offers a definition that differs from Zajonc's. He suggests that cognition involves learning and memory (see also Izard, 1994). This captures some of our pretheoretical intuitions, but it does not hold up to analysis. First of all, learning and memory are not necessary for cognition. It seems coherent to postulate innate cognitive abilities (cognitive scientists do that all the time), and innate abilities are, by definition, unlearned.

Second of all, learning and memory are insufficient for cognition. "Learning" can be defined as the process of forming new representations (or enacting new skills) as a result of experience or mental activity and encoding them in memory. "Memory" can be defined as a faculty that allows representations (or skills) to be used at some point after they were initially formed (or enacted). On these plausible definitions, some insects are capable of learning and memory. Fruit flies, for example, can be conditioned to avoid electrical shocks (Tully & Quinn, 1985). We might even attribute learning and memory to individual neurons. In order to make the notions of learning and memory do any work, Lazarus would have to distinguish these forms from more advanced forms. Drawing that boundary is difficult. What matters is not memory as such but those memory systems that preside over cognitive states. Of course, one cannot make progress by defining cognition in terms of *cognitive* memory systems. Learning and memory lead to another circle.

Scherer (1993) suggests that cognition occurs when information processing goes beyond the physical features of the stimulus. The first thing to notice about this definition is that it cannot be a necessary condition. We can surely have cognitive states that refer to physical features. For example, a biochemist can reflect on the chemicals that we detect through taste and smell.

Scherer's claim must be that going beyond physical features is *sufficient* for cognition. Perhaps so, but what counts as a physical feature? Psychologists inspired by J. J. Gibson (1979) say that we perceive "affordances," that is, possible ways of interacting with objects. When we see a chair, we perceive its sit-ability. Is this a physical feature? Or consider pheromones, which may be used to detect fertility. Is fertility a physical feature? The visual system detects ego-relative location of external objects. Is that a physical feature? If all these features count as physical, it seems reasonable to say that the dangerousness of a snake is a physical feature. If the features driving emotional response (e.g., dangers and threats) qualify as physical, and being physical is merely a necessary condition for identifying noncognitive states, then we cannot adjudicate the cognition/emotion debate using Scherer's definition.

To give Scherer's definition some bite, we might define physical features more narrowly as, say, the intrinsic surface properties of objects. Since dangers and threats do not qualify as surface features, emotions that respond to dangers and threats count as cognitive on this refinement of Scherer's definition. But perceptual systems that detect affordances, fertility, and even egocentric locations may qualifies as cognitive on this analysis. Visual determination of three-dimensional form from a pattern of two-dimensional light qualifies as cognitive too. If colors are not real properties of objects, visual response to color also becomes a cognitive activity. There may be reasons for thinking perceptual systems can engage in cognition, but their mere ability to detect features that go beyond the surface is not a good reason.

The final definition I will consider here associates cognition with concepts. Concepts are widely presumed to be the primary currency of cognition. Perhaps cognitions can be defined as states that contain concepts. Armon-Jones (1989) defends a definition along these lines. In her terms, all cognition involves conceptualization.

This definition is, like its predecessors, faced with some difficulties. Imagine glancing at an empty suitcase in an effort to evaluate how much luggage you can pack. This seems to be a cognitive activity, but it is not *obvious* that it involves anything that we would want to call concepts. Showing that concepts are involved would take some work. One wants to know: What are concepts such that these activities qualify as conceptual? If a concept is merely a mental representation that can be used to identify something on more than one occasion, then edge detectors in early vision qualify. But mere activity among a population of edge detectors does not appear to be an especially cognitive event. One is tempted to supplement the initial definition of concepts by saying that concepts are mental representations that can combine together to form thoughts. This is an improvement, but it offers no help in this context. We cannot define cognition by appeal to conceptualization if concepts are defined by appeal to thoughts, because thoughts are a folk term for cognitions. To escape the circle, we would need another definition of what concepts are. I return to this in a moment.

For now, let us pause to absorb a rather surprising conclusion. Many of the most immediately plausible definitions of cognition fail. Some are circular, others are too widely applicable to draw an interesting cognitive/noncognitive distinction, some exclude things that would fit into a pretheoretical conception of the cognitive, and others include things that would not. The longstanding debate about the cognitive status of the emotions rests on terms whose definitions are frightfully unresolved.

## Organismic Control

I think we can find a substantially better definition of cognition. To cut to the chase, I think the crucial construct is organismic control. Cognitive states and processes are those that exploit representations that are under the control of an organism rather than under the control of the environment.[2] A representation is under organismic control if the organism has activated it or maintains it in working mem-

---

[2]This is related in letter, though perhaps not in spirit, to McDowell's (1996) suggestion that human mentality involves spontaneity, rather than receptivity.

ory. A cognitive state is one that contains such a representation, and a cognitive process is one that activates, maintains, or manipulates such a representation.

This suggestion is related to the proposal that cognition involves concepts. A moment ago, I said we need an alternative account of what concepts are before we can clarify the link between cognition and conceptualization. I think organismic control is the key here too. Elsewhere, I argue that concepts are mental representations that can come under organismic control (Prinz, 2002). By that I mean a representation that is residing in memory or one that has been activated from memory. A representation under organismic control is a representation in or drawn from memory. In Prinz (2002), I am mainly interested in distinguishing concepts from percepts. The difference is that we can activate and manipulate concepts in thought. This definition allows that percepts can be stored in memory and used as concepts on future occasions. Suppose we see a peculiar shape, and we store a copy of the percept so that we might recognize instances of that shape on future occasions. When we encounter the shape for a second time, two things happen. The shape causes a perceptual state, and that state is matched with a representation in memory. The representation in memory is a concept, but the perceptual state is not. The perceptual state is not under organismic control, but the representation drawn from memory is. If this definition of concepts is adopted, cognitions can be defined as states containing concepts.

The organismic control definition allows one to draw a distinction between cognitions and the act of cognition—between thoughts and thinking. A cognition must contain a concept, and a concept must be amenable to organismic control. But a concept needs to be under organismic control at the time that one has the cognition. Consider the case of thoughts that are triggered by perceptual experiences. You see a dog and automatically form the thought that there is a dog in front of you. This thought, and its constituent concepts, does not occur as a result of organismic control. It is a reflex-like response to your experience. It qualifies as a thought because the representations it contains are under organismic control in a *dispositional* sense. You *can* willfully form thoughts using your dog concept. Being a thought only requires being made up of representations that are capable of being controlled by the organisms that has them. Thinking, in contrast, requires actual effort. A cognitive act is an act of generating a thought under top-down control. Thoughts produced automatically in the course of perception are unthought thoughts. We have them without thinking. They are cognitions, but not acts of cognition.

The appeal to organismic control may seem to invite a regress. To say that an organism can control a mental representation implies that the organism is somehow situated inside the brain. It implies that there is a little inner homunculus calling all the shots. In reality, the brain is a big bureaucracy comprised of many simple subcomponents. No little decision-making homunculus can be found (Dennett, 1991; Minsky, 1986).

The homunculus problem can be overcome by treating "organismic control" as a synonym for "top-down control." Top-down control can itself be explicated in different ways. As a first approximation, one might say a representation is controlled top down just in case it is controlled by centers of the brain that lie farther away from the sensory periphery than that representation itself. This is not quite adequate. It assumes we can always tell what levels of processing qualify as further away from the senses; it makes it impossible to count interactions between states at a single hierarchical level as cognitive without intrusion of some higher level; and it leaves no way to call activities in the highest brain areas cognitive, for lack of anything higher.

A more promising tact defines "top down" by appeal to some specific psychological systems or neural structures. Many cognitive neuroscientists believe we can identify executive centers in prefrontal cortex. These centers may play a special role in manipulating and maintaining representations in working memory (D'Esposito, Postle, Ballard, & Lease, 1999). They may also play a special role in initiating the formation or activation of representations when those representations are not elicited by environmental stimulation. I propose that we call a state cognitive just in case it includes representations that are under the control of structures in executive systems, which, in mammals, are found in the prefrontal cortex.

A few notes about executive systems are in order. First, the plural counts. There is no single piece of prefrontal real estate that is responsible for activating all mental representations. Different kinds of representations (e.g., verbal and nonverbal) may be under the control of different centers. Second, I am not suggesting that cognitive states are necessarily implemented in prefrontal areas. Cognitive states may be distributed throughout the brain (Damasio, 1989; Prinz, 2002). Their cognitive status depends only on frontal control. Third, executive centers are not homunculi. They do not necessarily *decide* what representations to activate or how to manipulate them. They are more like contractors than architects. There is no single architect or decision-center in the brain. Fourth, while executive systems are far away from sensory transducers, there may be no interesting sense in which they count as farther away than some of the representations that they activate.

These speculations help distinguish direct and indirect organismic control. Executive centers can exercise indirect control in several ways. First, they can influence the representations we form by changing the orientation of our bodies. If I decide to look at the moon, I will form a moon representation. Second, executive centers can influence representations by shifting attention. If I visually scan a room trying to find my can of Coke, I might elect to focus attention on red objects. My visual experience of the room is affected by that choice of focus, but the ensuing visual representations are not directly constructed by executive systems. The mental representations in these examples are not, as I intend the term, created under organismic control. To count as cognitive, control must be direct.[3]

---

[3]Directness of control may, however, be graded. Our ability to activate, manipulate, or maintain certain mental representations may be *enhanced* by focusing attention or changing our position in the world. In this case, one might say the states involved are less controlled, hence less cognitive, than some other states.

Organismic control captures some of the intuitions behind the previously considered definitions of cognition. First, consider the intuition that access-conscious states are cognitive. Access-conscious states are poised for reporting, deliberating, and controlling actions. These processes all may qualify as cognitive under the definition I proposed. Access consciousness entails the possibility of organismic control. Also consider the intuition that pains are not cognitive, whereas doing long division is. Long division problems are presumably orchestrated by executive centers, and pains occur automatically, without executive intervention. Next, consider the intuition that cognition involves mental work. The idea of mental work evokes the idea of effort—operations that cannot be carried out passively. Executive functions are experienced as active. They participate in operations that involve effort. For example, frontal cortex executive centers contribute to strategic selection between competing goals. This may account for the intuition that deliberation is a cognitive process as well. Deliberation may involve effortful choice. The suggestion that cognition involves memory is captured here as well. It is not the cases that memory processes are all cognitive, but any act of cognition must use representations drawn from a memory store.

This definition of cognition has advantages over the other definitions. First, it is not circular. It defines a cognition as a mental state that is under organismic control, and organismic control can be defined without reintroducing the term *cognition* or its cognates. Second, it does not seem too narrow. Imagine a creature whose mental life is driven entirely by exogenous forces. Every inner state is an automatic consequence of some event in this creature's environment. My intuitions dictate that this creature lacks cognitive states and processes.

Critics may complain that this definition of cognition is too inclusive. Consider mental images. If I choose to form an image of a red expanse, that image is under organismic control, and thus it counts as a cognition. This may sound odd to some ears, but I think it is not incompatible with our pretheoretic understanding. Earlier, I appealed to the intuition that the use of imagery in science is cognitive. One might say the science case is irrelevant, because scientists use images in the context of deliberating, problem solving, and developing theories, all of which are paradigmatically cognitive activities. An image that is not put into such service may strike some people as noncognitive. I disagree. Some people do clever things with their mental images, and others do not. Cognitive status does not depend on what we do with the images that we electively form. If we think Einstein's images are cognitive, we cannot decree that their cognitive status depends on the extraordinary theories that they helped him derive. The very act of electively constructing an image is a cognitive act, I maintain, even if the cognitive activity stops there. If we had killed Einstein just after he formed an image and before he drew any conclusions from that image, we would not say he was not thinking at the time of his death.

It must be emphasized, finally, that while this account offers an inclusive definition of cognition, it is not all-inclusive. Some mental states and processes are not under organismic control. For example, there is little reason to believe that we can control activity in early sensory areas except by manipulating orientation or attention. Cognitive states, on this analysis, require that representations be activated or maintained by executive centers. Early sensory states are not. It may also turn out that certain representations fairly far from the sensory periphery are outside of organismic control. It is well known that recognition far exceeds recall. I cannot perfectly recall the face of Rosalind Carter, the former first lady, but I could recognize her. The representations by which I recognize her may not be under my control. Perhaps many mental representations are like this. They aid us in making our way through the world, but we cannot manipulate them by act of will, as it were.

### *Resolving the Debate*

### Are Emotions Cognitive?

We come, at last, to the question of emotion and cognition. A cognitive theory of the emotions is one that says emotions involve cognitions essentially. I have now argued that cognitions are states containing representations that are under organismic control. I have also suggested that there is a difference between a cognition (or thought) and a cognitive act (or thinking). One can have thoughts without thinking. Thus, the question "Are emotions cognitive?" divides in two. We can ask "Do emotions necessarily involve acts of cognition?" and "Do emotions necessarily involve cognitions?"

The answer to the first question should be obvious. Emotions often do not occur as acts of cognition. Most of the time, emotions are passive. We seem to be helpless spectators to our emotional responses. When we react emotionally to a snake or an exam, it is not by act of will. We do not choose to be afraid. In fact, we often explicitly try not to be afraid (as when one addresses a large audience for the first time). But fear takes over. The same can be said for other emotions. In many of their instances, emotions are paradigm cases of automatic responses: neither orchestrated nor fettered by the executive centers within. This is even true when emotions arise in planning. While we can willfully imagine being afraid, we more typically enter an imaginative fear state as an automatic consequence of imagining a frightening situation. We visualize standing over a ravine, and fear follows. Thus, while emotions may qualify as cognitions in human adults, they generally do not qualify as cognitive acts.

What about the second question: Are emotions cognitive? According to cognitive theorists, the answer is yes. Emotions are unthought thoughts. Or, as Descartes puts it, emotions are "thoughts which are not actions of the soul" (1649/1988, xxviii). If emotions are cognitive, they must be under cognitive control. Is there any reason to think that they are? One line of support comes from the fact that we can generate emotions in imagination. Try to imagine the feeling of fear. Now try anger or disgust. Form a vivid image of joy or amusement. I think such directives can be met. We can imagine being in emotional states.

The ability to imagine emotions suggests that we may exercise cognitive control over our emotions. This does not mean we willfully elect the emotions we have. It only means that we can generate emotions spontaneously, as when we plan for the future. One might willfully imagine feeling afraid and elated to determine whether the emotional costs of a roller-coaster ride will outweigh the emotional benefits. If emotions can be deployed under organismic control, then they qualify as concepts, and states containing emotions qualify as thoughts. Or so it might seem.

On further reflection, our ability to willfully generate emotions does not entail that every episode of emotion is conceptual. Recall the example of seeing a shape. First, the shape causes a percept, and then that percept is matched against a representation in memory. Only the memory representation counts as conceptual. The percept is not a concept, because it is under exogenous control. Likewise for emotions. When we generate an emotion by act of will (imagine being angry!), that emotion is a concept. It is drawn from memory. But the emotions that are caused in us by events in our day-to-day life are not concepts. They are more like percepts. They are under exogenous control. The fact that we have stored copies of our emotions in memory does not render exogenously controlled emotions cognitive. By comparison, the fact that we have a concept of redness does not make ordinary red experiences conceptual. Recognizing red involves concepts, but merely experiencing it does not. Moreover, we may have emotions that we never store copies of in memory. We have no concept, no capacity to recognize, some of our emotions. Infants and animals may have no emotion concepts at all. Their affective lives may always be under exogenous control.

I conclude that emotions are not in fact cognitive, most of the time. They are not generated by acts of cognition, and they are not conceptual. We have conceptualized versions of our emotions, and we can use these in cognitive acts, but in ordinary cases emotions are not cognitive at all. This bolsters the interim moral that I drew earlier. Emotions are unlikely to have the complex structure that cognitive theorists presume that they have. They do not decompose into meaningful, propositionally structured parts. They are not propositional attitudes. Nor, I have now argued, are they cognitions of a more primitive variety.

### Raising Lazarus

My conclusion echoes Zajonc. Lazarus's theory is wrong. But perhaps he is not completely wrong. Like other cognitive theorists, Lazarus defends three hypotheses: emotions are conceptualized; emotions are disembodied; and emotions are appraisals. As a package, these hypotheses are threatened by neuroanatomical evidence and by cases in which emotions arise through direct physical induction. Under certain circumstances, subcortical structures can trigger bodily responses, which are felt as emotions, without the intervention of concept-laden, disembodied appraisals. Nevertheless, I do not think that we are forced to abandon all of the hypotheses that defenders of those theories hold dear.

The disembodiment hypothesis is threatened by that fact that emotions can be caused by direct physical inductions, such as facial feedback. The concept-ladeness hypothesis is threatened by that fact that emotions are under ordinarily exogenous control and by the fact that emotions seem to involve primitive brain structures that do not harbor complex propositional attitudes.

But what about the third hypotheses, the hypothesis that emotions are appraisals? An appraisal is a representation of the relation between an organism and its environment that bears on well-being. I might appraise that the environment presents a physical danger to me. Many appraisals are disembodied. Appraising that I am in physical danger does not require states that control or register changes in the body. But there is no principled reason for insisting that appraisals need to be disembodied. In chapter 3, I will explain what it would mean to say that appraisals can be embodied. I will also go a step farther and argue that emotions *are* embodied appraisals.

If the arguments in chapter 3 succeed, I will have demonstrated that Zajonc and Lazarus and both partially right about the nature of emotions. Zajonc is right to reject the disembodiment and conceptualization hypotheses, but Lazarus is right to defend the appraisal hypothesis. The position that will emerge in the next chapter lies squarely between the theories defended by these two researchers. It reconciles prevailing cognitive theories with the theories of their most ardent opponents.

# 3

## Embodied Appraisals

### *Emotions as Representations*

Chapter 2 ended with a promise. I said that I would present and defend an embodied appraisal theory of emotion. Appraisal theories claim that emotions necessarily comprise representations of organism-environment relations with respect to well-being. An embodied appraisal theory says that such representations can be inextricably bound up with states that are involved in the detection of bodily changes. In this chapter, I show that such a theory is tenable.

To show that emotions are appraisals, one must first establish that they are mental *representations*. To appraise is to represent something as having some bearing on one's interests or concerns. As I showed in chapter 1, some theorists claim that emotions are mere feelings, which do not represent anything at all (e.g., Hume, 1739/1978). Others argue that (at least some) emotions are changes in modes of information processing rather than information-bearing states in their own right (Oatley & Johnson-Laird, 1987). I think that these views are wrong. Once we see what mental representations are, it is clear, even obvious, that emotions represent. I thus begin with some general considerations about mental representation.

### Psychosemantics

A mental representation is a mental state that represents something. Emotions are mental states. They are temporally bounded occurrences in the mind. To show that they are representations, one must show that they represent. But how can a mental state, any mental state, represent something? There is a large philosophical literature on this question (see the articles in Stich & Warfield, 1994). Fodor (1987) has called a theory of how mental states represent a theory of "psychosemantics." I will not survey competing theories of psychosemantics here. Instead, I will focus my attention on one theory that has been influentially articulated by

Fred Dretske (1981, 1986). I defend a version of that approach in greater detail elsewhere (Prinz, 2000, 2002).

Dretske argues that mental representations are mental states that satisfy two conditions: they carry information, and they can be erroneously applied. Dretske's notion of "carrying information" is appropriated from Shannon and Weaver's information theory. On this approach, a state carries information about that with which it reliably cooccurs. In the most typical cases, the cooccurrence in question is causal. A state carries information about that which reliably causes it to occur. Reliable causation does not entail perfect correlation. To say that one thing is reliably caused by another thing just means that, were that second thing to occur, then, all things being equal, the first would have a high probability of occurring as a result.

Information in this technical sense is ubiquitous in the natural world. Smoke carries information about fire, because fire reliably causes smoke. Spots on the face carry information about measles. Tracks in the woods carry information about deer. Rings inside a tree carry information about the age of the tree. Carrying information comprises a "natural sense" of meaning (Grice, 1957). We can say that the smoke on the horizon *means* there is a fire. But carrying information is not sufficient for representation. Smoke does not represent fires.

The reason for this, Dretske argues, is that it does not make sense to say that smoke can be wrong or false. Suppose that I live in an environment where smoke can be reliably caused by lava or dry ice in addition to being caused by fires. In such an environment, smoke means fire-or-lava-or-dry-ice. It carries information about anything that causes it. This is not the case with bona fide representations. Suppose I have a concept that represents dogs. On Dretske's view, a dog concept is a mental state that is reliably caused by (i.e., becomes active as a result of) encounters with dogs. But a mental state that is reliably caused by dogs may also be reliably caused by wolves, foxes, or well-disguised cats. All of these creatures are similar in appearance, so any state that can be caused by one of them stands a reasonable chance of occasionally being caused by the others. Consequently, my dog concept carries information about all of these creatures. To count as a dog representation (and not a dog-or-wolf-or-fox-or-cat representation), there must be a way to say that I am making an *error* when my dog concept activates in response to wolves, foxes, and cats.

To explain how mere information carriers come to be genuine representations, Dretske appeals to the idea that some information carriers *have the function* of carrying certain information. To have the function of carrying certain information, something must be set in place for that purpose. Smoke is not set in place to be caused by fire; it *just is* caused by fire. A dog concept is different. It is set up—that is, learned—in order to reliably respond to dogs. A dog concept is a mental state that is reliably caused by dogs *and* was acquired for that purpose. In the simplest cases, this just means that the mental state was initially formed as a result of dog encounters, rather than encounters with something else (see Prinz, 2000). After such a state is formed, it *carries information* about dogs, foxes, and wolves, because all these things can cause it to activate, but it only *represents* dogs, because it was set up as a result of dog encounters. When a wolf causes a dog concept to activate, the response is considered erroneous.

Dretske (1986) argues that mental representations can be set up in different ways. Some are set up by learning (as in the dog concept case), and others are set up by evolution. For example, evolution may furnish our visual systems with cells that respond to edges. These cells *can* be activated by something other than edges. For example, they can be activated by seeing thin cracks (Burge, 1986). But they were almost certainly passed down from our ancestors as a result of successfully responding to edges. When one of these cells is activated by seeing a crack rather than an edge, it is firing in error—it is misrepresenting a crack as an edge.

This general idea has been refined in various ways, but the refinements are not essential here (see Dretske, 1981, 1986; Prinz, 2000). It is enough to say that a mental representation is a mental state that is reliably caused by something and has been set in place by learning or evolution to detect that thing. Put more concisely, a mental representation is a mental state that has been *set up* to be *set off* by something.

Dretske's approach is controversial. The most common objection is that it cannot assign very precise contents to our mental states. A single mental state ends up representing a disjunction of different things rather than one thing (see Fodor, 1990). The concern is sometimes illustrated by considering mental representations in the minds of frogs. Frogs eat flies, and, to do so, they must have mental representations that tell them when flies are present—an internal fly detector. But frogs cannot discriminate between flies and pellets shot from a bee bee gun. The mental representation in a frog's head that is reliably caused by flies would also be reliably caused by pellets. Should we say it is a fly representation or a pellet representation? Clearly, the former makes more sense than the latter. The representation in question was probably formed through natural selection, and natural selection is much more likely to have furnished the frog's mind with a fly detector than a pellet detector. But evolutionary considerations cannot rule out other possible contents. Perhaps the representation in question represents insects in general, rather than just representing flies. Or it may represent the property of being a small, dark, airborne object. If flies evolved in an environment where most small, dark, airborne objects were flies, representing the latter would have been a good way to detect the former. Or perhaps we should say that this mental representation represents nutrition. After all, it is set in place to help frogs find the food that nourishes them. The point is that each of these possible contents seems to satisfy Dretske's conditions on representation. There is no way to decide whether the state in the frog's head represents flies or insects or small, dark, airborne objects, or nutrition. Perhaps it represents the entire disjunction of these things. This is an embarrassment for a Dretske-style account.

This is not the place to solve the disjunction problem. I defend a solution elsewhere (Prinz, 2000, 2002). Here I will just briefly underscore resources that are available. First, on Dretske-style accounts, content is constrained by past history. Pellets were not around during the frog's ancestral past, so they cannot be what representations in the frog's brain were designed to detect. Second, bear in mind that the contents of a representation reliably correlate with that representation. Frogs receive nourishment from crawling insects as well as flying insects, but these may trigger different detectors, so neither detector deserves to be called a nutrition detector. Both are more specific than that. Likewise for insects in general. Insects in general would be what frogs represent only if insects in general caused a detector in the frog's brain to activate. But in all likelihood they do not. Things are a bit trickier for dark, airborne objects. The detector in the frog brain may be reliably set off by these. Moreover, if those detectors were set up as a result of fly encounters, they were set up by dark, airborne object encounters, because flies are dark, airborne objects. Now it's true that some dark, airborne objects will not trigger activity in a frog's brain (consider a dark airplane), but objects within certain size constraints will. In this case, I would suggest that there is one more resource available to disambiguate the representation.[1] We can look to see how the organism uses it. Millikan (1993) has emphasized this point in her discussions of "consumer-side" constraints on representation (see also Prinz, 2002, on semantic markers). It is not insignificant that the fly shoots out its tongue when its detector goes off. The fly engages in eating behavior. Flying black dots are not reliably edible, so they have no special relationship to eating. But flies are edible to frogs, so it makes better sense of a flies behavior to assume that its detectors detect flies rather than flying black dots.

I intend these informal remarks to show that a semantic theory of the kind I presented may place considerable constraints on content determination. These constraints rule out certain candidate contents. My goal now is to see whether such constraints could lead to a plausible story about what emotions represent.

## Do Emotions Represent Bodily Changes?

To show that emotions are representations, one must show that emotions are set off by certain things, and that they are set up to be set off by some of those things. Consider these issues in turn.

What are emotions set off by? What, in other words, reliably causes our emotions to occur? In chapter 1, we encountered a possible answer to this question. James and Lange argued that emotions are the effects of changes in the body. If their theory is correct, then it is reasonable to conclude that bodily changes reliably cause emotions. If fear is the feeling of a pattern of changes in the viscera,

---

[1]Note that there is no reason to insist that mental representations always have perfectly unambiguous on nondisjunctive contents. Some degree of indeterminacy, polysemy, or semantic untidiness may be inevitable, especially within frog psychology. The point of this exercise is to show that some contents are excluded.

then that pattern should reliably cause fear. But what reason is there for thinking that James and Lange are right? Why should we think that bodily changes are reliable causes of emotions? Couldn't it turn out that bodily changes are effects of emotion? Or that bodily changes merely accompany emotions on some occasions? To answer these questions, let's examine the reasons that James and Lange offer in favor of their somatic theory.

A number of arguments can be discerned in the pages of James and Lange. The most famous is the subtraction argument mentioned in chapter 1. James writes, "If we fancy some strong emotion, and then try to abstract from our consciousness of it all the feelings of its characteristic bodily symptoms, we find we have nothing left behind, no 'mind-stuff' out of which the emotion can be constituted, and that a cold and neutral state of intellectual perception is all that remains" (1884, p. 193). Lange offers a nearly identical argument: "If from one terrified the accompanying bodily symptoms are removed, the pulse permitted to beat quietly, the glance to become firm, the color natural, the movements rapid and secure, the speech strong, the thoughts clear,—what is there left of his terror?" (1812/1985, p. 675). The point is that emotion phenomenology seems to be exhausted by sensations of bodily changes. This suggests that bodily changes are the causes of our emotions, rather than the effects.

James also supports his theory by appeal to parsimony. We know that the mind can register bodily changes. If emotions are constituted by such mental states, we do not need to postulate some further faculty to explain affective phenomena.

In a third argument, James points out that voluntary change of bodily states can impact our emotions: "If we wish to conquer undesirable emotional tendencies in ourselves, we must assiduously, and in the first instance cold-bloodedly, go through the *outward motions* of those contrary dispositions we prefer to cultivate" (1884, p. 198). This passage augurs the lesson of facial feedback research, discussed in chapter 2. Smiles produce happiness.

A related argument is offered by Lange. He notes that emotions can be induced by taking certain drugs. Alcohol can "combat the closely related states of grief and fear, and . . . replace them with joy and courage" (1885/1912, p. 676). Never mind the fact that alcohol is actually a depressant. The point is that it, and other substances, can influence emotions by having a somatic affect. This supports the conjecture that emotions register changes in our bodily states, including our neurochemistry.

Lange also points to linguistic evidence for linking emotions to bodily states. He notes that many words for emotions also refer to bodily changes. His examples include "shudder" and "feverish." Of course many more can be produced: "heartache," "shocked," "tense," "agitated," "choked up," and so on. This pattern suggests that the correlation between emotional states and bodily states is strong.

In another argument, James appeals to cases of pathology. He notes that some psychiatric patients experience emotions with no identifiable cognitive cause, suggesting the state has a bodily origin. More significantly, some patients who report emotional insensibility also report a reduction in bodily feelings.

James says that the crucial empirical test for his theory involves people who suffer from complete bodily anaesthesia. If emotions register bodily changes, such an individual should show reduced emotional response. In his 1884 article, James writes of one such individual. That individual's doctor maintained that he continued to show signs of strong emotions. In response, James complains that the doctor based his conclusion of behavior rather than introspective testimony from the patient. In a later article, James was reassured by findings of a French physician who maintained that people with global bodily anesthesia due to injury or hypnosis show a major reduction in emotion (James, 1894, p. 314).

In more recent decades, researchers have revisited this issue. Damasio (1999), a vocal neo-Jamesian, cites a study of patients with spinal cord injuries, conducted by Hohmann. Hohmann (1966) found that spinal cord patients report subdued experience for many emotions (sadness being an exception). More strikingly, he finds that the degree of attenuation is a function of where the spinal lesion is located. Higher lesions, which degrade bodily feedback to a greater degree, correlate with greater reduction in affect. This result is also consistent with work by Valins (1966), who gave healthy subjects false audible feedback about their heart rates while viewing erotic photographs. Subjects who thought their hearts were beating rapidly rated the pictures more attractive and frequently chose to take home the pictures in lieu of payment for participation in the experiment.

These results have not gone unchallenged. Chwalisz, Diener, and Gallagher (1988) performed a similar study and got profoundly different results. Spinal patients reported having intense emotions, and their rating of at least one emotion, fear, was higher than that of control groups. Why such inconsistent results? Chwalisz et al. have several suggestions. First, Hohmann's patients may have provided inaccurate reports about their own emotional states. Therepeutic practices in the 1960s encouraged people to adopt stoic attitudes toward their disabilities. Hohmann's patients may also have fallen prey to a contrast effect: the trauma of getting injuries may have been so great that all subsequent emotions seemed dull in comparison. The patients may also be reporting a reduction in affect as a natural consequence of the aging process. And, finally, the reported reduction may stem from the fact that their medical conditions prevented them from conducting active lives. We now encourage people with spinal cord injuries to live more actively, which may result in richer emotional experiences.

When studies conflict to this degree, it is hard to know where the truth lies. The patients of Chwalisz et al. may report their emotions disingenuously to avoid stigma. Alternatively, they may simply be unable to recall their past emotions, because recollection may require reactivation of bodily states that are no longer accessible to them. In any case, the Chwalisz et al. findings do not refute somatic theories of emotion. As in chapter 1, both Damasio and James believe that emotions will be experienced whenever there is activity in brain centers that has the function of detecting bodily changes, however such activity is produced. Both authors think that we can have somatic feelings without bodily changes, just as we can have visual images without seeing any actual object. In Damasio's idiom, somatic states of the brain can be set off by an as-if loop, which bypasses the body. Damasio also notes that the bodily changes underlying our emotions include changes in facial expression and neurochemistry, both of which can be detected after spinal cord injury.

Damasio has further advanced the Jamesian cause by offering some direct evidence for the bodily basis of emotion. He points to functional neuroimaging studies that show activation in somatic brain centers during emotion induction (Damasio et al., 2000). When people experience emotions, brain areas that detect bodily changes apparently activate. These brain centers may be the neural correlates of our emotional states. Together with the arsenal of low-tech arguments devised by James and Lange, there seems to be overwhelming reason to believe that there is, at least, a regular correlation between emotions and bodily states. Evidence from bodily induction of emotion, spinal cord injury, and neuroimaging suggest that emotions are causal *consequences* of bodily changes. They are states that register bodily changes. If this is the case, then bodily changes must be capable of causing emotions. That does not mean that every emotion is the result of some prior perturbations in the body, but it does suggest that bodily perturbations are reliable causes of emotions. Indeed, emotions seem to be perceptions of bodily changes. In this, I believe that somatic theories are exactly right.

I can now return to the issue of representation. If bodily changes reliably cause emotional states, then bodily changes are candidates for the things that emotions represent. Perhaps anger represents dilated blood vessels and a scowl. This conclusion seems to follow directly from somatic theories. If emotions are *perceptions* of bodily changes, then it seems they represent bodily changes; after all, aren't perceptions representations?

Things are actually a bit more complicated. In saying that emotions are perceptions of bodily changes, I mean only to say that they are states within our somatosensory systems that register changes in our bodies. That is what all of the evidence just adduced seems to show. But it is helpful to distinguish "registration" from "representation." As I will use the term, a mental state registers that which reliably causes it to be activated. Emotions clearly "register" changes in the body, but there is still a further question about what such states represent. By analogy one might say that a state in the visual system *registers* a particular luminance discontinuity, but it *represents* an edge. On the theory of representation under consideration, reliable causation is not sufficient for representation. A representation must also have a function. Visual states have the function of representing shapes. The claim that emotions represent bodily changes requires a further premise. If anger represents dilated blood vessels, it must have the function of detecting them.

Do emotions have the function of detecting bodily changes? Might they have been set up for this purpose? At first, the answer seems to be affirmative. We can reasonably presume that the link between emotions and the body is a consequence of natural selection. Certain correlations between emotions and bodily states are basic and universal features of our biological constitution (see chapter 5). Thus, we have reason to ask whether emotions were woven into our genome in virtue of detecting bodily changes. Did evolution furnish us with emotions in order to carry information about our viscera, faces, and skeletal muscles? Such evolutionary questions are difficult to answer (see more on this later), but there is at least some room for doubt.

Evolution chooses things that confer a survival advantage. If evolution furnished us with emotions in order to detect bodily changes, then detecting bodily changes must confer a survival advantage. This is a strange hypothesis. It is not clear why it is advantageous to know when my blood vessels are constricting. That knowledge is not, in itself, especially useful for survival.

The problem can be further compounded by considering how emotions are used—the consumer side of emotional response. Emotions promote behavioral responses. We run when we are afraid. If emotions represented bodily changes this would be unintelligible. We should we flee when our hearts race? Emotions also play a role in decision making. This has been a central theme in Damasio's research. He has taken a special interest in patients with lesions in the ventromedial parts of their frontal lobes. The most famous of these is Phineas Gage, a nineteenth-century construction foreman who sustained a ventromedial lesion when he accidentally tamped down on exposed gunpowder with a long metal rod. The powder combusted, sending the rod hurling through his head. Gage survived the incident, but his capacity to make reasonable decisions was seriously compromised. It turns out that patients with ventromedial lesions lead disastrously unsuccessful lives, despite having no serious impairments in memory, IQ, language, or perceptual abilities. They form alliances with untrustworthy partners, fail to preserve close relationships, and make other bad decisions. This is just what happened to Gage, and to a number of contemporary patients with similar injuries. Damasio thinks their problems stem from an emotional deficit. In particular, ventromedial patients are unable to anticipate the emotional consequences of these actions. I think this account is broadly compelling, but it actually raises a puzzle for Damasio's theory of emotions. The fact that emotions are used in decision making is ostensibly at odds with Damasio's insistence that emotions represent changes in bodily states.

Let's assume that a failure to anticipate the emotional consequences of our actions leads to bad decision making. Couple this with the proposal that emotions represent bodily states. We are left with the conclusion that we reason badly when we cannot anticipate how our bodies will change when we choose certain actions. It is not clear why this should be the case. Suppose I do not know whether a certain course of action will make my blood vessels dilate or constrict? Does my ignorance lead me into recklessness? If so, it is not clear why.

Damasio (1994, p. 139) recognizes the problem and makes a move that I want to resist. Turning his back on James and Lange, he recommends that we identify emotions with perceptions of bodily changes *coupled with* evaluations. Emotions are perceptual/cognitive hybrids. He implies that we can only make sense of the role that emotions play in reasoning if we assume that they contain a cognitive component. I think this move is unnecessary. We do not need cognitive evaluations to explain how emotions are used by their consumers. Instead, we should accept the premise that emotions are bodily perceptions but deny that they represent (or exclusively represent) bodily changes. We should insist that emotions detect something more than the vicissitudes of vasculature. Otherwise, they would confer no survival advantage, and we could not make sense of the seemingly intelligible uses to which they are put.

## Emotion Elicitors

Rather than assuming that emotions represent bodily states, I want to explore the possibility that they represent things that are external to us. After all, emotions rarely begin from the inside. They are ordinarily elicited by some external situation. In order for emotions to represent external conditions, it would have to be the case that emotions are *reliably* caused by those conditions. There is reason to think that emotions can be reliably caused by bodily states, but is there any reason to think they have reliable causes that extend outside of us?

On the face of it, the answer is no. The external causes of emotions vary considerably. The things that cause fear or anger in me may cause feelings of comfort or joy in you. Political disagreements often pivot around such discrepancies. Likewise, the things that one culture finds endearing or pleasant another may find disgusting. Geertz (1973) reports that the Balinese are disgusted when they see a baby crawling, because it reminds them of nonhuman animals (cited in Johnson-Laird & Oatley, 2000). Food preferences are another famous example of variability in disgust. The Western taste for dairy products is considered repulsive in large parts of the world.

Underlying these differences, one can also find some agreement. All people are frightened by scary things, angered by offensive things, disgusted by disgusting things, and elated by pleasing things. We may disagree about what counts as scary, but we are all afraid of what is scary *to us*. The "to us" is important. It implies that emotions are elicited by things as they relate to us. This suggests that emotions represent relations between external states and our selves. They represent organism-environment relations.

It is not unusual for mental representations to represent organism-environment relations. Examples can be found among our perceptual states, concepts, and beliefs. I might perceive an object as being in front of me. I might categorize an object as being delicious to me. I might form the belief that the meal in front of me is delicious to me. In each case, I am representing something in relation to myself. Likewise, fear may represent something as scary to me.

This is a promising start, but the proposal is uncomfortably circular. Saying that fear represents the property of being scary to me is like saying fear represents whatever scares me. But that is like saying that fear represents whatever causes fear. A vacuous insight. What's worse, the proposal makes it look as if fear can never occur in error. If fear represents anything that causes fear, then whenever I am afraid, my fear is accurate or correct. This violates Dretske's stricture on representation. Representations must be able to misrepresent.

There are a couple of ways one can try to escape this circle. One option is to argue that emotions are secondary qualities. Locke (1690/1979), who coined this term, applied it to colors, saying that the property of being red is the property of having the power to cause a certain kind of experience in us. Red things are things that cause us to have red experiences. This is not circular, because a red experience can be characterized by its distinctive feel, without mention of red things. Secondary qualities also permit error. We can say that red is anything that causes *normal* humans to have red experiences in *normal* viewing conditions. If I have a red experience as a result of pressing my finger against my eye for a few seconds, it doesn't mean that my finger is red, because finger-pressing is a not a normal viewing condition. In a similar spirit, we might say that fears represent secondary qualities. We might say fears represent the property of having the power to cause fear experiences in normal human beings under normal conditions.

I think the secondary quality view is unsatisfying when put this way. First, the proposal that fear represents things that cause a certain kind of experience in us does not reveal anything about what those things have in common. Why do certain things and not other arouse fear?

Second, there is an important difference between fear experiences and color experiences. The conscious feelings associated with mental states that represent colors are projected out into the world. When we experience redness, we experience it as if it were out there on the surfaces of objects. Not so with emotions. The feeling of rage, for example, is not projected onto the object of rage; it is experienced as a state within us.

A third concern stems from the fact that the secondary qualities are response-dependent properties in a strict sense. A response-dependent property, P, is one that would not exist without being represented as P by a human experience, judgment, or other mental state. Being red is sometimes thought to be a response-dependent property. Something cannot be red without being represented as red (under ideal conditions). I do not think that emotions represent response-dependent properties in this strict sense. If I am right, this shows a weakness in the seemingly tautological claim that fear represents the property of being scary. Scariness is arguably a response-dependent property. Something is scary only if it is represented as scary. The property that fear represents is not response dependent. To show this, I will present an alternative to the secondary quality view.

One can generally find a common theme behind the range of things that elicit any given emotion. Consider a number of things that might cause sadness: a child's death, a report on political crises in the Middle East, a divorce, being fired, a rejection letter, a low grade, misplacing one's favorite sunglasses, a bad weather forecast, and so on. These elicitors range from the tragic to the trivial, and they involve utterly different kinds of events. Still, they are alike in one respect: they all involve the loss of something valued. We can lose loved ones, hopes for world peace, relationships, careers, prized possessions, self-esteem, access to resources, and many other things. The things themselves differ, but each can be lost, each one is valued and in each case the loss leads to sadness. It makes sense to say that sadness is elicited by loss, where loss is defined as the elimination of something valued. This analysis explains why different things sadden different people. The sadist who smiles at a child's death is not sad, because he does not value the child's life. But, should the sadist lose something he values, such as the freedom to prey on victims, he will become sad too.

Some terminology will be helpful here. Emotions can be elicited by actual environmental conditions impinging on an organism or by imagined conditions, as when an emotion is caused by contemplating a future event. The conditions (real or imagined) that elicit an emotion can be referred to as its objects. Invoking a distinction from scholastic philosophy, Kenny (1963) points out that emotions can have two kinds of objects. A *formal object* is the property in virtue of which an event elicits an emotion, and a *particular object* is the event itself. The death of a child can be a particular object of one's sadness, but it causes sadness in virtue of being a loss. Being a loss is the formal object of sadness. Emotions represent their formal objects, not their particular objects. An episode of sadness may concern any number of distinct particular objects, but the sadness in each episode represents loss.

There is some confusion about this in the philosophical literature. Arguments for the claim that emotions have intentionality often appeal to the fact that emotions can be directed at some particular event. Sadness must be intentional, on this line of reasoning, because one is always sad about one thing or another (e.g., Pitcher, 1965). In contrast, moods, such as depression, are sometimes said to be nonintentional because they are not directed at any particular thing (see chapter 8). This is a flawed form of argument. While there is a sense in which emotions are directed at particular events, that does not mean that they represent those events, or anything else for that matter. The events are represented by mental states that combine with emotions. When I am sad about the death of a child, I have one representation of the child's death and I have sadness attached to that representation (a similar point is made in chapter 2). The sadness doesn't represent the death. Saying that my sadness is *about* the death does not mean that my sadness represents the death; rather it means that the death is what has caused me to become sad. I can continue to think about the death after my sadness subsides, and I can continue to be sad after my thoughts of the death subside. The mental representation of an emotion's particular object can be doubly dissociated from the emotion it elicits.

This does not mean that emotions lack intentionality. Emotions are intentional in their own right, independent of any representations that happen to accompany them. This is where Kenny's formal objects come in. Sadness represents the loss of something valued. If I am sad about the death of a child, I have one mental representation that corresponds to the child's death and another, my sadness, that corresponds to there having been a loss (see fig. 3.1). Together, we can think of

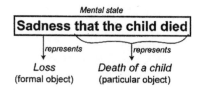

**Figure 3.1.** Formal and particular objects of an emotion.

these as constituting a complex representation that means the child's death has been a loss to me. We might think of the compound as meaning something like: a child has died, *and* what a loss! I will have a bit more to say about how emotions link up to representations of their particular objects in chapter 8. For now I want to leave particular objects to one side and explore the thesis that emotions represent their formal objects.

This proposal can be used to escape circularity. Rather than saying that sadness represents things that are sad to us, we can say that sadness represents loss (or some disjunction of closely related properties, including loss, privation, defeat, and so on). Loss is not a state of an organism. It is not a bodily condition. Nor is it something purely external. The case of the sadist shows that something only counts as a loss relative to what an organism values. Loss is a relational property. It is the elimination of something valued by an organism. Sadness represents the elimination of something valued by me.

On the face of it, this proposal is consistent with the claim that emotions represent response-dependent properties. Being valued is a response-dependent property. Something cannot be valued without being the object of a mental state (namely, being valued). Thus, something cannot be a loss, in the operative sense, without being the object of a mental state. But notice a difference between being valued and being a loss. If one represents something as valued, its being so represented constitutes its being valued. If I stopped valuing my pet turtle, my pet turtle would not be valued by me. But suppose I value my pet turtle, and that he dies. I may be sad about this. I may represent it as a loss. But it would be a loss even if I didn't represent it as a loss. It is a loss before I make the discovery that my turtle is dead. Being a loss depends on valuing something, but it does not depend on being represented as a loss. Being a loss *encompasses* a response-dependant property, namely being valued, but being a loss is not a response-dependant property *in its own right*.

This point applies equally to other emotions. Fear, for example, may represent the property of being dangerous. Being dangerous, like being poisonous, is a relational property, and a relative property. Something can be dangerous only *to* some creature or other, and whether or not something is dangerous depends on the creature in question. But being dangerous does not depend on being represented as dangerous. Radiation would be dangerous even if we didn't know that it is. Fear represents the property of being dangerous even though that property is possessed by some things that we do not in fact fear. Fear, like sadness, does not represent a response-dependent property.

A harder case is surprise. Surprise may represent a violation of expectations, and, intuitively, something cannot be unexpected if it is not represented as such. Here intuitions lead us astray. Something is unexpected if it does not conform to one's expectations. Something can have this property even if we don't happen to notice it. Pressing the point, one might object that surprising things, like red things, are secondary qualities, because they are dispositions to cause a certain state in us. Something would not be surprising if it didn't have the power to cause surprise. This may be true, but it only exposes a flaw in the formulation that says surprise represents the property of being surprising. If a surprise reaction meant "This event has the property of causing this state (surprise) in me," it would not be much help. Surprise is more likely to mean "I didn't expect this event," which could be true of events that do not happen to surprise me. Like sadness, this analysis of surprise makes direct reference to my psychological states (expectations). That does not entail that sadness represents a response-dependent property. It entails that sadness represents a relational property, which seems to be the case for emotions quite generally.

If emotions do not represent response-dependent properties, then they do not represent secondary qualities, because, on the standard definition, secondary qualifies are response dependent. It has always been difficult to explain how representations of secondary qualities can occur in error. If redness is the power to cause red experience, then it seems to follow that every red experience represents something red. As I remarked earlier, error in the perception of secondary qualities is usually explained by appeal to normal viewing conditions. This kind of strategy may succeed, but it faces many hurdles. Specifying what conditions count as normal is a difficult task. No such difficulty arises for the hypothesis that sadness represents loss. Sometimes we are sad when there has not been any loss. This might occur under the influence of certain drugs (e.g., alcohol), while listening to music, or even while making a sad facial expression. Some cases of clinical depression may involve chronic sadness without any loss (for more discussion, see chapter 10). These examples do not threaten the proposal that sadness represents loss. To the contrary, they show that the proposal can satisfy Dretske's stricture that representations must be capable of occurring in error.

The claim that sadness represents loss echoes a suggestion made by Lazarus. As I showed in chapter 1, Lazarus speculates that each emotion corresponds to a different core relational theme. He characterizes sadness as a state that occurs when one has "experienced an irrevocable loss." The word "irrevocable" is a nice embellishment of the proposal I have been considering. Sadness may indeed represent losses that are, in some sense, irrevocable. Death, rejection, and bad grades all fit this mold.

The other entries on Lazarus's list of core relational themes are good candidates for what some of our other emotions represent (glance back at table 1.2).

Each entry can be regarded as a thoughtful proposal about what the correspon-ding emotion was set up to be set off by. Sadness is about irrevocable losses, disgust is about real or metaphorical indigestibility, and fright is about concrete dangers.

Lazarus would not necessarily characterize things this way. He might agree with the claim that emotions represent core relational themes, but this is not his main goal in presenting the list. For Lazarus core relational themes are not just the external conditions that elicit emotions; they correspond to the inner judg-ments that we make in arriving at emotions. More accurately, they are summaries of judgments made along six appraisal dimensions. I have already argued against Lazarus's dimensional appraisal approach. I do not think that core relational themes capture inner judgments at all, much less judgments along six appraisal dimensions. Core relational themes do not capture the structure of our emotions or the structure of any other mental representations that are necessary concomi-tants of emotions. We can form the judgment that there has been an irrevocable loss, but we seldom do. Sadness can occur without that judgment. But sadness represents what that judgment represents. It has the same meaning but a different form. Judgments are propositional attitudes. Lazarus thinks that emotions are bound to propositional attitudes, and his list of core relational themes gives a rough approximation of the kinds of concepts those attitudes contain. In chapter 2 I argued that emotions are not propositional attitudes. If I am right, then Lazarus's list should be reconstrued as an account of emotional content rather than emotional form.

Dretske's theory shows how something quite complex, such as a core rela-tional theme, can be represented by something quite simple. To make this point, Dretske often appeals to simple mechanical devices. Consider "fuzz busters," which people place in their cars to determine when they are driving in zones monitored by police radars. A beep emitted from a fuzz buster represents the presence of a police radar. But the beep itself is utterly lacking in structure. It cannot be analyzed in to meaningful subbeeps. There is not a tone meaning "radar" and another tone meaning "police," which merge together to form a "po-lice radar" tone. In other words, the beep emitted by a fuzz buster does not de-scribe what it represents. It represents police radars because it is reliably caused by police radars, and it is set up for that purpose.

Likewise, emotions can represent core relational themes without describing them. Sadness can represent irrevocable loss without having some part that rep-resents irrevocability and another part that represents loss. Nor does sadness need to be preceded by any representation that can be analyzed into those two compo-nents. A *fortiori*, sadness does not need to be preceded by any inner states with the structure of Lazarus's six appraisal dimensions. Appraisal theorists often mis-take the complex property represented by emotions for the inner representations that constitute or precede our emotions. If Dretske's story is right, the com-plexity of that which is represented need not be mirrored by the complexity of the representation.

In summary, I follow Lazarus in submitting that emotions correspond to core relational themes. Core relational themes are what our emotions represent. But core relational themes need not capture the inner structure of emotions or the inner structure of any mental states that lead up to our emotions. For the moment, I remain neutral about the structure of emotions and other inner states that contribute to emotional response.

### From Information to Representation

My argument for the claim that emotions represent core relational themes is missing one premise. Emotions are certainly set off by core relational themes. That is, they are reliably caused by relational properties that pertain to well-being. But representation requires more than reliable causation. On Dretske's account, a mental state represents something that reliably causes it only if the state has the function of being caused by that thing. I need to show that emotions have the function of being caused by core relational themes. They must be set up for that purpose.

Sadness may track loss, but why think it has been set up to do so? One strategy for defending this premise would be to appeal to cultural universality. If the same themes elicit emotions in all cultures, then it is plausible that emotions are set up to track those themes by evolution. But I will argue that many emotions are not culturally universal (chapter 6). Moreover, universality is not sufficient evidence for evolutionary purpose. Emotions are universally caused by changes in bodily states, but I argued that they do not represent changes in bodily states. To say that fear represents a racing heart fails to explain the important role that fear plays in our lives. It fails to explain why an inability to predict emotional consequences makes us bad decision makers. The claim that emotions represent core relational themes fares much better. Fear seems to be a danger warning system, not a heart monitor. We flee because we are faced with dangers, not because we have palpitations. This is the key.

The ability to detect core relational themes does a better job of explaining behavior. It also does a better job of explaining why emotions are acquired. Fear may be acquired (through genes or learning) because it confers a survival advantage by protecting us from dangers. Anger may be acquired because it helps us cope with challenges from conspecifics. Sadness may be acquired because it allows us to register the loss of things for which efforts have been extended. These suggestions are just first approximations. The point is that core relational themes are directly relevant to our needs and interests.

I offer one more argument. Let's suppose that emotions did not reliably detect core relational themes. Suppose emotions tracked bodily changes, and our bodies made such changes in situations that had no significance for well-being. It is not clear why those states would be genetically transmitted or acquired through learning. It is not clear why they would be set up. Suppose, conversely, that we had mental states that tracked core relational themes but did not track bodily changes. Those states would still confer a survival advantage, and they would have been passed down (through genes or culture) to future generations.

In sum, emotions are reliably caused by both bodily changes and core relational themes, but they seem to have the function of detecting only the latter.[2] If this is right, then core relational themes satisfy the second criterion for being represented by emotions. They are what emotions are set up to be set off by. I conclude that emotions represent core themes.

### Bringing Back the Body

### Real Contents and Nominal Contents

Lazarus's core relational themes offer a good approximation of what emotions represent. Lazarus's mistake is that he thinks core relational themes correspond to complex judgments in the head. This is not obligatory. Something can represent a property, even a very complex property, without describing that property. Dretske's discussions of simple mechanical devices show us how.

The beeps emitted by fuzz busters are a limiting case. As noted, those beeps represent complex properties (the presence of a police radar) without having any internal structure. There are no meaningful subbeeps. I call unstructured representations "indicators" (see Prinz, 2002). Other representations have structure. They represent in virtue of having meaningful parts. I call such representations "detectors."

Among detectors, it is useful to make a further distinction. Some detectors have parts that represent parts of the property that the detector represents. Consider, for example, a letter-detecting device that identifies letters by identifying lines and edges. It may have inner states that serve as indicators for horizontal lines (of various lengths and positions), vertical lines, diagonal lines, and curved lines. Clusters of these indicators serve as letter detectors. Two converging diagonal lines with a horizontal line between them serves as an "A" detector. This detector detects As by having parts that indicate A parts. Having such parts is, one might suppose, constitutive of being an A. We can call a device of this kind an "essence-tracking detector."

Other detectors work differently. They track appearances rather than essences. Consider, again, a concept that represents dogs. To be a dog, something must have a complex biological property. It must have a particular genome or belong to a particular clade. We, as individuals, have no idea how to describe the dog genome or trace the dog evolutionary tree, but we can represent dogs. People

<hr>

[2]One might want to add to this story an account of emotional intensity (a point raised by Barry Smith, personal communication). Emotional episodes vary in their intensity, and, intuitively, the variations are semantically significant. Minor fear may represent a minor danger, and intense fear may represent a more serious danger. Intensity seems to have the function of tracking seriousness. I leave this topic for another occasion.

could represent dogs before the concepts of genes and clades were even developed. Our dog concepts represent a particular genome in virtue of being reliably caused by objects that have that genome. This does not mean that our dog concepts do not describe any features of dogs. They may explicitly represent dogs as having fur, as barking, as wagging their tails, and so on. Dog concepts are reliably caused by objects with the dog genome, because such objects reliably possess certain appearances. We track dogs by those appearances. Dog concepts are "appearance-tracking detectors."

I offer another terminological distinction. The dog genome, or any other property essential to being a dog, can be called the "real content" of a dog concept. The features by which we detect dogs can be called the "nominal content" of our dog concepts (see Prinz, 2000, 2002). Detectors represent their real contents by *registering* their nominal contents. Essence-tracking detectors have real contents and nominal contents that coincide, but with appearance-tracking detectors, these come apart. Dog concepts are reliably caused by dogs *via* their appearances.

Mental representations often work this way (Prinz, 2000). They track real contents via more superficial nominal contents. This raises a question about emotions. I have already argued that emotions do not detect core relational themes by explicitly describing those themes. They are not essence detectors. But, this does not mean that emotions are unstructured; it does not mean they are indicators. Perhaps they represent core relation themes by registering something else. But what could they possible register? What are the superficial features of core relational themes? Wherein lie the fur and wagging tails of emotion?

The answer marks a grand reconciliation between the appraisal tradition and the tradition inaugurated by James and Lange. I submit that emotions track core relational themes by registering changes in the body. Earlier I presented a barrage of evidence in favor of the view that emotions are perceptions of the body. On the face of it, this seems to be incompatible with the claim that emotions represent core relational themes, but that tension can now be lifted. Just as concepts of dogs track dogs via furriness, fears track dangers via heart palpitations. Emotions are embodied. They represent core relational themes, but they do so by perceiving bodily changes.[3] Core relational themes are the real contents of emotions, and bodily changes are their nominal contents. The proposal is depicted in figure 3.2.

This proposal raises a question. Why should we be able to track core relational themes via changes in the body? For this to occur, it would have to be the case that certain bodily changes reliably cooccur with core relational themes. Why should this be so? The answer has already been intimated in chapter 1. Bodily changes occur because they prepare us for response. Our hearts race to increase blood flow, which prepares us for fleeing, fighting, or engaging in other kinds of behavior.

---

[3]In chapter 10, I will ask whether emotions can be considered perceptions of core relational themes, or whether they represent core relational themes in a nonperceptual way.

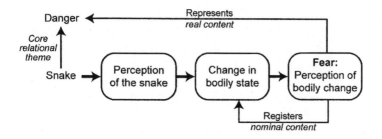

*Figure 3.2.*    The real contents and nominal contents of an emotion.

Evolution has undoubtedly endowed us with distinctive physiological re-sponses to various situations that our ancestors encountered. The heart is predis-posed to race (along with several other physiological responses) when we see looming objects, snakes, crawling insects, or large moving shadows at night; or when we hear loud noises or the screams of conspecifics; or when we smell the odor of a predator. The racing heart and the other physiological changes that oc-cur under these conditions collectively serve as a danger detector. They occur un-der these situations because of how we are wired. Perceptual experiences of dan-gerous situations are wired to cause appropriate physiological changes to occur. Some of this wiring is innate, and some is learned. Learned fear responses capi-talize on phylogenetically primitive machinery.

Consider the chain of events leading to fear. Something dangerous occurs. That thing is perceived by the mind. This perception triggers a constellation of bodily changes. These changes are registered by a further state: a bodily perception. The bodily perception is directly caused by bodily changes, but it is indirectly caused by the danger that started the whole chain of events. It carries information about danger by responding to changes in the body. That further state is fear. This is just like the somatic theories of chapter 1, with a new story about the semantic properties of the bodily perception.

If this proposal is right, it shows that emotions can represent core relational themes without explicitly describing them. Emotions track bodily states that reli-ably cooccur with important organism-environment relations, so emotions reli-ably cooccur with organism-environment relations. Each emotion is both an in-ternal body monitor and a detector of dangers, threats, losses, or other matters of concern. Emotions are gut reactions; they use our bodies to tell us how we are faring in the world.

## The Adrenaline Objection

The theory that I have been presenting identifies emotions with inner states that register changes in the body. This proposal will be revised, elaborated, and de-fended against objections in the chapters that follow. One objection, however, cannot be delayed. In saying that emotions are states that register bodily changes, I am vulnerable to a complaint that plagued defenders of the James-Lange theory. Different emotions, it has been alleged, can be associated with the same bodily states. Moreover, nonemotional states can cause bodily changes of the kind we associate with emotions.

The allegation was made by Walter Cannon in 1927. Cannon (1927) argued that fear, rage, chilliness, hypoglycemia, asphyxia, and fever all affect the viscera in similar ways. The same changes can even be caused by intense bouts of joy, sorrow, and disgust. In defending these claims, Cannon calls on a study by Gregorio Marañon (1924). Marañon injected subjects with adrenaline without telling them what effects they could expect. Subjects who had been reflecting on emotionally significant life events (e.g., the death of a loved one) reported feeling as if they were experiencing the relevant emotion (e.g., sadness). The reported emotions varied with the interpretations—not, Marañon presumed, with changes in physiology. Physiological changes were under the control of the adrenaline injections, which were the same for all subjects.

This seminal experiment was the inspiration behind the experiment of Schachter and Singer (1962) described in chapter 1, in which subjects injected with adrenaline (and ignorant of its effects) showed signs of anger when they were given an insulting questionnaire and showed signs of happiness when they were placed in a room with someone engaged in silly antics. Different contexts cause the same physiological state (e.g., heart palpitations) to be interpreted in different ways. It is the difference in interpretation, not physiology, that accounts for the difference in emotional state.

If Marañon, Cannon, and Schachter are right, bodily states cannot distinguish between different emotions. They cannot even distinguish between emotions and nonemotions. If the inner states that constitute our emotions are simply responses to bodily changes, we should not be able to tell one emotion from another. Call this the adrenaline objection.

Defenders of the adrenaline objection make two crucial assumptions. First, they assume that the subjects who *display* distinct emotional behavior are actually in different emotional states. Second, they assume that the subjects who display different emotional behavior are actually in the same physiological state. Both assumptions can be challenged.

The second assumption is based on the fact that all the subjects in the experiment are injected with the same drug. The same drug at the beginning of the experiment is thought to entail the same physiological changes throughout the experiment. This inference is far from secure. Suppose two people are injected with adrenaline and then placed in a mildly amusing or a mildly aggravating situation (as in the Schachter and Singer experiment). Under ordinary conditions, such situations may be too mild to induce an emotion. The adrenaline, however, may serve as a catalyst that increases the likelihood of an emotional response. Once that response occurs, there is no reason to assume that the physiology in the amusing and aggravating situations will remain the same. Generic physiological arousal may be modified or supplemented, resulting in physiological states that are distinctive to happiness or anger.

Now consider the assumption that subjects who display different emotional behavior actually experience the emotions they display. When Schachter and Singer did their experiment, they measured the emotions of their subjects in two ways. They observed subjects' behavior and they asked them to report on their emotional states. The behavioral measures supported Schachter and Singer's predictions. Subjects in the anger condition behaved angrily, and subjects in the euphoria condition behaved as if they were happy. In particular, subjects in the anger condition expressed agreement with a stooge who complained about an insulting questionnaire, and subjects in the euphoria condition joined a stooge in silly antics. When asked to report their emotions, however, subjects in *both* conditions reported that they were happy! In fact, even subjects who were forewarned of the physiological effects of adrenaline reported experiencing happiness. This is at odds with the assumption that emotions depend on interpretations rather than physiology alone. Perhaps all subjects experience mild happiness because the adrenaline causes the same physiological responses, and those responses are sufficient for happiness.

Schachter and Singer explain this embarrassing result by arguing that subjects in all the experimental conditions report happiness because they are all trying to please the experimenter. This explanation is not credible. Why assume that subjects in the anger condition would try to please an experimenter who just gave them an insulting questionnaire? Why assume that their verbal reports are false while assuming the sincerity of the angry behavior they exhibit earlier in the experiment? That behavior may be disingenuously performed to appease the confederates in the experiment. Subjects may exhibit angry behavior in an attempt to express sympathy with the outraged stooge, despite feeling rather joyful. In short, the Schachter and Singer results actually support the view that emotions do not vary across physiologically identical states. (For a more detailed critique see Reisenzein [1983], who reviews several unsuccessful attempts to replicate Schachter and Singer's results.)

There is, I conclude, reason to doubt the two key assumptions made by defenders of the adrenaline objection. We cannot be sure that subjects in adrenaline experiments experience different emotions, and we cannot be sure that they have the same physiological states. As it turns out, the adrenaline objection fails even if both of these assumptions are true. The theory of emotions that I have proposed says that emotions are internal states that register changes in the body. It is consistent with this proposal that those states sometimes occur in the absence of the bodily changes they are designed to detect. Suppose, for example, that happiness ordinarily involves general arousal plus some other physiological change, $P1$. Suppose that anger involves general arousal plus physiological change $P2$. Despite some overlap, anger and sadness involve different changes overall. Now suppose that the actual brain state of happiness, $B1$, is a state that is generally triggered by arousal plus $P1$, and the brain state of anger, $B2$, is one that is generally triggered by arousal plus P2. B1 and B2 are distinct brain states. Finally, assume that B1 and B2 can occur without the physiological states that ordinarily cause them. If all these assumptions are correct, subjects in the Schachter and Singer experiments could be in different emotional states, B1 or B2, without being in different physiological states P1 and P2.

General arousal may be enough to prime both B1 and B2 (i.e., it may temporarily dispose us to experience both anger and happiness). Subsequent context-based interpretation may then finish the job by leading the brain to enter state B1 or B2, even though the current physiology is neutral between these. The brain is duped to thinking that the body is in a physiological state that is specific to one emotion or the other, even though it is not.

This proposal is similar to Damasio's (1994) suggestion that the brain contains as-if loops. As-if loops can cause activation in brain states that ordinarily register physiological changes even in the absence of those changes. They are like mental images of physiological changes. If as-if loops exist, the existence of different emotions under comparable physiological conditions poses no threat to Damasio's theory or to mine. The adrenaline objection fails.

## Emotion-Specific Physiology

The preceding considerations undercut one objection to the proposal that emotional states are brain states that register physiological changes. This point is only defensive. I have not provided positive evidence for the claim that emotions are physiologically distinct. That supposition is a matter of ongoing controversy. At present, there has been no decisive evidence for the physiological distinctness of all emotions. Nevertheless, existing evidence is suggestive.

Notice that the position I am defending does not require that each type of emotion always be accompanied by the same physiological responses. In laboratory animals, fear sometimes causes flight behavior and sometimes causes freezing. These two responses may be underwritten by distinct physiological changes, such as heart rate increase, in the first case, and blood vessel constriction and muscle tension, in the second. The same division in fear responses and attendant physiology may be found in humans. This does not show that fear lacks distinctive physiology. Fear and other emotions may each correspond to several physiological patterns.

Because of such variability, I think it is best to associate emotions with body state prototypes. A prototype is a mental representation made up of parts that correspond to a range of "diagnostic features." Diagnostic features are features that provide good evidence for something but are not always essential for that thing. The ability to bark is a diagnostic feature for being a dog, because, while some dogs do not bark (e.g., dingos), many barking things are dogs. A dog prototype is a mental representation of dogs, whose parts correspond to a set of such features (barking, being furry, having four legs, tail wagging, playing fetch, etc.). Prototypes are used to categorize things. A prototype becomes active when a sufficient number of its diagnostic features are detected. Likewise for the mental representations associated with emotions. A fear representation (i.e., a representation of danger) becomes active when a sufficient number of the many bodily changes that can occur in a dangerous situation is detected. A freezing reaction may be sufficient on one occasion, and a fleeing response may be sufficient on another. The hypothesis, then, is that each emotion has a corresponding prototype that responds to different patterns of bodily changes and thereby comes under the causal control of core relational themes.

But why think bodily patterns can discriminate between emotions? After all, both fleeing, associated with fear, and fighting, associated with anger, benefit from many of the same bodily changes. An increased heart rate is needed to provide extra blood flow for either of these responses. If physiological changes are linked to behavioral dispositions, could emotions really be physiologically distinguishable? The answer seems to be yes.

Levenson, Ekman, and Friesen (1990) performed a study in which they measured the physiological states associated with six different emotions. Ostensibly, they were interested in finding out whether changes in facial expression caused changes in affect. They instructed subjects to form faces that have been independently found to cooccur with emotional states. Subjects were then asked to report any emotions that they experienced. During this process, heart rate, finger temperature, and electrical conductivity of the skin were all measured. When subjects formed emotional facial expressions, they often reported experiencing emotions. These reports were well correlated with physiological changes.

Levenson, Ekman, and Friesen found the following physiological patterns. First, there were differences between the changes that accompanied happiness and the changes that accompanied the other measured emotions, which were all negative. Heart rate acceleration was greater for anger and fear than for happiness. Skin conductance increase was greater for fear and disgust than for happiness. This suggests that positive emotions can be physiologically distinguished from negative emotions. There were also physiological distinctions between negative emotions. Anger, fear, and sadness all had greater heart rate acceleration than disgust. Finger temperature increase was larger for anger than for fear. The sixth emotion measured was surprise, which the authors regard as neither negative nor positive. Surprise has lower heart rate acceleration than happiness.

The results of this study suggest that no single physiological dimension is unique to any emotion. This has led some researchers to doubt whether emotions can be physiologically distinguished (see, e.g., Cacioppo, Bernston, Larson, Poehlmann, & Ito, 2000). But this conclusion is unfounded. The results suggest that each of the tested emotions has its own *pattern* of effects. This result was obtained using a small handful of physiological measures. Had Levenson et al. measured other physiological responses (such as changes in digestive organs, blood vessel constriction, respiration, or hormones), further differences might have emerged.

There are two limitations with the data collected by Levenson et al. First, the experimenters did not manipulate levels of arousal. All emotions were induced through voluntary changes in facial expression, and such changes may only induce weak emotional states. For all the experiment shows, intense emotions may blur the physiological differences between emotions. Perhaps intense happiness has the bodily profile of despair or rage. There is no obvious reason to assume such blurring would occur, but it calls for further testing.

More seriously, the Levensen et al. studies are limited to six emotions, which are alleged to be especially fundamental. It is difficult to predict what would happen if the study were expanded to include emotions such as shame, jealousy, contempt, embarrassment, and indignation. Perhaps these emotions have no distinctive physiology, or no strong physiological responses at all.

I address this issue in chapters 4 and 5. For the moment, I will have to be content with the conclusion that some emotions appear to be associated with distinctive patterns of physiological response.

### *Locating Appraisals*

#### Inner Causes of Emotion

There remains one more lingering concern. When an external object causes an emotion in us, there is no direct causal link between the object and the changes in the body. A slithering snake cannot cause one's skin to crawl without a mediating link in between. There must be some inner state that detects the snake and then causes the physiological change to take place. Emotions must have inner causes. Supporters of Lazarus might say that this is where disembodied appraisal judgments come in. Our hearts begin to race only after we use disembodied concepts to evaluate a situation as dangerous. Perhaps the model I am proposing covertly demands that emotions have disembodied appraisals as causes.

There is something to this objection. Disembodied appraisal judgments certainly enter into the equation on some occasions. When someone reacts fearfully to the sight of a college exam, for example, disembodied judgments may mediate the link between the external danger and the racing heart. One may judge the exam to be incongruent with one's motives, potentially damaging to one's self-esteem, and so on.

This is not a precondition for all fear responses, however. In the case of snake phobia discussed in chapter 2, the link between the external danger and the racing heart may be mediated by nothing more than a primitive visual representation of the snake. Merely seeing the snake gets one's heart racing. The inner cause of an emotion is not a judgment in the snake phobia case but a perceptual state. Cases like this are, I believe, more fundamental than cases like the fear of exams.

The upshot is that emotions can have different kinds of inner causes. Snake phobias lie at one end of the spectrum. Studies of nonhuman primates suggest that snake phobia has a basis in the genes. When young macaque monkeys witness a conspecific displaying an aversive response to snakes, they develop snake phobias (Mineka, Davidson, Cook, & Keir, 1984). Macaques that never see such a display do not develop snake phobias. Macaques who see conspecifics showing aversive response to various things other than snakes do not develop phobias for those things. This suggests that macaques are born with a predisposition to become snake phobic and the predisposition can be triggered by a particular kind of experience. Once triggered, the mere sight of a snake makes the heart race. The same may be true in humans.

The snake case shows that emotions can be triggered by perceptual states. Fear begins as soon as a perceived snake causes activity in brain centers involved in early visual processing. Other examples, such as fear of insects or fear of looming objects, may owe a special debt to the genes as well. There may also be genetically prepared elicitors for other emotions. Joy may naturally issue from physical stimulation, and a glaring look from a conspecific may be a natural trigger for anger.

Given such examples, one might infer that innate emotional responses are perceptually induced and learned emotional responses are induced via nonperceptual states (see Damasio, 1994). That would be a mistake. Many of our learned emotional responses are perceptually mediated. Zajonc's examples of food aversions are a case in point. If you feel disgusted by the sight of a food that once made you ill, it may be because your brain has set up a shortcut between the appearance of that food and a negative reaction. The ability to acquire emotional responses in this way probably evolved in creatures that were incapable of cognition. An organism merely requires the ability to associate a perceptual state (e.g., seeing a food) with an affective response that has occurred in conjunction with that perceptual state (e.g., disgust).

Associative learning can probably forge a link between emotions and any perceptual experience that occurs in conjunction with them. Food aversions can be formed after a single experience with a noxious food. Other experiences become emotion triggers after repeated or protracted exposures. Imagine a person who develops a lifelong aversion to the color yellow after being domiciled in a yellow room during a long childhood illness (compare Locke, 1690/1979, II.xxxiii.12). One can experience pleasure seeing the face of a loved one, or anger seeing the face of an enemy. In each case, a visual experience that frequently coincided with an emotion in the past serves to respark that emotion.

Emotions can also be triggered by cognitive states. Recall that a cognitive state is just a mental representation that is under organismic control. Mental images qualify as cognitive. When one intentionally forms an image of a noxious food, a loved one, or an enemy, one may feel the appropriate emotional response. These are cognitively induced emotions. Imageless thoughts of pleasant and unpleasant situations can be effective emotion triggers as well. For example, one can enter an emotional state by merely uttering an emotionally charged sentence in one's head. Thinking about anything that once caused an emotion in the past can cause the emotion in the present. Memory forges links between emotions and representations of the particular objects that elicited them.

It cannot be the case that every emotional response depends on some prior memory. Sometimes we form emotional responses upon encountering an object for the first time. Sometimes we have emotional responses to objects that we have just conjured up in imagination. Sometimes reflecting on a novel situation can cause an emotional response. How do these cases occur?

The answer may shed some light on the allure of cognitive cause appraisal theories. Cognitive cause theories say that emotions occur only after we have evaluated a situation. Defenders of these theories assume that the evaluations in question are disembodied; they are propositional attitudes built up from concepts that have no intrinsic connection to the states that cause or register changes in the body. I argued that this is not always the case. That does not mean it never occurs. Disembodied propositional attitudes can become emotion triggers through learning.

Imagine the following developmental sequence. Initially, one is biologically disposed to experience certain emotions under a restricted range of perceptually detectable circumstances. Darkness and a sudden loss of support may both be triggers of the state we come to know as fear. As our cognitive skills develop, we learn acquire a host of disembodied concepts for reflecting on the world around us. We acquire a concept of danger, and a corresponding word. At some point, while experiencing fear in a darkened room, we entertain the verbally mediated thought that we are facing a dangerous situation. This happens on a number of subsequent occasions. At first, the thought "I am in danger" is an effect of fear. It is an assessment of the situation that triggered an emotional response. But, through associate learning, that thought becomes a trigger for fear as well. Eventually, the explicit thought "I am in danger" becomes capable of initiating fear responses in situations that lack the physical features that are predisposed to upset us as a function of our biology. A well-illuminated room with no visible threat can send us into a state of terror if a series of dispassionate judgments lead us to infer that we are facing some invisible threat. In sum, a narrow range of biologically programmed, perceptual emotion elicitors can induce states that lead us to deploy concepts that capture the features unifying those elicitors; those concepts then become emotion elicitors of their own.

In this way, explicit, disembodied judgments about core relational themes can become inner causes of our emotions. Cognitive cause theorists have hit upon one of the ways in which emotions occur. This method of emotion induction is quite powerful. It allows us to consider actual and nonactual situations that have no immediate emotional impact, reason about them, and arrive at an appropriate emotional response. There is nothing intrinsically scary looking about an exam book, a gun, or a politician with fascist tendencies, but thinking about any of these things can instill fear. In each case, the fear may be caused by a belief that the object in question is dangerous.

I thus concede that emotions are often caused by disembodied judgments. But these cases are not the model on which a theory of emotion should be built. If I am right, such cases are parasitic on cases in which emotions are caused by perceptual responses. Propositional attitudes representing core relational themes induce emotions only because they are associated with emotions in the past. Other kinds of propositional attitudes and perceptual states can become emotion elicitors by associative learning as well. Suppose I become terrified upon seeing a bowl of spaghetti. It may be that I was eating spaghetti during a traumatic earthquake, and the mere sight of it has instilled terror in me ever since. It may be that I have a food aversion caused by prior consumption of rancid spaghetti sauce. It may be that I believe the spaghetti has been poisoned, and I reason that I am in danger. Explicit, disembodied judgments are just one kind of cause among many. They have no special value in our inner emotional economies. They are neither necessary nor the gold standard from which other kinds of causes are derived. Cognitive cause theorists erroneously treat an ontogenetically sophisticated class of emotion elicitors as fundamental.

It turns out that emotions can have a variety of inner causes. This is illustrated in figure 3.3. The box in between danger and the bodily response can be filled by complex judgments or simple percepts. Because of this variety, it is a mistake to look for a universal causes of emotions within the mind. Different kinds of mental states do the trick on different occasions.

### Appraisals Embodied

The preceding considerations do not bode well for the prevailing appraisal theories of emotion. Most of those theories assume that emotions always follow on the heels of disembodied propositional attitudes. I suggest that such cases are parasitic on emotion episodes caused by states that are neither propositional attitudes nor appraisals. This does not mean that appraisal theories of emotion should be abandoned.

In the conclusion of chapter 2, I promised to show that appraisals can be embodied. To qualify as an appraisal, a state must represent an organism-environment relation that bears on well-being. On the view I have been defending, emotions qualify as appraisals in this strict sense. They represent core relational themes.

I have also argued that emotions monitor our bodily states. Emotions represent

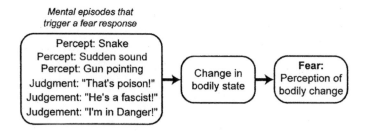

***Figure 3.3.***    Fear and its many inner causes.

# Basic Emotions and Natural Kinds

## *The Disunity Thesis*

### Emotions and Natural Kinds

In the preceding chapters, I have assumed that all emotions are essentially alike. Obviously fear, sadness, anger, guilt, jealousy, and elation are different in some sense. They all play different roles in our lives. But I have assumed that they also have something in common. I have assumed there are some shared features in virtue of which they all qualify as emotions. The very idea that there can be *a* theory of emotions, as opposed to several different theories, carries this presupposition. The presupposition is virtually forced on us by the English language. The word "emotion" is used as an umbrella term for many different states. We assume, without ever reflecting, that those states form a coherent class.

Other languages lack a word for "emotions" (Wierzbicka, 1999). Languages all seem to have a word translatable as "feelings," but this is a more general term that subsumes sensations, drives, moods, and pains along with emotions. The idea that there is a certain class of feelings, the emotions, that constitutes a coherent domain of inquiry is not codified in every languages. Indeed, the word "emotion" was only introduced in English at the end of the sixteenth century (Crespo, 1986). This fact should raise some eyebrows. Do the things we call emotions really share some properties in virtue of which they all belong together and can all be distinguished from other kinds of feelings? Or is the category just imposed on us by English? The assumption that emotions form a coherent class needs to be examined.

Amelie Rorty opens the introduction to her (1980) anthology *Explaining Emotions* by remarking that "emotions do not form a natural class." Call this the *disunity thesis*. If the disunity thesis is correct, it calls for a significant change in the way emotions are studied. Most emotion researchers work under the assumption that emotions form a natural class—or "natural kind," to use the preferred term of art. Working under this assumption, researchers often develop theories of the emotions based on a few choice examples. Those theories are expected to generalize to all other cases. If emotions do not form a natural kind, there cannot be a single theory of the emotions. It may even be impossible to develop a single science of the emotions. Different kinds of explanatory resources may be needed to handle different emotion subcategories.

De Sousa (1987) develops an argument for the disunity thesis. He argues that emotions cannot form a natural kind because they have no unifying formal objects. Beliefs form a natural kind because they all aim at truth; they have a shared criterion for success. Emotions all have different formal objects—fear is about danger and sadness is about loss—so they have no shared criterion for success. I think this argument can be answered. First of all, there is a sense in which emotions all share the same formal object. All emotions are about core relational themes. Emotions have a shared criterion of success, because each emotion is appropriate when it responds to a relationship between its possessor and the environment that bears on well-being. While beliefs aim at the True, emotions aim at Relations that Matter. Second, having a shared formal object is not a good criterion for determining whether a class of things forms a natural kind. It is not a necessary criterion. Tigers are a natural kind, and they do not have formal objects. And it is not a sufficient criterion. Beliefs and indicative sentences both aim at truth, but they are very different kinds of entities. To prove or refute the disunity thesis, we must look elsewhere.

Paul Griffiths (1997) has developed a more compelling case for the disunity thesis that emotions do not form a natural class. Before discussing his arguments, we must get a bit more clear on what the disunity thesis maintains. Disunity is defined in terms of natural kinds. Many philosophers (and scientists) presume that certain categories have boundaries that derive from nature, not from the way we human beings happen to group things together. Nature is thought to have built-in divisions, or joints. It is the job of science to identify those joints. Lions, tigers, and bears are all thought to be natural kinds. Water, gold, and galaxies are others.

The category of good actors, funny jokes, and bad restaurants may be non natural kinds. They are things that get grouped together on the basis of how we classify. There are also some controversial cases. There is a debate about whether mental illnesses are natural kinds, for example (Murphy & Stich, 2000). Sometimes things that were once thought to be natural kinds turn out to be nonnatural. The category of fire is an example. We use the word "fire" to subsume activity on the sun, the northern lights, fireflies, and burning logs, none of which derive from the same physical phenomenon (Churchland, 1992). The heterogeneous conditions we group under the word "pneumonia" may also fail to comprise a natural kind. These conditions have similar symptoms but different underlying etiologies. The same is true of the class of lilies, which turn out to be superficially similar but not closely related biologically (Griffiths, 1997).

Philosophers have disagreed about what distinguishes natural kinds from nonnatural kinds. A standard view used to be that members of a natural kind all share a common underlying essence (Kripke, 1980). All samples of water qualify as water, on this model, in virtue of being made of $H_2O$. All lions are lions in virtue of having a certain genome or a certain ancestral lineage (a common clade). The underlying essence view may be appropriate for certain categories, but it is hard to apply to others. The class of rivers, for example, may not be made out of the same underlying materials. Even water samples may vary in constitution. Many things we call water have "impurities," and many things that are predominantly $H_2O$ are not called water (Malt, 1994). Tea, for example, probably contains more $H_2O$ than the "water" in the Red Sea.

Boyd (1989; see also Keil, 1989) has developed a more liberal definition of natural kinds. He says that natural kinds are homeostatic property clusters. Certain properties, such as being a clear, tasteless liquid, often cluster together in nature. They are highly correlated. Often property clusters are not accidental. Some properties in a cluster tend to promote the presence of the others. In such cases, there are generally causal mechanisms increasing the probability of cooccurrence. Whatever promotes the properties of being liquid and tasteless also promotes the property of being clear. Properties that cluster together in virtue of causal mechanisms are said to be homeostatic. These, Boyd, argues are natural kinds.

Homeostatic property clusters need not have a common underlying essence. It is not necessary for all water samples to have the exact same proportion of $H_2O$, and it is not necessary for all lions to have the exact same genome. They only need to have similar collections of properties bound by causal mechanisms. Rivers are a natural kind, because flowing water, beds, banks, tributaries, and other properties of rivers cooccur because each of these properties is causally supported by the existence of the others.

Griffiths endorses Boyd's definition of natural kinds. By using this definition, instead of the underlying essence account, he makes it harder to demonstrate disunity. To show that emotions are a natural kind, one does not need to show that they have, for example, a common neurochemistry. One only needs to show that they tend to share a cluster of properties that are causally homeostatic. Griffiths thinks emotions fail to satisfy this condition. His disunity thesis amounts to the claim that emotions do not share a common cluster of homeostatic properties. I will ultimately argue that emotions are a natural kind in both the Boydian sense and in the stronger sense. Emotions have a unifying essence.

## Affect Programs and Commitment Clinchers

Griffiths's central argument for the disunity thesis rests on an analysis of distinctions within the class of states we call "emotions." He tries to show that this class splinters into at least two incongruous subcategories. The first subcategory can be explained by appeal to Paul Ekman's notion of "affect programs." As I showed in chapter 1, affect programs are complex responses that involve appraisals, bodily changes, and action dispositions in response to perceived stimuli. Affect programs are also culturally universal, are underwritten by specific neural circuits, and have homologues in nonhuman species. They are generally associated with specific facial expressions.

According to Griffiths, the most distinctive feature of affect programs is their modularity. Modules are fast[1] processing systems that respond to proprietary inputs and cannot be directly influenced by information in other processing systems. They are informationally encapsulated (Fodor, 1983; see chapter 10 for more discussion). For example, the visual system is said to be modular because it responds to proprietary inputs (light coming in through the eyes) and is impervious to direct manipulation by our thoughts and beliefs. In looking at an optical illusion, for example, our eyes cannot help but be fooled, even if we believe that appearance is illusory. Likewise, Ekman's theory suggests that affect programs are modular. Activity in our affect program is triggered by a restricted class of inputs and cannot be overridden by conflicting beliefs. A looming object will cause the fear affect program to run, even if we know that the object is harmless.

As this last example illustrates, affect programs offer a reasonable account of certain things we call emotions. Ekman has focused on six affect programs in particular. He calls these fear, anger, happiness, sadness, surprise, and disgust. Recently, he has argued that there is an affect program corresponding to contempt (Ekman & Friesen, 1986). As I will show in chapter 5, these labels are somewhat loose. They do not correspond perfectly to ordinary English expressions. The "happiness" affect program may subsume states that we call joy, ecstasy, amusement, contentment, gratification, and so on. In ordinary usage, all of these states are subtly different. The affect program of happiness is an overarching positive emotion that may lie behind each of these folk categories.

Griffiths believes that Ekman's theory captures one subset of things that we call emotions. Emotions in this subset can be easily handled by the embodied appraisal theory presented in chapter 3. These emotions are associated with identifiable and distinctive patterns of bodily change. Those bodily changes comprise part of an affect program on Ekman's account. On my theory, emotions are identified with inner responses to bodily changes. So emotions that lend themselves to explanation by appeal to affect programs lend themselves to explanation by appeal to somatic appraisals. But Griffiths does not think that Ekman's theory generalizes. Certain emotions cannot be identified with affect programs. Most notably, he thinks that Ekman's theory will not accommodate "higher cognitive emotions." This term refers to emotions such emotions as envy, guilt, shame, pride, feelings of loyalty, and vengefulness.[2] If these emotions cannot be associated with affect programs, then there is also little hope for explaining them by appeal to embodied appraisals.

---

[1]Griffiths sometimes mentions speed and duration in arguing that emotions are not a natural kind. Some are fast and short, and some are slow and long. I think speed is a red herring. Members of a coherent category can be highly variable in onset time and duration. Consider the temporal variability of migraines, hurricanes, and copulations.

[2]This list includes some items that Ekman now tries to explain in the affect program framework.

As the name implies, higher cognitive emotions seem to be intrinsically cognitive.[3] It is hard to imagine having them without having advanced cognitive abilities. We would not be surprised to find that rats can be angry or afraid, but we would be very surprised to discover that they can be ashamed or jealous. The capacity for shame and jealousy seems to carry a degree of conceptual sophistication. To be ashamed, you must be capable of thinking that you did something wrong. To be jealous, you must be capable of believing that someone has something that is rightfully yours. There is no reason to think that rats can entertain such thoughts.

Griffiths regards the cognitive prerequisites of higher cognitive emotions as a tipoff. Unlike affect programs, higher cognitive emotions do not seem to be modular. Not only can beliefs influence a state of shame but they also seem to be obligatory for shame. If you do not believe you did anything wrong, you will not feel ashamed. Shame can be caused by beliefs and cured by beliefs. If you discover that your actions were beneficial rather than harmful, you can trade shame in for pride.

Griffiths argues that cognitive involvement in higher cognitive emotions does not render them less amenable to evolutionary explanation than affect programs. He is open to the possibility that higher cognitive emotions are products of natural selection. At the same time, Griffiths is refreshingly cautious about evolutionary explanation in psychology. He warns that it is too easy to weave evolutionary yarns. Sometimes we come up with a compelling story about why some psychological trait evolved before we have even established that the trait exists. Sometimes we buy into a compelling story about a well-established trait without any evidence for thinking the story is true. We cannot infer traits from evolutionary stories or evolutionary stories from traits. Griffiths cautions that any thesis about the adaptive function of a trait must be measured against quantitative evidence concerning the time and environment in which that trait emerged. Despite such pitfalls, Griffiths is willing to speculate a bit. He speaks with some sympathy of a particular adaptationist story that has been defended by Robert Frank.

According to Frank (1988), many of our emotions evolved as solutions to "commitment problems." Commitment problems emerge whenever two or more parties negotiate. Evolution cares about reproduction, and in order to reach a reproductive age, organisms must struggle for their interests. But the interests of two organisms are not necessarily identical. Both you and I might want all the cookies in the jar. If we both try to take all the cookies, we will fight, harm each other, and walk away losers. As a result, we negotiate. We both promise to take only half the cookies. If I am lying when I make the promise, I can get all the cookies. If you are lying, you can do the same. We need some way to predict honesty, and some bias against negotiating with cheaters. That is where emotions come in. Emotions encourage fair trades and help us identify fair traders.

---

[3] Though whether they really do involve higher cognition is a matter of debate, as this chapter will show. The term "higher cognitive emotions" should be treated as a name for emotions that *seem* to involve higher cognition rather than a name for emotions that necessarily involve higher cognition.

To do their work, emotions must override simple means-ends reasoning. Suppose you offer to give me two of the ten cookies in the jar and keep the rest. If I say yes, I get two cookies. If I say no, you will grab the jar and eat them all. Means-ends reasoning tells me to accept the bargain. Two is better than none. But Frank has found that people routinely avoid unfair bargains. They would sooner have no cookies than accept an unfair deal. Somehow our means-ends reasoning is short-circuited. Frank explains this by saying that emotions are "irruptive motivations." They sacrifice immediate gains in the interest of long-term benefits by temporarily silencing plans based on expected utility. We refuse to accept unfair deals because we are overwhelmed by feelings of honesty and integrity.

Similarly, we may feel vengeful when we are wronged, even though seeking revenge is a high-risk activity (higher risk than simply walking away). Merely displaying feelings of vengefulness (which are very hard to fake) shows potential negotiating partners that we will not tolerate any mischief. Irruptive motivations increase the likelihood that everyone will avoid unfair deals and wrongful acts. The long-term payoff is a net reduction in cheaters and meanies. The remaining nice folks can live in reciprocal harmony. Emotions ensure that most commitments will be kept.

Griffiths thinks that Frank's theory may provide a good account of the higher cognitive emotions (for critique, see chapter 5). That endorsement provides a crucial premise for his main point. Affect programs are rapid, modular response systems with homologues in nonhuman animals. Higher cognitive emotions are commitment clinchers that interact with beliefs and may be unique to human beings (though see de Waal, 1996, on chimpanzees). These two kinds of emotions are underwritten by different mechanisms and lend themselves to different kinds of evolutionary explanations.[4]

Griffiths is convinced that these differences make a difference. Affect programs and higher cognitive emotions do not belong to a common natural kind. They do not share a common cluster of homeostatically bound properties. Griffiths speculates about why people call them both emotions. Why does folk psychology treat higher cognitive emotions and affect programs as belonging together? The answer, he suspects, is that they can both function as irruptive motivations. Affect programs, like feelings of honesty or vengefulness, can interfere with means-ends reasoning. When we become afraid, for example, we may run away from situations that could be rewarding.

According to Griffiths, this similarity between higher cognitive emotions and

---

[4]Griffiths goes on to identify a third class of states that we may call emotions. These consist of emotion-like displays that are actually intentionally performed for some strategic purpose. We often exhibit such displays without realizing that they are intentional (as when we display anger during a lovers' quarrel). Griffiths regards such emotion-like displays as disclaimed actions—actions that we do not take responsibility for. He admits, however, that these may be not be true emotions. They are feigned emotions rather than the real thing. Therefore, they cannot contribute to his disunity argument.

affect programs is not enough for true unity. These two classes of states may both be irruptive motivations, but they are underwritten by different causal mechanisms. Affect programs are modular, and higher cognitive emotions are not. True natural kinds require similarity in causal mechanisms. Griffiths concludes that emotions are not a natural kind.

I am not convinced by this argument. The very fact that affect programs and higher cognitive emotions can both be described as irruptive motivations *constitutes* a unifying causal mechanism. Irruptive motivation is a causal role that is responsible for correlations between many of the "superficial" properties of emotions. It explains why emotions seem passive, drive action, and influence practical reasoning in seemingly irrational ways. It may also explain why higher cognitive emotions and affect programs get grouped together in folk psychology. They seem alike to us because they play a similar role in our mental lives. The irruptive motivation account also allows for projectability. If we were to identify an unlexicalized state that serves as an irruptive motivation, be it modular or nonmodular, we would have a principled reason for grouping it with familiar emotions.

Notice that grouping affect programs and higher cognitive emotions together is compatible with Griffiths's conjecture that they are importantly different. I interpret Boyd's approach to natural kinds as quite liberal. There are many features that cluster together in similar ways. When two sets of states share some projectable homeostatic mechanism and not others, we can say they constitute both two distinct natural kinds *and* a common natural kind. Familiar examples of superordinate categories give an obvious case of this. Kiwis and bananas are different natural kinds, but they also belong to the common natural kind, fruits. We can also have compatible kind divisions at a single taxonomic level. Marsupials and mammals may belong to a single natural kind in virtue of being warm-blooded and having a common ancestry, but they are also distinct in virtue of the way they reproduce and in virtue of a split at some point in their ancestral line. They belong to both the same natural kind and different natural kinds. For certain purposes, coclassification may be most informative.

This reply to Griffiths is not fully satisfying. I suspect that the irruptive motivation proposal will fail in the end. The problem is that it casts the emotion net too wide. Consider fatigue. Like fear and feelings of loyalty, fatigue can figure into decision making in a way that departs from means-ends reasoning. For example, imagine cases where fatigue causes one to stop working on an important assignment. Fatigue, it would seem, is an irruptive motivation but not an emotion. The search for a principle that unites all and only emotions must go on.

Even if the irruptive motivation proposal were to succeed, Griffiths's argument would have important ramifications. First, it puts another nail in the coffin of dimensional appraisal theories. Those theories analyze each emotion into a number of appraisal dimensions, which are thought to capture actual judgments made before an emotional response. Dimensional appraisal theories assume that every emotion is associated with different values along the very same appraisal dimensions (e.g., Lazarus, 1991). Griffiths's argument suggests that the mechanisms that set off affect programs differ considerably from the mechanisms that set off higher cognitive emotions. Affect programs respond to a restricted range of perceptual inputs, and higher cognitive emotions respond to complex thoughts. The suggestion that both are driven by a shared set of appraisal dimensions is not easy to reconcile with this apparent difference in their etiology.

The postulation of shared appraisal mechanisms suffers from a further problem. If emotions such as anger and fear were generated from the same appraisal dimensions as guilt and pride, we should not find creatures that have the former but lack the latter. On dimensional accounts, higher cognitive emotions are not generally presumed to differ in complexity from the emotions associated with affect programs. All derive from the same dimensions. But, in nature, there seem to be many creatures that have affect programs but lack higher cognitive emotions. Dimensional accounts have difficulty explaining that fact.

If Griffiths's argument undermines dimensional appraisal theories, it might be regarded as grist for my mill. After all, I reject those theories as well. Unfortunately, his argument also raises a concern about my embodied appraisal theory. In chapter 3, I proposed that emotions be identified with mental states that track core relational themes by monitoring changes in the body. Lazarus's table of core relational themes (reproduced as table 1.2) includes emotions associated with affect programs as well as higher cognitive emotions. For example, it contains both sadness and jealousy. In presenting my embodied appraisal story, I focused on emotions associated with affect programs (especially sadness and fear). But by invoking Lazarus's table I implied that all emotions, including higher cognitive emotions, could be identified with embodied appraisals. Griffiths's argument calls this into question. Affect programs involve physiological changes and thus may involve embodied appraisals, but higher cognitive emotions are driven by phylogenetically recent, nonmodular systems that may have no intimate connection to physiological changes. If the embodied appraisal theory has any hope of encompassing all emotions, the concerns raised by Griffiths's argument must be answered.

### *Basic Emotions*

#### What Are Basic Emotions?

One way to find unity within the class of emotions is to postulate a set of "basic emotions." Basic emotions are hypothesized to be a privileged set of emotions from which all others are derived. If a small class of basic emotions can be identified, then all other emotions can be characterized as members of that class or states that contain members of that class. The basic emotion theory has an advantage over the dimensional appraisal approach. By distinguishing basic and nonbasic emotions, it provides an explanation for the fact that higher cognitive emotions are not found in many other species, while the emotions associated with affect programs are. Higher cognitive emotions may be nonbasic. It is possible that most nonhuman animals are limited to the basic emotions. The capacity for nonbasic emotions requires resources that they simply lack.

The suggestion that some emotions are more basic than others has been defended by various researchers over the years. It was even defended by Descartes. In *Passions of the Soul* (1649/1988) Descartes argues that six emotions are "primitive": joy, sadness, desire, love, hatred, and wonder. Descartes believes all other emotions can be derived from these. For example, he defines fear as the belief that there is only a small probability that one will obtain what one desires (Descartes, 1649/1988, II.58). He subsequently defines jealousy as a fear relating to the desire to keep something that one values (III.167).

Spinoza (1677/1994) also believes in basic emotions, but reduces Descartes's list to the first three: joy (or pleasure), sadness (or pain), and desire. Love and hatred are not primitive, argues Spinoza, because they can be respectively defined as pleasure or pain accompanying the thought of an object. Spinoza removes wonder from the list because he does not regard it as an emotion. He defines wonder as the contemplation of a single object considered independently of any others.

In the twentieth century, psychologists began to defend basic emotions as well (for a critical review, see Ortony & Turner, 1990). McDougall (1908) identifies anger, disgust, elation, fear, subjection, tender-emotion, and wonder as primitive. Interestingly, wonder is the only item that his list shares with Descartes's. Mc-Dougal has the unusual view that joy and sadness are not basic. Another list is offered by Izard (1971), under the influence of Tomkins (1962): anger, contempt, disgust, distress, fear, guilt, interest, joy, shame, and surprise. If we interpret "distress" as sadness, Izard's list encompasses the emotions that Ekman identifies in his studies of affect programs. "Interest" may be an analogue of "wonder." Surprisingly, Izard also includes guilt and shame, which are paradigmatic higher cognitive emotions. Oatley and Johnson-Laird (1987) prune these from their list of basic emotions, offering just: anger, anxiety, disgust, happiness, and sadness. They exclude surprise, whose status as an emotion has been contested. Panksepp (2000) provides a less orthodox list comprised of: care, fear, lust, panic, play, rage, and seeking. In recent writings, Ekman (1999a) has gone beyond his initial list of six affect programs to include fifteen basic emotions: amusement, anger, contempt, contentment, disgust, embarrassment, excitement, fear, guilt, pride in achievement, relief, sadness, satisfaction, sensory pleasure, and shame.

Basic emotions theorists differ from each other in various ways. As just demonstrated, they include different items on their lists. They also use different criteria for inclusion. Ortony and Turner (1990) note a major division between approaches to basic emotions. Some authors maintain that basic emotions are psychologically primitive, and others maintain they are biologically primitive. One version of the psychological approach is exemplified by the early theories of basic emotions developed by philosophers. In this tradition, to say an emotion is basic is to say that it contains no other emotions as parts. This wording is slightly restrictive because it assumes that basic emotions must be related to nonbasic emotions as parts are related to wholes. More neutral wording would say that an emotion is basic if it is not *derived* from another emotion.

In more recent emotion research, biological criteria have taken center stage. The central idea behind biological theories is that basic emotions are innate or present in all normally developing members of the species. (I say more about innateness in chapter 5.) They are evolved patterns of response.

Rather than choosing between psychological and biological approaches, I think the two should be integrated. Basic emotions are innate emotions that are not derived from other emotions. The biological criterion is insufficient on its own, because evolution could have furnished us with responses that integrate two previously evolved and separable emotion systems. Intuitively, such compound emotions would fail to be basic even if they were innate. The psychological criterion is also insufficient on its own. It allows that one could acquire, through learning, a new basic emotion that was not dependent on previously existing emotions. This is counterintuitive. The idea that a new emotion could be created *ex nihilo* is not conceptually incoherent, but there are no obvious examples.

How can we identify basic emotions? One approach, associated with Ekman, is to look for culturally universal facial expressions. If the same faces are elicited by the same conditions across cultures, there is reason to believe that the response is mediated, at least in part, by an innate emotion. But this kind of evidence is neither necessary nor sufficient for basicness. It is not necessary, because, as Ekman (1999a) admits, some innate emotions may lack corresponding facial expressions. It is not sufficient, because, as just remarked, some innate emotions may be nonbasic. Ortony and Turner (1990) also complain that facial expressions may be a bad test for innateness. It is possible that the component features of a facial expression are driven by innate response systems, while the whole ensemble depends on the fact that the conditions that elicit those responses often happen to cooccur.

Plutchik (1980, 1984, 2001) argues that we can identify basic emotions by first identifying adaptive functions. He thinks that each basic emotion corresponds to a fundamental environmental challenge faced by our ancestors. For example, he relates fear to protection and joy to reproduction. The trouble with this approach is that it is hard to know what challenges are truly fundamental. If mate selection is essential for procreation (which is what genes care about), then jealousy should be basic. Conversely, Plutchik says sadness is basic because it relates to "reintegration" behaviors. But it is unclear why reintegration is a fundamental evolutionary challenge. Plutchick's assumptions about what emotions are basic seem to drive his choice and interpretation of what challenges are fundamental. If one adds these worries to the more general concern that evolutionary analyses are easy to generate and difficult to test (see chapter 5), prospects for Plutchik's criterion look dim.

A third approach identifies basic emotions by searching for neural circuits. Panksepp (2000) believes that basic emotions are those for which we can locate dedicated anatomical regions and neurochemicals. If we find circuitry dedicated to a particular emotional response, that is good evidence that the response is both innate and cannot be broken down into further emotions. In pursuing this strategy, Panksepp has come up with a list of basic emotions that differs from other leading accounts. For example, he distinguishes panic from fear because there is evidence that these two forms of danger response are mediated by different neural machinery. That insight illustrates the value of grounding an approach to basic emotions in the brain.

The major limitation of this approach is that the neural circuitry condition is not necessary for basicness. While no two emotions could involve exactly the same neuronal *activity*, there is no reason to assume that two emotions could not involve the same anatomical structures and chemicals. It is a familiar feature of neural networks that different states can supervene on distinct patterns of activation over the same populations of neurons. Distinct emotions could, in principle, occur in shared circuitry. I am not suggesting that this is, in fact, the case. It could turn out all basic emotions have unique circuitry, but we cannot make this assumption in advance.

I think we need convergent evidence to identify basic emotions. There are various kinds of circumstantial clues for thinking that a given emotion is not derived from other emotions. Neurobiological findings of the kind Panksepp uses can be helpful. One can see whether the neural correlates of one emotion include the neural correlates of another. If not, there is reason to suppose the emotion is basic. Developmental evidence may also help. If an emotion appears before other emotions in development and no other emotions appear before it, there is reason to think it is basic.

One can also study emotion concepts as evidence for basicness. Emotion concepts should not be confused with the emotions themselves. We all have a concept of anger, which is encompassed by our beliefs about what anger is like, when it arises, what sorts of behaviors it causes, and so on. Someone who is congenitally incapable of experiencing anger could possess an anger concept, and someone could have the capacity for anger without having an anger concept. Nevertheless, we form our anger concept, in part, by observing instances of anger, just as we form our concepts of gorillas, in part, by observing gorillas. This does not mean our concept is completely accurate. We may have false beliefs about anger, just as we have false beliefs about gorillas (see Putnam, 1975, on the latter). But we are likely to have true beliefs about anger as well. These can tell us something about the emotion.

Much emotion research is conducted by analyzing emotion concepts. This methodology is the norm in philosophical research (e.g., Gordon, 1987; Kenny, 1963; Thalberg, 1964). But it is also true of experimental work. Psychologists ask people to verbally describe their emotions, to rate similarities between emotions, or to convey the meanings of their emotions. All these exercises that require reflection and verbal report inevitably tap into emotion concepts. Such methods are limited when used in isolation (recall chapter 3), but, conjoined with other evidence, they can contribute a bit of evidence pertaining to which emotions are basic.

Here is a simple "possibility test." For every pair of emotion terms, ask subjects: Could you experience emotion $x$ without experiencing emotion $y$? Could you experience jealousy, for example, without experiencing anger? Could you experience anger without experiencing jealousy? My guess is that most people would answer the first question negatively and the second question affirmatively. The emotions that can be experienced without experiencing any other emotion are quite possibly basic.

Another way to identify basic emotions through emotion concepts is to conduct crosscultural linguistic research. One can look for words that appear in many different languages. If basic emotions are universal building blocks for all others, they are likely to be experienced in all cultures. If they are experienced, they have a reasonably high chance of being named. Overlap in the emotion vocabularies of the world's languages can be used as a clue for basicness. One can also do sublexical analyses. We may be able to analyze some emotion terms into discrete features. We can look for features that seem to correspond to emotions in their own right (e.g., indignation could be analyzed as anger at an injustice). The units of meaning in English emotion terms can be compared to the units of meaning in emotion vocabularies of other languages. Universally shared units may help us identify basic emotions (see Wierzbicka, 1999).

In sum, I do not think there is any decisive test for basicness. The best strategy is to look for converging evidence. Identify emotions that pass the possibility test described earlier. Then see whether they have analogues in other languages. Then try to find a neural correlate for that those emotions that have universal analogues. Make sure the correlates do not encompass any parts that qualify as emotions in their own right. If one follows this procedure, one is likely to find a viable list of basic emotions.

### Should We Believe in Basic Emotions?

Some researchers think that the search for basic emotions is going to come up empty. Ortony and Turner (1990) present a trenchant critique of the basic emotion literature. They begin by noting the diversity of items included on basic emotion lists. If researchers arrive at different lists, basic emotions may be unprincipled. The emotions counted on such lists may simply reflect the most prevalent emotions in Western culture (where much of the basic emotion research is conducted). Ortony and Turner also spend considerable energy trying to show that some emotions commonly regarded as basic may contain other emotions. For example, anger seems to contain distress.[5]

---

[5]Ortony and Turner also cast doubt on the inference from facial expressions to basic emotions, because each of the features comprising a single facial expression may correspond to unique emotions in their own right. I have argued that we need converging evidence. I agree that inferring basicness from the face alone is risky.

I think a lack of consensus is no cause for skepticism. Ortony and Turner favor a dimensional appraisal approach to emotions, but they fail to note that researchers in that tradition disagree about the basic appraisal dimensions.[6] If disagreement were evidence against a theory, the dimensional appraisal view would be equally vulnerable. Indeed, every scientific theory would be vulnerable. Disagreement is rampant in science. Disagreement shows that someone must be wrong, but it does not show that everyone is wrong. The diversity of basic emotions lists does not cast doubt on the basic emotion program, any more than Aristotle's theory of four elements casts doubt on the modern periodic table. Emotion science is in its infancy, and current lists reflect early speculations.

This point defuses other arguments presented by Ortony and Turner. Their suggestion that lists of basic emotions may reflect cultural bias is probably correct, but such biases can be reduced by doing crosscultural psychology and crosscultural linguistics. Their suggestion that anger contains distress might also be correct, but that would only show that anger is not a basic emotion. Basic emotion lists must be subject to revision.

I will not offer a list of basic emotions here, though I offer some speculations in chapter 6. It is too early to identify the basic emotions with complete certainty. Whatever emotions turn out to be basic, I conjecture that all of those will turn out to be embodied appraisals. I base this hypothesis on the following two observations. First, we can consciously experience all emotions. I am not claiming that all emotions are conscious—that is matter of debate—only that all emotions can be conscious. Second, as James observed, the conscious feelings of emotions are apparently exhausted by feelings of bodily changes (see chapter 9). Therefore, all emotions potentially occur with feelings of bodily changes. This suggests that bodily changes are intimately connected to emotions quite generally. This can be explained by the hypothesis that basic emotions are embodied appraisals. If nonbasic emotions are derived from basic emotions and basic emotions are embodied, nonbasic emotions will be embodied as well. They will inherit bodily correlates from basic emotions.

## Nonbasic Emotions

Anyone who believes in basic emotions must explain how they give rise to nonbasic emotions.[7] Different researchers have offered different answers. One proposal compares emotions to colors. Basic emotions are like primary colors, and

---

[6]It is worth noting that dimensional appraisal theories are not incompatible with basic emotions (see, e.g., Arnold, 1960; Frijda, 1986). One can hold, for example, that basic emotions are the emotions that can be generated by a set of appraisal dimensions, while nonbasic emotions are combinations of these.

[7]Some defenders of basic emotions try to skirt this issue by arguing that all emotions are basic (Ekman, 1999a). This thesis implies that no emotions have other emotions as parts. I am skeptical. For reasons that will be increasingly clear later, it is hard to see what would prevent emotions from combining to form more complex states that also qualify as emotions.

nonbasic emotions are blends of basic emotions. Plutchik (2001) defends a version of this approach. He argues that the basic emotions can be organized into a wheel, like the color wheel. Similar emotions are adjacent, and every basic emotion is situated across from an opposing basic emotion. Plutchik then argues that pairs of basic emotions can combine together to form composite emotions. He calls the emotions formed by combining pairs of basic emotions that are adjacent on the emotion wheel "primary dyads." For example, sadness and surprise combine to produce disapproval, while anger and disgust combine to produce contempt (see fig. 4.1).

Plutchik's blending theory has not been immensely popular. Some problems stem from the specific details of his proposal. Some readers may take issue with some of Plutchik's choices of basic emotions. For example, it is not obvious that trust and anticipation are true emotions, much less basic emotions. This concern infects secondary dyads derived from these two, such as optimism and aggressiveness, which sound more like personality traits than emotions.

These problems may require us to abandon Plutchik's specific proposals, but they do not vitiate the idea that some emotions are generated through blending. Contempt and disapproval are plausible candidates. The feeling of "thrills" or exhilaration may be a blend of joy and fear. Carroll (1990) has argued that the feeling of horror blends fear with disgust. Feeling sadistic may involve a blend of anger and joy.

Griffiths (1997) identifies a more serious problem with the blending theory. It is implausible that all higher cognitive emotions can be generated by simply mix-

**Figure 4.1.** Plutchik's basic emotions (center) and primary dyads, based on figure 6 in Plutchik (2001), p. 348, with permission of *American Scientist*.

ing basic emotions together. Consider romantic jealousy, which may involve ideas of infidelity, sex, and entitlement. It is hard to see how any of these ideas could emerge from basic emotions. None of these ideas are contained within the emotions that are usually catalogued as basic. If emotions were all basic or blends of basic emotions, some of the ideas that constitute romantic jealousy would have to emerge *ex nihilo*. To take another example, consider *Schadenfreude*—joy in another person's suffering. The joy in *Schadenfreude* is presumably borrowed from a basic emotion, but the representation of another person's suffering presumably is not (note the subtle difference with sadism; one drives behavior and the other is a response to particular kinds of events).

The obvious explanation of these cases is that some nonbasic emotions emerge by combining basic emotions with other mental states that are not emotions in their own right. Put differently, many nonbasic emotions may involve *cognitive elaborations* of basic emotions. A view of this kind is defended by Oatley and Johnson-Laird (Oatley & Johnson-Laird, 1987; Johnson-Laird & Oatley, 2000). They argue that some are basic and others are combinations of basic emotions and beliefs. A natural example is *Schadenfreude*, which might be thought to contain both joy and a thought about the suffering of another person, that serves an elicitor for that joy.

For purposes of illustration, it is worth considering the emotions listed on Lazarus's table of core relational themes (see table 1.2). Some of the emotions on his list may be basic. Anger, anxiety, fright, sadness, happiness, and disgust are all included. These terms correspond to Ekman's list of basic emotions. Guilt, shame, envy, jealousy, pride, relief, hope, and love are good candidates for being nonbasic. One can easily generate plausible hypotheses about their relationship to the basic emotions on the list. For example, guilt may be sadness brought on by the belief that one has committed a harmful transgression. Pride may be happiness brought on by the belief that one has achieved a difficult task. Jealousy may contain several basic emotions, including anger, sadness, and disgust, all brought on by the belief that one's lover has been unfaithful. In chapter 3, I criticized Lazarus for assuming that core relational themes correspond to inner judgments. If Oatley and Johnson-Laird are right about how nonbasic emotions are derived, then those emotions involve inner judgments. Basic emotions are embodied appraisals, but nonbasic emotions may require both judgments and embodied appraisals. On this hybrid view, guilt, pride, and jealousy involve cognitive states, while sadness, happiness, and anger do not.

The proposals that I have been considering provide ammunition against Griffiths's disunity thesis. Griffiths would have us believe that the category of emotions is a hodgepodge. There is no scientifically respectable reason for grouping all emotions together. I have been suggesting that there may be a way around this conclusion. There may be basic emotions from which all others are derived. Those basic emotions may be united in virtue of being embodied appraisals. All other emotions may be blends of basic emotions or cognitive elaborations of basic emotions. If these suggestions pan out, then all emotions are united in virtue of having a common set of basic parts. Is there any reason to doubt that emotions are unified in this way?

## *Resisting Unity*

### Against the Basic Emotion Thesis

Griffiths is familiar with the hypothesis that all emotions are basic emotions or basic emotion derivatives, but he does not think it has any merit. He considers and rejects the related proposal that all higher cognitive emotions have affect programs as parts. His response can be translated into an argument against the view that all higher cognitive emotions are derived from embodied appraisals.

One common objection is that higher cognitive emotions often occur without the pronounced physiological changes and facial expressions that are associated with embodied appraisals (e.g., Griffiths, 1997; Harré, 1986; Solomon, 1976). There is no obvious physiological or facial response associated with guilt or jealousy. If higher cognitive emotions contain embodied appraisals, one would expect them to have associated facial expressions and visceral responses.

This objection can be met. Higher cognitive emotions are often ascribed as dispositional states. Much of our mental vocabulary is systematically ambiguous between occurrent and dispositional states. When we say Matilda believes that George Washington was the first president of the United States, for example, we do not necessarily mean that she is entertaining that belief right now. She is disposed to entertain that belief when the topic comes up. Likewise, being jealous of one's lover can be disposition to have certain feelings when one's lover comes home later than expected. When we have an occurrent state of jealousy, short-lasting physiological changes presumably do occur. We have flashes of jealousy and pangs of guilt. We swell with pride and hang our heads in shame. The apparent lack of bodily involvement in higher cognitive emotions vanishes when one considers felt experiences of those states.

The hypothesis that higher cognitive emotions contain embodied appraisals can be tested in various ways. The easiest test would be to give people questionnaires that ask whether various physiological symptoms are associated with different higher cognitive emotions. In a study that was principally designed to study cultural variation in emotions, Scherer and Wallbott (1994) administered a questionnaire that included questions about physiological symptoms for guilt and shame, which are generally regarded as higher cognitive emotions. The three thousand respondents in 37 countries "frequently" associated physiological states with these two emotions. For example, 28.1 percent associated a lump in the throat with guilt and 34.2 percent associated increased heart rate with shame (Scherer & Wallbott, 1994, table 8). These numbers were higher than any reported for disgust, which is a paradigmatically basic and somatically based emotion.

In an informal pilot study of my own, I tested for overlap between basic and higher cognitive emotions by administering a questionnaire that asked respondents to read emotion scenarios and then rate the applicability of several photographs of facial expressions. Classic basic emotions tended to get high rating for just one face, whereas higher cognitive emotions got high ratings for several. For example, a jealousy scenario, which describes a situation in which a lover is unfaithful, yielded high ratings for faces that are characteristically associated with anger, sadness, and disgust (fig. 4.2). This trend, which should be replicated in a more formal experiment, suggests that higher cognitive emotions are associated with the faces of basic emotions and that some of them blend several basic emotions together.

Another experimental strategy is to employ cognitive tests. Different emotions are known to interact differentially with memory, attention, and reasoning strategies (see chapter 1). For example, sadness tends to promote focused, analytic, flaw-sensitive thinking processes. I predict that the same affects would be found in higher cognitive emotions presumed to contain sadness, such as guilt and shame.

One can also look for priming, or facilitation effects. If contempt contains disgust, then eliciting disgust should make it easier to subsequently elicit contempt. Imagine asking people to assess political speeches while they are smelling noxious substances. My prediction is that they would express more contempt. Alternatively, one could present subjects with stories designed to elicit contempt

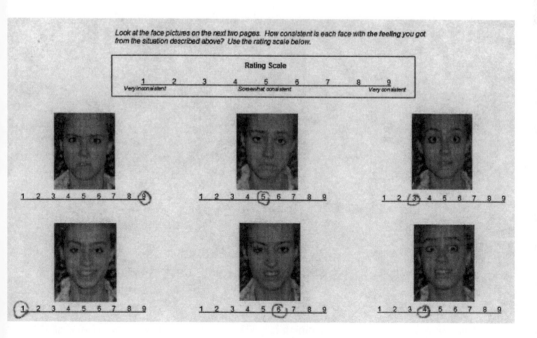

*Figure 4.2.* A typical subject's response when asked to rate how well various facial expressions go with a scenario involving romantic jealousy.

(e.g., a story about hypocrisy), right after presenting them with stories designed to elicit other emotions, and then ask them to rate how much contempt they feel. My prediction is that contempt ratings will be higher when contempt stories follow stories that elicit disgust and anger, as opposed to sadness or fear.

Support for the claim that higher cognitive emotions overlap with basic emotions can also come from studying the brain. Shin et al. (2000) performed positron emission tomography scans on people as they recalled experiences in which the felt extreme guilt. They found activations (especially in paralimbic areas) that have been associated with negative emotions in other studies. Participants in the study by Shin et al. also reported experiencing sadness and disgust when they experienced guilt. Bartels and Zeki (2000) performed a functional magnetic resonance imaging study of people who reported being in love. As they showed these people photographs of their loved ones, the researchers found activation in the insula, a structure that registers activity in visceral organs. This explains why people in love experience "butterflies" in their stomachs. Insula activation has also been detected in studies of more basic emotions, such as joy and fear (e.g., Damasio et al., 2000). Perhaps being-in-love inherits its somatic components from these emotions.

Less conclusive but highly suggestive evidence also comes from work by Damasio (1994) and LeDoux (1996). They have emphasized pathways from higher cognitive centers into regions associated with phylogenetically primitive emotions. If these areas can be activated by high-level cognitive states, then high-level cognitive states could invoke processes essential to embodied appraisals. This wiring is consistent with the view that nonbasic emotions are cognitive elaborations of basic emotions.

It would hardly be surprising to find experimental evidence for the claim that higher cognitive emotions derive from basic emotions. A number of independent considerations favor this hypothesis. First, as I remarked earlier, higher cognitive emotions seem to include bodily responses when they are consciously experienced. Second, the fact that all emotions function as irruptive motivations could be neatly explained by the discovery that all emotions overlap. Third, *pace* Griffiths, there is anecdotal evidence that higher order emotions are, at least, partially modular. In chapter 2 I mentioned cases where an emotional feeling remains even after the belief that gave rise to the feeling is reversed. This can occur with higher cognitive emotions. For example, though jealousy may arise in response to unencapsulated reasoning processes, once it is there the feeling of jealousy is hard to dispel by further deliberation. If one feels jealous of a lover and suddenly realizes that the grounds for jealously were mistaken, a negative feeling may linger or be converted into some other emotion. If higher cognitive emotions were entirely nonmodular, this should not occur. On this view, higher cognitive emotions are not entirely nonmodular. They contain embodied appraisals, and embodied appraisals are modular (see chapter 10). When one rescinds the hasty thoughts that spawned a bout of jealousy, the anger that had been contained in the jealousy may remain. Anger, unlike beliefs about infidelity, cannot simply be erased by a change in judgment.

Griffiths is wrong to think the basic emotions thesis is hopeless. It is consistent with existing evidence, capable of being tested, and likely to prove explanatorily fruitful.

## Are Emotions Natural Kinds?

Even if everything I have been suggesting is correct, Griffiths's disunity thesis may still be defensible. The chapter began with the question: Are emotions a natural kind? All along, I have been assuming that we could answer this question affirmatively if we could show that all emotions are or derive from basic emotions. That assumption may not be warranted. To see this, it will help to consider an analogy.

On the view I have been describing, emotions are like alcoholic beverages. Alcoholic beverages have a common unifying core: they are beverages, they contain alcohol, and they come in a variety of flavors. Alcohol has a common microstructure and it gives rise to common effects (intoxication). Flavors have two sources. They derive from the stuff used in the distillation or fermentation process, or they are added after that process, as in the case of mixed drinks.

Like alcoholic beverages, emotions have two basic components: alcohol and flavoring. The alcohol of emotion is valence. All emotions are either positive or negative. That will be the topic of chapter 7. Emotional flavoring comes from appraisal. Appraisals can be purely embodied, or they can include cognitive elaborations of embodied appraisals. Basic emotions are embodied appraisals. Higher cognitive emotions, one might suppose, are either blends of two basic emotions (just as martinis are blends of two spirits), or combinations of basic emotions and cognitive elaborations (just as a screwdriver combines a spirit and a fruit juice).

Basic emotions and blends of basic emotions form a coherent class. All emotions in this class derive from the same parts. But that is not the case when we consider basic emotions and cognitively elaborated emotions on the picture that I have been presenting so far. On the face of it, there is an inelegance. I have said that cognitively elaborated emotions contain both embodied appraisals *and* cognitive mental representations, such as judgments. If this is right, cognitively elaborated emotions are the mixed drinks of our emotional life. But that sets them apart from the pure spirits. If embodied appraisals are states of modular systems, and higher cognitive emotions are states of modular systems *plus* cognitive elaborations, then they have very different psychological properties. They are not completely informationally encapsulated, they are dependent on concept possession, they are directly susceptible to cultural influence, and so on. If we are seeking a unified science of emotions, these differences present a problem. They implicate very different kinds of mechanisms. Likewise, a science of alcoholic beverages would be hard to achieve without keeping pure spirits and mixed drinks apart.

There are three possible replies to this objection. The first invokes the definition of natural kinds introduced earlier. Following Boyd, Griffiths maintains that natural kinds are homeostatic property clusters. The members of a natural kind are comprised of clusters of properties that tend to cooccur in virtue of causal mechanisms. The fact that some higher cognitive emotions contain something other than embodied appraisals does not show that they cannot belong to a natural kind that includes embodied appraisals. The properties associated with an embodied appraisal include bodily changes, conscious somatic feelings, and motivational effects. Cognitive elaborations may tend to cause such states, and those states may tend to promote cognitive elaborations by association. If so, cognitively elaborated emotions are causally homeostatic with embodied appraisals. They belong to a common natural kind.

One can also reply by distinguishing two kinds of unity. A category can be unified in virtue of the fact that its members belong to a single natural kind or in virtue of the fact that its members can be explained within a unified scientific theory. Griffiths tends to run these together. In actual fact, emotions would form a unified category in the latter sense, even if they failed to qualify as a unified category in the former sense. Embodied appraisals and higher cognitive emotions demand the same explanatory resources.

If some higher cognitive emotions have embodied appraisals as constituents, a science of higher cognitive emotions must clearly encompass a science of embodied appraisals. It turns out that the converse is also true. At least in humans, embodied appraisals generally occur with accompanying cognitive states. While we are sometimes frightened by loud noises and looming objects, we are more often frightened by cognitively apperceived dangers. For example, one might become afraid while walking down a desolate city street and recognizing that one could be attacked without anyone around to help. This complex fear-inducing thought is not fundamentally different from the kinds of cognitive states involved in higher cognitive emotions. Emotions of any kind can be embedded in rich cognitive episodes. Therefore, a full science of embodied appraisals depends on an understanding of their interactions with the cognitions that buffer, elicit, and elaborate them.

Still, my plea for a unified science of emotion cannot override a nagging inelegance. It remains an odd fact about folk psychology that some emotions are individuated by embodied appraisal while others are individuated by embodied appraisals *plus* disembodied judgments.

Here is where a third reply comes into focus. In introducing the idea that some emotions may be comprised by cognitively elaborated embodied appraisals, I implied that those emotions are composite states: states whose token instances contain both an embodied appraisal and a cognitive state. This conception is not obligatory. I propose that cognitively elaborated embodied appraisals are not composite states at all. They are comprised of nothing but embodied appraisals. The cognitions that elaborate them are *prior conditions*, not *constituent parts*.

When romantic jealousy occurs, there is first a judgment to the effect that one's lover has been unfaithful and then an embodied appraisal. The emotion, jealousy, is comprised entirely by the embodied appraisal. Under other conditions, an embodied appraisal of the kind that comprises a state of jealousy may qualify as another emotion. When an embodied appraisal occurs as a response to judgments regarding infidelity, it constitutes jealousy; when it has another cause, it may constitute another emotion. On this proposal, the cognitive concomitant of a cognitively elaborated emotion is not part of the emotion, but it plays a role in determining the identity of that emotion.

This proposal can be clarified by importing another idea from Dretske's (1986) psychosemantics. As I have noted, Dretske argues that some mental states represent what they do in virtue of having an evolved function to carry information. But, he also argues that those mental states can come to represent things other than what they are evolved to represent. We can put evolved representations to new uses. In Dretskean terminology, representations are "calibrated" to certain causes, and they can be "recalibrated." To get the idea, consider a case outside the mental realm. Coughing has the evolved function of clearing the throat. But a spy might also use a cough as a secret code in communicating with an accomplice. A spy's cough might represent the fact that the microfilm has been delivered. Likewise, an embodied appraisal that usually represents a demeaning offense (anger) may represent an infidelity (jealousy) when used under the direction of the right judgment. We can recalibrate our embodied appraisals to occur under conditions that are somewhat different than those for which they were initially evolved.

All this suggests that higher cognitive emotions are not cognitive elaborations, after all. They are not compounds of judgments and embodied appraisals. Instead, they are embodied appraisals that have been recalibrated by judgments to represent somewhat different relations to the environment. A more accurate depiction is offered in figure 4.3.

When an embodied appraisal has been recalibrated by judgments, it does not lose the meaning it had before it was recalibrated. When a spy uses a cough as a code, it is still a cough, and, as a cough, it is a state that has the function of clearing the throat. Likewise, when an embodied appraisal that usually comprises anger comes under the control of a judgment about infidelity, it continues to have

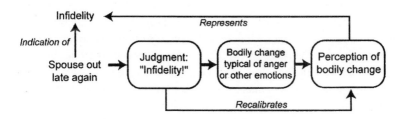

***Figure 4.3.***    Higher cognitive emotions as recalibrated embodied appraisals.

the function of representing whatever anger represents; it remains a state of anger. So, when anger is caused by a judgment about infidelity, it would be accurate to say that it is both a state of anger and a state of jealousy. It simultaneously represents the fact that there has been a demeaning offense (the content of anger) and the fact that one's lover has been unfaithful (the content of jealousy).

This proposal raises a question. I just claimed that jealousy is comprised of anger (or some other embodied appraisal) recalibrated by a judgment about infidelity. Anger can be triggered by many other judgments. Suppose Jones becomes angry when she learns that she has lost her job. Why doesn't this state qualify as a higher cognitive emotion? Why do we call jealousy an emotion and fail to identify a special emotion associated with losing one's job? Why is there no emotion of job-loss rage? We regard some cognitively induced appraisals as emotions in their own right but refuse this special status for others. This suggests that the class of higher cognitive emotions is arbitrary.

Two replies. First, I think it is a linguistic accident that some cognitive elaborated embodied appraisals have names and others do not. Metaphysically, job-loss rage and jealousy may be comparable. The class of higher cognitive emotions is quite open-ended. Many cognitively induced embodied appraisals qualify as higher cognitive emotions even if we do not have names for them.

Second, there is a difference between embodied appraisals that *happen to be* caused by judgments and those that are *calibrated* by judgments. To be calibrated by a judgment, an embodied appraisal has to be reliably caused by judgments of that kind. One must have a mental mechanism in place that establishes a link between judgments of a particular kind and embodied appraisals. I call such a mechanism a calibration file. Calibration files are data structures in long-term memory. Every calibration file contains a set of representations that can each causally trigger the same (or similar) patterned bodily response. The perceptions of the bodily responses caused by representations in a calibration file are emotions. Their content is determined by the representations in a calibration. Emotions do not represent the content of any individual representation in a calibration file but rather the more abstract property that those representations collectively track. The calibration file for jealousy is a collection of representations that can track infidelity. It includes the explicit judgment that one's lover has been unfaithful. When representations in this file are activated, they trigger a somatic response, and that response triggers an embodied appraisal. If an embodied appraisal just happens to be caused by an isolated judgment on some particular occasion, it is not yet calibrated by that judgment. If an appraisal is reliably caused by a judgment of a certain kind, then it will come to be reliably caused by whatever external conditions are represented by that judgment. For that, we need calibration files. There must be a link in memory between judgments and somatic responses in order to get those somatic responses to represent the property designated by the judgment. By establishing new calibration files, an embodied appraisal can be said to represent something beyond what it is evolved to represent. Thus, while the set of possible higher cognitive emotions is open-ended, it is not the case that every time we have an embodied appraisal triggered by a different judgment it counts as a distinct emotion.

One final objection must be considered. The distinction between calibrating causes and constitutive causes looks like a cheap verbal trick. If a judgment reliably triggers an embodied appraisal to occur, there seems to be little reason to deny that it is part of the resulting emotion. After all, such a judgment would occur whenever the emotion occurs, and it would play an essential role in determining what core relational theme the emotion represents. Denying that such judgments are constitutive parts of emotions is ad hoc.

This objection is grounded on a false assumption. To say that a higher cognitive emotion is reliably triggered by a particular judgment does not entail that the same emotion is always triggered by that very judgment. Jealousy can be triggered by the judgment that one's lover has been unfaithful, but it can also be triggered by other judgments, such as the judgment that one's lover has been staying unusually late at work. Jealousy can even be triggered by perceptual states, such as the smell of an unfamiliar perfume on a lover's clothes. Many different judgments and perceptions can be used to reliably track cases of infidelity. Calibration files contain a variety of representations, ranging from explicit judgments to sensory states. There is no internal state that always plays the role of triggering a higher cognitive emotion. Different items in our calibration files play that role on different occasions. There is, therefore, no pressure to say that any particular judgment comprises a constituent part of any higher cognitive emotion. Two instances of jealousy may be triggered in very different ways. Instances of jealousy are united not by the fact that they share judgments but by the fact that they share similar somatic states and those somatic states represent infidelity. Two instances of jealousy represent infidelity in virtue of being calibrated by the same mental file, but the actual representations from that file that do the calibrating work can be highly variable.

This point about calibration files reveals an even greater unity between basic and nonbasic emotions. I said that basic emotions are genetically set up to be set off by certain kinds of things. Fear, for example (or the closest basic emotion to fear, if fear itself is not basic), may be predisposed to be set off by loud noises, sudden loss of support, visual cliffs, darkness, insects, and snakes. All of these things can be detected by our senses. We can think of the sensory representations of noises, cliffs, and the like as making up a calibration file. In saying that fear (or something like fear) is innate, one is actually committed to the view that there is a genetic predisposition to form a calibration file comprised of certain kinds of representations. Basic and nonbasic emotions both have calibration files; their files just differ in etiology and content. The difference between basic and nonbasic emotions is that basic emotions are calibrated through files that have been fostered by natural selection. Nonbasic emotions emerge when new files are set up to hijack the emotions that are already in place (or when basic emotions are blended).

I conclude that there is no inelegance in the category that contains both basic emotions and higher cognitive emotions. All emotions are states of the same type. All emotions are embodied appraisals under the causal control of calibration files. The chief difference between basic and nonbasic emotions is that the latter take on new contents as a result of being *re*calibrated. New calibration files re-tune existing emotions to respond to properties that they were not genetically predisposed to detect. For both basic and nonbasic emotions, calibration files are causes, not constituents. All emotions are constituted by embodied appraisals alone. In making this case, I observed other related commonalities. In addition to having meanings of a similar kind, all emotions are associated with expressive behavior, all are associated with autonomic responses, all seem to involve related structures in the central nervous system, and all are eruptive. To this it might be added that all emotions are associated with action tendencies, all are motivating, all engage attention, and (as I discuss in chapter 7) all are valent. The case for unity is actually quite overwhelming. When one reflects on the many things that emotions share in common, it is rather surprising that many philosophers have been tempted to divide up the category. It is really no wonder that we have a single English word for the spectrum that runs from animalistic ecstasy to aesthetic delight. Emotions are a natural kind in a strong sense. They share a common essence. It is rare for nature (and folk psychology) to offer such a neat category.

# 5

# Emotions and Nature

## *Biological Reductionism*

### What Reductionists Claim

For much of the twentieth century, it was widely assumed that emotions differ from culture to culture. This assumption owed much to the impressive examples of cultural diversity reported by anthropologists. In her pioneering study of Samoan culture, Margaret Mead (1928) had arrived at the conclusion that Samoans live a life free of anger, sexual jealousy, and other emotions that we consider perfectly natural. Colin Turnbull (1972) claimed that the Ik people of Uganda were without love. In the face of such examples, one might be tempted to conclude that all emotions are products of learning and culture. That is now a minority position in emotion research. These days, the prevailing wisdom is that there are universal emotions. These universals are presumed to be biologically based. For convenience, I will label this contention "biological reductionism." In this chapter I will critically assess biological reductionism. I think many of the arguments used in its defense are wrong. Biology makes an important contribution to emotions, of course, but there is more to the story than reductionists would have us believe.

To say that emotions are biologically based is, in part, a conjecture about how we should go about studying their acquisition. Biologically based psychological traits can be most fruitfully explained by appeal to biology, rather than psychology (Cowie, 1998). This methodological recommendation is the implication of a more specific thesis. Biological reductionists assume that universally shared emotions are innate. Those emotions are a consequences of our genetic makeup, rather than our sociocultural environments. Most biological reductionists also assume that universal emotions got into our genes in virtue of the functions they serve. These emotions are adaptations.

Some reductionists shy away from the term "innate," preferring to call emotions "species-typical" (Griffiths, 2002). This language preference reflects a growing view that the division between innate and learned is unprincipled; phenotypes are products of both nature and nurture. I wholeheartedly agree with the claim about phenotypes, but I don't think that vitiates innateness as an explanatory construct. Consider the case of snake phobia. This is in some intuitive sense innate in primates, but it takes specific environmental conditions to arise. A primate will become snake phobic only if it sees a member of its species exhibit an aversive reaction to snakes during a critical period (Mineka, Davidson, Cook, & Keir, 1984). Such examples certainly show how genes and environment can depend on each other, but it is still sensible to say that snake phobia is innate. The term "species-typical" does not suffice. If "species-typical" means widely found across the species, then it subsumes many traits that can be explained by appeal to observational learning. The belief that the sun rises is widely found in members of our species, but it is very different from snake phobia. We need some way of capturing what's special about snake phobia, and innateness seems like the right construct. If "species-typical" is interpreted in a technical sense, that transcends statistical regularity; it becomes a euphemism for "innate."

As a starting place, we can define innateness operationally. Snake phobia is said to be innate because once acquired it is very hard to get rid of, and that recalcitrance cannot be explained by appeal to any general fact about primate learning. If a primate sees a conspecific grimace in the presence of a handgun, it will not develop handgun phobia. Innate psychological traits cannot be fully explained by appeal to the environmental conditions under which they are acquired or general-purpose learning mechanisms (see Cowie [1998] on poverty of the stimulus definitions).

This definition characterizes innateness by appeal to a certain kind of evidence. I think we can do even better than that. Snake phobia is ultimately attributable to a collection of genes. Some set of genes is causally responsible, in appropriate genetic and external contexts, for whatever it is that helps primates to develop a very strong reaction to snakes despite limited exposure. Snake phoia increased fitness in the past, so its genetic facilitators managed to be replicated more than other genes. Those genetic facilitators code for snake phobia, despite their need for environmental complicity, because they reliably cooccur with snake phobia and, unlike the environment, have the function of doing so. More generally, we can say that a phenotype is innate if its existence is causally facilitated by a collection of genes that have been replicated in virtue of having causally facilitated such phenotypes in the past. Snake phobia is innate, but fear of guns isn't, because whatever genes allow for the latter did not end up in us because of their contribution to fear of guns in our ancestral past.

Nonadaptive traits can have genetic facilitators as well. Sickle cell anemia is not adaptive, but it is the byproduct of a gene that helps protect against malaria. In such cases, we need to be careful when we specify what is innate. Sickle cell anemia is not innate, but it is a byproduct of a particular kind of disease protection, which is innate. Such cases need not concern us. Most biological reductionists regard emotions as adaptations. If we restrict our definition of innateness to adaptations, we can define biological reductionists as those who think emotions are innate.

Biological reductionists do not think that emotions are unaffected by culture. The way we convey our emotions and the specific conditions that elicit them may vary. Nor are biological reductionists necessarily reductionists about all emotions. Evolutionary psychologists are among the few who try to provide evolutionary accounts of higher cognitive emotions. Call this "comprehensive reductionism." Others are more cautious. Some reductionists assume that only a small group of *basic* emotions are innate (e.g., Damasio, 1994; Plutchik, 1984). Call this "constrained reductionism."

Both comprehensive and constrained reductionists tend to make a further assumption. They tend to assume that the innate emotions map, reasonably well, onto emotion terms in English. They might say that fear and anger are innate, for example. Call this "the translatability thesis." Any reductionist, comprehensive or constrained, who believes in translatability I will call a "strong reductionist."

### Evidence for Reductionism

Darwin was one of the first to provide careful evidence for reductionism. Much of that evidence appears in his book *Expressions of Emotion in Man and Animals* (1872/1998). As the title suggests, most of Darwin's discussion is about expression and not the underlying emotions that are expressed. But evidence for the biological origins of expressions is certainly suggestive. If expressions are innate, and they are produced by all healthy people under the same circumstances, then it is not unreasonable to assume that emotions are innate as well.

To support his hypothesis that human emotional expressions are innate, Darwin sought to prove that they are universal. He was especially interested in finding evidence for similar facial expression among members of isolated cultures. If people who are cut off from Europe make faces like Europeans, those faces are unlikely to be culturally derived. Darwin asked Englishmen living in remote parts of the globe to answer questions about the facial expressions they observed. They reported that the facial expressions of people who had been isolated from the West were readily identifiable. Darwin's study was very innovative. It is an early landmark in crosscultural research. But Darwin's reliance on the testimony of English informants left room for skepticism about his results.

Silvan Tomkins (1962) predicted that Darwin's results would be replicated in a more carefully designed experiment, and he instilled this prediction in two of his students, Paul Ekman and Carroll Izard. In an academic climate where cultural relativism reigned, they set out to find evidence for universality (Ekman, 1972; Ekman & Friesen, 1971; Ekman, Sorenson, & Friesen, 1969; Izard, 1971; see also Sorenson, 1975). Ekman's studies are of particular interest, because he chose to investigate expressions among the Fore, a preliterate people in the highlands of New Guinea. The Fore had existed in isolation from the West until twelve years before his studies began.

In one series of experiments, Ekman and his collaborator Wallace Friesen (1971) had bilingual interpreters read stories to members of the Fore describing various emotion-eliciting events. One story described the death of a child, another described an encounter with an old friend, and a third described smelling something bad. With each scenario, Ekman and Friesen also showed their Fore subjects three photographs of different facial expressions. When subjects were asked to select a face to go with each story, their answers were similar to answers that American and European respondents would give. A frowning face was chosen to go with the death of a child scenario, a smile was chosen for the encounter with a friend, a face with a wrinkled nose was chosen for the rotten smell scenario. Ekman studied six expressions in all: those corresponding to joy, anger, sadness, surprise, disgust, and fear (see fig. 5.1 for examples). The Fore tended to confuse the surprise expression with the fear expression, but performance was otherwise impressive. Ekman concluded that some facial expressions are universal. He concluded that the corresponding emotions are universal. If the same faces are used under the same circumstances, then the intermediating inner state is likely to be the same as well.[1]

Earlier I said that universality is not always evidence for innateness. The belief that the sun rises is universal but not innate. In this case, however, the inference is on pretty firm ground. Unlike beliefs about the sun, facial expressions are not easy to acquire through casual observation. We can pick up an expression by imitating people around us, but those people must get the expression from somewhere too. There must be a first instance. It is incredibly unlikely that members of completely isolated cultures *invented* the very same expressions generations ago. Moreover, there is evidence that infants make emotional facial expressions, and that they do so even if they are congenitally blind (Galati, Scherer, & Ricci-Bitti, 1997). These expressions must have a genetic basic.

Further evidence for the innateness of expressions comes from research on nonhuman animals. Despite some pronounced differences, there is continuity between chimpanzee and human facial expressions (Chevalier-Skolnikoff, 1973). Even greater continuities can be found if we look beyond the face. Bodily expressions of emotion show continuity across animals with considerably different morphology. For example, Darwin (1872/1988) observed that both humans and other mammals have body hair that bristles when we are faced with a threat. One can also observe freezing behavior in both humans and laboratory rats. Clearly rats didn't pick up such behavior from immersion in human cultures. The response seems to be innate.

Cross-species comparisons also go beneath the skin. The neural circuitry of emotions has homologues in different species. Papez developed an important early model of the emotional circuitry in the brain, which MacLean (1952) expanded and dubbed the limbic system. MacLean (1993) believes that the limbic

---

[1]Ekman also believes that emotions are partially constituted by facial expressions, so he regards universality of facial expressions as direct evidence for universality of emotions.

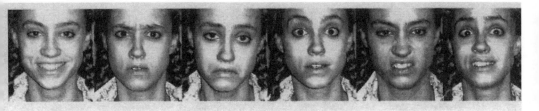

***Figure 5.1.***     Facial expressions of joy, anger, sadness, surprise, disgust, and fear similar to those used by Ekman and Friesen (1971).

system is shared by even the most primitive mammals and that even more ancient circuits associated with instinctive fight and flight responses can be found in the brainstem, which we share with reptiles. LeDoux (1996) has found that limbic structures, especially the amygdala, play similar roles in responding to emotionally significant stimuli in both humans and rats. The very fact that the brain contains circuits that are dedicated to emotions supports the case that emotions are biologically specified. The presence of similar circuits in other creatures suggests that some of our emotions may derive from ancestors far back on the phylogenetic tree.

Evidence for the biological basis of emotions also comes from studies of genetic inheritance. Genetic inheritance is usually measured by looking at trait correlations. Investigators look for correlations between traits within members of the same gene line. Emotions are usually brief responses to external conditions. They are states, not traits. Inheritance of emotions is, therefore, hard to measure. But emotions are closely related to traits. Most obviously, they are related to traits of personality (or temperament) and to affective disorders. Both of these are thought to be heritable (Jang, Livesley, Vernon, & Jackson, 1996; Tellegen, Lykken, Bouchard, Wilcox, Segal, & Rich, 1988). If constructs related to emotion are heritable, then it is reasonable to conclude that emotions are genetic in origin. If depression is heritable, for example, then some constellation of that makes people especially prone to depression. Depression seems to be related to sadness. This suggests that sadness is an aspect of human nature, not human culture.

If the capacity for certain emotions is written into our genes, one might wonder how they got there. Many emotions seem arbitrary or irrational. Why would they have been passed down from generation to generation? The question also arises for emotional expressions. Some physical responses to emotion make sense. It makes sense that we run or freeze when we are afraid. But others are more inscrutable. There is no obvious reason why certain facial contortions get assigned to one emotion and not another. Nor is there any obvious explanation for why emotions correlate with bodily changes that are not directly related to instrumental behavior. To address such questions, defenders of reductionism need to tell a story about why emotions evolved.

Darwin was the first to address such questions, focusing on the evolution of expressions. He claims that some expressions have an adaptive function. When an animal bears its canines, it signals to an aggressor that it is equipped to fight back. When hairs stand on end, a threatened animal appears larger. Darwin offers a Lamarckian explanation of how such expressions are inherited. He claims that they begin as voluntary responses, become habitual, and, as a result of their adaptive utility, get passed on to future generations. Darwin calls this the principle of serviceable habits. Lamarckian theories of inheritance are now unpopular, but Darwin's analyses can be reconciled with the non-Lamarckian account of inheritance that Darwin himself is famous for defending. It is possible that canine-baring and piloerection began as random mutations that got passed on through natural selection. One can translate talk of serviceable habits into talk of propitious mutations.

Darwin does not claim that every expression of emotion is the result of a serviceable habit. He claims that some expressions are due to excessive nerve forces caused by experiencing an emotionally significant stimulus. This is dubbed the principle of actions due to the constitution of the nervous system. Darwin invokes this principle to account for trembling and the whitening of hair after shock. Other expressions are explained by the principle of antithesis. When one emotion opposes another emotion that has an associated expression, the former can result in an opposite expression. Darwin offers this explanation of shoulder shrugging, when used to express an apology. Feelings of indignation impel us to move our arms forward in a stance of attack. The opposing feeling of apology causes us to retract our arms and hunch our shoulders.

There is little evidential support for Darwin's principles of nervous system response and antithesis. Neither remains a common explanatory strategy in emotion research. But the principle of serviceable habits, retooled as a principle of natural selection, is alive and well. Many emotion researchers find explanatory purchase in appeals to adaptation. This camp includes the evolutionary psychologists.

Evolutionary psychology is a movement that has gained tremendous support (Barkow, Cosmides, & Tooby, 1992; Pinker, 1997). Its practitioners typically make three assumptions: the mind is an information-processing system that can be broadly characterized as computational; higher cognition can be divided into highly specialized, modular subsystems that are relatively impervious to direct influence from one another; and the processes in those subsystems include rules and reputations that are adaptive responses to survival challenges faced by our ancestors in the Pleistocene or other earlier environments. These working hypotheses go beyond Darwin. For one thing, Darwin does not offer a computational or modular view of the mind. For another, Darwin's evolutionary claims tend to focus on externally observable traits, such as emotional expressions, rather than inner mental states (though he does take expressions to correlate with inner states). Evolutionary psychologists argue that emotions themselves, not just emotional expressions, are products of evolution (Tooby & Cosmides, 1990). They even claim that the class of evolved emotions extends beyond the classic basic emotions discussed in chapter 4 to include higher cognitive emotions, which may be unique to our species (e.g., Buss, 2000; Frank, 1988; Trivers, 1971). In general, evolutionary psychologists think that adaptationist explanations will subsume far more than Darwin dared to imagine.

To illustrate how evolutionary psychologists approach the emotions, consider Robert Frank's (1988) analysis of romantic love. When searching for goods, Frank says, we must often settle for the best thing that has come our way rather than the best thing possible. The same is true with romance. The people we happen to have met when on the marriage market probably do not match our absolute ideals. If we settle for one of those people, it is always likely that a better mate will appear sometime down the line. But why should that person settle for us if we are still shopping? According to Frank, love is nature's solution to this commitment problem. If you fall head over heels for someone, that person will have more confidence that you will stick around. Love is a way of signaling that you are devoted and that you would incur a great cost (misery) if the relationship should come to an end. If two individuals "fall in love," they make the cost of a breakup prohibitively high, which makes the risk of investing in the relationship seem worthwhile. Love forges commitments by saddling infidelity with mutually assured despair.

Frank's analysis of love typifies explanations in evolutionary psychology. It analyzes emotions as nature's clever tactics for increasing fitness. Love helps ensure pair bonding by making it seem less risky. That increases prospects for reproduction. Frank also implies that true love, like other emotions, is hard to fake, so evolution has made it difficult to dupe another person into a sexual alliance that will not last. Emotions are not just universal, according to evolutionary psychologists; emotions play leading roles in the biological programs that ensure our survival.

Strictly speaking, arguments from evolutionary psychology presuppose biological reductionism; they don't seek to prove it. They assume that love is innate, and then seek to find an explanation of why it is innate. But, dialectically, these arguments are sometimes deployed as part of the evidence for reductionism. If one can show that an emotion is adaptive, then one can remove a potential barrier that would otherwise obstruct innateness claims. One can think of evolutionary psychologists as urging a kind of gestalt shift. If we begin to look at aspects of psychology as if they were adaptations, we may arrive at an evolutionary story whose explanations are so satisfying and whose predictions are so accurate that we have little choice but to take that story as true. Theory construction always involves this kind of leap of faith, insofar as theories always postulate hidden variables. We embrace a theory because it makes sense of what we observe. Evolutionary psychologists are just another group of sense-makers.

In summary, there are a number of different kinds of arguments for reductionism. Some researchers appeal to universal expressions of emotion across human cultures. Others make comparisons across species. And still others try to find evidence that emotions are transmitted genetically, by measuring the heritability of affective traits. Though quite distinct, each of these strategies works by finding a correlation between two groups and then postulating innate capacities to explain these correlations. In crosscultural studies, the correlations are between different peoples' responses to facial expressions. In animal studies, the correlations are between features of distinct species. In heritability studies, the correlations are between individuals who are genetically related. Arguments from evolutionary psychology have a different form. Rather than relying on quantitative analyses, they tend to deploy a narrative methodology. Stories about why emotions may have evolved are presented as evidence that they did evolve. I will evaluate the success of each of these argument strategies.

### From Facial Expression to Gene Expression

#### Emotion Universals?

Crosscultural research on facial expressions has a privileged place among arguments for reductionism. These results have been celebrated in numerous textbooks and are often presented uncritically as supporting the claim that emotions are universal. The argument is simple: members of different cultures make similar faces under similar circumstances; this suggests they are experiencing the same emotions; if so, the best explanation is that those emotions are biologically based; therefore, some emotions are biologically based.

The argument from facial expressions rests on the implicit assumption that there is a tight link between facial expressions and emotions. Can we assume that people who make the same faces under the same circumstances are experiencing the same emotions? Can we assume that facial expressions are emotional expressions? This assumption has met two important challenges.

The first is expressed by Ortony and Turner (1990). They have argued that facial expressions are actually complex, and their individual parts correspond to appraisal dimensions. A face associated with anger may be comprised of a furrowed brow, which reflects consciousness of an inability to attain a goal, and a square mouth with exposed teeth, which reflects a tendency toward aggression. If this analysis is correct, the prevalence of the so-called angry face across cultures may support the universality of those components, not of anger itself.

This alternative explanation of facial expressions is not fatal to reductionism. A reductionist can argue that the states alleged to underlie an angry expression on Ortony and Turner's account are emotions in their own right. Consciousness of an inability to attain a goal may be tantamount to frustration, and a tendency toward aggression may reflect a feeling of pugnacity. Anger itself may be a blend of frustration and pugnacity. If so, Ortony and Turner's proposal could be used to challenge the thesis that anger is basic, but it cannot refute the claim that some emotions are basic.

Fridlund (1994) has defended a more radical departure from the assumption that faces and emotions are tightly linked. He argues that facial expressions are communicative, rather than expressive. In particular, facial expressions convey our behavioral intentions or elicit behavioral responses from others. The face we ordinarily call an expression of anger is not an outward sign of an inner feeling but a message that that its bearer may strike and its viewers had better watch out. A frown expresses supplication, beckoning the viewer to hold and comfort the frowner. The mapping between expressions and emotions is quite contingent, on Fridlund's view.

In support of his hypothesis, Fridlund (1994) cites evidence that we do not always make expressions when emotions are intensely felt. Fernández-Dols and Ruiz-Belda (1995) found that Olympic athletes rarely smile just after winning gold medals; they only smile reliably when they are standing on the award podium facing an audience. Kraut and Johnston (1979) found that bowlers also tend to smile most when others are watching them, not when they bowl a strike. A smile is not an expression of happiness, Fridlund concludes, but an invitation for others to approach. If he is right, this is damning for the evidence from Ekman and Friesen's studies. Universal facial expressions may show only that people in different cultures have similar intentions in similar circumstances, leaving the question about emotions unanswered.

Ekman (1997) has responded to Fridlund. He notes, first, that emotions sometimes occur more when a person is alone than when that person is in public. For example, people from Japan tend to express negative emotions more when they are alone than when they are with another person, especially if they view that person as an authority (Ekman, 1972; Friesen, 1972). Ekman also offers an explanation of why certain expressions increase in the presence of an audience. Such "audience effects" reflect the social nature of certain emotions. People smile when confronted with an audience, because happiness can be elicited by positive responses from others. Far from showing that expressions do not express emotions, the fact that we smile more when we are being watched may show that social approval is an especially good elicitor for happiness. Fridlund may be right that expressions serve communicative functions, but he tends to exaggerate the disconnection between expression and emotions. It is possible that expressions are used to communicate intended actions *precisely because* they are naturally linked to emotions that typically accompany those actions. Moreover, in chapter 2 I presented evidence that changing facial expressions changes one's emotion, suggesting an especially intimate link.

Russell (1994) has developed a more convincing critique of research on emotional expressions. He argues that the crosscultural findings are considerably less robust than they are often presumed to be. I will only mention a few of his arguments. One complaint concerns the forced-choice method employed by Ekman and Friesen. If members of the Fore are asked to select expressions from a group of three photos, they may be able to do so by a process of elimination. Their response does not mean necessarily that the selected photo is a perfect choice but that it is the best given the options. The experimenters make the decision easier by avoiding very difficult contrasts (e.g., asking subjects to choose between a "surprise" and a "fear" face). Russell also argues that the Fore subjects who participated in the experiments were not completely isolated from Western contact and may have been inadvertently exposed to Western facial expression by the experimenters themselves. He notes that Fore who had less contact with Westerners tended to perform less well in the experiments.

The problems with the forced-choice method can be avoided by using a free-choice paradigm, in which subjects view images of facial expressions and come up with their own names for them. Some experimenters have used free choice and reported reasonably good results (see, e.g., Izard, 1971; Boucher & Carlson, 1980). Russell argues that these results depend on liberal coding criteria. One can show high agreement about the meaning of a given facial expression only if a variety of very different words are treated as equivalent. For example, Izard treated "loneliness," "pain," "pity," and "worry" as equivalent, grouping them under the generic label *distress*. Izard also says that "distress" should be treated as a synonym for "sadness," implying that subjects in his free-choice experiment consistently regarded a frown as a sad face. This is surely a stretch. Free-choice experiments simply have not shown that specific emotions, such as sadness, are consistently associated with faces. Rather they show that broad "clusters" of emotions are associated with faces. This makes it difficult to determine whether particular emotions are universal or whether broader affective dimensions uniting those clusters are universal. A frown may express a range of negative emotional states that includes sadness along with culturally specific analogues that may differ in important ways.

In an effort to drive home the nonspecificity of expressions, Russell (1993) conducted an experiment in which American respondents were shown a standard set of emotion faces and asked to chose between emotion words that did not include the words that are canonically associated with those faces. For example, respondents shown an "angry" face labeled it "contempt" when "anger" was not included in the set of words from which they had to choose. Subjects also labeled a "sad" face "fear" when "sadness" was not an option. Respondents showed high agreement in their responses, despite the fact that the canonical words were not included. This shows that expressions may be ambiguous and context sensitive.

Russell also points out that the actual percentages of agreement in crosscultural studies are lower than one might expect if emotions were biologically based and universal. For example, in a study in which Fore named emotions to go with photographs of facial expressions, 56 percent chose the Fore word that corresponds to "anger" when they saw what we would consider an expression of sadness (Ekman, Sorensen, & Friesen, 1969). It may be significant to note, in this context, that some African languages have a single word for anger and sadness (Leff, 1973). Perhaps these emotions are not strongly differentiated for the Fore. In the study that used stories rather than verbal labels, percentages went up. Fore chose the sad face for the story about the death of a child 81 percent of the time (Ekman & Friesen, 1971). But even this percentage may be unimpressive, given that a forced-choice method is used. Cross-cultural studies yield the best results for recognition of "happy" faces. Happiness is the only positive emotion tested, so stories and words can be associated with "happy" faces by process of elimination. Russell concludes that the experimental literature fails to provide conclusive evidence for the universality of facial expressions.

Unsurprisingly, Ekman has responded to Russell (e.g., Ekman, 1994, 1999b). In addition to addressing each of Russell's individual objections, he drives home the central point that agreement across cultures is vastly greater than could be the case if the link between facial expression and emotions was arbitrarily determined by culture. The findings suggest that nature has a hand in determining which face goes with which emotion. While there might be minor cultural and individual differences here and there, the general pattern is robust and replicable.

This response is effective against extreme forms of cultural relativism, but it is not sufficient for supporting comprehensive reductionism. The massive agreement across cultures concerning the faces in Ekman's experiments would be dwarfed by massive disagreement about the facial expressions of other emotions. A huge number of expressive faces seem to be culturally specific. Early research on expression included faces for interest, wonder, religious devotion, romantic love, and scores of other emotions (e.g., Feleky, 1914; Langfeld, 1918). Within the West, some of these expressions might be recognizable. Consider depictions, in Christian paintings from the Renaissance, of devoted believers staring heavenward with wide eyes and heads cocked slightly to one side. Religious devotion is pancultural (Boyer, 2001), but this expression almost certainly is not. To take another example, Menon and Shweder (1994) found that people in Orissa, India, associate tongue biting with shame. In South China, brief tongue protrusions are associated with feeling apologetic (Morris, 1994). If shared facial expressions are evidence of biological universality, culturally specific expressions may be evidence for sociocultural influence. Thus, Ekman's research program can only support constrained reductionism: some emotions are universal while others are not.

But which emotions are universal? A casual read of reductionist research might lead one to think that every culture has such emotions as joy, fear, disgust, sadness, and perhaps surprise and anger. But foreign words that are presumed to be synonyms for these demonstrate impressive correlations with the predicted facial expressions only in forced-choice experiments. Results of free-choice experiments are unimpressive unless nonsynonymous words are grouped together. Ekman (1993) has a surprisingly conciliatory response to this objection. He says that emotions come in "families." These families are universal, but their specific members—the discrete emotions that get lexicalized in the world's languages—may vary to some degree as a function of culture. Ekman's emotion families seem to be equivalent to what Russell calls "clusters." Both authors seem to agree that English emotion labels may not correspond perfectly to emotions in other cultures. Instead, we find *similar* emotions across cultures.

The emotion family hypothesis it is a departure from stronger forms of reductionism. In particular, it is a departure from the translatability thesis, hence from strong reductionism. If our emotion terms name culturally influenced instances of universal emotion families, then we cannot assume they map onto terms in other languages.

The difference between Russell and Ekman seems to come down to the question of how many universal families or clusters exist. Russell thinks there are very few, and that the clusters may ultimately correspond to major dimensions within emotion space (e.g., valence and arousal) rather than particular emotions. Ekman thinks there may be up to fifteen universal emotion families (Ekman, 1999a; see chapter 6). The cross cultural experiments on facial expressions have provided evidence for fewer than half that number, but some of these families have not been adequately investigated, and some may lack characteristic facial expressions. However many clusters there are, Ekman's current view seems to concede that a pure form of reductionism that insists on translatability is not tenable.

It is very easy to extend this general conclusion to studies of infants and nonhuman animals. Reductionism seems to get a significant boost from infant and animal studies, because infants and animals do not operate under the influence of culture. Infants smile when stimulated, rats freeze when threatened, and cats bristle their hairs when a predator approaches. These expressions probably operate under the control of brain structures that are homologous to structures found in adult humans. If emotional circuits and expressions like ours are found in organisms that operate outside our cultures, then it is odd to attribute emotions to culture. Clearly emotions have a biological basis.

The problem with this argument is that the conclusion is ambiguous. There is a trivial sense in which emotions have a biological basis. They must be grounded in the brain. There is also a substantive interpretation that is perfectly acceptable. The nature of adult human emotions derives in part from emotion-specific neural circuits that have homologues in other creatures. The emotions we experience in daily life build on resources in our innate neural architecture. But there is an interpretation of the claim that emotions have a biological basis that goes much farther than this. On the stronger interpretation, emotions are biologically determined, and humans share emotions with infants, apes, and laboratory rodents. This conclusion is unfounded.

Continuity between the expressive and neurobiological aspects of adult human emotions and other creatures does not prove identity. Differences at the expressive and anatomical levels are often as striking as similarities. First consider expressions. Human infants make familiar expressions, but the emotions they experience when they do so may not correspond to those that adults experience. For example, Camras (1992) reports that infants make what look like surprise expressions when viewing familiar stimuli, and expressions associated with discrete negative emotions in adults (anger, fear, sadness) are correlated with undifferentiated distress in infants. By the second year, correlations between emotion and expression are closer to the adult pattern but not perfectly consistent (Camras, 1994). This does not prove that emotions are culturally acquired, but it demonstrates the risk of drawing conclusions about innateness by appeal to adult-infant comparisons.

Evidence from neuroanatomy is equally shaky. Adult human brains have more developed frontal lobes than the brains of infants and nonhuman animals. There is extensive connectivity between frontal areas and more primitive emotion circuits (e.g., Amaral, Price, Pitkaner, & Carmichael, 1992; Devinsky, Morrell, & Vogt, 1995). MacLean's triune brain model is frequently criticized for assuming that old neural circuits function the same way as newer brain circuits are added. The dynamic nature of neuronal activity and evolution makes this implausible. Likewise, the links between old circuits and adult frontal cortex are likely to impact emotions. Frontal areas are receptacles for higher cognition, including cultural knowledge. When old emotion circuits interface with these, they may function differently.

If infants and animals behaved just like human adults, we might have reason for thinking our emotions are shared. This simply isn't the case. Infants and animals are emotionally affected by different things, and they express their emotions in different ways. Similarities across different kinds of creatures are just similarities. Arguments from cross-species comparison and human development can show only that our emotions are related to states found in other creatures. Emotions can exist outside of human culture, but we have no reason for believing that adult human emotions can exist without culture. Following Ekman's conciliatory response to cultural variation, we might even speculate that some infants and animals have emotions that belong to the same "families" as nonhuman emotions. Rats may have something like a fear response. But we should not conclude that rats have "fear" where this word is defined as the very same aversive response to danger that we find in us. If would be better to say they have a homologue of fear or a fear-like emotion.

## Emotion Genes?

The preceding arguments attempt to support reductionism by appealing to similarities across human populations or species. Reductionists hope to identify universals so that they can say that certain emotions are innate. Another way to provide evidence for innateness is more direct. One can try to find emotion genes. Ironically, the search for genes usually involves a search for differences, rather than universals. Genetic psychologists look for traits that vary across individuals, and then they try to explain the variance. When variance across individuals can be correlated with variance in a factor associated with genes, genes are held to be responsible.[2] Heritability is the percentage of variance that can be correlated with genetic factors.

---

[2]Note though that heritability does not entail innateness, because it is a correlational measure. A trait can abe correlated with a biological property without being innate. Having dark skin pigmentation is a biological property that happens to be correlated with being the victim of bigotry, so being the victim of bigotry is heritable. But being the victim of bigotry clearly isn't innate. Having light skin is correlated with skin cancer, which makes skin cancer somewhat heritable but not innate. In other words, heritable traits can be acquired byproductas of innate traits.

Looking for emotion genes is difficult, because emotions are states, not traits. But emotions have been associated with certain traits that are known to be heritable. As noted earlier, two classes of finding are especially relevant. The first involves personality or temperament. Personality traits are known to be quite stable over the life span, and there is evidence that they can be passed down through the genes (Tellegen et al., 1988). Some major dimensions of personality seem to be intimately connected to emotions. For example, neuroticism seems to be linked to fear. Neurotics tend to be anxious about various things. Another major dimension, extroversion, may be related to happiness. Like someone who is experiencing a temporary bout of happiness, extroverts tend to think positively, to approach others, and to actively explore their environments. Both neuroticism and extroversion are believed to have genetic components. Cloninger (1994) has even offered specific speculations about what those genetic components are. Cloninger uses constructs such as novelty seeking and harm avoidance rather than extroversion and neuroticism. He associates novelty seeking with a gene that influences dopamine receptors, and he associates harm avoidance with a gene that influences serotonin. If affective personality traits are genetically based, the corresponding emotions may be as well.

The second class of findings involves psychopathology. Vulnerability to certain mood disorders is widely believed to be genetic. Everyone has heard, for example, that depression is highly heritable (Sullivan, Neale, & Kendler, 2000). Depression is associated with sadness. Depressed people, like people experiencing sadness, tend to view things negatively, to cry, and to feel unmotivated. If depression has a genetic component, then sadness may as well.

The arguments from heritability are open to challenge. Consider the argument pertaining to personality traits. Even if personality traits are highly heritable, they provide weak evidence for the innateness of particular emotions. Personality traits are linked only to broad affective dimensions such as valence and arousal. For example, neuroticism may derive from negative valence, while extroversion derives from positive valence or low baseline arousal (Eysenck, 1967; Meyer & Shack, 1989). Most personality theorists draw the link between emotions and character traits using these broad dimensions rather than discrete emotional states, such as happiness and fear. And these links may themselves vary a bit from culture to culture. For example, Lucas, Diener, Grob, Suh, and Shao (2000) found that the correlation between extraversion and happiness is lower in the Far East than in the West. Moreover, there is some controversy about the claim that personality traits are genetic. Richard Nisbett and his colleagues have spent decades arguing that environmental factors can contribute to behaviors that are traditionally explained in terms of character traits (Ross & Nisbett, 1991). If he is right, then research on "personality" actually provides evidence against biological reduction.

Research on the heritability of mood disorders is also insufficient for defending reductionist theories of emotion. First, one can raise doubt on the evidence for the genetic basis of depression. Some of the studies that have been used to support the claim that depression is highly heritable are based on correlations between identical twins. Upward of 30 percent of the variability in identical twins can be accounted for by genetic factors. But this assessment fails to take into consideration the fact that identical twins may experience many of the same environmental influences (Kendler, 1993). If they are put up for adoption, they will both endure that stigma, and if they are not put up for adoption, they will be raised in the same homes. More important, identical twins tend to be treated in similar ways. Shared physical traits and psychological traits that are unrelated to mood may promote similar patterns of interaction with others. This may explain why identical twins sometimes show higher degrees of correlation for depression than fraternal twins (which, by the way, is not always the case; Sullivan et al., 2000).

Even if depression has a genetic basis, it is not fully determined by biology. Symptoms of depression vary as a function of culture. Depressed Nigerians tend to report feelings of worthlessness less often than Americans, depressed Chinese may report more physical weakness, and depressed Latinos may complain more about nerves (American Psychiatric Association, 1994; Kleinman, 1988). The fact that depression is found in all cultures suggests that it has an innate basis (Kleinman, 1988). But genes may provide a core condition that gets fleshed out under the influence of cultural factors.

In short, depression is another family concept. It corresponds to a collection of similar conditions whose specific incarnations are sensitive to culture. If depression involves some of the mechanisms that underlie sadness, then we shouldn't be surprised to discover that sadness is culturally sensitive as well. This is the conclusion that I already drew from crosscultural facial expression research. The term "sad" only refers to a genetically based universal if we use it as a family concept, referring to a superordinate category whose members vary across cultures. If we use sadness to name a discrete emotion, as vernacular use would seem to demand, then there is no reason to regard it as a universal. It may be a culturally nuanced instantiation of a broader category.

Evidence from heritability, like evidence from emotional expressions and physiology, provides compelling evidence for the conclusion that biology has a significant impact on human emotions. Biology may even partition affective space into a small group of fundamental categories. But differences across cultures, age groups, and phyla suggest that these categories are susceptible to non-biological influences. Strong reductionists claim that the discrete emotions named in English are innate. There is little support for this claim in the evidence I have reviewed. Weaker forms of reductionism may still be viable.

### *Evolutionary Psychology*

Arguments from evolutionary psychology differ from those I have been considering. They try to support innateness claims (or claims about species-typicality) by developing intuitively plausible stories about the adaptive functions of various states and traits. Evolutionary psychologists also tend to support more comprehensive forms of reductionism. They argue that higher cognitive emotions are products of natural selection. So far, I have only considered arguments for the innateness of emotions that are widely regarded as basic. I have granted that these emotions may be related, if not identical, to emotion categories whose boundaries are preordained by genes. Might this be true for higher cognitive emotions as well?

Before coming to that question, I want to illustrate the difference between arguments from evolutionary psychology and arguments from heritability by considering evolutionary approaches to depression. There are a growing number of evolutionary explanations of why people become depressed (see Nesse, 1998, for review). Evolutionary psychologists do not try to demonstrate this fact by searching for genes. Instead they come up with stories to explain why depression might have been selected for. Where clinicians tend to regard depression as a defect, evolutionary psychologists regard it as an adaptation that may be better suited to the demands of our ancestral environments.

According to one typical theory, depression evolved as a response to loss of status (Price, Sloman, Gardner, Gilbert, & Rohde, 1994). In hierarchically organized populations, depression serves an adaptive function for individuals who vie unsuccessfully for a rank increase. Depression signals one's current place in the hierarchy. In nonhuman animals, such as deer, individuals who have lost rank battles do indeed show symptoms of depression (Raleigh, McGuire, Brammer, Pollack, & Yuwiler, 1991; though see Marrow, Overton, & Brian, 1999). The rank theory also explains a couple of mysterious facts. It explains why depression diminishes motivation: if one has just been knocked down by a dominant individual, it would be too risky to try to advance one's station again. This theory also explains the fact that depression is on the rise in our society. With all the increases in quality of life that the modern world affords, one might think we would be happier. The reason we are not, according to some evolutionary psychologists, is that we are constantly bombarded by media images of people who are better off (Price et al., 1994). Television, movies, and magazines present an endless pageant of people who are wealthier, prettier, more powerful, and more fabulous.

The rank theory of depression is captivating, has experimental support in deer, and explains some mysterious facts. But I think it is probably too narrow. Rank is just one of the challenges we face, and I see little reason to think that depression was designed for rank disputes alone. Intuitively, the rank theory would predict that more successful people are less depressed, which is not the case (Diener, Sandvik, Seidlitz, & Diener, 1992). The theory also predicts that people who watch more television should be more depressed. More important, it predicts that other struggles, stressors, and losses should be less reliable causes of depression than rank battles. The loss of a loved one or a traumatic experience should cause depression only insofar as they mark a diminution in one's ability to advance in the social hierarchy. Admittedly, any trauma could potentially have such consequences, but it is contrived to say that the death of one's spouse leads to depression because it makes one less equipped to take on the alpha male. Rather than associating depression with any one fundamental adaptive challenge, one can see it as a response to any major losses.

Some evolutionary psychologists would agree that depression serves a variety of functions (Nesse & Williams, 1997). This alternative perspective is perfectly consistent with the hypothesis that depression is an adaptive response. I introduced the rank theory because it typifies a general tendency in evolutionary psychology. Its adherents tend to look for very specific adaptive explanations for psychological traits. Our mind is a Swiss army knife comprised of tools that have been carefully shaped for unique evolutionary purposes (Pinker, 1997). An alternative view, which is perfectly consistent with evolution but ideologically at odds with evolutionary psychology, says that our mind is equipped with a more general set of tools and biases that can help us cope with a great variety of challenges and can be shaped by experience to meet challenges that nature may not have anticipated. On this view the mind is more like an erector set: it gives us pieces to work with, but we can build them up in different ways to face new demands. These two perspectives on evolution are not radically different, but the contrast between them has bearing on whether emotions are biologically reducible.

The two perspectives, Swiss army knife and erector set, lead to different predictions about the emotions. The Swiss army knife model predicts that each emotion is a solution that as been evolved for a specific challenge. The erector set model predicts that many emotions will be built up from simpler parts to meet unexpected demands. The hypothesis that we have a small set of innate emotions and a large set of emotions that are built up from these falls somewhere between these two pictures. Predictably, evolutionary psychologists aim for a more comprehensive account. They tend to be comprehensive reductionists. On this approach, each of our emotions, from fear to falling in love, is honed by natural selection to serve us in some way.

I gave an example of this tendency in Robert Frank's theory of love. Frank (1988) argues that love is an evolved solution to a commitment problem. It is away of forming and conveying strong and lasting bonds to others. If we chose to form sexual alliances dispassionately, they would not last. We would leave our lovers as soon a more attractive hairless ape came along. If we form pair bonds out of love, however, they can endure, and two people in love can risk making the sacrifice associated with commitment because their emotional bond promises long-term payoffs through an enduring alliance.

The story sounds perfectly plausible, but is it true? Those who idealize love might resist Frank's analysis on the grounds that it degrades love to a tool for material exchange. Frank's economic account seems to rob love of all its magnificent splendor. I think Frank's analysis actually suffers from the opposite problem. It is based on a very romantic view of love that may be specific to Western culture. Frank assumes that love can play a role in forging long-term commitments (or at least an illusion thereof) because love instills a desire for long-term bonding. Love, on his analysis, is an overpowering and seemingly irrational force that is experienced as having the potential to endure forever. This is consistent with how love is described in the West, but it is not true crossculturally. Dion and Dion (1988) review findings from Chinese culture. In China, love is reportedly deemphasized in long-term relationships. It is associated with illicit affairs (Hsu, 1981). Marriage is built on things closer to trust and friendship. When Chinese women are asked to describe traits they look for in a partner, romance is not mentioned (Chu, 1985). If these studies are accurate, some people in China regard love as a sign of something ephemeral and unreliable, not the kind of thing to build a relationship on. If love were really an evolved way to forge and signal commitment, we would not expect such dramatic variation. Love may help solve a commitment problem in the West, but it is not necessarily evolved to do so. It may not be a product of natural selection at all.

Let's consider another example of the kinds of analyses offered by evolutionary psychologists. Sticking with the relationship theme, consider romantic jealousy (hereafter just "jealousy"). Jealousy has received considerable attention within evolutionary psychology (Buss, 2000). One might wonder why such an unpleasant emotion would ever evolve? Jealousy (the "green-eyed monster") certainly doesn't exist to make life more enjoyable. But evolution doesn't care about enjoyment. Evolutionary psychologists say that jealousy evolved in order to maximize the success of our genes. Genes only "care" about being replicated. In our species, gene replication depends on sex. But the future success of the genes replicated through this method depend on our offspring living to reproductive age. So, as agents of gene replication, we are programmed to reproduce and to protect our offspring. We care more about our own offspring than any others because they are most likely to have our genes. Our genes don't want us to waste energy and resources caring for other genes. They only care about themselves and the replicas; they are selfish (Dawkins, 1976). All this explains sex drive and parenting, but where does jealousy come in? According to evolutionary psychologists, jealousy is just another part of the program that helps us guarantee that our own genes have a fighting chance.

In keeping with this principle, evolutionary psychologists predict a gender difference in jealousy. Women who have offspring know that those offspring are theirs. If they invest resources in their offspring, they will be investing in close genetic relatives. Men have no such guarantee. If their female partners give birth, men cannot be certain about their own paternity; their partners could have had other sexual partners. When a man invests resources in a child that he takes to be his, there is some risk that he is investing in someone who isn't genetically related. For men, then, sexual infidelity is a very big threat. Men want to make sure their female partners are not promiscuous so they do not end up helping someone else's genes. Women face an entirely different risk. They have no doubts about their maternity, but they do worry that their male partners will not be there to help with the burden of childrearing. So women care more about emotional infidelity. If a male partner is showing affection for someone else, he may also be planning to allocate his resources elsewhere.

In sum, evolutionary psychology predicts that men will be more jealous of sexual infidelity, and women will be more jealous of emotional infidelity. Buss, Larson, Westen, and Semmelroth (1992) conducted a series of studies that seemed to bear this out. Given the choice between these two kinds of infidelity, men say sexual infidelity is worse and women say emotional infidelity is worse. Buss and Larsen even measured autonomic responses and found that men show greater autonomic response when contemplating sexual infidelity. They consider this an experimental demonstration of their evolutionary hypothesis. If they are right, jealousy is a biologically based emotion that was selected for its adaptive role.

This account of jealousy is seductive, but the evidence does not hold up under scrutiny. Consider another explanation. Assume that men and women have the same priority rankings: access to financial resources is most important, access to sex comes after that, and emotional ties to others come in third. The similarities stop there. Men have more economic power in most cultures, and until recently women have been extremely dependent on men financially. Women know that an emotionally unfaithful man poses a serious financial risk, whereas as a sexually unfaithful man just poses a risk to one's access to sexual gratification. Men do not generally depend on women financially. In our culture, men actually do better financially when they divorce (Holden & Smock, 1991). So emotional infidelity has emotional costs but it does not threaten the bank account. Given the choice, men would prefer this to sexual infidelity, because they, like women, value access to sex.

A slightly different, but compatible, proposal has been developed by Harris and Christenfeld (1996; see also DeSteno & Salovey, 1996). They argue that the difference in jealousy may derive from gender stereotypes about the link between sex and love. Men may believe that women only have sex when they are in love, while also believing that they can be in love without having sex. If so, they will regard sexual infidelity as worse because it always indicates both sexual and emotional infidelity. Conversely, women may believe that men can have sex without being in love, and that men in love always have sex. This would make emotional infidelity worse that sexual infidelity, because the former implies the latter, while the latter does not imply the former. Harris and Christenfeld found that men and women do indeed draw these inferences. This explains the gender difference without supposing that jealousy is innate.

Buss, Larsen, and Westen (1996) reply that this account still requires innate gender differences to explain the differences in gender stereotypes. Why does our culture think that men (but not women) can have sex without love? Mightn't this be routed in a genetic difference? In a more recent paper, Harris (2000) offers a very deflationary account of genetic contribution to the gender differences in jealousy. Perhaps men are just genetically disposed to be more preoccupied with sex. If so, they will be bothered by any threat to their access to sex, and they will be more prone to having sex without love. On this account, the gender difference in jealousy has a genetic source, but jealousy is not innate.

Harris also uses the sex drive theory to explain why men show more autonomic response when considering sexual infidelity. Perhaps the response is just sex arousal that occurs whenever men think about sex. To test this hypothesis, Harris measured autonomic response in men as they contemplated their female partners cheating on them and when they contemplated having sex with their female partners. Autonomic response was about the same under these two conditions. The initial physiological results of Buss et al. may have little to do with feelings of jealousy.

The evidence for the innateness of jealousy is weak at best. In fact, other evidence seems to suggest that it varies considerably across cultures. In the Netherlands and China, both men and women report that they would be more disturbed by emotional infidelity than sexual infidelity (Buunk, Angleitner, Oubaid, & Buss, 1996; Geary, Rumsey, Bow-Thomas, & Hoard, 1995). Buss regards such findings as consistent with the evolutionary account, but in fact it renders that account unnecessary by inviting cultural explanations. In the Netherlands, which is more sexually liberal than the United States, this may reflect the fact that sex is not regarded as a very big deal. In China, gender invariant concern with emotional infidelity may reflect a cultural emphasis on social relations. Even more radically, Hupka (1991) has shown that the Todas people in India showed very little jealousy for within-group sexual infidelity. The same may be true, in general, for avunculate cultures in which women have many sexual partners and raise their offspring with male siblings (Hill & Hurtado, 1996). In the end, then, studies of jealousy actually tend to support sociocultural models more decisively than they support reductionist models. While there is little evidence that jealousy is innate, there is good evidence that it is influenced by culture.

Evolutionary psychology has been criticized on many other grounds (e.g., Dupré, 2001; Griffiths, 1997; Rose & Rose, 2000; Scher & Rauscher, 2002). Critics complain that evolutionary psychologists often mistake the narrative cleverness of their evolutionary explanations for evidence. Numerous evolutionary stories can be devised for any psychological phenomenon, and without knowing the specific conditions under which that phenomenon arose, those stories are at best untested guesses. In this example, Buss and his colleagues assume that women acquired jealousy to ensure that male partners would help rear the kids. It is equally possible that early hominid clans raised offspring collectively, rendering any one male's contribution unimportant. Buss also assumes that men want to retain sexual access to a female partner with whom they have already had sexual relations, when in fact pressure for genetic diversity may have fostered an evolutionary drive to find new sexual partners after copulation. The presumed gender difference in jealousy conforms suspiciously to marital values in our own cultures.

Buss and his colleagues also fail to establish that jealousy is innate before devising their explanations of why it might have evolved. The explanation is treated as evidence for what it is designed to explain. Griffiths (1997) points out that this is a frequent fallacy in evolutionary psychology. In this context, this fallacy is especially relevant because it defuses the argument for the innateness of jealousy. This example is representative of reasoning in evolutionary psychology. I described an evolutionary explanation of why we fall in love. It sounds plausible, but it is worthless unless we can show that love is innate. It would have been advantageous if evolution had equipped the human mind with knowledge of farming techniques, but that does not mean such knowledge is innate. Jealousy and other cognitive emotions certainly have value, but, like crop rotation, they could be cultural inventions.

What would it take to show that romantic love is innate? What would it take to show that jealousy is innate? A hint can be garnered from the definition of innateness proposed in the first section of this chapter. I said there that innate traits are ones whose acquisition cannot be explained by appeal to the stimuli on the basis of which we learn together with general learning mechanisms. Both jealousy and romantic love seem to fail this test. If we think of jealousy as an aversive emotional reaction to a lover's infidelity, we can explain its acquisition quite easily. Assume that an organism has a set of negative emotions (anger, disgust, sadness, fear). Assume, further, that an organism values sexual access and intimacy. If those are threatened, aversive emotions will be felt. If jealousy is just a special name for such an aversive response (see chapter 6), then there is no reason why it needs to be innate. As long as one can explain how other aversive emotions came to be (they may be innate), jealousy may come along for free.

A similar story can be told about romantic love. It may have its basis in a more fundamental emotion known as attachment. Attachment is a positive emotion associated with being near another person. It may be specially suited for forging bonds between infants and their caregivers. Shaver, Hazan, and Bradshaw (1988) demonstrate suggestive parallels between attachment and romantic love. For example, lovers, like infants and their caregivers, coo and use baby talk. Lovers seek proximity and feel distress when separation occurs. Shaver et al. also show that well-documented differences in infant-to-caregiver attachment styles have parallels in styles of adult romantic love relationships. All this suggests that love is actually an outgrowth of attachment. But, as Shaver et al. recognize, more is needed. One difference between romantic love and attachment is that mere attachment lacks romance. This missing ingredient may be provided by coupling attachment with another affective state: lust (compare Sternberg, 1986). The link between romantic love and lust is sometimes denied. We are often cautioned against confusing the two. But lust almost certainly plays a role. The physiologies of love and lust almost certainly overlap (Hatfield, 1988). People get flushed, flustered, excited, and even euphoric when they are in love.

Lust and attachment are happy bedfellows. Lust tends to bring us into close contact with people, which can lead to the development of close, nurturing bonds. Attachment tends to bring us close to people, some of whom may be recognized as suitable sexual partners. So attachment can increase the probability of lust, and lust can increase the probability of attachment. When the two cooccur, the combination may answer to one of the meanings of romantic love. Some cases of love may be nothing more than lascivious attachment. Sometimes other emotions are probably involved as well. If every example of love can be characterized as a blend of other emotions, it is plausible that love is a learned response. Evolutionary psychologists often hypothesize that an emotion is an adaptation before providing good grounds for thinking that it is innate.

To drive home this moral, I will consider one final emotion. Like love and jealousy, evolutionary psychologists have argued that guilt is an evolved adaptation. Especially noteworthy are the accounts of Frank (1988) and Trivers (1971). According to Frank, guilt evolved to facilitate reciprocal altruism: making self-sacrificing choices to serve others who may end up helping you as a result. Behaving altruistically is a challenge because life presents us with so many opportunities to cheat. It is easy to steal from business associates, plagiarize a term paper, or have an extramarital affair. Cheating is advantageous for the cheater. This presents a puzzle. Natural selection favors self-interested behavior and should, therefore, favor cheating, but many of us do not cheat. The puzzle can be solved by considering what would happen if natural selection created an entire population of cheaters. Members of such a population would never trust each other, and consequently they would not be able to reap the benefits of cooperation and exchange. So natural selection confers an advantage to those who do not cheat. But natural selection cannot eliminate cheaters entirely. In a world of noncheaters, cheaters always stand to gain more than noncheaters by pretending to be honest. To prevent being wiped out by cheaters, cheating must be detectable. But it cannot be perfectly detectable.[3] If we had to monitor everyone all the time, we would waste too much energy. Equilibrium is achieved when there are some cheaters, some noncheaters, and good but imperfect ways of telling the two apart.

If you are a noncheater, you need a way to convince others that you are honest. If you cannot convince others that you are honest, being honest will not be of much use. Merely saying that you are honest will not work, because cheaters can lie. Frank describes two ways in which we can convince others of our honesty, and both involve guilt.

First, we can convince others of our honesty by making facial expressions. Facial expressions are notoriously difficult to fake. Unfortunately, there is no facial expression of honesty. This is where guilt comes in. According to Frank, there are facial expressions of guilt. He says, for example, that guilt causes people to blush and avert their gaze. When dishonest people cheat, they do not feel guilty. As a result, they do not make these characteristic facial expressions. This provides a way to distinguish honest people from dishonest people. If we catch a

---

[3]Evolutionary psychologists have argued that there are innate mechanisms for detecting cheaters (Cosmides, 1989; Gigerenzer & Hug, 1992). This evidence has been challenged (Liberman & Klar, 1996). Though I side with the challenges, I will not discuss these issues here, because the alleged cheater detection mechanisms do not involve guilt detection or any other emotion.

person doing something wrong, we know that the person has moral sentiments if they show signs of guilt. It would be better to cooperate with that person than with the person who commits transgressions with a poker face or a smile.

The second way to convince others that you are honest is to establish a reputation for not cheating. Establishing such a reputation is difficult, because we have a strong tendency to favor immediate gains over larger future gains or future costs. This bias is the product of natural selection. In our ancestors' risk-filled environment, a bird in the hand was worth two in the bush. When one is presented with an opportunity to cheat, the payoff of cheating is immediate, and the payoff or cost of not cheating (increased or reduced reputation) is remote. The bias in favor of present rewards makes cheating very attractive. Establishing a reputation requires a mechanism that mitigates temptation.

This is another job for guilt. According to Frank, we are evolved to feel guilty because it tips the balance in favor of honesty. If you want to overcome the temptation to cheat, it had better be the case that the costs of cheating outweigh the benefits. It had also better be the case that the costs can be appreciated in the present, because we tend to discount costs that occur in the future. Guilt counterbalances our bias for present rewards. Cheating feels bad. That feeling serves as a punishment, which makes cheating seem unattractive. People who experiences guilt when they cheat—that is, honest people—will resist cheating in spite of a general temptation to reap present rewards. People who do not feel guilt will have no mechanism for tempering that temptation. They will tend to cheat. Honest and dishonest people behave differently. The behavior of honest people confers a good reputation. The behavior is permitted by the presence of guilt. As a result, the behavior is also a good indicator of guilt. A good reputation indicates that a person is motivated by unselfish motives, because people who lack such motives are likely to tarnish their reputations by giving in to selfish temptations. Being truly unselfish, and not just faking it, leads to a pattern of behavior that signals reliability to potential negotiators. Being unselfish creates more opportunities for negotiation. True selflessness is self-serving, and guilt plays an integral role in undercutting the allure of selfish acts.

In sum, Frank thinks that guilt was selected because it helps convey important information about one's character. It causes us to make facial expressions that show we are morally sensitive, and it allows us to establish good reputations by placing a prohibitive tariff on cheating. Frank's account builds on the work of Trivers (1971), who was the first to suggest that guilt facilitates reciprocal altruism. Trivers's account assigns a slightly different role to guilt. Guilt compels cheaters to make amends. When a cheater is caught, she will try to repair a damaged relationship by engaging in altruistic behavior toward the affected party. This can restore trust and heal a damaged reputation. In support of this hypothesis, Trivers cites evidence that people who are caught doing something wrong are more likely than others to engage in self-sacrificing acts. Wallace and Sadalla (1966) found that individuals who broke an expensive piece of equipment were more likely to volunteer for a painful experiment.

Together, Frank and Trivers offer three roles for guilt in facilitating reciprocal altruism. Guilt signals moral character through facial expressions, guilt enhances reputation by deterring us from cheating, and guilt plays a reparative role when we do in fact cheat. If these authors are right, guilt is a very useful emotion. It increases fitness by facilitating reciprocal altruism. If guilt did emerge as a result of random genetic mutation, it may well have conferred enough of an advantage to have been selected for.

Thus far, however, we have only heard a just-so story. Frank and Trivers tell a plausible tale about how guilt may increase fitness, but we need more. We need evidence that guilt does, in fact, increase fitness for the reasons they have given, and we need evidence that guilt is innate rather than learned. To assess the evolutionary account of guilt, we should compare it to nonevolutionary accounts. Consider two alternatives.

According to one nonevolutionary account, guilt is foisted on us by culture. Members of a culture or a kin group have a stake in making sure that new members (such as children) conform to the rules that are in place. A convenient method for encouraging conformity is to encourage people to feel badly when they break a rule. Guilt may be constructed for just this purpose. Children may be taught to feel badly when they break rules. This account makes sense of the fact that guilt is often explicitly encouraged by others. People, especially caregivers, often pressure others into compliance by laying on "guilt trips."

According to a second nonevolutionary account, guilt is a learned byproduct of more basic traits. Human beings are social animals. We seek the support of others. When we do things to harm others, they will not give us support. That loss of support may cause sadness. Sadness at the loss of support gets tied, through association, to the transgression that led to the loss of support. This—sadness at our own transgressions—is the essence of guilt. This nonevolutionary account is actually compatible with the first. Guilt may be a learned byproduct that is further engrained and fine-tuned by caregivers and culture.

To choose between the evolutionary account of guilt and its nonevolutionary rivals, we must look at the evidence. Is there reason to think guilt is an innate adaptation to play the three roles described by Frank and Trivers? First consider Frank's suggestion that guilt causes facial expressions that help others assess our moral fiber. According to Frank, a guilty face is an indicator of moral sensitivity. The person who looks guilty can reveal that she feels badly when she does something wrong, and this can increase the probability that others will negotiate with her.

This story faces two problems. First, Frank's list of facial expressions for guilt lacks adequate support. There is not a good experimental literature on guilty expressions. In any case, the expressions that Frank mentions are not unique to guilt. Gaze averting is associated with social submission quite generally, and blushing is more often associated with embarrassment and shame. To show that guilt is an evolved emotion, and to show that its evolution depended, in part, on our ability to convey guilt to others, it would be helpful to establish a unique expression of guilt. Frank provides no evidence for the existence of such an expression. The fact that guilt borrows expressions from other mental states is just what a nonevolutionary story would predict. It fits in with the hypothesis that guilt is a previously existing negative emotion (or complex of negative emotions) that is set up through learning to be set off by our own transgressions.

The second problem with the expression story is that facial expressions of guilt are unlikely to help in building trust and forging cooperative alliances. As Frank notes, we are better off dealing with people who never make guilty expressions, because we are better off dealing with people who never do things that are worthy of guilt. Therefore, we need another indicator of honesty. Frank says one strategy is to look for signs of sympathy. He says sympathetic people are unlikely to deceive those with whom they sympathize. The problem with this proposal is that sympathy has no characteristic facial expression. Detecting sympathy in an honest person may be just as hard as detecting guilt. In conclusion, the evidence that guilt evolved for its role in conveying information about character through facial expressions is very weak. Facial expressions of guilt do not facilitate reciprocal altruism, and they lack the distinctiveness that would support the claim that guilt is innate.

What about the other alleged evolutionary functions of guilt? Might guilt have evolved to discourage cheating or to encourage reparation? These proposals are more promising. Guilt seems to play both of these roles, and, in playing them, it increases fitness. But this only shows that guilt is adaptive. Frank and Trivers want us to believe that guilt is an adaptation. The problem is that adaptiveness cannot distinguish between traits that are evolved and traits that are learned. Many learned responses are acquired because of the advantages they confer. Recall crop rotation. Cultures may have developed guilt precisely because it facilitates group living by keeping cheaters in line.

Defenders of evolutionary accounts need to provide evidence that guilt is innate rather than learned. This sounds plausible to many pet owners. Everyone has seen a dog looking sheepish after relieving itself on the carpet instead of outside. It seems plausible to say that dogs feel guilty about their behavior, and that guilt is, thus, likely to be innate.[4]

One might be tempted to respond to such anecdotal evidence as follows. Guilt seems to require sophisticated concepts. It is hard to imagine a true case of guilt in a creature that lacks a concept of self, other, and moral transgression. Apparent cases of canine guilt may be spurious. The conceptual prerequisites of guilt have lead many researches to conclude that guilt does not exist in nonhuman animals (Hauser, 2002) or in human infants (Lewis, 2000; Sroufe, 1984). Most developmentalists speculate that human guilt emerges no earlier than the second year of life. If guilt has significant cognitive prerequisites, then it may be learned.

---

[4]Paul Griffiths has rightfully complained (personal communication) that little would follow about our own biological makeup from innate traits in dogs. Dogs have been selectively bred by us to exhibit interpretable social emotions. To draw conclusions about the natural phylogeny of biologically based emotions in humans, it would be better to consider the emotions of primates.

I am not persuaded by this argument, because I am not convinced that guilt requires such concepts. Emotions get their meaning by reliably tracking core relational themes. Guilt may get its meaning by reliably tracking personal transgressions.[5] This does not require a self-concept or a transgression concept. A creature can track its own transgressions in other ways. Suppose Fido, a dog, has a calibration file that triggers an emotional response to any action for which he has previously punished. When Fido pees on the carpet in the presence of his human caregiver, he enters a negative emotional state. This could be regarded as a primitive form of guilt because it is reliably caused by personal transgression. Fido does not enter this state by thinking "Gee, I violated a moral norm." He perceives the event, which happens to be a norm violation, and he responds by feeling bad. Animal guilt cannot be dismissed so easily.

The real problem with appeals to animal guilt is not that guilt requires sophisticated concepts. Guilt may be conceptually inexpensive, and it may have analogues in dogs and nonhuman primates. The problem is that this is not evidence for innateness. There is a tendency to think that anything found in animals must be innate. We like to think of animals as our primitive biological selves, free from the adulterating marks of learning. This Romanticist fantasy is easily dismissed. Animals can learn. They can learn to feel badly about their actions, just as they can be conditioned to fear electrical grids or conditioned to get excited when their caregivers open the front door. This is consistent with the byproduct theory of guilt and with the cultural imposition theory. We may train animals to feel bad when they violate our cultural norms. To date, there has been no uncontroversial demonstration of guilt in nonhuman animals, but should such demonstrations come, the innateness question will not be settled.

The best strategy for showing that something is innate is to show that it couldn't be learned. This is how poverty of the stimulus arguments in linguistics work. Linguists argue that this is an innate language faculty by showing that children develop linguistic skills that outstrip the sentences that they hear during learning. By parity of reasoning, evolutionary psychologists could try to argue that guilt could not possibly be acquired, in the time frame in which it is acquired, without the help of innate resources *that are specific to guilt*. But no such argument seems possible. If guilt is just sadness at one's own transgressions (as the byproduct account suggests), then the acquisition of guilt requires three in-

---

[5]This may seem to neglect survivor guilt, which is experienced by those who do not think they have done anything wrong. Survivor guilt arises when harm comes to those we care about and we are unharmed. I think that survivor guilt is not really guilt at all. It is confused with guilt because it shares two important features with paradigm cases of guilt: harm to others and subsequent thoughts to the effect that "I deserve to suffer because of that harm." But these two features are insufficient for guilt. Thoughts about punishment are not even necessary for guilt. One can feel guilty about taking a wallet found on the street without explicitly entertaining thoughts about punishment. Survivor guilt gets its name because its paradigm instances have a family resemblance to paradigm instances of bona fide guilt. If emotions are individuated by the properties that they reliably detect, these emotions are importantly different.

gredients: sadness, a concept of transgression, and associative learning. In other words, it does not require any innate resources that are specific to guilt.

One might try to prove that guilt is innate by showing that some people are born without a capacity for it. Psychopaths have just such a deficit. This may look like evidence for the claim that guilt is a genetic trait. I think there is an alternate explanation. Let's suppose guilt is built up from sadness. It is sadness calibrated to harms that one has brought to others. If this analysis is correct, then a sadness deficit would result in a guilt deficit. That points to a plausible explanation of psychopaths' moral retardation. Psychopaths are known to have flattened emotional responses quite globally (Hare, 1993). That means they have abnormally low levels of sadness. Consequently, guilt has insufficient raw materials to emerge. In developmental terms, the story might go something like this. When a your child does something wrong, parents and caregivers become upset. They may respond in various ways: getting angry, drawing the child's attention to the harm she has caused, or withdrawing love and affection. Children are gregarious and want their parents' affection. Being scolded or cast off naturally cause sadness, because they lead to loss of that affection. Being oriented toward someone who has been harmed also causes sadness through emotional contagion. Thus, each form of ordinary parental response leads to sadness. This forges a link between sadness and transgression in memory, and thus guilt is born. Subtract sadness from the child's emotional repertoire, and guilt goes too. The result is a lifetime of antisocial behavior.

Elsewhere, I develop this account in more detail (Prinz, 2003, in progress). My point here is to show that we can explain the emergence of guilt without innateness. Putting guilt in the genome is simply unnecessary. Guilt *could* be innate, but, short of positive evidence for that conclusion, we should accept a more conservative hypothesis. Guilt is a product of nurture that builds on other emotions, a desire for affection, and a general capacity for learning.

This echoes the moral from love and jealousy. Evolutionary accounts are gratuitous when plausible learning stories can be developed. There is no reason to put something in the genome if it can easily come about through learning. If some of our ancestors happened to have innate resources that were specific to the development of love, jealousy, or guilt, they would have had no significant survival advantage over those who acquired these emotions by means of resources that were initially designed to serve some other purpose.

I conclude that arguments for biological reductionism are not very successful. Arguments from evolutionary psychologists rest on especially shaky ground, leaving little support for comprehensive reduction. The evidence for shared facial expressions, shared physiology, and genetic factors is more credible. It suggests that there is a significant biological contribution to some emotions. But this evidence does not show that the emotions we have names for in English exist in all cultures. Thus, we have seen no support for the translatability thesis. Strictly speaking, the evidence we have seen does not even provide adequate support for

# 6

# *Emotions and Nurture*

### *Constructionism and Compatibilism*

#### Social Constructionism

While some researchers have been impressed by the apparent universality of emotions, others have been impressed by the diversity. In some cultures there seem to be emotions, or at least words for emotions, that are quite alien to those found in the Anglo-American world. The Dutch have the word *gezellig*, which is close to the English word "cozy" in meaning, but it is a coziness that occurs only in the presence of other people (Harré, 1986). In Japan, there is an emotion called *amae*, which is characterized as a feeling of dependency akin to that which infants feel toward their mothers (Doi, 1973; Morsbach & Tyler, 1986). In Japan, *amae* is regarded as a common and important emotion that bonds individuals to each other and to cherished institutions. The Ifaluk people, who live in a Micronesian atoll, have an emotion that they call *song*, which is their primary analogue of our emotion "anger" but is more like a feeling of admonition, with moralistic overtones and no disposition to revenge (Lutz, 1988; Wierzbicka, 1999).

Some of our own emotions might appear completely exotic to another culture. Consider feelings of patriotism, as they are expressed in the United States. Patriots stand erect and become teary-eyed when they hear the national anthem. These bodily responses may seem as natural as any others associated with our emotions, but to an outsider they may look exotic. Why should a song, or a flag, or thoughts of one's country produce such a strong visceral response?

Some researchers believe that emotions such as *gezelligheid*, *amae*, *song*, and patriotism are unique to particular cultures. They are social constructions, devised and disseminated by human groups. To say that an emotion is socially constructed is to say that its identity conditions depend on features that have come about as a consequence of the sociocultural environment in which the possessor of that emotion resides. The identity conditions for such an emotion advert to a property that emerged through the influence of beliefs, values, practices, or institutions that are specific to a particular human group. Culture makes a constitutive contribution.

Ian Hacking (1999) observes that constructed kinds are kinds whose instances are affected by how we classify and regard them. Gender categories are a familiar example. What we consider masculine or feminine seems to be partially determined by culture. In Western culture, femininity is associated with such arbitrary symptoms as dresses, love of flowers, manicured nails, and the color pink. More disturbingly, femininity has been associated with submissiveness, manners, and frivolity. Being feminine is being placed under a label that carries with it a set of characteristics, appearances, and behaviors. Femininity is a role. Its players don't always realize that they are playing out culturally ordained behaviors, but they are. Gender roles require choices that are not rendered obligatory by biology.

Social constructionists about the emotions think that *amae*, *song*, and patriotism are a lot like femininity. When people put their hands to their hearts during the national anthem, they may feel like they are being passively moved to do so by the music, but a moment's reflection suggests that the behavior is, in some sense, voluntary. Averill (1980) calls emotions disclaimed actions. They are culturally scripted behaviors that people carry out under the unconscious pretense that they are as reflexive as a cough or a sneeze.

The notion of a script is especially dear to social constructionists. Emotions are not simple bodily responses, according to most researchers in this tradition. They are complex behavioral "practices," which are supposed to occur under certain conditions and include a range of behavioral sequelae. Within cognitive science, the notion of script is most associated with Schank and Abelson's (1977) work in artificial intelligence. Schank and Abelson argue that human knowledge is often based on script-like instructions about what to do under various circumstances. Our knowledge of what to do in a restaurant, to use their example, involves instructions that tell us we must first select from a menu, then order, then eat, then pay, and so on. Social constructionists think that human emotions are orchestrated by instructions of this kind as well (D'Andrade, 1992; Shaver, Hazan, & Bradshaw, 1992; see also Tomkins, 1979, and Goldie, 2000).

In the same spirit, Averill (1980) describes emotions as transitory social roles. The roles are governed by rules that tell us what can elicit our emotions, and how we should behave once they are elicited. A member of our culture may know that recipients of insults should enter a state we call anger, which includes confrontational behavior, threats, and often a protracted form of social interaction we call "holding a grudge." Members of the Ifaluk culture know that the corresponding emotion, *song*, should be triggered by violations of taboos and should be expressed by reprimands, pouting, or even a refusal to eat.

Anger illustrates another dimension found in constructionist accounts. There is a link between emotions and moral values. Anger is elicited by moral transgressions; the angry person feels that she has been wronged. But what counts as being wronged depends on the values of a particular culture (Harré, 1986). Spousal abuse might incite rage in our culture, but it is allegedly regarded as a welcome sign of affection among the Yanomamö of South America (Chagnon, 1968). In either culture, a person who exhibits anger under the wrong circumstances will be morally censured. Cultural variation in anger is especially striking, because anger is widely regarded as a biologically basic emotion with analogues in other species. If emotions depend on moral values, they are not animalistic instincts but intellectual skills that reflect some of the most sophisticated forms of human thought.

Because constructionists regard emotions as intellectual skills, they tend to favor cognitive theories of emotion. Armon-Jones (1986, p. 36) says that constructionism requires a theory of emotions that is "cognition-based." Constuctionists also tend to diminish the role of physiology. They admit that emotions can be accompanied by bodily changes and that the body may factor into how emotions are conceptualized. But constructionists do not think that bodily changes are obligatory parts of emotions (Harré, 1986). The emotions that tend to have bodily components also contain culturally informed cognitive components. These cognitive components are essential.

To contrast the constructionist approach with evolutionary psychology, it is instructive to see reconsider romantic love. Some constructionists have endorsed C. S. Lewis's (1936) provocative thesis that romantic love was invented in medieval France (see Oatley & Jenkins [1996] and Averill [1985] for discussion; similar views were advanced by Finck [1887]). Apparently, during the twelfth century it became very fashionable for Frenchmen to become infatuated with married women of higher social station. To confess their feelings, these Frenchmen would write passionate letters to the objects of their affection. Of course, these advances could never be consummated; they were the seminal expression of unrequited love.

The idea that love is sᴛ.ongest when unrequited is just one of several motifs that have entered into the Western conception of romantic love. A second is that romantic love can be sparked instantaneously (Averill & Boothroyd, 1977). We believe in love at first sight. A third motif, consistent with Averill's notion of disclaimed action, is that we are passively struck, swayed, and blinded by love. A fourth motif is undying devotion. Those who are acting out the love script should devise demonstrations of commitment (Averill, 1985). It is hard to know which is more cynical, reductionism or constructionism. On the former, love is an evolutionary insurance policy, and on the latter, it is a French fad that happened to stick.

Like reductionism, constructionism comes in a variety of strengths. Comprehensive constructionists claim that all emotions, from alleged basic emotions to the most overtly cognitive, are socially constructed. Constrained constructionists say that only some emotions are cultural products. Armon-Jones (1986) says the constrained view may be easier to defend, because it allows one to more easily compare human emotions with affective states in nonhuman animals, but some constructionists prefer the stronger view. They are skeptical of close comparisons between human and nonhuman. Constructionists of both varieties generally defend a "nontranslatability thesis," according to which emotion terms in one language do not map perfectly onto terms in the languages spoken in different cultures.

## Compatibilism

Constrained constructionism and constrained reductionism are evidently compatible. One can hold that a set of basic emotions are innate universals, while holding that certain higher cognitive emotions are driven by culture (see Griffiths, 1997).

This thesis has it that some emotions are socially constructed while others are not. Call this "scope compatibilism," because it reconciles constructionism and reductionism by giving them different scopes of application. Another kind of compatibilism is possible as well. Rather than focusing on the scope of application, one can focus on the parts that make up an emotion. If emotions are complex entities, one can hold the view that some of their parts are biologically based, while others are socially constructed. Call this "componential compatibilism." One can also hold a combination of scope and componential compatibilism, saying that some emotions are purely biological while others merely have biologically based parts (Damasio, 1994; Frijda & Mesquita, 1994; Johnson-Laird & Oatley, 2000).

Componential compatibilism comes in different forms. One can hold that the physiological component of emotions is biologically based, while the cognitive component is culturally informed. This may be Damasio's (1994) position, though he says little about culture. Another possibility, favored by some appraisal theorists, is that emotions consist of cognitive dimensions, some of which are universal and others of which are cultural. Some emotions may consist entirely of the former, while others contain both (Frijda & Mesquita, 1994).

Paul Ekman's (1992, 1999a) recent position sounds like a form of componential compatibilism. He now claims that particular emotions belong to emotion families. Those families are biologically universal, but the family members (variations within a family) are influenced by culture. It is not entirely clear from Ekman's writings how these cultural differences manifest themselves. One clue comes from Ekman's acknowledgment of the fact that culture can influence the way emotions are expressed (more on this later). Ekman also believes that expressions are components of emotions rather than mere effects of emotions (Ekman, 1977). Putting these two points together, Ekman's view may be that cultural variants of emotions are biologically based emotions whose facial expressions have been influenced by sociocultural environments.

Compatibilist proposals of this kind may be the rule in emotion science rather than the exception. Extreme forms of constructionism and reductionism, which preclude compatibility, are hard to come by. Most researchers tend to admit that both biology and culture contribute to emotions. But this is more a point of policy than practice. Research programs tend to focus on one side of the nature/nurture divide, and detailed proposals of how the two intermingle are few and far between. Moreover, componential and scope compatibilism may not exhaust the options.

## Assessing Arguments for Constructionism

In chapter 5 I suggested that prevailing arguments for strong forms of reductionism do not succeed. Those arguments fail to show that any of the emotions we have labels for in English are immune to cultural influence. But the relative contributions of nature and nurture have not been identified. I have not shown how culture contributes to our emotions. It will be my position in this chapter that many constructionists mischaracterize the nature of that contribution. In this section, I raise objections to constructionist arguments. After that I will see whether some form of constructionism can survive those objections.

Most constructionists defend their view by pointing to examples. If emotions in other cultures seem different from our own, we have reason to conclude that culture exerts a constitutive influence. The diversity of emotions in the word is quite impressive on the face of it. Some examples have already been mentioned, such as the Ifaluk emotion of admonition, *song*, and the Japanese emotion of dependency, *amae*.

Even more exotic are "culture-bound syndromes." Simons and Hughes (1993, p. 75) define these as "recurrent, locality specific patterns of aberrant behavior and experience that appear to fall outside conventional Western psychiatric diagnostic categories." Psychiatric disorders are widely regarded as medical conditions that reflect abnormal brain function. Constructionists think this perspective may be overly biological. Cultural variation suggest that psychiatric syndromes may include symptoms that are not directly attributable to an organic pathology. Consider *witiko* (also knows as *windigo*), a condition reported among Algonquin Indians (e.g., Chippewa, Cree, and Ogibwa), whose victims develop the fear that they have been transformed into cannibal monsters with a craving for human flesh (Trimble, Manson, Dinges, & Medicine, 1984). In China there is a condition called *p'a-leng*, which is a morbid fear of the cold. associated with a yin/yang imbalance (too little yang). Victims bundle up and sleep under layers of blankets even in warm weather (Kleinman, 1980). Middle-aged Malaysian women sometimes experience *latah*, which manifests itself in an exaggerated startle reflex, outbursts of profanity, and a disposition to repeat whatever they hear (Simons, 1996). Unfortunate members of Greenland's Inuit population suffer from *pibloktoq*, which causes them to scream, tear off their clothing, break things, and eat feces before collapsing in seizures, followed by a deep sleep. Victims usually have no memory of the episode (Yap, 1974; though also see Dick, 1995). The Assam and the South Chinese sometimes suffer from *koro*, which is an intense anxiety that the penis or breasts and vulva will retract into the body (Yap, 1965). Among the Gururumba in New Guinea, young men occasionally

"become wild pigs"; they are said to have been bitten by ghosts of their ancestors, and they run wild, looting, stealing, and shooting arrows for a few days. The
cure for this condition involves being held over a smoking fire (Averill, 1980;
Griffiths, 1997; Newman, 1965). Many of our own diagnostic categories would
sound equally exotic in other parts of the world. Anorexia nervosa is one example; its victims suffer from an extreme fear of weight gain and distorted body image, which lead to a refusal to eat (Nasser, 1988).

All of these syndromes have emotional components, and they all reflect cultural beliefs and values. Anorexia reflects a Western preoccupation with weight,
*witiko* reflects a mythology and cultural history of cannibalism, and *p'a-leng* is
attributed to a yin/yang imbalance (too little yang). Culture-bound syndromes are
especially instructive because they show how we may be misled into thinking a
condition is natural and entirely passive (Averill, 1980). Victims of these disorders probably feel that they are no more responsible for their symptoms than they
would be if they had a cold or a flu. We tend to think of emotions in the same
way. Confronted with the variety and apparent cultural influence on emotions and
emotional disorders, constructionism begins to look very plausible.

In some cases, apparent differences between emotions across cultures may turn
out to be purely verbal. Pinker (1994) remarks that *Schadenfreude* is perfectly
familiar in countries that do not have a word for it. Even *amae*, the feeling of
dependency, and *gezelligheid*, coziness in the company of others, are probably
experienced outside of Japan and the Netherlands. Indeed, one might feel both
at the same time when one goes out for a beer with an old friend. Differences in
vocabulary do not entail social construction. They do not even support the nontranslatability thesis. We can certainly describe *amae* or *gezelligheid* in English.
They are not ineffable. Nor do they cast any doubt on the translatability of other
emotion words, such as anger, joy, or fear.

The culture-bound syndrome of *pibloktoq* may also derive some of its apparent uniqueness from its lexical label. *Pibloktoq* has analogues in other cultures,
such as *amok* in Malaysia and *phii pob* in Thailand (Simons & Hughes, 1993). A
syndrome like *latah* can be found in other cultures as well: *mali-mali* in the
Philippines, *yuan* in Burma, *ikota* in Siberia, and jumping mania among the
French Canadians of Main (Simons, 1996). It is possible that these syndromes
have a shared physiological basis, which happens to be labeled and explained differently across cultures. In our culture, these states have not been labeled by clinicians, but a variety of informal diagnostic categories may be related. We talk of
"nervous breakdowns" for symptoms that overlap with *latah* and "going postal"
for symptoms that overlap with *amok*. People who go on the shooting sprees that
are reported on the nightly news may be suffering from a condition very much
like what people in Malaysia experience when they run *amok*.

Constructionists believe that crosscultural differences in affective states are
substantive, not verbal. They often base this conclusion on the assumption that
affective states are structured entities. When one looks at all the components
making up an emotion in one culture, one may find no perfect analogue in an-

other. This form of argument gets constructionists into trouble. The assumption that emotions are structured entities is open to question. Where constructionists see essential parts, reductionists may see continent concomitants. Constructionists tend to blur the boundary between emotions and things that merely accompany emotions. More specifically, constructionists tend to blur the boundary between emotions and their causes and effects. Both causes and effects can be culturally influenced without altering the emotion itself.

Consider causes first. In chapter 3, I distinguished particular and formal objects. The objects of our emotions are the real or imagined conditions that elicit them. A particular object is a specific event, consideration of which elicits an emotion. A formal object is the general property in virtue of which a range of particular objects elicit an emotion. Emotions represent formal objects. *Witiko, p'a-leng,* and *koro* are all directed at different particular objects (cannibalism, cold, and genital retraction), but they have the same formal objects. They all represent danger. Consequently, they are all fears. The same emotion can have different particular objects. The fact that I love my spouse and you love yours does not mean that our loves are different emotions. Likewise, the fact that members of different cultures fear different things does not qualify as evidence for different emotions across cultures.

This lesson also applies to an example mentioned earlier. Spousal abuse causes anger in our culture but not, allegedly, among the Yanomamö. In both cultures, however, anger may be exactly the same emotion. Anger represents demeaning offenses. Culture influences what we take to be demeaning or offensive, but anger always tracks this core theme.

Culture influences the effects of emotions as well. Consider facial expressions. If one works as a flight attendant, smiling may be encouraged, and if one works at a funeral parlor, smiling may be discouraged. Cultures also tell us when it is appropriate to exaggerate or inhibit our facial expressions. Ekman and Friesen (1971) call such influences "display rules." In an influential study, Friesen covertly recorded the facial expressions of Japanese and American students as they sat alone watching a graphic film of a surgical procedure (Friesen, 1972; summarized in Ekman, 1972). Both groups showed equal disgust. He then recorded them as they watched the same film in the presence of an authority figure. This time the Japanese students showed far fewer negative facial expressions. This smacks of cultural influence, but there seems to be no reason to infer that disgust is different in these two cultures, much less that it is culturally constructed.

Constructionists will be quick to point out that culture can influence the effects of emotions in much more dramatic ways. Even if facial expression do not evidence construction, other behaviors may. Consider the Gururumba syndrome called becoming a wild pig. This syndrome is not an emotion in its own right, but it may be caused by an emotion. According to Newman, young men "become wild pigs" when they come under financial stress associated with the newfound responsibilities of adult life. Stress may cause irritable behavior, tantrums, or even suicide in our culture, but people do not run around acting as if they were wild pigs. Also consider *latah*. This syndrome may serve as a release for Malaysian women who are frustrated with their culturally prescribed roles. That frustration is all too common in the West, but frustrated Western women do not seem enter a hyperstartle trance. In our culture, we experience anxiety about fiscal responsibilities, and we experience frustration at culturally proscribed social roles. But we express these emotions very differently. We don't shoot arrows in the woods or enter trancelike states. We have profoundly different scripts for anxiety and frustration. Doesn't this show that anxiety and frustration are not uniform across cultures? Doesn't it show that these emotions are socially constructed?

Evidently not. The constructionist conclusion would follow only if there were reason to think that emotions are scripts. There is no doubt that culture teaches us to engage in a variety of complex behaviors when we experience emotions, but we mustn't confuse those behaviors with the emotions themselves. It is part of a cultural script to get married if you (and a member of the opposite sex) are in love. But marriage is not part of love. They may go together like a horse and carriage, but you *can* have one without the other. If marriage were part of love, love could not be regarded as a motive for marriage. Nor could we talk about love between people who have no plan to marry (consider a gay couple who don't want to fight restrictive marriage laws). Other ideas associated with the love script are equally contingent. The idea of love at first sight is diametrically opposed to the idea of growing to love someone. Each of these is a different love script, but we recognize the underlying emotion as the same. It is, in short, a grave mistake to infer that emotions *are* scripts from the fact that they *have* scripts. The script theory of emotions is sometimes defended as if it were a conceptual truth (see Armon-Jones, 1986), but we seem to have a clear conceptual handle on emotions that retain their identity while violating scripts.

Emotions may be a bit like eating. What we eat, where we eat, how we behave when eating, and what we do after eating may all be culturally influenced. There is, famously, a script for eating at a restaurant. But eating itself is a biological process that is roughly the same in all cultures. We chew and we swallow. Our mouths may be open or closed, our foods may be spicy or mild, our belches may be amplified or repressed, but eating itself is an evolved process underwritten by universal mechanisms. Constructionists need to show that the inputs and outputs of our passions contribute to their identity conditions. Too often this argumentative burden is unmet.

To make the case for constructionism, one has to show that emotions are the kinds of things that culture can affect. This is why constructionists strongly favor cognitive theories of emotion. Even those who concede that emotions are not scripts may cling to the idea that emotions contain beliefs or values. Culture can certainly affect such cognitive states. If emotions contain belief or values, then culture can make constitutive contributions to our emotions. In previous chapters,

I have expressed doubt about the claim that emotions contain cognitive states. Do constructionists provide any reason to overrule that doubt? I will consider two arguments.

First, Harré (1986) advances a version of an argument that I considered, in another context, in chapter 4. He says that emotions must have a cognitive dimension, because while some emotions are associated with both bodily states and cognitive states, others are associated with only cognitive states. He gives the example of loneliness (see also Wood, 1986). Certain attitudes go along with loneliness, but our bodies seem to be quite unaffected. This suggests that emotions are cognitive, hence vulnerable to cultural influence.

I am unconvinced. First, it is not obvious that loneliness qualifies as an emotion. Unlike paradigm cases, such as anger and fear, it tends to have a slow onset, to lack perceptual triggers, and to endure for a long time. But let's call it an emotion for the sake of argument. Harré says it lacks physical symptoms. This is an empirical claim. I would be surprised to discover that someone who reported feeling lonely did not have a correlated somatic condition. It is hard to imagine feeling lonely while one's heart is racing, for example. This suggests that loneliness may involve parasympathetic response. Now a lonely person may not be in this condition for the entire duration of her loneliness, but, in accord with arguments I put forth in chapter 5, loneliness may always carry this disposition. If someone merely judged that she was isolated from others but had no bodily feeling associated with this, we might not say she was lonely.

We should also be reluctant to concede that loneliness has a necessary cognitive dimension. It is conceivably, though we have no evidence, that loneliness is a rather primitive response that is triggered by the pheromone system. When we do not detect pheromones of other people for a period of time (or pheromones of people with whom we have some intimacy, if our vomeronasal systems can discriminate), then we enter a somatic state akin to sadness. We may have thoughts of isolation under such conditions, but these are neither necessary nor sufficient for loneliness. Given the possibility that loneliness works this way, we have no grounds for assuming it has cognitive components.

Harré claims that bodily states are contingently associated with emotions while cognitive states are necessary. This is at odds with crosscultural evidence. One of the most striking findings in the crosscultural literature is that every culture uses bodily metaphors for emotion (reviewed in Heelas, 1986, and Wierzbicka, 1999). The Chewong of central Malaysia associate emotions with the liver (Howell, 1981); the Gahuku-Gama of New Guinea locate emotions in the stomach (Read, 1967); Tahitians and the Maori locate emotions in the intestines (Levy, 1973; Smith, 1981); and the Ilongot of Luzon echo us in associating emotions with the heart (Rosaldo, 1980). The pervasiveness of bodily metaphors does not show that every emotion is linked to a particular somatic state, but it does point to an intimate link. In emphasizing the cognitive, constructionists often leave this unexplained.

The first constructionist argument for saying that emotions have a cognitive component is unconvincing, because it rests on the questionable assumption that some emotions lack a somatic component. The second constructionist argument for a cognitive component does not make this assumption. It is compatible with the possibility that all emotions have a somatic component. This argument has it that emotions must be at least partially cognitive because they are normatively penetrable. I use this phrase to capture the idea that emotions manifest themselves in ways that reflect cultural value systems. Values are generally transmitted through higher cognitive states. They require the comprehension of codes and customs. If emotions are normatively penetrable, then they may include cognitive components that are culturally infused.

To illustrate normative penetrability, consider how morality interacts with disgust. Some instances of disgust are largely independent morality (e.g., being disgusted by rotten food), but others are intimately tied to morality. Moral values can produce or intensify disgust. We are disgusted by such things as incest and racism (Haidt, Rozin, McCauley, & Imada, 1997). Moral vegetarians are more disgusted by meat than health-concerned vegetarians (Rozin, Markwith, & Stoess, 1997). Anything having to do with cigarette smoking now seems more disgusting than it did before our culture deemed smoking immoral (Rozin & Singh, 1999). We are even disgusted by harmless objects that have come into contact with evil people. Nemeroff and Rozin (1992) found that people were horribly disgusted by the idea of trying on Hitler's sweater. Here moral views affect disgust. In other cases, disgust seems to affect moral judgments. Haidt, Koller, and Dias (1993) found that some people find certain harmless acts (victimless crimes) immoral because they are disgusting. For example, some people think it is morally wrong to have sex with a chicken carcass. Haidt et al. (1993) also found that such judgments vary as a function of socioeconomic status and culture. While most people find acts of necrophilic bestiality disgusting, privileged American college students were considerably less likely to find it immoral than low-income Americans and people with varied incomes in Brazil.

A second example of normative penetrability issues from the well-documented division between cultures that highly value the independence of people (individualism) and cultures that highly value interdependence between people (collectivism) (Triandis, 1988). The United States and Western Europe value individualism at the expense of collectivism, and the reverse pattern is found in much of the Far East. This distinction impacts our emotions (Markus & Kitayama, 1991). The centrality of *amae* in Japan may reflect the Japanese emphasis on interdependence. The Japanese also have an emotion called *ijirashii*, which arises on seeing someone praiseworthy overcome an obstacle (Matsumoto, 1994). Emotional reactions to the accomplishments of others is also a collectivist tendency. Collectivists take pride in others. Markus and Kitayama share an anecdote (described by Hsu, 1975) in which an employee at a Japanese company took a visitor into the opulently furnished office of his boss and pointed to a desk, proudly boasting, "This is the desk of my section chief." In the West, pride is usually self-directed, and when it is directed at the achievements of another person, that person is usually a family member.

Negative emotions also vary as a function of individualism and collectivism. When Americans or Europeans violate a rule, we tend to feel guilt, which is a very personal sense of wrongdoing. In collectivist cultures, rule violation is more likely to produce shame, which has negative consequences for those associated with the wrongdoer. One can bring shame to one's family (Benedict, 1946; Creighton, 1990). Collectivists tend to be wary of negative emotions that create rifts between individuals. Anger is especially shunned in this regard. Japanese infants are more inhibited than American infants after hearing angry tones in their mother's voices (Miyake, Campos, Kagan, and Bradshaw, 1986). The Ukta Inuits, another collectivist culture, repress anger as much as possible (Briggs, 1970).

These examples of normative penetrability certainly suggest that emotional reactions are sensitive to our moral values. This is clear evidence for the claim that emotion is influenced by cognition, including cognitive states that are shaped by culture. But none of this shows that emotions are culturally constructed. The examples of morally influenced disgust fail to prove that disgust itself is a product of morality. In every case, disgust seems to represent something physically or figuratively unpalatable. Moral values contribute to our beliefs about what particular things have these properties. Moral vegetarians find meat unpalatable in both figurative and literal senses, increasing their disgust reaction, but the meaning of that reaction is constant. Brazilians and low-income Americans tend to think disgusting things are immoral even when they are harmless, but this only shows that the concept of morality varies across cultures and socioeconomic groups. Disgust remains the same.

The individualism/collectivism contrast is more promising, because it seems to show that cultures with different values have different emotions. Western cultures seem to lack *ijirashii*, and the Ukta Inuits seem to lack anger. But these differences may be illusory. Levy (1973, 1984) introduces the useful concepts of hyper- and hypocognized emotions. An emotion is hypercognized if it is strongly emphasized and valued within a culture and hypocognized if it is ignored or disvalued and repressed. Ukta Inuits probably experience anger, but they try not to experience it or discuss it. Westerners may experience *ijirashii* (as when a talented underdog wins an Academy Award); we just don't experience it often.

In summary, I have argued that the arguments for constructionism fail to establish that culture makes a constitutive contribution to our emotions. Culture can influence the particular objects that elicit emotions and the effects of emotions (including complex behaviors that may conform to cultural scripts). Culture can also affect attitudes toward emotions, which bears on their frequency, how often they are noticed, and the vocabulary we have to describe them. These effects are often profound, and they provide important information for understanding cultural variation, but they do not show that emotions themselves vary from culture to culture.

### *Reconstructing Constructionism*

#### Habits of the Body

The preceding discussion may look like a victory for reductionism. Prevailing arguments for constructionism show that emotions have causes and effects that are culturally influenced, but they fail to show that culture influences emotions themselves. The major flaw with these arguments is that they presuppose faulty theories of emotion. They begin by pointing to emotions that come along with thought-patterns or behaviors that are not found in our culture. This premise would show that emotions are socially constructed only if thought patterns and behaviors were constituent parts of emotions. Once cognitive and script theories of emotion are rejected, the arguments for constructionism seem to lose their footing.

Yet the reductionist victory party must be short-lived. Even if standard constructionist arguments fail, the examples they bring forward may help advance their cause in some other way. Suppose we begin with a better theory of emotion. In chapter 3, I argued that emotions are embodied appraisals. This is a somatic theory. Embodied appraisals are mental states that represent core relational themes by registering bodily changes that cooccur with those themes. The theory implies two ways of individuating emotions. We can individuate them by the bodily changes they register (their nominal contents) or by the core relational themes they represent (their real contents). Sadness represents irrevocable loss via some patterned response in the body. Every emotion has both kinds of contents. An alteration in real or nominal content would be an alteration in the emotion. It turns out that both kinds of contents can come under cultural influence. Many of the examples that are deployed by constructionists who reject somatic theories of emotion can be redeployed to show that embodied appraisals are culturally informed. I will consider cultural influences on nominal content in this subsection and turn to real content later.

Nominal contents include changes in respiration. The way we breathe can vary as a function of our emotions: the heavy breathing of sorrow, the constrained breathing of panic, and so on. Lyon (1999) argues that breathing can alter as a function of learning and culture. She notes that breathing can be controlled by the neocortex, and breathing often must be controlled in this way in order to talk and sing. If we can willfully control respiration, and culture can control our will, then respiration can come under cultural influence. Lyon gives the example of trance induction through rhythmic breathing used in ritual contexts by the Samburu and Mole tribes of northern Kenya. She also cites research on the !Kung, who use rapid deep breathing to intensify emotions. Perhaps such practices become habitual. Through cultural conditioning, the !Kung may develop emotional experiences that are different from our own. Lyon describes culturally conditioned breathing practices using a phrase borrowed from Marcel Maus: they are "habits of the body."

The notion of bodily habits can be used to resuscitate arguments for constructionism that I rejected earlier. Consider culture-bound syndromes such as *latah* or becoming a wild pig. I said that these syndromes do not provide evidence for constructionism, because the exotic behaviors they contain are not constituent parts of their concomitant emotions. This response overlooks an important possibility. The bodily states that determine an emotion's nominal contents are states of preparation for action. Fear, for example, involves bodily changes that prepare the body for flight. The same may be true of emotions that accompany culture-bound syndrome behavior. A Malaysian woman who is about to enter a state of *latah* may experience a prior state of anxious frustration whose bodily profile is a preamble to the trance that characterizes that syndrome. Likewise, a distinctive bodily state may arise just before a member of the Gururumba becomes a wild pig. There may also be emotions that occur during these syndromes whose nominal contents are determined by bodily patterns that are unfamiliar in this culture. This is pure speculation of course. The point is that cultural differences in emotional behavior can affect the somatic concomitants of our emotions. If these concomitants determine nominal contents, and nominal contents contribute to the identity conditions of our emotions, then culture can influence our emotions.

A second argument that I rejected earlier can also be rescued by appeal to habits of the body. Ekman and Friesen's research on display rules shows that facial expressions can be influenced by culture. Culture conditions us to exaggerate and repress our facial expressions. Earlier I argued that variation in display rules does not support constructionism. The same emotion might be displayed in different ways. But this response needs to be reexamined. If the embodied appraisal theory is right, than any bodily change that accompanies an emotion, including a facial change, can contribute to the nominal content of that emotion. Facial changes can affect how an emotion is experienced. Imagine training yourself to make an exaggerated facial contortion just before you sneeze. Once this is habitual, your experience of sneezing will be different; it will include the experience of your contorted facial muscles. Now imagine training yourself to keep your facial muscles as still as possible when you sneeze. Your experience will now include the feeling of muscular control. Likewise for the emotions. Habitual facial behavior has an impact on what our emotions are like. That impact may be compounded by the phenomenon of facial feedback. If making faces causes patterns of physiological change, then expressing emotions may also serve to intensify them. Imagine the difference between keeping a straight face when watching a comedy and allowing yourself to smile. Studies have shown that Japanese subjects, who repress public displays of negative emotions, experience emotions less intensely than American subjects (Scherer, Matsumoto, Wallbott, & Kudoh, 1988).

These arguments are vulnerable to an objection. Constructionists claim that culture makes a constitutive contribution to our emotions. That means that the identity of an emotion can be a result of sociocultural influences. Showing that culture can affect nominal content does not prove that culture can make a constitutive contribution. Intuitively, two emotions with distinct nominal contents can count as the same. The label we choose for an emotion generally has more to do with real content than nominal content. Imagine a culture whose members puff out their cheeks whenever they face a danger. This behavior could surely affect the emotion they experience in dangerous situations, but one might be inclined to say the emotion still counts as fear. Intuitively, any somatically mediated representation of danger qualifies as fear. That is one reason why we don't hesitate to ascribe fear to animals whose bodies differ significantly from our own. So arguments from habits of the body do not offer proof of constructionism.

In response, we need only descend to a more finely grained level of categorization. One can categorize emotion at various levels of abstraction (fig. 6.1). At a high level, we can partition affective space into negative and positive emotions. At a somewhat lower level, we can group together emotions that have similar real contents, like those in the emotion families or clusters that I discussed in chapter 5. There might be a family of emotions that are related to anger, for example, but are somewhat variable across cultures. At a lower level, we can partition these families into discrete emotion categories whose members have the same real contents. We usually presume that most of our emotion words pick out emotions at this level, such as anger and joy. At an even finer level, we can distinguish different kinds of anger and different kinds of joy. These are emotions that have the same real contents but different nominal contents. Emotions at the fine level can be regarded as "somatic modes" of the same intermediate-level emotion. But they can also be regarded as distinct emotions. There is no contradiction in this. It is like saying that rottweilers and Chihuahuas are the same kind of animal (dogs) and different animals (breeds). The foregoing arguments show that culture can impact emotion breeds. As I will show now, culture can promote variation at the intermediate level of abstraction as well.

### Blending

To show how culture can influence the real contents of our emotions, I need to deploy some of the machinery I introduced in chapter 4. There I defended the view that some emotions are basic while others are derived. The derived emotions include those that are called higher cognitive emotions. I described two ways in which new emotions can be derived from the basic set: blending and calibration. Both of these processes are amenable to cultural influence.

Blending occurs when two basic emotions are combined together. Examples may include contempt, exhilaration, and horror. Contempt may be a blend of anger and disgust. In principle, a blended emotion can be innate. That is to say, an advantageous mutation might lead to a genetic predisposition to bring certain emotions together. But even if a blend is pancultural (as contempt may be), that does not show it is innate. Showing that a blend is innate requires showing that it cannot be learned. Certain blends may be so easy to acquire that they emerge all over the globe.

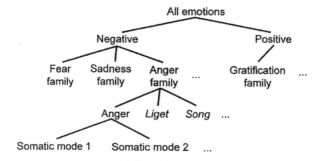

**Figure 6.1.**   A hierarchy of emotion categories. *Liget* and *Song* are variants of anger found among the Ilongot and the Ifaluk, respectively.

This may explain the prevalence of contempt. Contempt is an especially likely blend. Disgust, I noted, can be applied to things that are figuratively unpalatable, as in the case of moral disgust. A morally disgusting person violates our social mores. This is generally regarded as offensive (consider the phrase "criminal offender") because it flies in the face of our personal values. Anger is directed at those who offend us. Therefore, individuals or actions that violate mores are likely to elicit both disgust and anger simultaneously, hence contempt. The prevalence of contempt can be explained without innateness.

The same is true of love. In chapter 5, I suggested that love is a blend of lust and attachment. If attachment is a basic emotion (see the next section) and lust is a basic motivation, then love is byproduct of two previously existing affective states. This is a departure from the standard constructionist story. I am not suggesting that love is a narrative script. It is a blended emotion. But, like narrative scripts, the love-blend may be fostered by culture. Feeling attachment toward the objects of lust is not inevitable. That would put the pornography business out of commission. But culture exerts pressure to keep these two in line, especially when lust leads to procreation. Some cultures encourage parents to share in the responsibility of childcare. If parents are bound to each other by attachment, their cooperative efforts will be easier to achieve. In our culture, we no longer believe that parents need to stay together in order to raise children. As a result, there is less pressure for attachments between parents to last, and we talk of "falling out of love." Culture may play a role in determining whether the love-blend will emerge, when it will occur, and how long it will last. Culture is not necessary for love, but it may have an influence.

Some emotional blends are difficult to acquire without unusual experiences or cultural influence. Combinations of anger and joy, for example, do not come to many of us naturally, but they can be cultivated. Some soldiers may develop such a blend to cope with the trauma of war. If you are angry at your enemy and enjoy that anger, you may find it easier to kill. Some children may develop this blend for the more innocent activity of playing violent video games. Something resembling an anger-joy blend may also lie at the heart of Yanomamö culture (Chagnon, 1968). Locked in an endless cycle of invasion, murder, and bloody revenge, members of this culture may find that joyful anger has the advantage of elevating motivation and keeping despair at bay.

Blending two emotions together has an impact on real content. Primitive mental representations (i.e., ones that do not have meaningful parts) represent what they have the function of detecting. When two primitive representations are combined, the real content changes. In some cases, the real content of a compound is a direct function of the contents of its parts. Mental representations that have "logical form," such as the mental equivalent of a sentence or phrase, often work this way. A mental version of the phrase "yellow and blue," refers to things that are both yellow and blue (presumably in different places), because it has one part that detects yellow things and another part that detects blue things. But blends of emotions, like blends of colors, do not have logical form. Therefore, they do not necessarily refer to the intersections of their component emotions. Blended emotions function like primitive emotions; they are derived primitives. They refer to whatever they have the function of detecting. They have the function of detecting those things that reliably elicit them and for which they were blended in the first place.

In some cases, a blended emotion may work like a mental phrase: it detects things that fall in the intersection of what its component emotions detect in isolation. Consider romantic love again. Suppose that love begins as a blend of lust and attachment. When we feel lust and attachment for a person, we enter a physiological state, which results from merging two simultaneous patterns of change associated with lust and attachment. That physiological state may occur for the first time when we first enter into a nurturing interaction with someone to whom we are sexually attracted. It is subsequently stored in memory and serves as an emotion in its own right. But the stored emotion continues to serve as a detector for concupiscent attachments. It does not undergo a transformation of meaning.

In other cases, blended emotions mean more than the sum of their parts. Consider the case of contempt. If contempt represented the Boolean compound of its parts, it would represent something that is both a demeaning offense and figuratively or literally unpalatable. In actuality, the real content of contempt may be subtly different from that. Suppose that one first experiences a combined state of anger and disgust as a result of seeing something that was morally offensive. Suppose further that after several other encounters with morally offensive things, the blend gets stored, as a unit, in memory. One's emotional circuits are now set up to produce this blend without going through the mixing processes anew. The blend of anger and disgust was set up in memory as a result of a particular class of disgusting and enraging things. It was set up as a *moral* offense detector. So the anger-disgust blend may represent moral offensives in particular rather than representing all unpalatable offenses as a Boolean semantics would predict. This may explain why contempt seems to transcend anger and disgust. It begins its life as a blend of these two emotions, but it serves a slightly different detection function. It is set up to detect a subset of unpalatable offenses, rather than the whole class.

Blending is one way for culture to exert influence on our emotions. The emotions that happen to get blended together depend, in some cases, on our sociocultural environments as much as our personal histories. Joy-anger blends were an example. One can also imagine other possibilities. *Amae* may be derived from attachment and joy. The Ifaluk value an emotion called *fago*, which seems to combine love, compassion, and sadness (Lutz, 1988). In a comparison of English speaking Ugandan subjects and Americans, Davitz (1969) found that Ugandans associate "anger" with crying. This suggests that they may use the English word to name a blend of anger and sadness, which may also be the case among the Fore, who associate frowning faces with "anger" scenarios. Conversely, situations of grief tend to cause *liget*, which is closely related to anger, among the Ilongot (Rosaldo, 1980). The death of a loved one can inspire a headhunting expedition.

Hyper- and hypocognizing emotions can have impact on blending. Hypercognized emotions are frequently instantiated, hence more available for blending. Hypocognized emotions are infrequently instantiated, hence less available. Cultures like the Ilongot that hypercognize an emotion related to anger may be especially likely to wind up with an emotion like contempt. Among Ukta Inuit, where anger is hypocognized, contempt may be less likely. The process of hypocognizing can also promote some unusual hybrids. In a culture that discourages sexual thoughts, concupiscence may be combated by drumming up disturbing images. A curious blend of lust, disgust, and shame could result.

The real and nominal contents of a blend differ from the contents of its components. Since cultures can foster blends, culture can impact the contents of our emotions. If emotions are individuated by their contents, and contents are determined, in part, through cultural influences, then culture can play a part in the construction of emotions. When cultures lead to emotional blending, they make a constitutive contribution.

## Calibration

Culture can also make a constitutive contribution through the process of calibration. In chapter 4 I argued that many of our higher cognitive emotions do not literally contain cognitions as constituent parts. *Schadenfreude* is not a feeling of joy plus a thought that someone is suffering. Rather it is a feeling of joy that has been triggered by a cognition (or perception) of someone suffering. The cognition is a cause, not a component. But it is a special kind of cause. Beliefs about suffering are set up in memory as triggers for happiness among those who experience *Schadenfreude*. We all have memory files that contain records of misfortunes that others have endured. People who are prone to *Schadenfreude* have a link between this file and happiness. They have a calibration file that compassionate people lack (chapter 4).

Calibration files contain representational states that serve as calibrating causes. They link emotions to sets of eliciting conditions. To form a new calibration file, we generally have to recognize that the items in that file relate to a core relational theme for an existing emotion. In the early stages of *Schadenfreude* acquisition, one might form the belief that the suffering of others satisfies one's goals. The thought that such-and-such satisfies my goals explicitly describes the core relational theme for joy. Thoughts that explicitly describe core relational themes can serve as triggers for the corresponding emotions (chapter 3). In the early stages of *Schadenfreude* acquisition, the emotional response may depend on explicitly believing that one's goals have been satisfied. Later those thoughts may become superfluous. In the mind of someone who has cultivated this sinister emotion, the mere sound of another person's screams can induce delight.

Some emotions are created through both calibration and blending. As I said in chapters 4 and 5, jealousy is a possible example. Suppose one discovers that one's lover has been unfaithful. One might entertain thoughts of loss leading to sadness, thoughts of offense leading to anger, and thoughts of contamination leading to disgust. Each of these emotions blends together into a stomach-turning, sob-inducing, fist-clenching amalgam. During the same process, one might establish a calibration file. Thoughts of infidelity or any perceptible signs of infidelity get recorded there and serve as triggers for the emotional blend. The file calibrates the blend by establishing a reliable causal relationship between it and infidelity.

Culture can certainly play a role in the calibration of our emotions. Take acedia (also known as accidia), which is defined as a spiritual torpor. Those who grow weary of the regular duties associated with religious practice are said to experience this emotion. Harré (1986) says acedia is socially constructed emotion, and I think he is right. It was a widely discussed emotion in the Middle Ages and early Renaissance, and it disappeared from emotion lists after the rise of Protestantism. I think acedia is constructed through culturally driven calibration. It is boredom that has been calibrated to religious contexts. Initially, ordinary boredom is induced by the repetitive nature of worship, and then a calibration file is set up so that the mere sight of a religious artifact or edifice can trigger a feeling of gloom. In the Middle Ages, such feelings were regarded as sad but morally acceptable. Within Protestant culture, they were shunned. Waning religious fervor became a source of shame rather than boredom, and with that reform went acedia (Harré, 1986).

Shame itself may be a culturally calibrated emotion. It may be a sadness that has been calibrated to one's own violations of a moral code. Unlike guilt, the calibration file for shame also contains thoughts of how one's transgressions can affect others. Shame is calibrated to contexts in which one's actions are likely to bring one's close affiliates into disrepute. Shame does not *contain* such thoughts, but it occurs when such thoughts (or situations that warrant such thoughts) arise.

The feeling of being dishonored may be another example of a calibrated emotion. Feeling dishonored is, arguably, a derivative of anger that has been calibrated to insults that violate an honor code. A malfunctioning computer may make you mad, but it won't make you feel dishonored. Even when we anthropomorphize them, malfunctioning computers do not disrespect any cherished set of social rules. The somatic state caused in us by a malfunctioning computer may be indistinguishable from the somatic state caused by an honor violation, but it is not triggered by activity in the dishonor file.

Nisbett and Cohen (1995) have argued that feelings of dishonor are especially common in certain subcultures. White Southern males in the United States seem to feel this emotion especially intensely. Nisbett and Cohen say white Southerners have a culture of honor. The emotion of dishonor may be culturally specific. It depends on having a calibration file that is culturally determined.

Feeling dishonored also carries behavioral consequences. Just as emotions have calibration files, they may have behavior files. These are the cultural scripts that tell us what to do when we experience a certain emotion. I have argued that such scripts may have subtle constitutive effects on our emotions. Anger produced by the dishonor file may be more likely to lead to revenge. Nisbett refers to hair-trigger responses and excessive violence in cultures of honor. The anger produced by being dishonored may involve physiological symptoms that are consistent with these behavioral responses.

To see another example of culturally facilitated calibration, consider *ijirashii*. As its core, this emotion may be a kind of pleasure, somatically comparable to happiness. It is elicited, however, by seeing a praiseworthy person overcome an obstacle. I said that Westerners experience this from time to time, but people in Japan probably have a significantly more entrenched calibration file for *ijirashii*. The very fact that this word exists in Japan may draw attention to cases that might otherwise be overlooked as sources of happiness. Calibration files are set in place so that the mere consideration of a praiseworthy person's successes becomes a likely happiness trigger. Happiness that is triggered in this way comes to have a new meaning.

These examples undermine one of my objections to standard constructionist arguments. Constructionists try to defend their position by noting that emotions can have different elicitors in different cultures. Earlier I suggested that these differences make no difference. I drew a similar moral about some culture-bound syndromes. For example, I said that the disorder called *p'a-leng* in China does not support constructionist conclusions, because the emotion it involves is just garden-variety fear. Like any fear, the fear in *p'a-leng* represents danger.

The notion of calibration shows that this dismissal of constructionist arguments is too hasty. Victims of *p'a-leng* have calibration files that promote fear in circumstances that bring coldness to mind. When a person with *p'a-leng* feels a mild breeze, she may enter a state of terror. That feeling is garden-variety fear in one sense; it may have the same general physiology. But it is far from ordinary in another sense; it is caused by a mental file that calibrates fear with coldness.

On this analysis, the emotion involved in *p'a-leng* is not fear but fear-of-the cold, a culturally calibrated derivative of fear. The real content of this emotion is not physical dangers *in general* but a particular kind of danger.

I have been arguing that culture can exert constitutive influence on emotions in three ways. Culture can set up habits of the body, promote blends, or lead to the creation of calibration files. Habits of the body can influence the nominal content of an emotion, and both blending and calibration can yield emotions with new, culturally determined, real contents. Many of the arguments for constructionism that were dismissed earlier turn out to support the case for these forms of cultural influence. The major problem with standard arguments for constructionism is that they rest on erroneous theories of emotion. Once those theories are corrected, the arguments can be redeployed with some success.

### Reconciling Constructionism and Reductionism

#### Basic Training

I conclude this chapter by revisiting the question of basic emotions. Calibration and blending need raw materials. There must be emotions in place for these processes to occur. Basic emotions are those raw materials. In chapter 4 I defined a basic emotion as an emotion that is not derived from any other. I declared my faith in basic emotion, in that chapter, but I did not offer a list. Emotion science is too young to verify which emotions are basic. Converging neuroscientific, psychological, comparative, and linguistic research is needed to settle that question. With the help of crosscultural evidence, however, one can offer a few provisional speculations.

I will begin by surveying the most popular candidates for basic emotions. These are the ones identified by Ekman in his early research on facial expressions: anger, disgust, fear, happiness, sadness, and surprise. Ekman himself has shifted to a longer list, alleging fifteen basic emotions: amusement, anger, contempt, contentment, disgust, embarrassment, excitement, fear, guilt, pride in achievement, relief, sadness/distress, satisfaction, sensory pleasure, and shame. I will mention all of these along the way. But the six-item list has become the textbook roster of basic emotions, and by Ekman's own lights, the other items have not been as well established.

Some ethnographic psychologists argue that the standard six-item list is strongly biased by our culture and language. Of the many emotion words that Lutz (1989) found among the Ifaluk, only ten appear to be synonymous with English emotion terms and of these only one (a word for disgust) aligned with an item on the standard basic emotion list. One can justifiably wonder whether that list would have ever been generated by an ethnographer from another culture (Wierzbicka, 1999).

We cannot infer that an emotion doesn't exist in a culture from the fact that the culture has no name for it. The hypothesis that vocabulary sets the bounds of experience was refuted long ago in the context of color terms. Speakers of languages with few color terms still experience the same universal set of colors as focal (Berlin & Kay, 1969). White (1993) criticizes the analogy between emotion and color. He argues that emotions, unlike colors, have complex social causes and effects, which contribute to their identity. I have argued that the causes and effects of our emotions do not always make constitutive contributions, but they can make constitutive contributions. White's basic point is correct.

It is useful to recall Hacking's suggestion that labeling can affect identity. When we call something "anger," we separate it out from other things, and we apply a variety of beliefs, expectations, and values. These attitudes influence the conditions under which anger arises and the way anger is expressed. Both of these influences can have constitutive impact on anger. Color experiences differ, in that they are more constrained by the cellular physiology of the early visual processing, which we cannot directly control. When we assume that a labeled emotion is basic or that it exists, unlabeled, in another culture, we neglect the impact of our own classificatory practices. We should not assume that the emotions we label are basic. The very fact of labeling may have a transformational effect. Ironically, entries on the standard list of alleged basic emotions may be unlikely candidates simply in virtue of having labels by which we can list them.

Let's begin with anger, which has received considerable attention in crosscultural studies. Analogues of anger are shunned in some cultures and exalted in others. The Ifaluk lack an exact word for anger, and crosscultural studies have shown that members of some cultures associate "sad" faces with situations that cause anger in the West. This casts doubt on the supposition that anger is basic.

Let me suggest an alternative possibility, inspired by remarks in Ortony and Turner (1990). Perhaps something like frustration is innate. There may be a universally experienced aversive reaction to things that constrain us or thwart our goals (see Watson, 1919). In the course of development, we discover that human beings can thwart our goals. Some of us experience frustration emotion in these situations. In some cultures, special emphasis is placed on frustrations caused by other people. Members of such cultures set up calibration files that link frustration to cases where another person has frustrated us intentionally. Those calibration files may encode eliciting conditions that range from physical threats to insults and moral wrongs. Since all cultures have moral systems, theories of agency, and frustration, anger is extremely likely to emerge but not inevitable. In some cultures, intentional wrongdoings by others elicit something closer to sadness.

Sadness itself may not correspond perfectly to a basic emotion. There is little question that sadness is rooted in a genetic program. Crying is a universal phenomenon and it is associated with the death of a loved one in almost all cultures (the Balinese are a possible exception; see Rosenblatt, Walsh, & Jackson, 1976). But that does not mean sadness is universal. Infants cry, but their cries can have different meanings. Some infant cries are associated with pain or discomfort. These cries indicate physical distress, which may be a universal emotion. There is little doubt that all healthy people have an aversive emotional response to physically noxious stimuli. This response cannot be equated with sadness. Physical distress may be a form of anxiety that has been calibrated, by evolution, to physical pathologies. If so, it is universal but not basic. It derives from anxiety, which is a basic emotion, as I will soon argue.

A second kind of crying exhibited in infants is associated with separation from a primary caregiver. Infants among the !Kung, who have almost constant physical contact with their caregivers, cry infrequently (Konner, 1976). Crying that occurs during separation is related to sadness; after all, separation is a kind of loss. To the mind of an infant, with no sense of the future, separation from a caregiver might even seem to be an irrevocable loss. Further reflection, however, suggests that the infant separation response should not be identified with sadness. Sadness refers to *any* irrevocable loss, not just the loss of a caregiver. For infants, the emotion appears more specific. It might be called separation distress, because it involves separation from a person. Later in life, we learn to be distressed about other kinds of losses (jobs, possessions, status). Toddlers may cry when someone takes away a toy, but this can easily be interpreted as a sign of frustration. I suspect that the aversive response to separation from a person is an independent emotion.

If I am right, the emotion we call "sadness" does not exist in the early months of life. It is possible that sadness is still innate. It may be a natural outgrowth of separation distress, programmed by the genes to appear sometime between the first teeth and puberty. It is equally plausible, however, that sadness is not innate. It may be a learned generalization of separation distress. In this respect, sadness would be the opposite of anger. Where anger starts with a broadly applicable frustration emotion and becomes a narrow, person-directed emotion, sadness starts with narrow, person-directed emotion and becomes a broadly applicable emotion.

Moving on, let us consider fear. Of all the items on the standard list, fear may have the best claim to being basic. Fear has obvious analogues in nonhuman animals, and it certainly increases fitness. Some triggers of fear (sudden loss of support, heights, darkness, snakes) certainly seem to get a boost from the genes. But fear elicitors can also be learned, and learned elicitors vary across cultures. In Japan, novel situations, relationships, and traffic are better fear elicitors than they are for American subjects (Masumoto, Kudoh, Scherer, & Wallbott, 1988). Reductionists will say that such differences are superficial. Japanese and Americans both fear dangers. They simply regard different things as dangerous.

All these findings are consistent with the hypothesis that fear is a basic emotion, but that conclusion is premature. There is evidence that our folk category of fear subsumes two distinct states, which can be labeled "panic" and "anxiety," provided those terms are understood in a technical sense. As I mentioned in chapter 4, Panksepp distinguishes panic and anxiety. Lazarus (1991) arrives at a related distinction, between anxiety and fright; Gray (1991) distinguishes fear induced by conditioned stimuli from fear induced by unconditioned stimuli; and

Heller, Nitschke, Etienne, and Miller (1997) use neuroimaging to draw a distinction between psychiatric disorders involving chronic worry and disorders involving panic attacks. Panic is a response to an immediate physical threat. It is associated with a fight-or-flight response (fight is likely when flight is impossible). Anxiety is more anticipatory; it detects impeding danger and is associated with freezing. This may be why anxiety is caused by conditioned stimuli. If an animal hears a bell whenever it receives an electrical shock, hearing the bell will cause it to prepare for being shocked. Gray (1991) suggests the innately aversive stimuli will cause panic, and they can probably cause anxiety as well. Sudden loss of support and glimpsing a snake are likely to trigger a fight-or-flight response, whereas the perception of darkness or heights may make us freeze. Darkness and heights signal impending danger, not an immediate threat. Earlier I said that pain may be bound to anxiety as well. There are three principled reasons for predicting that pain involves anxiety rather than panic. First, we cannot flee or fight our illnesses and injuries. Second, the true danger of an injury is the threat it poses to life or to the capacity to access vital resources, both of which are anticipatory in nature. Third, injuries are often more likely to heal if we arrest behavior. Panic incites behavior, whereas anxiety makes us pause. The prediction is borne out by empirical research. Rhudy and Meagher (2000) tested for differential affects of panic and anxiety on pain, and they found that pain reactions increase with anxiety and decrease with panic. Anticipating danger makes pain worse than encountering danger. By demonstrating different effects, this study also confirms that anxiety and panic are distinct. I conclude that fear is a superordinate emotion category (an emotion family in fig. 6.1) that subsumes two dissociable basic emotions.

These remarks about fear help us assess the status of surprise, which is also alleged to be basic. As noted in chapter 5, people in some cultures have difficulty distinguishing the face of fear from the face of surprise. Fear and surprise have an obvious connection. Things that surprise us are often dangerous, and things that are dangerous are often surprising. The link between panic and surprise may be especially close. Some of the best candidates for innate panic elicitors (sudden loss of support, snakes) are generally surprising, and in ancestral environments, fight and flight may have been the safest response to anything completely novel or unexpected. It is tempting to conclude that surprise and panic begin as one emotion. Surprise may be a mild form of panic (low-arousal panic). Over time, people in cultures that do not feel especially threatened by novelty may dissociate these two emotions. In some cultures, many stimuli that elicit low-arousal panic are perfectly safe. That is the case in our culture of incredible variety, but it is less likely to be true in Fore culture. The bodily changes associated with panic are primarily associated with fight and flight, but they also include a cluster of states that allow us to receive information (open mouth, inhalation, open eyes). When facing a threat, we must be able to obtain information relevant to selecting a response. This cluster can gain independence and become the foundation of the surprise response. The facial expressions of panic and surprise are consistent with this story. Both panic and surprise tend to have furrowed brows and open mouths, but in panic, the corners of the mouth are often turned down, as in a frown. Surprise looks like panic minus distress. If these highly speculative conjectures are correct, then surprise is not a basic emotion. It is derived from panic. Notice that it is not derived by calibration or blending. It is extracted from the patterned bodily responses making up another emotion. I will not discuss this kind of emotion derivation further, but I would recommend it as an important area for future research.

Now turn to disgust. Some languages, including Polish, lack an exact word for this emotion (Wierzbicka, 1999). Nevertheless, people seem to find things disgusting in all cultures. Rozin, Haidt, and McCauley (1993) demonstrate that disgust has a universal logic. Disgust is typically associated with animals or animal products. People find every substance excreted by animals disgusting with the exception of tears. Feces, vomit, urine, sweat, and blood are all disgusting. There is some culturally variability in this. Some people in India drink urine, and infants are known to eat fecal matter, but it is universally true that the best disgust elicitors involve animals. Disgust is also governed by rules of contagion. People refuse to drink a beverage after a cockroach has been dipped in it, even if the roach is sterilized first (Rozin, Millman, and Nemeroff, 1986). This suggests that disgust was evolved to protect us against germs. Long before we discovered germs, we needed a way to avoid these invisible killers. Reviling things that have come into contact with something disgusting (such as a bug or a dead animal) is a simple mechanism for achieving this end.

Despite such universals, there may still be reason to think that disgust is a culturally influenced emotion. Our word "disgust" refers not only to things that are physically unpalatable but also to things that are figuratively unpalatable. As I have shown, there is a category of moral disgust, which seems to occur crossculturally (recall the study with Brazilians). But our concept of moral disgust, hence of disgust itself, may not be universal. Haidt et al. (1997) compared moral disgust among Japanese and Americans and found interesting differences. Americans tended to express moral disgust at things that harm people (e.g., a mass murder, racism) and Japanese tended to express moral disgust at personal failure (e.g., failing an entrance exam).

On close examination, the notion of figurative unpalatability may be too vague to explain the real content of disgust. What does it mean to say something is figuratively unpalatable? One answer is that something is figuratively unpalatable if it is a nonnoxious cause of disgust. This definition is circular. In chapter 3, I argued that we should define core relational themes without circularities of this kind. It would be better to say that something is figuratively unpalatable if it defies our moral code. This is an improvement, but it is a bit too broad. Our emotion of disgust seems to apply to particular kinds of moral code violations, especially those that are cruel (mass murder) or "against nature" (bestiality). The real core relational theme of disgust is things that are literally unpalatable and moral transgressions that are cruel or unusual.

Now here's the rub. In Japan, there is an emotion that we liken to disgust, but it seems to have a different range of application. It applies to things that are literally unpalatable *and to personal failures*. This suggests that the word "disgust" and perhaps the emotion itself has no exact counterpart in Japan. To the extent that the meaning of "disgust" includes these moral dimensions, it is a culturally specific emotion. I think there is a basic emotion related to disgust, but it should not be called "disgust" because it is restricted to cases of literal unpalatability. Strictly speaking, disgust is not a basic emotion. It is an extension of a basic emotion that has been recalibrated by a calibration file that includes a restricted range of moral transgressions.

The only remaining emotion on the standard six-item basic emotion list is happiness. Ekman (1999a) himself no longer seems to count happiness among the basic emotions. His revised fifteen-item list replaces happiness with several positive emotions: amusement, personal pride, contentment, satisfaction, excitement, relief, and sensory pleasure. I doubt whether most of these are basic emotions.

Pride may be acquired through calibration: we can learn to take pleasure in our own achievement. Relief may be pleasure caused by the elimination of something disvalued. The fact that we sigh with relief does not prove that relief is basic; sighing may simply mark the cession of shallow breathing after distress. Contentment is probably an umbrella term for low grades of various positive emotions, rather than an emotion in its own right. Excitement may be pleasure plus high arousal.

Amusement is probably related to Panksepp's notion of play. As I mentioned in chapter 4, Panksepp (2000) thinks play is a basic emotion, because it is found in all mammals, it has identifiable neural correlates, and it has a universal behavioral response, namely laughter. In both amusement and play, there seems to be an element of panic. The infant game of peekaboo is an obvious case in point. Rough-and-tumble play also causes panic because it mimics real fighting. But in both cases, the apparent threat is benevolent. It is tempting to say that amusement is an emotion blend (perhaps one toward which we have an innate disposition). The ingredients may be panic and pleasure. It may be a counterpart to exhilaration, which combines anxiety and pleasure.

I have said that various nonbasic emotions contain pleasure as ingredients. That implies that pleasure is a basic emotion. As it turns out, pleasure is not a monolithic concept. It splinters into several innate varieties. Sensory pleasure certainly looks like a basic emotion. Infants coo when they are stroked. The adjective "sensory," however, may be too broad. We seem to have a variety of different pleasurable states. We are satiated by consumption of food and drink, we are gratified by sexual interactions, and we are delighted by certain sounds, strokes, and sights. This last form of pleasure needs to be further subdivided. Sometimes delight arises when something satisfies an urge, goal, or wish. Here Ekman's term "satisfaction" seems appropriate ("gladness" might also do). Sometimes delight arises when there is no preexisting goal, as when we are physically stimulated. Stimulation, unlike satisfaction, may cause us to orient attention toward a source. Satisfaction may lead to complacency or pursuit of other goals.

It is possible that sexual gratification and food satiation are forms of stimulation and satisfaction, respectively. These states may be blends of basic emotions and nonemotional states. Sexual gratification may combine stimulation with sensation in sexual organs and lust (a motivation). Food satiation may combine satisfaction with gustatory sensation and inhibition of eating behavior. If so, stimulation and satisfaction comprise two fundamental states that lie behind many sensory pleasures. But notice that neither stimulation nor satisfaction requires a sensory component. Thinking about a problem can be stimulating, and solving it can be satisfying. "Sensory pleasure" is not an innate emotion but an amalgam of innate emotions and other states. The innate emotions are stimulation and satisfaction.

I would add attachment to the set of innate positive emotions. Attachment is a response to nurturing, physical interactions with another person. Its somatic concomitants may include pheromone signals, muscle relaxation, staring (especially at another person's eyes, which would be threatening under other situations), and preparation for physical contact. It seems to appear very early in life and may be the complement to separation distress (see Bowlby, 1973).

If I am right, the pleasure pie can be cut into three slices: satisfaction, stimulation, and attachment. Do any of these pleasures correspond to "happiness"? Yes and no. If happiness is a superordinate term for all kinds of pleasure, then happiness is innate. Or, more accurately, a variety of happinesses is innate. If, on the other hand, happiness is regarded as a discrete emotion in its own right, then it is not part of our innate repertoire. Like other terms on the standard six-item list of basic emotions, "happiness" may be misleading.

What about other emotions that are not included on the standard six-item list? Are any of these basic? One popular candidate is embarrassment. Embarrassment has a distinctive physiological signature. When we are embarrassed we blush (Miller, 1996). But blushing may not be restricted to embarrassment. As Keats notes, "There's a blush for want, and a blush for shan't / And a blush for having done it." Wierzbicka (1999) provides linguistic evidence for the claim that embarrassment is a derived emotion that builds on a basic emotion that has no exact name in English. Some languages have no word for embarrassment, but they have other words for social emotions that involve unwelcome attention from others—an aversive self-consciousness.

Wierzbicka argues that aversive self-consciousness lies at the root of both embarrassment as well as shame. Some Eastern languages have a single word covering both of these emotions. Other languages have words that overlap with embarrassment but have importantly different eliciting conditions. Fessler (1999) describes *malu*, an emotion experienced by people in Dusun Baguk, Malaysia, which overlaps with shame and embarrassment but can also be elicited by being in the presence of a person of higher rank.

Ekman includes both embarrassment and shame on his recent list of basic emotions. Following Wierzbicka, I regard both of these as nonbasic. Embarrassment may actually subsume several related emotions. Sabini, Siepman, Stein, and Meyerowitz (2000) present evidence that people are embarrassed by three distinct triggers: committing a faux pas, being the center of attention, and threatening another person's social identity. These may be distinct discrete emotions generated by calibrating a basic emotion that occurs when we get attention from others. We group them together because they all lead us to blushing and a desire for self-concealment. Shame is a sense of unwelcome attention that occurs when one has committed a transgression that will disappoint others. The concern that we will disappoint others may instigate an element of sadness or separation distress. This sets shame apart from the three species of embarrassment. Sadness also seems to lie at the heart of shame's cousin, guilt. Ekman now regards guilt as a basic emotion, but I think it is more likely a species of sadness calibrated to one's own transgressions (see chapter 5).

As I pointed out in chapter 5, Ekman prefers to talk of universal emotion *families* rather than universal emotions. I think this is helpful, because it implies that English emotion terms may not correspond perfectly to the emotions that are biologically basic. The terms on Ekman's standard six-item list do not map perfectly onto our innate endowment. Using these terms loosely to refer to emotion families is perfectly acceptable, and in that sense I have no qualms with Ekman's general approach to the basic emotions. I think he may be wrong about some of the families, however, and he underestimates the power of blending and calibration.

The final list of basic emotions may go beyond those that I have mentioned. My proposals are primarily intended to drive home a pair of methodological cautions. We should always ask whether a putative basic emotion could be explained through blending or calibration, and we should be wary about using our own emotion vocabulary to divide affective space at its genetic joints.

Summarizing this discussion, I offer the following, highly speculative list of basic emotions. On the negative side, we have frustration, panic, anxiety, physical disgust, separation distress, and aversive self-consciousness. On the positive side, we have satisfaction, stimulation, and attachment.

### Integrative Compatibilism

In chapter 5, I argued that biology makes some contribution to our emotions, but strong forms of reductionism lack support. In this chapter, I filled some promissory notes by proposing a list of innate emotions and identifying three ways in which culture can exert a constitutive influence. The resulting view is obviously compatibilist. Emotions depend on both nature and nurture. But what kind of compatibilism is this?

At the beginning of the chapter, I identified two different kinds of compatibilist theories. Scope compatibilism is the view that some emotions are biologically based, while others are cultural. Componential compatibilism says that a single emotion can have both culturally derived and biologically derived parts. Neither of these alternatives aligns perfectly with the kind of compatibilism I have been trying to defend.

I do endorse a form of scope compatibilism. I think there is a set of innate basic emotions. Unlike typical scope compatibilists and reductionists, however, I do not think that these emotions can be easily labeled using English emotion vocabulary. I also think that most emotions experienced in adult human life bear the influence of culture. Adult emotions are both cultural and biological. One needs a notion of compatibilism to capture this interaction.

Componential compatibilism looks promising in this regard, but it too comes up short. Most componential compatibilists, like most constructionists, assume that emotions are at least partially constituted by judgments. I reject this view. I also deny that emotions can be divided up into meaningful parts. One cannot say: Here is the component that owes to culture, and here is the component that owes to evolution. I favor an integrative compatibilism. The contributions of nature and nurture are so seamlessly integrated that we cannot easily tease them apart.

From a brain's-eye point of view, basic and nonbasic emotions are alike. All emotions are all neural responses to patterned bodily states. To identify the relative contributions of nature and nurture, one must look an emotion's history, not its internal organization. Many of the bodily patterns associated with our emotions are genetically predetermined. Culture can exert an influence by shaping habits of the body, by blending, or by recalibration. When blending and recalibration occur, our body patterns become detectors for new classes of external elicitors. In the latter case (recalibration), the genetically predetermined bodily pattern may remain unaltered. An emotion that has been culturally tuned may look just like one that has been set up by our genes. To see the difference, one must see how the elicitation conditions of that emotion have been transformed over time. Such an emotion should not be called cultural or biological, because it integrates these two seamlessly.

On the integrative compatibilist position that I favor, there are different ways to individuate emotions. On the one hand, we can individuate by the somatic states to which an emotion responds (nominal content). On the other, we can individuate emotions by the relational properties that they represent (real content). Earlier I mentioned that emotions with the same real contents can have different nominal contents. The discussion also entails that emotions with the same nominal contents can also have different real contents. To see that, it is useful to divide real contents into two distinct varieties. Basic emotions are innately tuned to certain properties (call these basic contents). But they can be recalibrated to pick out new properties (call these derived contents). Two emotions that have the same nominal contents can have different real contents because real contents can be specified in terms of innate dispositions or learning.

Two emotions with the same basic contents may also have different derived contents. Consider *Schadenfreude*. It may have the same nominal content and the same basic content as some form of pleasure (say stimulation). This means there is a perfectly good sense in which we can talk of *Schadenfreude* as a form of pleasure. But the derived content of *Schadenfreude* is another person's suffering. That means there is an equally good sense in which we can talk of *Schadenfreude* as distinct from pleasure. Likewise, we can describe jealousy as a blend of (the basic emotions underlying) anger, sadness, and disgust, or we can describe jealousy as an independent emotion. These different ways of individuating emotions are perfectly compatible, insofar as we specify the kind of content we have in mind. On this view, emotions have three layers of content or meaning. The only layer that is immune to the influence of culture and experience is the basic layer, which is innately determined by definition. The other two layers, nominal and derived, can reflect the disparate ways in which nature is nurtured.

# 7

# *Valence*

### Good Times, Bad Times

#### Introducing Valence

Consider George W. Bush on election night 2000. After an astonishing reversal, television networks declare that Bush has won the electoral votes in Florida, which are sufficient for securing the presidency. Bush's brother, the governor of Florida, has assured him that this is indeed the case. Then a concession call comes in from his adversary, Al Gore. Gore congratulates Bush on his victory. After an exhausting campaign and an agonizingly long election night, the news must usher in a storm of positive affect: tremendous relief, bubbling pride, humbling gratitude, and, above all else, elation.

But then the phone rings again. Gore reports that the Florida contest has been deemed too close to call. He retracts his concession. Now the storm winds change direction. Elation turns to frustration, then aggravation, bewilderment, and crushing disappointment. All of this is followed by renewed anxiety about what will happen next.

We have no difficulty discerning a fundamental difference between the emotions after Bush's two conversations with Gore. The emotions in the first set are positive, and the emotions in the second set are negative. Most of us like having emotions such as pride and elation and dislike having emotions such as aggravation and disappointment. The distinction between negative and positive emotions crosscuts many other distinctions. Anxiety and disappointment are surely distinct, but they are both disagreeable. The same may be true for terror and tedium. Conversely, glee and gratitude are both agreeable. The difference between negative and positive emotions is called a difference in "valence." There are two different valences an emotion can have, negative or positive, and all emotions seem to have one or the other.

Emotion researchers have tried to find empirical support for the intuition that valence is a fundamental feature of emotion. One form of support comes from studies of emotion similarity space. In order to see how we think about emotions, researchers sometimes ask subjects to form similarity judgments for pairs of emotion terms. Statistical techniques are then used to plot large sets of similarity judgments on a graph. Emotions that are rated more similar are placed closely together, and emotions that are rated dissimilar are placed farther apart. When this is done, a circular structure, or "circumplex," emerges (Larsen & Diener, 1992; Russell, 1980). In order to see what is driving similarity judgments, researchers try to organize the circumplex along meaningful dimensions of comparison. In study after study, two dimensions seem to emerge (fig. 7.1).

One dimension is "arousal": emotions that seem to involve high degrees of arousal can be grouped on one side of the circumplex, while low arousal emotions group together on the other. Plutchik (1984) persuasively argues that all emotions can vary in arousal—what he calls "intensity." Anger, for example, can span from minor irritation (low intensity) to violent rage (high intensity). Happiness can span from mild contentment to ecstasy.

The second dimension, orthogonal to arousal, is sometimes termed "hedonic tone."[1] Hedonic tone is equivalent to valence. Positive emotions are placed on one side, and negative emotions are placed on the other. The fact that valence emerges as a dimension of the circumplex suggests that valence underwrites our implicit beliefs about the organization of emotion space. Negative emotions, such as anger, fear, and sadness, are regarded as similar. This fact is so obvious that it seems unworthy of mention. But, on reflection, it is quite surprising. After all, the core relational themes associated with these emotions are quite different. Anger represents offense and fear represents danger and sadness represents loss. They are unified by the fact that they are all negative.

Some circumplex theorists have assumed that negative and positive valence are two ends of a common continuum. Others have argued that they are independent (Watson & Tellegen, 1995). Negative and positive valence tend to inhibit each other, but they derive from dissociable systems. Support for this conclusion comes from cognitive neuroscience. A number of researches have tried to find the neural correlates of valence. To date, these attempts have failed to produce consistent results. Different labs have published different findings. But one trend has consistently appeared. In every study, positive and negative valence seems to involve activity in independent brain areas. Elliott, Friston, and Dolan (2000) used fMRI to measure neural response to rewards and losses during a gambling task. They found activity in the right midbrain and ventral striatum, when subjects had attained high rewards,[2] and they found bilateral hippocampus activation when subjects received high penalties. Lane, Chua, and Dolan (1999) found somewhat different results in a PET study. They measured regional cerebral blood flow as

---

[1]Some circumplex researchers assume that two dimensions are enough to differentiate all emotions. As Larsen and Diener (1992) point out, this is implausible. Distinct emotions can have the same location on the circumplex. For example, fury and terror are both negative in valence and high in arousal. Such emotions can only be distinguished by the appraisals they embody.

[2]Some further areas connected to these structures, including bilateral globbus pallidus, right anteroventral thalamus, and subgenual cingulate cortex, became active during a winning streak.

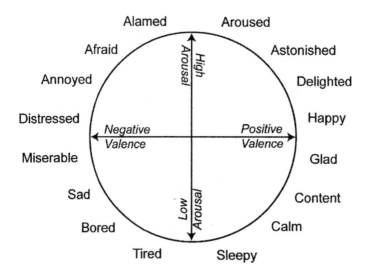

*Figure 7.1.* A circumplex model of the organization of emotions, adapted from Figure 4 in Russell (1980, p. 1169), with permission. Copyright by the American Psychological Association.

female subjects viewed neutral, pleasant, and unpleasant pictures. Negative pictures caused activation in the bilateral occipito-temporal cortex, left parahippocampus gyrus, left amygdala, and cerebellum. Lane et al. did not identify any structures unique to positive affect. In another PET study, Paradiso et al. (1999) found that pleasant pictures tended to cause more activation in neocortical areas (dorsolateral, orbital, and medial frontal cortex) than unpleasant picture, and unpleasant pictures tended to cause more subcortical outside the neocortex (amygdala and cerebellum).

Other laboratories have found neocortical activation for both negative and positive emotions. In a combined fMRI/MEG study, Northoff et al. (2000) found that negative pictures caused medial orbitofrontal activation, and positive pictures caused lateral oribitofrontal activation. In other studies, Davidson has found evidence that valence-sensitive frontal activations are lateralized. In EEG and PET studies, he his and colleagues have found increased activity in the left prefrontal cortex during positive emotions and increased activity in the right prefrontal cortex during negative emotions (Davidson, 1992; Sutton & Davidson, 1997). These asymmetries can be found when subjects view emotionally evocative filmstrips and are also consistent with neural patterns found in subjects suffering from emotional disorders and brain injuries (see review in Davidson & Irwin, 1999).

Obviously, the exact anatomic substrates of negative and positive valence are still unresolved. But it is equally apparent that negative and positive valence involve different structures. The studies also consistently show that distinct emotions with the same valence cause overlapping brain activations. For example, Paradiso et al. (1999) obtained their results using pictures that elicit a sense of happiness, appetite, satisfaction, beauty, and success on the positive side, while using pictures that elicit fear, disgust, sorrow, and disappointment on the negative side. Despite this variety, distinct patterns emerged for the positive group and for the negative group.

One might wonder why different labs have obtained such different results. One possibility is that negative and positive valence supervene on complex networks that implicate a large number of brain areas. Minor differences in testing techniques may produce disparate neuroimaging results because different parts of those networks are being activated. In any case, these studies provide good evidence for the reality of emotional valence, and for the independence of positive and negative valence.

None of this should be taken as evidence for the conclusion that all emotions with the same valence have exactly the same neural correlates. This is not the case. For example, studies of different negative emotions have found different patterns of activation. Sometimes these differences occur within a common anatomical region. In a PET study, Liotti et al. (2000) found that memories of sad events caused activation in the right posterior insula, and memories of anxiety-inducing events caused activation in the right ventral insula. In an fMRI study, Phllips et al. (1997) found that perceiving facial expression of disgust caused anterior insula activation. These studies also show distinctive activations in other brain areas. I mention the insula, because this region is associated with the response to bodily changes, especially changes in viscera organs. Variation in insula activations suggests that different negative emotions correspond to distinctive patterns of bodily response. This supports the embodied appraisal theory defended in chapter 3.

The upshot is that emotions seem to contain *two* distinctive parts. Every emotion has a valence, which it shares with other emotions. But every emotion also has a distinctive bodily profile reflected by (sometimes subtle) differences in neuronal activity. In defending the embodied appraisal theory, I have been focusing on this second part—the embodied appraisal themselves. The evidence concerning valence suggests that the embodied appraisal theory needs to be supplemented. In addition to embodied appraisals, every emotion seems to have what can be termed a "valence marker." On this revised model, sadness is a compound state, containing both an embodied appraisal that detects loss and an activation that represents the loss as something negative.

The two components of an emotion may be dissociated in certain cases. Consider surprise. Surprise can be regarded as an embodied appraisal representing a violation in one's expectations. When expectations are violated, various bodily changes take place. Most obviously, the mouth tends to drop open and the eyes widen. Darwin (1872/1998) speculates that the widened mouth is a way of quieting breathing and increasing respiration. Opening the mouth may also increases access to the nasal cavity in order to be better smell the source of the surprise. Some surprises involve the unexpected intrusion of harmful entities, and some involve the unexpected intrusion of beneficial opportunities. Correlatively, one can be pleasantly and unpleasantly surprised. Extremely positive surprise can yield amazement, and extremely negative surprise can yield shock. Parallel points can be made about such states as curiosity or interest, both of which are frequently included on lists of emotions. Intuitively, these states qualify as emotions only when they are valent. Consider the positive state of interest one has when studying a beautiful painting or, conversely, the negative interest one has when looking at the wreckage and mutilation of a car accident on the roadside.

The case of surprise strongly supports the conjecture that appraisal and valence are two separate components of emotion. Surprise also provides evidence that valence is essential to emotionality. Laypeople are often perplexed when they learn that emotion researchers commonly count surprise as an emotion. Surprise seems different from fear, sadness, and joy. That difference stems from the fact that surprise often lacks valence. Ortony and Turner (1990) give the example of being surprised to discover that several people at a meeting share a birth date. Intuitively, surprise can only become an emotion when accompanied by positive and negative marker. Ordinary intuitions would not be compromised by calling surprise an emotion when it follows news of winning the lottery or news that one's home has burnt to the ground. I think valence is a real feature of our psychology and it is essential to emotionality.[3]

Unlike surprise, some emotions tend to involve just one valence marker. Sadness, for example, is generally negative. This makes sense, because sadness is a loss detector. We would gain little benefit from an evolved loss detector if that detector were not prewired to be held in negative regard. Likewise for fear and other trademark negative emotions.[4]

## Mixed Feelings

I just argued that all emotions are valent. Some emotions may be intrinsically negative (sadness, fear), some may be intrinsically positive (joy), and some may have variable valence markers (surprise). On some occasions we experience both a negative emotion and a positive emotion concurrently. Greenspan (1980) gives the case of feeling both happy and sad when a friend wins a contest that one was also competing in. It also turns out that some emotions are *intrinsically* both negatively and positively valent. Some emotions are intrinsically mixed.

---

[3]Of course, there is some risk in using pretheoretical intuitions as a guide in scientific theory construction. It would be useful to empirically investigate various instances of surprise and compare them to paradigm cases of emotion. For example, one could look for neural correlates of valence and test for their presence in cases of positive, negative, and neutral surprise. In the interim, the intuitions can be used to support the working hypothesis that surprise can be valent and that valence is found in all clear cases of emotion.

[4]It is sometimes said that thrill-seekers experience fear as a positive emotion. I doubt that this is the case. Fear is probably intrinsically negative for all of us. The apparent thrill of fear, experienced by some people, may have another explanation, which I will touch on later.

Consider nostalgia. When we reminisce on the past, we often experience a whirl of joyful sadness. The very structure of reminiscence seems to make this inevitable. Suppose you call up a fond memory. Recalling happy times is sure to cause joy. At the same moment, one is keenly aware that the past is no longer available to us. Reminiscing is recalling a good time while recognizing its absence. This gives us a sense of loss, which triggers a sadness response. This combination of joy and sadness is nostalgia. There is every reason to think it is a state that carries two conflicting valence markers.

Another mixed emotion occurs when one feels "touched." For example, imagine arriving at your workplace for the first time after a long absence due to illness only to discover that your colleagues have left a bouquet of flowers on your desk. It is touching to be thought of by others, especially when we do not assume that others will think of us. The feeling one experiences of such occasions seems simultaneously happy and sad. We are happy for the kind gesture and sad, perhaps, because the gesture points to the feeling of isolation, uncertainty, or hardship that preceded the gesture. This may put one in an ambiguous state of valence. In a way, this is the inverse of nostalgia. When we feel nostalgic, we relive the joy of the past, while thinking that the object of our joy is no longer present. When we feel touched, a present source of joy brings a past hardship to mind.

Some mixed emotions are even more dramatic. Consider those instances of joy that bring one to tears. We cry when we are saved from peril, win lotteries, witness spectacular human achievements, or reunite with long-lost friends. Crying is itself an unsolved mystery in emotion research. There is no universally accepted theory of why we weep. Descartes argued that tears come when sadness is followed by love or joy (1649/1988, II. cxxviii–cxxxi). First, sadness contracts the pores of the eyes, bringing them close together; then, joy or love increase the excretion of bodily vapors; and finally, the contracted pores bring these vapors together around the eyes, turning them into liquid. Darwin (1872/1988) thought crying was an accidental result of putting pressure on one's tear ducts in an effort to protect the eyes while screaming. Infants, he observed, do not tear in the first months of life. When tears finally come, as protection during screaming, they come to be associated with sadness, a leading cause of screaming during infancy. According to an even stranger hypothesis, crying is a response that dates back to the time when we burned dead relatives on funeral pyres. The smoke of the pyres caused us to tear naturally, and that bodily defense mechanism become associated with moments of great loss (MacLean, 1993). All of these proposals are almost certainly wrong. What they share, however, is the natural assumption that crying involves feelings of sadness.

This makes joyful crying quite puzzling. One provocative response to the puzzle alleges that all crying is actually joyful. Something like this may lie behind Descartes's claim that crying comes when sadness is followed by love or joy. A more explicit formulation owes to Efran and Spangler (1979). They argue that crying always involves recovery from stress or tension. This has some intuitive appeal. In sadness, tears often come when feelings of impending loss are followed by news that brings finality. We cry when the worries that we naturally harbor for our loved ones is laid to rest by news of their death. Wonderful news can cause crying too, because it often marks the elimination of a burden. Winning the lottery may bring forth tears, because it marks an end to our financial woes.

I am not convinced by the recovery model. First, it makes little sense of the tears that infants emit. Crying in infancy is often a distress call. It does not co-occur with moments of relief. Second, the recovery hypothesis predicts that the sympathetic part of the autonomic nervous system will become less active when we cry. The sympathetic nervous system generates arousal, which counteracts any calm that might be associated with recovery. Experimental evidence shows, unsurprisingly, that we actually become more aroused while crying (Gross, Frederickson, & Levenson, 1994).

The key to understanding joyful tears may be found in the examples of nostalgia and feeling touched. In both these cases, a mixed feeling is produced by a glance backward. Feeling touched provides an especially good model. An unexpected outpouring of love from one's colleagues may bring to mind a prior hardship. Likewise, the elation that comes from escaping peril, winning a lottery, or reuniting with an old friend may bring to mind the misery of certain doom, financial burdens, or separation. Tears evoked by witnessing spectacular human achievements may call up thoughts of human frailty: how can feeble creatures be capable of this? Joyful tears often involve relief, because relief involves glancing back at a hardship.

This proposal is vulnerable to an objection. If joyful tears reflect the unhappiness of a remembered hardship, then the hardship itself is the source of those tears. But that implies there should be even more tears during the time when that hardship is occurring. This is true some of the time. When infants cry in distress, they probably aren't mourning over something that happened in the past. But we sometimes cry after the worst part of the hardship has passed. A person trapped in a burning building may cry after being rescued rather than during the ordeal.

Infant tears may help us understand this phenomenon as well. I said that infants cry as a distress call. If crying serves a communicative function, it is more likely to occur when there is someone with whom we can communicate. It is more likely to occur in the presence of a nurturer who can answer a plea for distress. Tears of joy often occur in the presence of a potential nurturer who was absent during a period of distress. This is especially obvious in the case of tears that occur after being rescued or tears that occur when reuniting with an old friend. Tears caused by winning a lottery may arise because the lucre itself can symbolically serve as a nurturer.

If I am right, crying is always a distress call. In that regard, it always expresses a negative emotion. But despair often arises when we are experiencing great happiness or relief. Good in the present brings old traumas to mind. That explains why crying often conveys mixed feelings. Tears of joy are also tears of sorrow. The underlying emotion is mixed.

I will consider one more mixed feeling. This one arises during some instances of laughter. Laughter is the counterpart of crying. Just as we generally cry when we are sad, laughter generally occurs when we are happy. Most people assume that laughter is essentially a humor response. Provine (2000) provides fascinating evidence against this view. It turns out that only 20 percent of our laughter follows jokes. Most of the time we laugh after we hear someone make an innocuous remark, as when we greet each other or express departing salutations. Provine concludes that laughter is a more general social signal. It expresses social bonding, and even dominance or submission. In our male chauvinist culture, the role of laughter in expressing submission is most alarmingly exhibited by the fact that women laugh in response to male speakers far more frequently than men laugh at female speakers. When submission laughter occurs, it hovers in an awkward position between joy and defeat. It expresses a mixed feeling.

Panksepp and Burgdorf (2000) have advanced a related idea. They claim to find analogues of laughter in laboratory rats. Laughter is an expression correlated with play. He induces laughter in rats by tickling them. Tickling is physical stimulation that would be very threatening if it were initiated by an enemy. When we are tickled by siblings, friends, and lovers, it is mildly pleasurable. But the fear is not completely lost. Panksepp (2000) speculates that play evolved as a system of mock combat, to train us for less friendly attacks. Laughter conveys that one is being playfully attacked. It is a submission cue that reminds the aggressor that we are not taking the attack too seriously. I would submit that the emotion experienced while being tickled combines a negative valence marker, imported with the fear of attack, and a positive valence marker, associated with the joy of physical interaction with our near and dear.

### *What Is Valence?*

#### Theories of Valence

Valence comes in two essential flavors: negative and positive. I have argued that some emotions are always negative, some are always positive, some are variable, and some are mixed. I have said nothing, however, about how the division between positive and negative valence should be drawn. The terms *positive* and *negative* are not terribly informative. One wants to know: What makes positive emotions so positive and negative emotions so negative? It would be useful to replace these generic terms with a more informative characterization. It turns out that there is little consensus about how this should be done. Several alternatives deserve consideration.

One possibility is that positive emotions are pleasant and negative emotions are unpleasant (e.g., Frijda, 1993). This seems true as far as it goes. Joy is pleasurable and fear is not. The problem is that "pleasant" and "unpleasant" are words that describe conscious feelings. We cannot have an unconscious unpleasant state. Any state that is unfelt is neither pleasant nor unpleasant. To identify positive and negative valence markers with pleasantness and unpleasantness implies that emotions can never be unconscious. Even those who think all emotions must be conscious agree that there can be unconscious analogues of emotional states. There can be unconscious states that share many properties with fear, for example, but lack the distinctive fear feeling (LeDoux, 1996). Unconscious analogues of fear are negative states. Therefore, negative valence markers cannot be defined by unpleasantness. Likewise for positive valence markers.

A second way of distinguishing positive and negative emotions owes to dimensional appraisal theories. Lazarus (1991) and others have claimed that positive emotions occur in response to things deemed congruent with our goals, and negative emotions occur in response to things deemed incongruent with our goals (see also Oatley & Johnson-Laird, 1987; Stein, Trabasso, & Liwag, 1993). Assessments of goal congruence can occur unconsciously, so this approach is better than the appeal to pleasantness. But it has a problem of its own.

It is not plausible that all emotions relate to goals. Suppose someone gives you a gift that you were not expecting. The joy you experience is certainly positive, but it is not plausible to assume that receiving the gift was a goal of yours. Likewise, suppose you are sitting at home and you suddenly hear the sound of a window breaking. The fear you will experience is surely negative, but it is implausible to assume that you had the goal of not being burglarized. There is an informal sense in which we might say that people do not want to be burglarized. But the absence of a desire to be burglarized and a negative attitude toward being burglarized do not add up to a goal of not being burglarized. To say one has that goal implies that one is in the active pursuit of achieving it. Attributing goals to people every time they experience an emotion seems overly cognitive. Some emotion episodes seem to be wholly independent of our goals and plans.

According to another popular approach, valence involves approach and withdrawal tendencies: positive emotions cause us to approach the things that elicit them, while negative emotions cause us to avoid them (e.g., MacLean, 1993).[5] This analysis does not presuppose that emotions are conscious. Nor does it presuppose that emotions always involve goals. But it remains problematic. Some negative emotions seem to involve approach behaviors, as well as withdrawal. Anger, which is popularly regarded as negative, often impels us to attack. Attacking is an approach behavior if ever there was one. Ostensibly, fear seems to involve withdrawal, because we tend to flee when we are afraid. But flight can also be interpreted as the active pursuit of safety, which is an approach behavior (Ikemoto & Panksepp, 1999).

Conversely, positive emotions do not always impel us to approach. If one is enjoying a piece of music, for example, there is no drive to get closer to it. Positive emotions often make us complacent. We want to stay put and continue enjoying the things that induce them. Approach is too active to capture this idea. Some authors have tried to defend the idea that positive emotions carry approach

---

[5] A similar idea is implied by those who use the terms "appetitive" and "aversive."

tendencies by noting that happiness often makes us want to explore. Happiness also tends to promote creative thinking (Isen, Doubman, & Novicki, 1987). On the face of it, these look like approach tendencies. But, one might retort, what is one approaching when one sets out to explore? Exploration and creativity both seem to involve receptiveness to new possibilities. Receptiveness may be more passive than the approach construct would suggest.

A different account of valence can by built on proposals made by Tomkins (1962). He notes that negative valence markers tend to promote an inward focus of attention, while positive emotions tend to cause an outward focus. When we are sad, we think about ourselves, and when we are happy, we think about the world. This is especially apparent in moods. Long-term focus on one's self, especially one's flaws, is characteristic of depression.

There are apparent counterexamples to this proposal. Contempt is an outwardly focused negative emotion, while pride is an inwardly focused positive emotion. One might reply by arguing that people focus on how they have been wronged when in a state of contempt, and they focus on the opportunities that the world affords when feeling proud. Even so, we could conclude only that both emotions contain both inward and outward objects of focus. It is not the case that direction of focus tracks valence perfectly. Moreover, it is not clear why inward focus should be negative and outward focus should be positive. Direction of focus seems to be orthogonal to valence. If they were bound, we should generally find self-focus unpleasant and outward focus pleasant.

The most detailed proposals about the basis of emotional valence may come from authors working within the framework of animal learning theory. This research program was initiated by behaviorists, who were often skeptical about explanatory models that appeal to inner mental or neural states. Recent researchers in the animal learning tradition have abandoned this methodological handicap and offered admirably explicit accounts of internal mechanism. Work by Jeffrey Gray (1982, 1987, 1991) is, perhaps, the best example.

To explain Gray's theory of valence, it is necessary to review some of the core concepts from learning theory. The underlying insight of learning theory is that properly selected stimuli can be used to regulate behavioral response. Certain stimuli increase the probability of response, and others decrease the probability of a response. All such stimuli are called reinforcers. Reinforcers can be positive or negative. Positive reinforcers are stimuli that increase appetitive response (e.g., food) and those that decrease aversive response (e.g., stopping an electrical shock). In other words, positive reinforcers are rewards or relieving nonpunishments. Negative reinforcers are stimuli that increase aversive response (e.g., an electrical shock) or decrease appetitive response (e.g., stopping supply of food). In other words, negative reinforcers are punishments or frustrating nonrewards.[6]

Many researchers have related emotion to reinforcement (e.g., Millenson, 1967;

[6]A nonreward, in learning theoretic terms, is what happens when a reward that has been sought or expected fails to occur.

Rolls, 1999; Watson, 1919; Weiskrantz, 1968). Gray's account has been especially influential in recent years. He proposes that the mammalian brain contains a behavioral inhibition system (BIS) and a behavioral approach system (also called the behavioral activation system, or BAS). The BIS responds to negative reinforcers and results in behavioral inhibition and increases in attention and arousal. For example, it might lead to a freezing response to a threatening stimulus. The BAS responds to positive reinforcers and results in approach behavior. It might lead an organism to move toward an object that has provided nourishment in the past.

Gray advances specific proposals about the neural correlates of these systems, which I can only summarize here. He says that the BIS principally involves the septohippocampal system (Gray, 1991). This is a network that includes two important circuits. The hippocampal formation (including hippocampus, entorhinal cortex, and the subicular area) receives information about the world. The subicular area sends that information to the Papez circuit (the mammilary bodies, anteroventral thalamus, and cingulate cortex), which monitors motor plans. The Papez circuit also passes information back to the subicular area so comparisons between word and plans can be made. When a mismatch occurs, a signal is sent to the anterior cingulate cortex, which can halt ongoing motor plans. An inhibitory signal can also be sent, via the septal area, to the hypothalamus, which participates in sympathetic autonomic response. Gray says that mismatches can also lead to modulations in arousal (via locus coeruleus) and attention (via entorhinal projections to neocortex).

The BAS also involves two major circuits. The caudate motor system (motor and sensory motor cortex, ventral thalamic nuclei, caudate-putamen, dorsal pallidum, and substantia negra) encodes relations between stimulus, response, and reinforcement in the steps of a motor program. The accumbens motor system (nucleus accumbens, prefrontal and cingulate limbic areas, dorsomedial thalamic nuclei, vental pallidum, and nucleus A 10 in the ventral tegmental area) monitors progress toward goals and switches between steps in a motor program. The nucleus accumbens is an especially important hub in the BAS. It receives inputs from the subicular area in the septohippocampal system when it detects a match between motor plans and the world. It then modulates motor response by sending outputs to the accumbens motor system, of which it is a part, and to the caudate motor system via the substantia nigra.

Gray makes two central claims about the relationship between emotion and the BIS and BAS. First, he implies that different emotions can be characterized by different kinds of reinforcement contingencies, and those contingencies can be related to activation levels in his BIS and BAS systems.[7] On this approach, relief

---

[7] Actually, Gray postulates three systems underlying all emotions: BIS, BAS, and a system that initiates fight-or-flight responses. Gray says that the BIS system is involved only in response to learned (conditioned) aversive stimuli. Unlearned (unconditioned) aversive stimuli activate the fight-or-flight system. This strikes me as an odd division of labor. I am inclined to believe that the fight-or-flight system, if it exists, is a special system for responding to immediate physical threats. Some immediate physical threats are unconditioned, but others may be unconditioned.

might come when a negative reinforcer is terminated and joy may come when a positive reinforcer in introduced. Call this the individuation claim. Gray's second claim is more relevant to this discussion. He says that negative and positive valence can be identified with high BIS and high BAS levels respectively. Call this the valence claim.

Both of these claims are very intriguing, but I think neither will pan out. I submit three objections. First, there is an unwelcome implication of accepting both the valence claim and the individuation claim together. If emotions are individuated with reference to BIS and BAS, and valence is identified with levels of BIS and BAS, then the same emotion cannot have distinct valence. Cases of positive anger, and the awe/shock contrast in surprise, would be difficult to explain on this model. I think there is reason to separate valence from the components that distinguish one emotion from another.

The second objection is directed at the individuation claim. Gray wants to individuate emotions by reinforcement contingencies and BIS/BAS levels. I think that reinforcement contingencies lack the variety and specificity of content to account for many of our emotions. No pattern of reinforcement can explain jealousy, resentment, shame, and the like.

My third objection targets the valence claim. Gray often implies a direct link between behavior and the BIS and BAS systems. As the names suggest, BIS is associated with cessation of behavior, and BAS is associated with behavioral approach. The proposal that valence relates to BIS and BAS is thus very close to the proposal that valence amounts to withdrawal and approach tendencies. The mechanisms underlying emotional valence cannot have such a simple link to action. As I argued earlier, approach is not necessary or sufficient for positive valence. The link between cessation and negative valence is a bit tighter. Negative emotions often dispose us to stop doing things. Fear experienced while walking along a path may cause us to stop in our tracks. Disgust may interrupt the process of eating. Sadness may cause us to stop doing anything at all. But one must exercise caution when equating negative valence with cessation. Negative valence is compatible with an increase in overall action. Indignation may lead one to join throngs of protestors in a jeering mob. This may count as a form of cessation in one sense ("I'm not going to take it any more!"), but it is not a shutdown in behavior.

This objection also plays out at the neuroanatomical level. Gray says that the nucleus accumbens plays a central role in the BAS. This is a natural hypothesis, because the nucleus accumbens is a hub in a dopaminergic network that has been associated with reward-modulated approach behaviors, such as feeding and addition. But the nucleus accumbens has also been associated with negative valence states. It contributes to negative defensive behavior (Reynolds & Berridge, 2001), environmental exploration in contextual fear conditioning (Fanselow & LeDoux, 1999), adaptive responses to stressors (Anisman, Zaleman, & Zachorko, 1993), and flight (Ikemoto & Panksepp, 1999). Gray himself has come to recognize that nucleus accumbens plays a role in aversive responses. He and his colleagues found rat nucleus accumbens activation triggered by cues associated with foot shock (Young, Joseph, & Gray, 1993).

One can also levy a more general complaint against Gray's attempt to link valence and behavior. Human emotional responses are extremely flexible. If I get annoyed by a bad movie matinee, I may avoid movies by that director, I may avoid movies altogether, I may avoid seeing matinees, I may avoid the theater where I saw the offending movie, I may buy more candy before the next movie, or I may decide to become a filmmaker to show Hollywood how movies should be made. Behavior depends, in other words, on at least two factors. It depends on what we identify as the source of past emotions (that director or all Hollywood movies), and it depends on what we identify as the best coping strategies (seeing fewer movies or making movies of our own). The behavioral options exercised by someone in a negative valence state raise doubts about the view that negative valence is merely inhibition.

I am not trying to cast doubt on the existence of the BIS and BAS systems. At the anatomical level, these systems are identified with circuits that have been studied extensively. I am resisting Gray's two claims about how BIS and BAS relate to emotion. On my view, emotions have two components, valence and an embodied appraisal. Because many emotions involve both inhibition and excitation, BIS and BAS cannot be equated with valence markers. And BIS and BAS cannot be equated with the appraisal components, because the range of BIS and BAS contingencies is smaller than the range of possible appraisals. But that does not mean that BIS and BAS play no role in emotion. It is likely that they play a role in emotion *initiation.*

BIS and BAS prepare us to respond to events that are punishing or rewarding; BAS initiates physiological changes that prepare us to start new behavioral responses, and BIS initiates physiological changes that interpret responses that are in progress. I have defended a somatic theory of the appraisal component in emotion. Appraisals are internal states that register patterned bodily changes. If BIS and BAS are involved in orchestrating such changes, then they are precursors to emotional states. They initiate physiological changes that are among those that form the basis of our embodied appraisals.

In this sense, Gray's individuation claim may have a kernel of truth; BIS and BAS may play an essential role in emotion individuation because of their role in orchestrating bodily changes. It is highly likely that different emotions characteristically involve different levels of BIS and BAS activation. Both joy and anger may involve high BAS, because both tend to involve preparation for approach. Fear and sadness may involve and high BIS, because they both tend to involve a shutdown in various behaviors and a reorientation of attention. Fear and sadness may typically involve low BAS as well, because they tend to hinder exploration. But that does not mean that BAS is entirely uninvolved in these negative emotions. Fear, in particular, may require some BAS activation when flight or escape is an option. The distinction between panic and anxiety, discussed in chapter 6, might be explained by variation in BAS. Both panic and anxiety are high-inhibition states, but in panic the perceived danger precludes escape, so behavioral activation stops. BIS and BAS can thus play a useful role in distinguishing emotions. Notice, however, that this falls far short of the individuation claim that Gray defends. Distinct emotions are often associated with comparable BIS and BAS levels. Mere activation and inhibition are insufficient for distinguishing between the patterns of bodily responses that set our emotions apart. Still, BIS and BAS may contribute essentially to the bodily patterns that distinguish emotions.[8] It is possible that every emotion is associated with some level of activation in the BIS and BAS systems.

There may also be a kernel of truth in Gray's theory of valence. All the theories of valence I have considered seem to fail. His is no exception. But Gray's invocation of constructs from learning theory may point us in the right direction.

### Valence and Inner Reinforcers

Gray's BIS and BAS systems orchestrate behavioral responses to reinforcers. In claiming that we can equate valence with differential levels of BIS and BAS activation, Gray assumes that valence is a feature of response modification. An alternative possibility is that valence belongs to the input side of systems that modulate response. Rather than equating valence with our responses to reinforcers, we can equate valence with the reinforcers themselves.

As I noted earlier, negative and positive reinforcers can come in different forms. Positive reinforcement can come in the form of reward or nonpunishment. Negative reinforcement can come in the form of punishment or nonreward. In addition, learning theorists distinguish those rewards and punishments that are innately specified from those that are learned. Innate or primary reinforcers include things like food consumption and pain. Just about anything else can become a reinforcer through classical conditioning. The implication of all this is that reinforcers take many shapes and forms. The brain needs a way of keeping track. It needs a way of recording which stimuli are positive reinforcers and which are negative. I propose that it does this by using a pair of internal labels. The brain contains a pair of inner reinforcers. These are states that get associated with representations of stimuli. Primary reinforcers are stimuli that have been genetically associated with inner reinforcers, and secondary reinforcers are stimuli for which the association is learned. These inner reinforcers are valence markers. A negatively valent state is one that includes an inner negative reinforcer (INR) and a positively valent state is one that includes an inner positive reinforcer (IPR).

In the animal learning literature, negative and positive reinforcers are presumed to be external stimuli, and they are defined with reference to future probability of behavior. Negative reinforcers decrease probability, and positive reinforcers increase it. On my account, reinforcers are inner states. They are behaviorist constructs reinvented for an age of cognitive science. But I need not abandon the be-

---

[8]Or at least basic emotions. Nonbasic emotions are often distinguished by their calibrating causes.

haviorist operationalization. Inner reinforcers can be characterized by their impact on future behavior, but that impact can now be explained in mentalist terms.

I think that IPRs and INRs serve as inner imperatives. An IPR serves as a command that says something like "More of this!" while an INR says "Less of this!" Positive emotions are ones we want to sustain, and negative emotions are ones that we want to get rid of. To obey these inner imperatives, we need to identify the source of our emotions. If I am overjoyed by a chocolate soufflé that I am eating, then I will recognize that the "More of this!" command would be best served by having more soufflé. If I am tormented by an awful movie that I am watching, the "Less of this!" command would best be served by leaving the theater.

Inner reinforcers have an impact on future behavior when they, and their attendant embodied appraisals, get stored in memory. When I think about having a chocolate soufflé, I recall my past experience, and the IPR prods me to value the option highly. When I think about seeing another movie by the director whose last product bored me to tears, the recalled INR tells me to skip it. This is very much like Damasio's (1994) suggestion that emotions serve as memory markers, which factor into decision making. In choosing a course of action, we anticipate the emotional consequences of our actions. In this way, valence markers can impact both present and future behavior. They influence the future in virtue of their ability to influence the present.

Identifying valence with inner reinforcers explains why emotions sometimes impel approach or withdrawal. Negative emotions encourage us to withdraw from situations that elicit them, and positive emotions encourage us to seek out the situations that elicit them. If some object in our environment is negatively reinforcing, we may try to relocate, and if an object is positively reinforcing, we may try to pursue it. At the same time, the reinforcement analysis can handle cases where approach and withdrawal do not map onto positive and negative valence. Anger impels us to attack, not withdraw, because attacking can be a way of eliminating the situation that elicited the anger. Fear has a negatively reinforcing influence, even though flight responses qualify as both withdrawing from threats and approaching safety. Happiness often promotes passivity, because there is no need to seek out a different situation when the present situation is positively reinforcing. In short, the inner reinforcer account does a considerably better job at explaining behavioral flexibility than other accounts of valence.

## Thrill Seekers and Ascetics

The inner reinforcer account may be better than the other accounts, but it faces one serious objection. If valence is constituted by inner reinforcers, then we should tend to repeat behaviors that cause positive emotions and avoid behaviors that cause negative emotions. On the face of it, this prediction seems perfectly plausible, but it may not accurately reflect human behavior. Consider ascetics, who avoid pleasure, masochists, who pursue pain, and thrill-seekers, who pursue fear.

There may be explanations of these behaviors. The first thing to note is that human behavior is a complex affair. The emotions caused by an activity are just one of the many factors that determine how likely one is to pursue that activity in the future. Ascetics who avoid pleasure and pursue discomfort may be seeking the great satisfaction of self-mastery or avoiding the unbearable guilt that comes with indulgence. People who repeat self-destructive patterns by entering into a series of abusive relationships may simply be choosing those situations that are most familiar. Freud (1920/1922) insightfully argues that the compulsion to repeat patterns can outweigh hedonistic pursuits.

Another possibility stems from my earlier assertion that valence and embodied appraisal are dissociable. I suggested earlier that certain emotions may be necessarily negative or necessarily positive, while other emotions can be either. It is an empirical possibility that this assumption is false. It could be the case that fear, for example, can become a positive emotion through learning and experience. Perhaps people discover that certain dangerous situations have benefits that outweigh the risks. This discovery could transform fear into a positive emotion under certain circumstances, which would explain some thrill-seeking behavior. There is as yet, so evidence for this possibility, so I consider it too speculative to embrace with any confidence.

There is a further possibility that enjoys some experimental support. Evidence suggests that there may be a psychological mechanism that tends to keep our emotional state at a state of equilibrium. Unbridled pleasure is tempered by negative aftereffects, and extreme distress is mitigated by positive aftereffects. This is the principle of "opponent processing" (Solomon, 1980). When a negative emotion kicks in, positively valent emotions automatically activate in response, and vice versa. For example, skydivers report extreme terror the first time they jump, but the fear is followed by giddy excitement. Conversely, drug users report extreme euphoria when they take drugs, but this is often followed by withdrawal. It seems that our affect systems want to avoid excess. When functioning normally, they tend toward balance. In extreme cases, such as drug addiction, the compensatory emotional responses begin to overshadow the initial triggering responses. Drug highs weaken, and withdrawal becomes worse. Conversely, in skydiving, the thrills eventually overshadow the chills.

Opponent processing explains why we may occasionally behave in ways that seem to be at odds with the reinforcement properties of our emotions. A positively reinforcing emotion can carry an overpowering negative aftereffect, and vice versa. Such cases are exceptional. Ordinarily, the reinforcing properties of the initial emotion induced by an activity will have greater impact than the reinforcing properties of a complementary emotion produced through opponent processing. All else being equal, one will avoid repeating activities that have caused misery in the past.

I conclude that the reinforcement proposal provides the most defensible account of valence. Negative emotions are negatively reinforcing, and positive emotions are positively reinforcing. Valence markers are inner reinforcers. When we experience an emotion, the valence marker contained in that emotion encourages continuation or cessation. When we consider an action during planning, we imagine the situation that the action will promote. If that situation has been associated with a valent response in the past, the valence of that response will factor into our decision to act. In this way, valence markers influence the likelihood that situations inducing our emotions will reoccur.[9]

## Does Valence Have a Distinctive Feel?

Earlier, I claimed that valence markers need not be conscious. That is why they should not be identified with felt pleasantness or unpleasantness. Even if this point is granted, one might be inclined to argue that valence markers *can* be conscious and that when they are they give rise to felt pleasantness or unpleasantness. On this view, the felt degree of pleasantness is always a consequence of valence.

The hypothesis that valence markers have a distinctive feel is certainly bolstered by intuition. It seems that negative and positive emotions feel significantly different in virtue of their difference in valence. There is, however, an alternative possibility. Perhaps the felt differences between negative and positive emotions is a consequence of the embodied appraisals they contain. If every emotion is an appraisal plus a valence marker, it could turn out that the feeling of the emotion is exhausted by the appraisal. Alleged commonalities between the feelings of different negative emotions could be an illusion. Perhaps there is no phenomenal thread linking disgust, betrayal, and grief.

I favor this view. I do not think that valence markers have any phenomenology in their own right. That claim may seem untenable. First, recall our earlier observations about surprise. It seems we can be pleasantly and unpleasantly surprised. Moreover, it seems that these two forms of surprise feel different. The surprise associated with winning the lottery feels much better than the surprise associated with discovering that a fire has decimated one's home.

This pair of examples shows that surprise can be a valent state and that the valence of surprise can vary, but I distrust the intuitions about phenomenology. If the lottery surprise feels better than fire surprise, it may be because lottery surprise is accompanied by bliss and fire surprise is accompanied by grief. The difference in feel is a difference is the phenomenology of an accompanying ap-

---

[9]One might wonder whether valence markers qualify as emotions in their own right. If they do, they are assuredly basic emotions. In chapter 4, I define a basic emotion as one that cannot be decomposed into other emotions. Valance markers do not decompose into other emotions, but they are constituents of all other emotions. Therefore, if valence markers qualify as emotions, they are the *only* basic emotions. This view has been defended by Frijda (1993). I do not think valence markers qualify as emotions. True emotions, I argued in chapter 3, represent core relational themes. If valence markers represent anything at all, they represent reminders to pursue or avoid certain situations. They are in the business of shaping behavior, not tracking organsim-environment relations. Valence markers are not appraisals.

praisal. Extreme cases of negative surprise (such as shock) do not obviously feel worse than extreme positive surprise (such as awe). The main difference is manifested in the fact that we tend to seek out situations that awe us and not those that shock us.

Another objection to the view that valence markers lack intrinsic feels comes from a well-known feature of pain. Pain is widely believed to be made up of two components: one sensory and the other affective (Melzack & Casey, 1968). The pain experience decomposes into a registration of pathology in the body (the sensory part) and an aversive feeling (the affective part). Ordinarily these two are inseparable, but they can come apart. When one endures an injury under the influence of morphine, for example, one will report feeling as if one were in pain but not minding it in the least. The experience of pain under morphine is apparently unlike the experience of pain under ordinary conditions, and that difference in feeling involves the presence of an affective state. It is tempting to believe that the affective component of ordinary pain experience is just a negative valence marker. If that were the case, it would be demonstrative evidence for valence having an intrinsic feel.

This pain objection can be answered in much the same way as the surprise objection. The feeling associated with the affective component of pain may derive from an embodied appraisal. It is possible that the affective component of pain is not simply a negative valence sate but a state of distress, which contains both an embodied appraisal and a negative valence marker. In chapter 6, I suggested that the physical distress may actually be a special case of anxiety. On this interpretation, pain feels bad because it contains anxiety, not because it is valent. The valence merely drives us to avoid pain-inducing situations. This explanation is consistent with the anatomy. The affective component of pain has been associated with activity in two familiar emotion regions, the anterior cingulate cortex and the insula (Berthier, Starkstein, & Leignarda, 1988; Rainville, Carrier, Hofbauer, Bushnell, & Duncan, 1999). Anterior cingulate cortex is also associated anxiety (Luu, Collins, & Tucker, 2000). There are also studies that show an interaction between pain and anxiety. Intensity of felt pain can increase if one is in an anxious state (e.g., Ploghaus et al., 2001). If pain contains anxiety, this is readily explained.

The strongest objection to the claim that valence has no intrinsic phenomenology comes from the apparent reality of pleasant and unpleasant feelings. If valence doesn't produce feelings of pleasantness and unpleasantness, what does? The feeling of pleasantness is the easier case. Most instances of pleasantness seem to involve some degree of joy. Joy, on my view, is an embodied appraisal, coupled with a positive valence marker. The feeling of pleasantness that seems to run through winning the lottery, seeing an old friend, running in the park, and doing well on one's chemistry final may all share a common core of joy.

The feeling of unpleasantness is more problematic. Negative emotions such as grief, disgust, and anger all involve their own embodied appraisals. The sense that they are all unpleasant cannot, on this view, reflect a common feeling that they all share. I do not think this is counterintuitive. We coclassify these emotions because they all lead to similar forms of aversive behavior. In particular, we tend to avoid all of these emotions and situations that lead to them. We do this because they all contain negatively reinforcing valence markers. There is no feeling of unpleasantness; there are just unpleasant feelings. Each of these unpleasant feelings feels quite different, but most of us try to avoid all of them.

I have been arguing that valence markers lack intrinsic feels. Hopefully, I have established that this position is tenable. But why, one might ask, should one reject the ostensibly appealing alternative? Is there any reason to deny that valence markers have intrinsic feels? My main motivation is introspective. Despite a strong intuition that there is a special feeling associated with unpleasantness, I cannot find anything that answers to this feeling when I introspect. When I mentally subtract away the feelings associated with the embodied appraisals of disgust, betrayal, and grief, I do not find any remainder. The foulness of disgust, the hopelessness of grief, and the stab of betrayal all strike me as different. Appeals to introspection are not strong arguments. Stronger support will come when I provide a theory of emotional consciousness in chapter 9.

### Conclusion: Emotions as Valent Embodied Appraisals

In chapter 4, I argued that emotions form a coherent class in virtue of the fact that all emotions contain embodied appraisals. The considerations presented in this chapter point toward a further source of coherence. All emotions contain valence markers. Putting these features together, one might say that all emotions are valent appraisals. Others have arrived at the same definition. It is precisely the definition offered by Ortony, Collins, and Clore (1988), but they equate appraisals with highly structured inner judgments rather than somatic states. On my view emotions are valent *embodied* appraisals.

Valence and appraisal hang together harmoniously. Appraisals represent relations that bear on well-being, but they do not represent such relations as bearing on well-being. Fear, for example, represents danger, but it does not represent the fact that danger is something that is undesirable. One can imagine being indifferent to danger. Appraisals represent things that matter to us, but they do not represent the fact that they matter. That's where valence markers come in. When one couples an embodied fear appraisal with a state that serves as a negative reinforcer, one represents the fact that the situation inducing the fear matters. Emotions without appraisals would lack content, and emotions without valence would have no punch. Repeating the metaphor from chapter 4, appraisal is the flavoring of our emotional states, and valence is the alcohol. Together, the two make up a tasty, intoxicating mix.

# 8

# A Typology of Affective States

I have argued that emotions form a coherent class. They are all valent embodied appraisals. Within that coherent class, however, it may be possible to identify important subcategories. Two such divisions have already been discussed. I distinguished basic and nonbasic emotions, and I distinguished positive and negative emotions. Other divisions within the category of emotions may be possible as well. In addition, it may be possible to distinguish emotions from other affective constructs, such as tickles, hungers, likes, and desires. In this chapter, I use the theory of emotions that I have been defending to map out the affective realm. I contend that all affective constructs can be characterized with reference to embodied appraisals and valence markers.

### *Further Distinctions Within the Class Emotion*

#### Attitudinal Emotions

In ordinary language, we have two very different ways of talking about emotions. On the one hand, we sometimes talk about emotions as if they are self-contained mental states. We say that Jones entered a state of fear after seeing a snake. Or the insulting remark sent Smith into an angry rage. In these cases, the object that caused the emotion may play little role after the emotion is under way. The emotion has a life of its own. On the other hand, we sometimes talk about emotions as if they were parts of more complex mental states. We say Jones was frightened of the snake, and Smith was angry about the insult. Locutions of this kind also include cases where emotion terms are used in conjunctions with that-clauses. We say that Jones was afraid that the snake would bite, and Smith was angry that someone insulted her. In these cases, we cannot fully separate the emotion from its particular object. Fear-of-snakes and fear-that-the-snake-will-bite seem to comprise unified wholes. They decompose into constituent parts—a fear and a representation of a particular object—but those parts hang together. If seeing a snake triggers a fear state, that fear state can remain after the experience of the snake subsides. If, on the other hand, Jones is afraid that a snake will bite, the fear in question disappears only after thoughts of being bitten subside.

I will use the term "state emotions" to label emotions that can persist as self-contained states. Those that are parts of larger wholes can be called "attitudinal emotions." Attitudinal emotions are ways of construing objects or states of affairs emotionally. This distinction, marked by ordinary language, corresponds to a real division in our affective lives. Much of what I have said in earlier chapters applies most naturally to state emotions. I have yet to provide a full account of attitudinal emotions.

One natural proposal is that attitudinal emotions are dispositions. Wollheim (1999) argues that all emotions are dispositions, and he distinguishes dispositions from states. Emotions can give rise to pangs and other bodily feelings (see also Ryle, 1949), which are states, but these are best regarded as effects of emotions rather than the emotions themselves. This analysis is clearly at odds with the story I have been defending. If emotions are embodied appraisals, then emotions are states, and they are states that can be consciously experienced in the form of bodily feelings. The apparent conflict between these two accounts can be reconciled by saying that Wollheim's story correctly characterizes attitudinal emotions, while the embodied appraisal theory correctly characterizes emotion states. Fearing that one will be bitten by a snake is a disposition, while fear caused by seeing a snake is a state.

This has a plausible ring, but it is too vague to assess. What kind of dispositions are attitudinal emotions? To what do they dispose us? One possibility is that attitudinal emotions are dispositions to behave in certain ways. Fear of snakes involves, on this analysis, a disposition to avoid snakes. This cannot do on its own. The disposition to avoid snakes is not sufficient for the snake fear.[1] Imagine someone who is incapable of experiencing fear due to a brain injury. Such a person might nevertheless realize that snakes pose a physical threat, and she may desire to avoid physical threats (not out of fear but out of the anticipated pleasure of a healthy, long life). This would result in a disposition to avoid snakes but not, ex hypothesi, fear of snakes. If attitudinal emotions are dispositions, they must be dispositions, in part, to have certain kinds of experiences. Dispositional fear must be a disposition to enter fear states, which, I have argued, can be identified with embodied appraisals.

This coheres with a proposal I advanced in chapter 4. Confronted with the objection that some emotions may not be associated with bodily perturbations, I ar-

---

[1]Neither is a behavioral dispositional necessary for snake fear. One can be afraid of snakes while not having the slightest idea what to do about that fear.

gued that they must at least be associated with the disposition to undergo bodily perturbations. I gave the example of longstanding jealousy concerning the fidelity of one's lover. Like fear of snakes, this is an attitudinal emotion. The argument that longstanding jealousy is a disposition to undergo somatic perturbations is just a special case of the more general observation that attitudinal emotions are inextricably bound to embodied appraisals.

The dispositional account of emotions requires a couple of embellishments. First, it must be emphasized that only nonoccurrent attitudinal emotions are dispositions. When an attitudinal emotion is actively entertained (e.g., when one experiences fear of snakes), an embodied appraisal is activated.

Second, attitudinal emotions, unlike state emotions, do not consist of embodied appraisals alone. Earlier I said that they seem to form wholes together with representations of their particular objects. When one is angry about an insult, one's thought about that insult is not merely a cause of one's anger, it is part of one's anger. This can be explained by saying that attitudinal emotions contain both embodied appraisals (or dispositions to embodied appraisals) and representations of objects or states of affairs. These two components are bound together in the mind. The actual nature of the binding has not been adequately investigated. Perhaps emotions are bound to representations of their particular objects via neural mechanisms like those that bind together components of a complex percept. A leading proposal is that such binding is achieved by synchronized firing of the relevant neural populations (Singer & Gray, 1995). In the case of attitudinal emotions, the proposal would be that the neural representation of an emotional bodily state fires at the same time as the neural realization of the representation of its particular object. However this binding is achieved, it must obey the right dependency relation. When an attitudinal emotion arises, the embodied appraisal (or appraisal disposition) must be caused by the representation of the particular object and, once caused, must be linked with that representation, so that the two persist simultaneously.[2]

Wollheim is right to observe that some emotions are dispositions. Nonoccurrent attitudinal emotions fall into this ontological category. But Wollheim is

----

[2]De Sousa (1987) has a more fine-grained taxonomy of emotion objects. For example, rather than talking of particular objects, he distinguishes the target of an emotion (an object toward which it is directed) from the property of that target that is especially implicated by the emotion. He also notes that some emotions are typically directed at propositions rather than, say, individual objects. My discussion of attitudinal emotions is most easily related to these latter cases, but it can easily be extended. Any adequate theory of how emotions get bound to other mental representations can explain bindings to various representations types. Variation in objects can be explained by variation in the representations to which emotions become bound. For example, if one is angry at a person for her political views, anger might be bound to a representation of that person and to a representation of the offensive views. There may be a contingency relation between these, such that anger toward the person subsides when the views change. These details would need to be worked out in any complete theory of how attitudes interrelate.

wrong to think that all emotions are dispositions. Occurrent attitudinal emotions and state emotions are not. Wollheim is also wrong to deny that dispositional emotions are dispositions to undergo bodily perturbations. This is precisely what they are, and, as a result, bodily perturbations are ontologically prior to dispositional emotions. Or more accurately, embodied appraisals, which are equivalent to state emotions, are ontologically prior. Attitudinal emotions only deserve to be called emotions because they contain actual or dispositional embodied appraisals. They are actual or potential emotions that have been linked to mental states representing particular objects.

Someone might object by declaring that attitudinal emotions are never mere dispositions. Solomon (1976) gives the example of enduring love. Imagine a man who declares he had been in love with his spouse every minute of every day since they first met. Clearly this man has not been experiencing an uninterrupted bodily perturbation all of that time. But neither can his situation be described as dispositional. A disposition is something that has not yet happened. If nonoccurrent emotions are dispositions, then there is a sense in which they should not count as emotions at all. They are potential emotions. On this analysis, long periods of love would be better described as occasional bouts of love. The man in Solomon's example has not really been in love, nonstop, for years. He has merely been disposed to be in love. This is counterintuitive.

This objection hinges on a faulty conception of dispositions. Dispositions are not mere potentialities. A disposition continues to exist even when it is not manifesting itself. Compare: the solubility of salt exists even when salt is not dissolving, because it is realized in some ever-present structural property of salt. Likewise, when one has an enduring love for another person, there is always, at every moment, a mental structure that represents that person in a way that disposes one to feel butterflies in one's stomach. The butterflies do not endure, but the representation that serves to trigger them does. It is as enduring as one's belief that the Earth orbits the sun. We do not entertain this belief at every moment, but it resides, uninterrupted in long-term memory. Likewise, attitudinal emotions are present, when nonoccurrent, in the form of enduring dispositions, concretely realized in the circuitry of the brain.

## Moods

Moods seem to be very similar to emotions. Moods often feel like emotions, they are named using some of the same words, and they have a comparable impact on thought and behavior. Like emotions, moods also seem to be decidedly nonpropositional. While moods may promote certain judgments (think of the depressive who judges that the everything is going wrong), no particular judgment seems to constitute a mood. Depression feels more like a somatic state; the body feels sluggish and drained. This raises the hypothesis that moods, like emotions, are embodied appraisals. The hypothesis is bolstered by the systematic correspondence between emotions and moods. For every mood, there apparently is a closely related emotion. Depression is related to sadness, free-floating anxiety is related to fear, and irritability is related to anger.[3]

Despite such obvious parallels, many people have the intuition that moods and emotions differ. So we are left with a challenge. We must explain the similarities between emotions and moods, while also preserving their differences. We need a mark of distinction that is consistent with a deep kinship. Three proposals appear again and again in the literature. The first invokes a temporal criterion: moods are just emotions that last for a long time. The second proposal appeals to dispositions: moods are dispositions to form emotions rather than emotions themselves (see Lormand, 1985). The third proposal involves intentionality: moods are like emotions, but they do not represent anything; one can be depressed without being depressed about anything in particular (Armon-Jones, 1989; Frijda, 1994; Sizer, 2000). I do not think that these proposals hold up to scrutiny. I consider them in turn.

Several emotion researchers have raised doubts about the temporal criterion. It cannot draw a boundary between emotions and moods. Lazarus (1994) argues, on the one hand, that some emotions are enduring. He gives the example of a couple who have an argument in the morning, and the argument gives rise to anger that subsides somewhat during the workday and then returns when they are reunited in the evening. Davidson (1994) speculates, on the other hand, that some moods are short-lived. He does not give an example, but one can imagine a situation in which one is sent into a gloomy state after peering out a window at a gray sky, only to have gloom interrupted by a welcome phone call from an old friend. The claim that moods are just long-lasting emotions does not hold up.

One can also raise doubts about the suggestion that moods are dispositions to have emotions. For one thing, the dispositional criterion makes it difficult to distinguish moods from sentiments and from nonoccurrent attitudinal emotions. The latter two are dispositions as well. There is, however, an apparent difference. One might propose that moods are dispositions to feel emotions toward lots of different particular objects, whereas sentiments and attitudinal emotions always have a single particular object or a single kind of particular object. If you hate Spielberg films (a sentiment), you will tend to respond negatively to Spielberg films. If you are in an irascible mood, you will tend to respond negatively towards anything that comes your way. John Updike (1965) gives another example in one of his short stories:

> Men traveling alone develop a romantic vertigo. Bech had already fallen in love with a freckled Embassy wife in Prague, a buck-toothed chanteuse in Rumania, a

---

[3]In this discussion I will periodically use emotional disorders as examples of moods. I regard depression an anxiety as moods. There are different accounts of what makes a mood count as a disorder. Their status as such may derive from the fact that they are inappropriate for their circumstances, harmful, or indicative of a biological dysfunction.

> stolid Mongolian sculptress in Kazakhstan. In the Tretyakov Gallery he had fallen
> in love with an entire roomful of girls. (p. 221)

Bech's romantic vertigo would be a mood on this proposal. It is a generalized
disposition to experience falling-in-love (an emotion). If moods are generalized
emotion dispositions, they can be distinguished from sentiments and nonoccurrent attitudinal emotions

The problem with this proposal is that moods can be occurrent. Depression, for
example, is notoriously miserable to endure. The misery is painfully present to
those who suffer from it. It is not merely a disposition to feel sad. Likewise, we
can imagine someone who is struck by an aching sense of ennui, or someone
who is bubbling with manic elation, or someone who is feeling blushingly bash-
ful, or grumblingly sulky. These can all be moods, but they are not dispositions
or emotional consequences of dispositions. They are occurrent states, through and
through.

According to the third proposal mentioned earlier, moods are like emotions
that lack intentional objects. This proposal avoids the implausible claim that
moods must be dispositions, while capturing the idea that they are generalized.
Perhaps moods seem to attach themselves to anything and everything precisely
because they are really about nothing at all.

I think the intentionality criterion is untenable, but it may point us in the right
direction. As I have argued, any mental state that has the function of being reliably caused by something can be said to represent that thing. If moods have such
a function, then they are intentional states. This supposition is highly plausible.
Moods do not occur at random. While they can be induced by diet, weather, hormones, and other seemingly arbitrary elicitors, they can also be caused by a life
event. One may go through a depression after the death of a loved one, the end
of a marriage, or the loss of a job. Even some of the chemical causes of depression may involve loss. Bad weather, for example, may be a sign that external
conditions will diminish access to valuable resources. Therefore, moods may represent just what corresponding emotions represent, and they may be caused
by the very same events. Ekman (1994) points out that moods are often induced
by episodes in which a corresponding emotion is strongly felt and repeatedly
experienced.

One might try to patch things up by saying that moods lack *particular* objects,
even though they have *formal* objects. They are intentional in only one of two
possible senses. Depression is about loss, but it isn't about any particular loss. I
do not think this saves the intentionality proposal. First, certain emotions (what I
called state emotions) lack particular objects as well. Second, it is at least an
open possibility that moods can have particular objects. We often use locutions
such as "Smith was depressed about her failing relationship."

The difference between emotions and moods should be captured by *what* they
represent, not *whether* they represent. Lazarus (1994) proposes that moods are
appraisals of the "existential background" of our lives. Less cryptically, moods

represent how we are doing in life overall (see also Lyons, 1980).[4] They may be induced by specific events, but their function is to inform us about how we are faring in general. I think this proposal is correct.

Emotions and moods can have the same particular objects. Sadness and depression can both be caused by the loss of a job. There is also a sense in which they represent the same formal objects. Formal objects, as I defined them, are the properties in virtue of which an emotion is caused. Both sadness and depression are caused by the same property, namely loss. The difference in what they represent has to be explicated by introducing a new term. Let me call the ontological class of things to which a term applies, the ontic object of that term. "Ontic object" refers to the kind of things that exhibit the property comprising the formal object of a term. Proper names refer to individuals, general nouns refer to properties or classes of individuals, temporal terms refer to periods of time, mathematic terms refer to abstracta, and so on. Emotions and moods have slightly different ontic objects.

Emotions refer to specific things or situations. Moods refer to things or situations quite generally. A properly applied emotion corresponds to a local occurrence, and a properly applied mood applies to a global condition. Emotions respond to isolated objects and events, whereas moods respond to one's general standing in the world. The difference is subtle but significant. Sadness represents a particular loss, while depression represents a losing battle. Fear represents a specific danger, whereas an anxious mood represents general peril. Anger represents a demeaning offense, while irritability represents the general offensiveness of the world. The formal objects are essentially the same, but the ontic objects differ.

One might object to this analysis by appeal to cases of moods that have particular objects. I mentioned the case of being depressed about a failing relationship. On the face of it, this looks like a mood that is directed toward a specific object rather than a general pattern. Fortunately, another interpretation is available. A failing relationship can certainly lead one to the conclusion that things are not going well over all. Access to intimacy, one of life's most central treasures, is in peril. When one is depressed about a failing relationship one is in a state that represents the generalized loss that results from that failing relationship. One can be both sad and depressed about the same particular object. The difference is that sadness represents its object as an isolated loss, while depression represents its object as bearing on one's general position in life.

This account makes sense of a curious fact. Some events elicit very strong emotions without inducing moods. For example, the "road rage" one feels after

---

[4]As an alternative to his nonintentionality thesis, Frijda (1994) occasionally suggests that moods can be construed as referring to everything. He sees these two extremes, moods refer to everything or moods refer to nothing, as similar in spirit. The suggestion that moods refer to everything may sound similar to Lazarus's proposal on the surface, but the two should not be confused. Lazarus regards moods as having the function of registering our general standing in life. He does not say moods represent everything.

being cut off on the highway is often intense but short-lasting. Other events, such as losing one's job, tend to elicit both a strong emotion and an enduring mood. The asymmetry can be explained by the fact that job loss, unlike discourtesy on the highway, can be construed as evidence that one is not faring well in life. Job loss marks a potential reduction in access to essential resources, not just a difficulty in the here and now.

If moods represent how one is faring in life, duration may play a role in the emotion/mood distinction after all. Emotions are responses to immediate challenges, and moods are responses to challenges that can be enduring. Thus, even if the duration criterion does not always apply to the length of affective states themselves, it may apply to the length of the core relational themes they represent. Emotions represent short-lasting relations to the environment, and moods represent long-lasting relations to the environment. This explains why moods tend to be longer lasting and less tied to specific elicitors, without saying that moods must be long-lasting or lacking in intentional content.

The account may also explain why moods are sometimes thought to be dispositions. Depression may dispose one to feel sad because it is a representation of the fact that life has been chronically disappointing. In situations that elicit such generalized appraisals, more specific appraisals are often likely to occur. An occurrent and intensely felt mood captures a general outlook that provides fertile breeding ground for congruent emotions.

In sum, the account of mood that I borrow from Lazarus explains intuitions motivating other theories of mood without the drawbacks of those theories. This argues strongly in favor of Lazarus's account. But, one might wonder, how can I adapt that account? Lazarus defends a cognitive theory of affect, and I do not. How does an embodied appraisal come to represent how things are faring overall? On the theory of intentionality I favor, a mental state represents whatever it has the function of detecting. Now suppose an affective state is caused by getting fired and another is caused by getting cut off on the road. Both involve the same bodily states. What distinguishes one from the other? What makes the former a mood and the latter an emotion? On Lazarus's theory, the difference can be explained by appeal to inner judgments. In one case, the victim judges that she has been threatened by a particular event, and in the other, she judges that she is threatened in a more global way. I do not want to equate emotions with judgments, so this explanation is not available to me.

The solution I offer begins with the assumption that emotions and moods are set up for different purposes. Emotions are set up to detect localized changes in organism-environment relations, and moods are set up to detect more global changes. This difference should lead to differences in the functional roles played by moods and emotions. If emotions and moods are set up to detect slightly different ontic objects, they should also be used in somewhat different ways by the mind-brain. The functional globality of moods has been emphasized in the literature on neurochemical changes and dysregulation in mood disorder. Griffiths (1989) says moods can be characterized in terms of chemically driven, global changes in state transition probabilities. Emotions, in contrast, may involve more localized changes, which pertain to processing that is related to their particular objects.

The global/local contrast brings to mind various empirically testable functional differences between emotions and moods. I give two examples. First, an affective state that is set up to detect global changes should be sensitive to trends. A creature with emotions, but no moods, would fail to pick up on general trends. It would be no more apprehensive after a tenth threat than after a first threat in the same environment. A creature with moods, but no emotions, would not experience fear when it faced an immediate physical threat, but it might experience an apprehensive mood after a series of threats in its environment. Such creatures do not exist, as far as we know, but the difference leads to testable predictions. In addition to affective states caused by a single event, there should be affective states caused by repeated affective states.

Second, an affective state that is set up to detect global changes should exert a special kind of influence on planning. Some threats can be dealt with immediately. Others require long-term strategies. We can think of the planning systems in the mind as a collection of hierarchically organized to-do lists. At one end of the hierarchy, there is a temporary work pad for upcoming actions. On the other end, we list our major objectives in life. One list contains plans about where to eat breakfast tomorrow, another contains such things as ongoing projects, a third contains career goals, and a forth contains information about what kinds of people we want to be. Emotions give rise to plans on the most immediate list, but moods can go higher up the scale. General anxiety may give rise to general wariness, which is more like an ongoing project than an immediate goal. If this hypothesis is correct, then we might expect to find differential effects of emotions and moods on levels in the planning hierarchy. Where emotions may cause us to reprioritize immediate goals, moods may cause us to reprioritize long-term goals.

Both of these proposals concerning the functional role of moods also help to explain why moods may have subtly different semantic properties than emotions. First consider the point about trends. If moods can be caused by repeated emotions, then they can represent a global feature of well-being. Anxiety caused by the distant sound of a predator (emotional anxiety) may represent an impending danger, while anxiety caused by several instances of anxiety (mood anxiety) represents a general pattern of dangerousness. Now consider the point about goal hierarchies. Affective states can be triggered by the outcome of goals (Oatley & Johnson-Laird, 1987). The affective states that come about in this way may have different semantic properties, depending on the hierarchical level of the precipitating goal outcome. The affective state caused by the failure of an immediate goal may differ in content from the affective state caused by the failure of a long-term goal. If one fails to achieve one's goal of being a good parent, the resulting emotion may represent that things are not going well overall. Good parenting is an encompassing aspiration, not an ephemeral demand.

These points can be summarized by saying that moods and ordinary emotions

have somewhat different functional roles. They were set up for different purposes. Moods are affective states that are set up to detect facts about how one is
faring overall. They succeed in reliably detecting such facts partially in virtue of
their tendency to be caused by trends and by outcomes of longstanding goals.
The difference between moods and emotions can be explained without appealing
to inner judgments. The affective state caused by getting fired (as opposed to getting cut off on the road) does not count as a mood in virtue of an explicit judge-
ment that the event has global ramifications for well-being. That state is a mood
because the getting fired clashes with a career goal, which, by its very nature, is
positioned high up in a goal hierarchy. I am proposing that our mind-brains avail
themselves of engineering shortcut. We are wired to experience moods when
longstanding goals are met or thwarted (and when we detect affective trends)
without explicitly judging that the outcome has global implications. Judgments
are unnecessary.

If this account is correct, the moods and emotions are distinct, but the distinction is very subtle. Both are valent embodied appraisals. Like emotions, moods
represent core relational themes. Depression represents the cup of life as half
empty. Moods are also valent. Depression is negatively reinforcing. One tends to
avoid those situations that have caused depression in the past. For example,
a person who had a depressing childhood may avoid the town in which she
grew up.

Emotions and moods differ only in the scope of their intentional contents. If
emotions are defined as valent embodied appraisals, then moods qualify as a special class of emotions. This explains why these two constructs are so closely
linked in folk psychology. It makes sense of the fact that moods and emotions are
often named by the same words. We can be irritated, elated, or sad about specific
elicitors or about life in general. I am inclined to conclude that moods are just a
special case of emotions. They are not an independent category. There is a sharp
distinction between moods and emotions that are not moods but no sharp distinction between moods and emotions. Moods are to emotions as sedans are to
cars. Every manufacturer makes a model with four doors. Wherever I have said
that emotions differ from moods, in the foregoing discussion, it would have been
better to say emotions that are not moods differ from emotions that are moods.
This way of talking honors the deep connection between moods and emotions,
while acknowledging the differences.

### Other Affective Constructs

#### Sentiments

There are, however, a variety of other affective constructs that seem to share
much in common with emotions but fail to qualify as emotions. I will explore
some of these other constructs here, and I will argue that they can be best understood by appeal to embodied appraisals. Let me begin with sentiments.

The term "sentiments" was once used as a synonym for emotions. It is now sometimes used in a more restrictive sense, to refer to states such as likes and dislikes. These, in turn, are often construed as affective dispositions. As a first stab, liking something is being disposed to feel certain emotions about that thing. If you like something, interactions with it should cause joy or other positive affects. Conversely for dislikes.

In this regard, sentiments are a lot like nonoccurrent attitudinal emotions. Both are dispositions. But there are two important differences. First, nonoccurrent attitudinal emotions can become occurrent. When one's longstanding jealousy toward one's spouse is sparked, one experiences a state of jealousy. But there are no states of liking and disliking. One cannot enter into a state of dislike. Sentiments exist only as dispositions. When those dispositions manifest themselves, it is an emotion that one experiences, not a sentiment.

On the face of it, it seems odd that we restrict the term "sentiment" to dispositions, whereas attitudinal emotions can exist as either dispositions or as occurrent emotions. This convention is less arbitrary than it appears. A second difference between nonoccurrent attitudinal emotions and sentiments is that the latter can manifest themselves in a variety of different emotional states. If you like someone, then you experience joy in her presence. But you may also experience amusement when she makes a joke, excitement when anticipating your next encounter, sadness when you are apart, distress when she is harmed, and so forth. If you dislike someone, you may experience anger, disgust, or contempt in her presence. You may even experience *Schadenfreude* when she falls victim to misfortune.

Some English words are systematically ambiguous between emotions and sentiments. "Love" and "hate" are excellent examples (see Frijda, 1994). One can enter a state of love or harbor a dispositional love for another person. In these contexts, love is an emotion. But one often says things like "I love peanut butter" or "I love rainy days." Here there is no specific emotion at work but a complex of different dispositional emotions. One may find rainy days joyful, desirous, tranquil, and so forth. Likewise, one can experience hate as an emotion. One can enter states of loathing, for example. Here, hate may be a special form of anger, calibrated to whole persons rather than to specific acts. But one can also say "I hate peanut butter," or "I hate rainy days." Here hate is a disposition to experience a variety of different emotions.

Frijda explains this ambiguity in our terms by pointing out that sentiments often dispose us to experience emotions that go by the same name. The sentiment of love may involve the disposition to experience love. I think this is a reasonable analysis. I differ from Frijda only in underscoring the fact that sentiments may dispose us to experience a variety of different emotions.

If this analysis is correct, sentiments and emotions are different kinds of states. They get blurred together in ordinary talk, but we would be wise to keep them apart. Sentiments are dispositions to have emotions. Because emotions can be dispositional, sentiments sometimes manifest themselves as second-order dispositions. Liking someone can be a disposition to take dispositional pleasure in her presence.

Despite these subtle differences between emotions and sentiments, it should be obvious that sentiments inherit their affectivity from emotions. They are affective constructs only insofar as they manifest themselves as emotions. Therefore, a theory of sentiments can be constructed from the basic building blocks of emotion theory. Sentiments bottom out in embodied appraisals.

## Valent Bodily States

In chapter 7, I concluded that emotions are valent embodied appraisals. That definition may be accused of overextending the folk category of emotion. It seems to fall prey to an argument I presented in chapter 4. There I rejected the proposal that emotions can be defined as irruptive motivations. Being an irruptive motivation is not sufficient for being an emotion. I made this case by appeal to fatigue. Fatigue is an irruptive motivation but not an emotion. My definition of emotions faces the same counterexample. On the face of it, fatigue is a valent embodied appraisal. It is negatively reinforcing ("Stop going, and get some rest"), it is embodied (feeling sluggish), and it represents a core relational theme ("I have not received adequate rest").

Parallel worries arise for certain bodily sensations. Pains, itches, tickles are all valent, and they certain involve changes in somatic condition. My definition of emotions has difficulty distinguishing all these states from emotions. It seems to cast the net too wide.

This concern can be put to rest by observing a semantic difference between fatigue and bodily sensations on the one hand and emotions on the other. Emotions involve bodily states, but they do not represent bodily states. They use bodily states to represent organism-environment relations. Fear, for example, uses the body to represent danger. In the language of chapter 3, fear has bodily states as nominal contents, not real contents. Now consider fatigue. Fatigue represents a bodily state; it has the function of detecting insufficient rest. Fatigue has a bodily state as its real contents and as its nominal contents. Fatigue is valent, but it is not an appraisal.

The semantic difference that I am proposing finds further support in the fact that emotions can typically be caused by a broad range of stimuli, perceived through a broad range of senses. We become afraid when we see, hear, or smell things. If fear represented a bodily state, it would not regularly require some external cause, perceived through externally directed sense. In contrast, fatigue is generally elicited by a condition that originates within the body. The same can be said about tickles. They may be valent, but they are not appraisals. Tickles are feelings that represent a distinctive bodily state (a pattern of excitation in cutaneous receptors).

This is not to say that emotions cannot represent conditions that involve the body. Emotions are very flexible, after all. Through calibration, an emotion can become a detector for an endless number of distinct properties. Some of these properties may relate to the body. Suppose Jones becomes happy whenever she walks in warm sand. Suppose that this feeling is so satisfying to her that she thinks of it often and seeks it out. Over time, a mental calibration file might be set up to link tactile encounters with warm sand to happiness. The happiness triggered by that file takes on a new meaning. It becomes feeling-of-warm-sand-on-feet happiness, just as *Schadenfreude* qualifies as other-people-are-suffering happiness. Jones's foot happiness represents a condition that involves bodily stimulation; it represents a sensation in her foot. But it does not just represent that sensation. It represents the relationship that the sensation has to Jones. It represents the fact that feeling warm sand on her feet satisfies a goal of hers. The somatosensory state she has when she walks on warm sand represents the physical state, but her emotional response represents a core relational theme that happens to include that physical state as a necessary component.

This example helps to understand the case of pain. In chapter 7, I said that pain may contain anxiety as a component part. This anxiety has been calibrated (presumably by evolution) to cases of physical pathology. Consequently, it is a pathology detector. It is reliably caused by physical pathologies. But it is not caused by pathology alone. It is caused by a relational property that has pathology as one of its relata. The anxiety in pain represents the dangerousness of pathology. It represents pathology-danger. On this analysis, pain is comprised of two components that are semantically distinct. The sensory aspect of pain represents disease or injury, while the affective component represents the danger posed by that pathological condition. If we ask "Is pain an emotion?" the answer is no. Pain is a complex state that *contains* an emotion. But it also contains a state that represents a bodily condition. If this analysis is correct, pain is slightly different from fatigue and tickles. Fatigue and tickles do not contain emotions; they just represent bodily conditions. All of these states are valent, but none satisfy the definition of emotion that I have been defending.

## Motivations

Motivations are the final affective constructs that I will consider. Motivations include states such as hunger, thirst, and the urge for sex. These are primitive motivations, because we are genetically predisposed to acquire them, and they serve fundamental life functions. The primitive motivations used to be called drives (after Woodworth, 1918), but the term "motivation" has gained currency. The class of motivations may extend beyond the biologically fundamental cases to include a variety of other urges and impulses. An urge to have a cigarette would probably fall in the same category. There may even be mechanisms that unite these simple cases with the urge to see a movie or the impulse to go on a shopping spree. All of these may be motivations in the same sense. Like emotions, motivations make us cease or continue acting. This suggests that they contain valence markers.

This does not mean that motivations are emotions. To see the difference, one might begin by noting that fatigue is a motivation. Fatigue compels us to seek rest, just as hunger compels us to eat. But fatigue is not an emotion. At the end of chapter 5, I suggested that fatigue differs from emotions semantically. It represents a state of the body, not a core relational theme. The same can be said of hunger, thirst, and sex drive. They represent something like undernourishment, dehydration, and arousal, respectively. It is tempting to define motivations as valent representations of bodily states. Unfortunately, the definition is inadequate. As I just showed, tickles and pains are also valent representations of bodily states, but they do not fit into the folk category of motivations. Being about the body is not a sufficient condition for being a motivation.

Neither is it a necessary condition. The class of motivations crosscuts the class of valent bodily states. It extends to include nonbodily drives and urges. There is a kinship between hunger and the generic states that we call "wants." People can want all sorts of things. We want food and sex, but we also want friendship, entertainment, success, intellectual stimulation, free time, and so on. Like hunger, wanting drives us to act. Both can be construed as negatively valent. Wants seek their own destruction by compelling us to satisfy them. If wants are motivations, then there can be motivations that do not necessarily represent the body. It may be theoretically costly to restrict motivations to body-directed states, because the kinship between hunger and wants cries out for explanation. We need a more general way of defining what motivations are and characterizing how they differ from other affective constructs.

Plutchik (1984, p. 214) offers an inventory of contrasts between emotions and motivations:

1. Motivations, unlike emotions, are aroused endogenously.
2. Motivations, unlike emotions, are aroused in the *absence* of survival-related events (e.g., we get hungry when food is absent).
3. Motivations, unlike emotions, are naturally directed at a very narrow range of objects (e.g., food and water).
4. Motivations, unlike emotions, occur before a search process, not after an evaluation.
5. Motivations, unlike emotions, often occur on rhythmic schedules, not after randomly occurring environmental events.

This list is an improvement over the suggestion that motivations are about the body. Paradigm cases of primitive motivations, such as hunger, generally satisfy every item. Nevertheless, Plutchik's list fails to cleave a sharp boundary between emotions and motivations.

The first distinction, that motivations are caused endogenously, is not always true. The sight of a potential sexual partner can cause a feeling of sexual attraction. The sight of a succulent fruit can spark hunger. People with anterograde amnesia, who cannot lay down new memories, will happily eat meal after meal if they think they haven't eaten yet (Rozin, Dow, Moscovitch, & Rajaram, 1998).

This point also counts against the second criterion: motivations can be triggered when we confront survival-related events (such as the hunger sparked by the sudden availability of food). Nor would it help to say that motivations represent absence, for emotions in the sadness family do as well.

Plutchik's third criterion, that motivations are narrower in range, is also open to challenge. Both emotions and motivations may begin, ontogenetically, with a narrow range, but both can expand considerably. If motivations include urges, cravings, and impulses, then their range is quite unlimited. This observation casts doubt on Plutchik's fifth criterion as well. Many of our urges and wants do not occur on rhythmic schedules. In fact, some primitive motivations are not rhythmic either. Human sex drive is a possible case in point.

Plutchik's fourth criterion can be divided into two parts: motivations do not follow evaluations, and motivations precipitate search. Both points are problematic. Motivations can follow evaluations (as when a craving follows the judgment "Now that looks tasty!"), and motivations do not always precipitate search (as when the object of one's want is already present). One might try to weaken the search criterion by suggesting that motivations impel us to search when and only when their objects are absent. This may be a necessary condition on motivations, but it is far from sufficient. It is equally true of many emotions. Fear impels us to seek safety when safety is absent, and love impels us to pursue to objects of our affection when she or he is absent.

At this impasse, one might simply concede that the line between emotions and motivations is blurred. Perhaps certain motivations, such as wants, straddle both sides of the fence. Perhaps all emotions really count as motivations, insofar as they are valent, and valence markers impel us to act. This would not be a terribly infelicitous conclusion.

Still, I think there is a theoretically useful way to draw a distinction between emotions and motivations. I want to begin by drawing another distinction—a distinction between motivations and motives. A motive provides a reason for action, and a motivation is that which impels us to act. I think that all emotions are motives. Being angry provides a reason, ceteris paribus, to attack. Being afraid provides a reason, ceteris paribus, to flee. But emotions are not always motivations. They do not always succeed in impelling us. One can be angry, it seems, without being disposed to revenge, and one can be afraid without being disposed to flee. In contrast, one cannot be hungry without being disposed to eat. The link between emotion and action tendencies is weaker than the link between motivations and action.

This difference can be brought out by reflecting further on the relationship between emotions and behavior. Some researchers have assumed that emotions simply are action tendencies. This tradition extends from Aristotle to contemporary researchers such as Frijda. I think the link between emotion and behavior is somewhat looser that these authors would have us believe. Consider anger. When a person is insulted, her skin may flush, her heart may accelerate, and her muscles may tense. These changes facilitate aggressive response, but they fall short of a disposition to revenge. Instead, it would be better to regard the changes as action *enabling*. The somatic component of an emotion prepares us for action, and the valence marker disposes us to act. In the case of anger, our bodies are prepared for aggression, and the valence marker tells us that we should maintain that state (positive valence) or change that state (negative valence). At this point in processing, no action has been selected, no strategy has been determined, no plan has been conceived. The somatic state and valence marker must be fed into a mental system that selects responses. Among the available responses is violent revenge against the source of our anger. The state of anger increases the probability of this response, but it is not constituted by this response. The decision to seek revenge is a choice that *follows* anger. Once that choice has been made, we can say there is action tendency at work. The action tendency is not itself a motive for action. It is a motivation. An active plan to seek revenge is an urge or a want; it is like hunger. On this analysis, emotions are motives. One can even describe emotions as motivating, because they drive us to select courses of action. In other words, emotions lead to motivations. But they are not to be identified with motivations. I think T. S. Eliot understood this when commenting on love in his poem "Burnt Norton." Eliot writes, "Love is itself unmoving / Only the cause and end of movement."

Now consider hunger. Earlier I tentatively proposed that hunger is a negatively valent representation of undernourishment. If this were correct, hunger would count as a motive, not a motivation. Further reflection suggests that hunger involves something more. Hunger actually commands us to eat. It is associated with cellular response in the lateral hypothalamus, which regulate eating behavior. Stimulation in this region causes us eat, and damage causes us to stop eating. If a person simply had a negatively valent representation of her undernourishment, say an unpleasant sensation of an empty gut, we would not necessarily say she was hungry. If we did use the term "hunger" here, it would be used in a different sense; it would not refer to a motivation. Ordinarily, "hunger" refers to a negatively valent representation of undernourishment *coupled* with an impulse to eat.

Put differently, hunger involves three things: a representation of a bodily condition, a valence marker, and an action command. The valence marker applies to the body representation. It says "Less of this!" Some subsystem is then assigned the task of coping with this command. Under usual conditions, that subsystem will address the situation by issuing another command, "Eat!" The compound state is hunger. Once hunger sets in, other subsystems search for strategies that will satisfy the behavior command, such as "Forage!" "Go to the refrigerator!" "Go to the deli!" and so on.

These points can be summarized by saying that emotions and motivations have a different imperative structure. Emotions contain valence markers, which are commands to change or sustain internal states. We generally regulate internal states by regulating behavior. Motivations do that work. They specify action goals rather than inner state goals. Valence tells us to change how we are feeling, and motivation tells us to change how we are acting. Motivation often issues action commands very abstractly. If one wants success, the motivation may be comprised by the command, "Seek success!" Using language from earlier in this chapter, this command belongs to a high level in a goal hierarchy. Many other decisions must be made before such a command translates into actual behavior.

Emotion and motivation are difficult to tease apart, because they tend to come together. Emotions often cause motivations, and motivations are often caused by emotions. Anger can cause a motivation to aggress. Hunger can be caused by distress about a lack of food. The link between affect and action is tight but not unbreakable. Berridge (1996) provides evidence that one can separate the affective component of hunger from the action-driving component. He calls the affective component "liking" and the action-driving component "wanting." Most of the time, we want those things that we like, and we like those things that we want. An animal that chooses to eat food will also find pleasure in doing so. But Berridge shows that liking and wanting are actually dissociable and, at least in the case of hunger, reside in different neural systems.

In rats, the liking system involves the shell of the nucleus accumbens, the ventral pallidum, and the brainstem region. Wanting involves the dopamine projection system from midbrain to nucleus accumbens. If one creates a lesion in the wanting system of a rat, the rat will not eat. It will starve to death. But if you force the same rat to eat agreeable food (e.g., something sweet) it will display behavior that suggests it enjoys the experience. It likes food, but it doesn't want food. Conversely, one can stimulate the wanting system to achieve wanting without liking. A rat in this condition will eat everything you give it, including foods that it dislikes. It will gorge itself on foods that cause it to display aversive reactions at every bite. Berridge compares this to addiction. Addicts often pursue their drug of choice even after that drug no longer induces pleasure.

Berridge's findings show that affect and action can be decoupled. This should come as no surprise, because many of our actions are performed without direct reward or punishment. Automatic behaviors, such as moving our legs in a particular sequence while walking, are a case in point. We do not experience a paroxysm of pleasure every time we place one foot before another. Only certain actions are motivated by hedonic considerations. I think the term "motivation" is best reserved for those cases.

Motivations are affectively motivated action commands. By affectively motivated, I mean that motivations are always initiated in response to an affective state. The affective state need not be an emotion. A negatively or positively valued body representation will do (e.g., a representation of dehydration or undernourshiment). An affective state is any state that contains a valence marker. Hunger is a motivation because it is driven by a valent response to undernourishment.

If motivations require affective causes, then Berridge's terminology is flawed. He refers to a dissociation between wanting and liking. Wanting is a motivation. On my analysis, wanting must always occur in the context of hedonic consequences (liking, hoping, fearing, etc.). When a command to eat is separated from pleasure, distress, or some other affective state, it is no longer a motivation. So I would say that Berridge's rats do not want to eat; they eat compulsively. They eat, despite not wanting to.[5]

One can distinguish two kinds of affectively motivated action commands. Some are driven by affective sates that an organism is experiencing *prior* to issuing the command. A command to eat that follows distress from undernourishment is an example. Other motivated action commands are driven by *anticipated* affective consequences. A command to eat may be driven by seeing delectable food. These two kinds of motivations are sometimes called pushes and pulls, respectively. We can be pushed to act by our inner states or pulled to act by features of our environment. Many of our actions are driven by both kinds of motivations. People are most likely to eat when they are both hungry and enticed by appealing food. The push/pull distinction helps review where Plutchik went wrong. Many of the features on his list are typical of motivations that push but not motivations that pull. The account I have been suggesting has greater breadth. It subsumes hungers and thirsts (primitive motivations) along with urges and simple wants.

It should be clear now that there is a way to draw a principled distinction between emotions and moods. Emotions are valent embodied appraisals. Motivations are action commands that are pushed or pulled by affective states. Motivations are often pushed or pulled by emotions. But when emotions cause motivations, those motivations never count as constitutive parts of emotions. The two constructs are thus closely entwined but independent.

### Concluding Remarks on Desire

By way of conclusion, I want to offer a few comments on desire. Desire has played a central role in philosophy. Philosophers often assume that human action is commonly driven by desires, working in concert with beliefs. We desire X, we believe we can get X by doing Y, so we do Y. Despite its centrality in action theory, however, desire is not well understood. There is no widely accepted account of what desires are. We now have the machinery on the table to address that question.

I think that desire is not a unitary construct. To desire something is, oftentimes, a motivation to attain it. On the account just offered, that means desire is an action command. If you have the desire to eat a good meal, eating a good meal will be entered as a goal state to the subsystems that guide your behavior. Barring impediments, auxiliary commands will then be rallied in place to satisfy that goal. You may go to the nearest purveyor of haut cuisine.

Yet desire cannot always be an action command. We sometimes us the word "desire" to describe our attitude toward things that we cannot strive to attain. One

---

[5] I would also quibble with Berridge's term "liking." He often seems to use "liking" as if it referred to a state rather than a sentiment (see discussion earlier).

might say *I desire good weather*. We cannot strive for good weather (except by prayer or travel), so this desire is not a motivation. "Desire," here, is a synonym for "hope." Both hope and desire, in the sense, are typically emotions. More accurately, they are attitudinal emotions—emotions that have been affixed to a representation of some particular object or event. Desire can also be a state emotion. The sumptuous contours of your lover's body may fill you with desire. In this concupiscent sense of the term, desire can even be a mood. A general appraisal to the affect that things are quite arousing overall—a kind of sexualizing stance toward the world.

Desire can also be a sentiment. It can be a disposition to feel various emotions if the desired state of affairs comes true. One may desire wealth in this sense. If wealth comes, one will be pleased; if it doesn't, one will be disappointed or even bitter.

If one wants to know how desire figures into the determination of action, one needs to be specific about what kind of desire one has in mind. Building a theory of action around desire, without such clarification, runs its risks. Construed as an emotion, desire is a motive, not a motivation. Qua motive, desire gives us a reason to act. It beckons us to make a decision. Qua motivation, desire directly drives us to act. One might say that emotional desires motivate motivations. The move from deliberation to action may require a move from emotional desires to motivation desires.

I offer these remarks as a cautionary note. Many of the words we use to describe affective constructs are polysemous.[6] In using these words, we must head distinctions within the affective realm. Emotions have a privileged place in that realm. They are causes or cores of every affective construct that I have discussed. In the remaining chapters, I will narrow my focus onto the emotions again, but the arguments therein clearly bear on kindred kinds.

---

[6]The word "want," which I have treated as naming a motivation, is as polysemous as "desire."

# 9

## *Emotional Consciousness*

### *Hidden Feelings*

#### The Case Against Unconscious Emotions

We are best acquainted with our emotions through the way they feel.[1] It feels like something to experience rage, joy, or despair. Some people hold that emotions simply are feelings and nothing more. This has never been an especially popular view in emotion research, but it sits well with many pretheoretical intuitions. The majority of contemporary researchers reject the simple equation of emotions and feelings. They emphasize thoughts, action tendencies, or physiological responses instead. On the view I have been defending, emotions are states that represent core relational themes by registering bodily changes. I join the majority in denying that emotions are mere feelings.

Yet it would be foolish to deny that emotions can be felt. Opponents of simplistic feeling theories often say too little about this topic. Up to now, I have said a lot about emotions, but I have said nothing about emotional feelings. This leaves my account incomplete. Emotional feelings must be explained, and they present the emotion research with a variety of questions. How does the brain give rise to emotional phenomenology? What do we feel when we feel an emotion? Why are emotions felt at all? Can emotions occur without feelings, that is, can they be unconscious? I address all of these questions in this chapter, beginning with the last.

The suggestion that emotions can occur unconsciously may strike some ears as odd. It is hard to imagine being in a state of rage, for example, without consciously experiencing it. But the difficulty in imagining such a situation cannot count as decisive evidence against it. In the last hundred years, we have all become acquainted with theories of mentality that afford a central role to unconscious activity. Freud may be credited with starting this trend. Under Freud's influence, most of us have come to believe that some of our actions are motivated

[1] Themes from this chapter are also discussed in Prinz (2003a).

by unconscious wishes. Since Freud, cognitive scientists have extended the range of unconscious states into less provocative domains. Unconscious processes abound in perception, memory encoding, motor control, and so on. Indeed, it is widely believed that the majority of brain activity is unavailable to consciousness. Information is processed behind the scenes. It has been suggested that consciousness encompasses only the *results* of information processing (Nisbett & Wilson, 1977). Consciousness is like a restaurant dining room: customers see only the final product of a meal that has been produced behind the kitchen door. We are forced to speculate about how the delicacies of experience were created.

With so much going on behind the scenes, one can't help entertaining the idea that emotions can occur unconsciously. When emotions are conscious, they influence behavior. A sudden bout of rage may cause one to yell out an obscenity. It is possible that behavior is driven by unconscious emotions as well. Returning to Freud, let's imagine the case of a man named Ed who marries a woman who reminds him of his mother. The explanation: Ed is in love with his mother but fails to realize this. He represses his incestuous love, but it still manages to influence his marital choice. Isn't this a case of unconscious emotion?

It is tempting to say that Ed is driven by hidden love, but there is another interpretation. Ed's love is perfectly conscious. What's hidden is the particular object of his love. Ed does not know that he loves his mother. Surely he knows that he is in love, however. Otherwise he would not elect to get married. On this interpretation, we repress the causes of our emotions but not the emotions themselves.

This proposal is consistent with many of Freud's own remarks. For example, in his discussions of free-floating anxiety, he says that the anxiety is conscious, sometimes devastatingly so, but its source had been concealed from view (1915/1984). Freud is the master of the unconscious, but he is reluctant to situate emotions in that hidden realm. He writes:

> It is surely the essence of emotion that we should be aware of it, i.e., that it should be known to consciousness . . . [But] it may happen that an affective or emotional impulse is perceived, but misconstrued. Owing to the repression of its proper representative it has been forced to become connected with another idea." (p. 179)

Freud distinguishes between two components: the judgments leading up to an emotion and the emotion itself. In the passage just quoted, he seems to say that the latter can be unconscious but the former cannot. Skepticism about unconscious emotions continues to this day. Clore (1994a) argues that emotions must be felt and that feelings are conscious by definition. Like Freud, he explains away apparent cases of unconscious emotions by appeal to unconscious emotion eliciting judgments. LeDoux (1994) also argues that there cannot be unconscious emotions, admitting only unconscious "emotion processes." LeDoux's term refers not to unconscious judgments, but to processes in primitive, preconscious brain structures that contribute to emotional response in humans and other animals.

Even some defenders of unconscious emotions seem to imply that *something* must be conscious when we have an emotion. Zajonc (1994) declares faith in unconscious emotions, but his view is not all that different from Clore's or LeDoux's. He defends unconscious emotions by arguing that affective responses (preferences and likings) can be influenced by subliminally perceived stimuli. This is good evidence for unconscious emotion elicitation but not unconscious emotions. To show the latter, Zajonc needs to show that the affective responses are unconscious as well. In his own experiments, however, those affective responses are measured by subjects' verbal reports and preference ratings, suggesting that they are conscious. Greenspan (1988) sometimes expresses faith in unconscious emotions, but her position seems close to Clore's as well. She defines emotions as evaluative thoughts coupled with primitive affects (pain and pleasure). The evaluative components can be unconscious, she says, but we always feel the pain or pleasure.[2] Strictly speaking, she should conclude only that emotions can be partially unconscious.

Why do so many researchers insist that emotions cannot be completely unconscious? One possibility is that they have been unable to shake their deep faith in the feeling theory. The feeling theory says that emotions simply are conscious feelings. On the face of it, this theory seems equally applicable to a variety of other mental states, such as itches, pains, and afterimages. According to pretheoretical intuitions, it does not make sense to say that there can be an unconscious shooting pain or an unconscious green afterimage. All of these examples are controversial, but it seems plausible, in principle, that some of our mental terms could refer to states that must be conscious. Emotion terms *could* fall into this category. But do they?

Clore (1994a) offers an interesting argument. Rather than simply declaring that emotions are conscious by definition, Clore argues that emotions must be conscious in order to serve their primary function in our mental lives. Emotions, Clore claims, alert us to things. They are mental red flags. If emotions were unconscious, they could not play this role. Imagine someone waving a red flag in utter darkness. If you can't see the flag, it cannot grab your attention.

Clore's argument is seductive, but it rests on some unstable premises. First, it is not obvious that emotions serve the function of grabbing our attention, and if they do serve this function, it is not obvious that they must do so in every instance. Emotions may be able to influence behavior without grabbing our attention. Indeed, Clore's own analysis raises questions about the attention-grabbing function. With Freud, Clore admits that we can be unconscious of the conditions that elicit our emotions. Ed's love must be conscious, but he may be oblivious to the fact that it is his mother who elicited his love in the first place. Now, suppose that emotions are designed to capture our attention. What good would this serve? The obvious answer is that emotions capture our attention to make us focus on the situations that elicit them. Fear, for example, may cause me to focus on the

---

[2]If pain and pleasure are supposed to capture emotional valence, Greenspan's view is in direct oppositon to the view I defend in chapter 7. I claim valence is unconscious.

snake in front of me, even though I was in the middle of some other activity when the snake appeared. The most sensible reading of Clore's proposal is that emotions have the function of making us focus on their elicitors. This conclusion undermines his argument against unconscious emotions. According to that argument, emotions must be conscious, because they cannot serve their proper function unconsciously. At the same time, he admits that we can repress knowledge of emotion elicitors. If it is the function of emotions to cause us to focus on elicitors, then emotions fail to serve their function when elicitors are repressed. So Clore is committed to saying that emotions can occur without serving their proper function. If that is the case, he has no reason left for denying that emotions can occur unconsciously.

There is a further problem with Clore's argument. He moves very rapidly from the premise that emotions grab our attention to the conclusion that they must be conscious. There is no reason to think that this inference follows. In order for it to work, Clore needs the auxiliary premise that a mental state can grab our attention only if it is conscious. But this need not be the case. We can imagine an unconscious warning system that detects problems and alerts us to them. The outcome of the warning system may be a conscious state, but the warning itself could occur outside consciousness. This provides one model for thinking of unconscious emotions. Rather than seeing emotions as red flags waved in darkness, we might regard emotions as light switches that can be turned on in darkness. Ordinarily, when the switch is turned on, we can see both the switch itself (the emotion) and the hand that turned it on (the elicitor). In some cases, however, the light may fail to illuminate the switch.

## Defending Unconscious Emotions

I have shown that one argument against unconscious emotions is unconvincing. But that's a far cry from showing that emotions can be unconscious. The idea of unconscious emotions may sounded bizarre. One might wonder why we should ever postulate such states. What grounds are there for extending emotions into the unconscious realm? In this section, I will offer several arguments.

Within philosophy, there has been considerable discussion of a related issue: the possibility of unconscious pains. Unconscious pains may sound even less probable than unconscious emotions, but some philosophers have presented plausible arguments. Rosenthal (1991), for example, asks us to think of a familiar kind of case. During an intense headache, you happen to focus on something else. Perhaps you are reading a gripping novel. For a brief spell, you seem to lose awareness of your headache. It no longer hurts. Now, we can either say that the pain went away for a spell, or we can say that it never stopped but temporarily vacated consciousness. The second option has an advantage. Suppose that during the episode in question, you were continuously pressing your fingers to your temples or wincing as if the pain were there. Suppose, in other words, that you exhibited overt behavior that was consistent with having a headache. Suppose further that nothing relating to the cause of the headache changed while you were reading. Perhaps the headache came from muscle tension, or a whack on the head, or a hangover. All these etiological factors were still in place. To say that your headache disappeared, when its cause and behavioral effects remain, is unmotivated.

The case for unconscious pain gains further support when we consider the best theory of what pain is. While pain is characteristically felt, pain involves more than feelings. Pain is the mind's way of registering physical pathology. Tension headaches, for example, register contractions of muscles in the head, face, or scalp. Migraines may register blood vessel dilation. All pains carry the information about particular physical conditions. When we get distracted from our pains while reading novels, the mind does not stop representing the state of the body. The pathology is continually represented (hence the continuity of behavior). If pains are mental states that evolved to represent physical pathologies, and mental states can represent physical pathologies outside of consciousness, then we have good reason to call such mental states unconscious pains.

These arguments can be adapted to the emotion case. Imagine that you are given to a particular phobia, say fear of flying. As your plane takes off on an intercontinental flight, you find yourself entering a state of acute anxiety. Your heart is racing, you clutch the armrests, your body stiffens against the seat as if it were being pulled back by gravity. Sensing your distress, the friend you are traveling with begins to tell you a humorous anecdote about her visit to a bald-headed barber. For a moment you lose yourself in her inane yarn. In that brief interval, you are not aware of your fear. In fact, you experience amusement. But then you recall where you are, and terror immediately returns. You notice that the whole while you have been clutching the armrests with equal vigor. Even during the moment of greatest absorption in the barber anecdote, you never stopped displaying the bodily signs of fear. Should we say that your fear briefly subsided during this episode, or should we say it endured unconsciously? The latter option certainly doesn't sound unreasonable.

The argument for unconscious pain profited from the observation that a primary function of pain (carrying information about pathology) can be served without consciousness. The same is true in the emotion case. I have maintained that emotions are primarily designed to carry information about core relational themes. There is no reason why one cannot represent core relational themes unconsciously. Emotions are also thought to play other roles that can occur unconsciously. They can prepare us for behavioral responses, they can initiate thinking processes, they can embody cultural values, and they can motivate moral conduct. None of these effects is intrinsically bound to consciousness. As I remarked in responding to Clore, emotions can even direct our attention to things without being felt. Imagine watching someone casually drop a piece of trash on the street. One might instinctively glare at the offender in contempt without consciously experiencing the corresponding feeling.

These arguments can be regarded as a coherence proof. It does not tax our concept of emotions too much to say they can occur beneath the threshold of awareness. But coherence and actuality are two different things. Hypothetical cases and anecdotes cry out for experimental confirmation. Toward this end, Berridge (1999) reviews a variety of laboratory findings that are suggestive, if not conclusive, evidence for unconscious emotions. In one study by Arntz (1993), for example, women with a spider phobia were asked to perform a series of tasks that required increasingly close contact with spiders. Before the test, some women were given an opioid antagonist drug, and others where given a placebo. Those who took that opioid antagonist were not able to complete as many of the tasks as the other group, but both groups reported the same amount of subjective fear. The behavior suggests a difference in their emotions, despite subjective reports being the same. In a study by Fischman and Foltin (1992), cocaine addicts are affixed with two intravenous lines, one containing saline and the other containing varying amounts of cocaine. The addicts could press a button to release infusions from either line. At very low doses of cocaine, subjects reported no subjective difference between the two lines, but they unknowingly pressed the button for the cocaine line more often. These finding in addicts and phobics can be compared to studies with healthy subjects. Strahan, Spencer, & Zanna (2002) found that subjects were more likely to select upbeat music after observing sad faces that had been presented subliminally. The subjects' behavior thus revealed an alteration in mood, but when asked, they did not report any subjective experience of mood change. In all of these studies, reports of occurrent emotions and emotionally driven behavior come apart, suggesting that subjects may not be aware of their true emotional states.

Experiments that purport to demonstrate unconscious processing are not immune to criticism. The studies I mentioned measure consciousness by verbal reports. If participants in an experiment report that two experiences are the same (e.g., by assigning the same numerical rating), we conclude that their conscious states are the same. This methodology is vulnerable to an objection advanced by Ned Block (1995). Block argues that there is more than one kind of consciousness. He distinguishes between our conscious access to information ("access consciousness") and our conscious qualitative experiences ("phenomenal consciousness"). Mental states are access conscious when they are poised for reporting and rational deliberation, and mental states are phenomenally conscious when there is something it is like to be in them. Block believes that there can be states that are phenomenally conscious but not access conscious (and conversely). He gives the example of experiencing the din of a distant drill without noticing it, and then suddenly realizing that one has been hearing the din all along. The sound is phenomenally conscious the whole time but not access conscious. The crucial observation about this case is that one cannot freely report on the sound of the drill until one notices it. This suggests that, while verbal reports provide reasonably good evidence for access consciousness, they are seriously limited when it comes to phenomenal consciousness.

If Block is right, we commonly have phenomenally conscious experiences that we cannot report. This calls all of the evidence for unconscious emotions into doubt. When cocaine addicts report that fluid from neither of two intravenous infusions causes hedonic elevation, we can conclude only that they lack access consciousness of an affective difference. They may be experiencing the difference phenomenally.

I think that this objection proves too much. If verbal reports cannot be trusted, then phenomenal consciousness is exquisitely hard to measure. Suppose we rely on nonverbal behavior to measure phenomenal consciousness. Cocaine addicts may be said to have phenomenal consciousness of the subtle drug-induced euphoria because they press the right button more often. The problem is that any mental states can potentially impact behavior. If nonverbal behavior is evidence for phenomenal consciousness, then we may be forced to conclude that every mental state is conscious. There seems to be no principled way for determining which nonverbal behavior counts as evidence and which does not. We are forced into a skeptical position. One can only detect phenomenal consciousness from the first-person perspective. Only the cocaine addicts in the experiment know if there was a phenomenal difference, and this is a queer kind of knowledge, because they are unable to report it. Block *could* be right that unreportable phenomenal consciousness occurs, but there is absolutely no way of confirming this.

The inability to confirm something does not prove its nonexistence (that would be crude verificationism). On the other hand, when something is impossible to confirm, one should only believe it exists if there is independent grounds for doing so. The independent evidence in this case is supposed to come from alleged dissociations between phenomenal and access consciousness, as in the drill example. But notice that, in the drill example, one does come to verbalize one's phenomenal experience retrospectively. One says, "Gee, I've been hearing that drill all along." This phenomenon has two competing explanations. First, the retrospective report could be a false memory, in which case we have no evidence for phenomenal consciousness without access. Second, it could be a true memory, in which case it may point to a general principle about the relationship between access and phenomenal consciousness. Barring brain injury or some other impediment, one can gain access to any phenomenal states if one tries. This principle has considerable introspective support. While we often lack the vocabulary to perfectly describe phenomenal experiences, we always seem to be in a position to try to describe them if we pause to reflect. There is no reason to believe that any portion of phenomenology is totally barred from access under ordinary conditions. When a drill is buzzing in the background, it takes hardly any effort to bring it into access consciousness and report on it.

Now consider the cocaine case and the spider phobia case. In both experiments subjects are asked to probe the contents of their experience. They are asked to report how they are feeling. This is not like the drill case, where one might be distracted away from a distant din by some more engaging object of attention. There is no reason why participants in these experiments should be unable to report on their phenomenal experiences, and no independent reason for thinking that unreportable phenomenal experiences ever exist without brain damage (e.g., damage to one's language centers). So even if we grant that phenomenal and access consciousness both exist and can come apart, there is no reason to think they come apart in these experiments. I conclude that we have reasonably good evidence for unconscious emotions.

At this juncture, a stubborn critic might concede that we do indeed have unconscious affective states, while denying that those affective states deserve to be called emotions. Those tempted by this response are truly in the grip of the feeling theory. The best reply calls on the points with which I began. If our best theory of what emotions are for suggests that they are for representing core relational themes (e.g., dangers and goal attainment), and unconscious states are playing that role, then we should, on methodological grounds, call those unconscious states emotions. The experiments reviewed by Berridge are useful precisely because they support this argument. The unconscious state driving the spider phobic's behavior is a modulation in a danger detector, and the unconscious state driving the cocaine addict's behavior is a modulation in a state that represents the attainment of a goal. These experiments provide concrete evidence for the claim that states with the same informational function as conscious emotions can exist unconsciously. We should call these unconscious emotions.

I think the easiest way to undercut skepticism about unconscious emotions is to recall that people were once skeptical about unconscious perceptions. The suggestion that one could see without awareness, for example, would have sounded bizarre in earlier times. The reason for this is simple. The instances of vision that we are aware of are, trivially, conscious visual states. We have no direct awareness of unconscious visual states (on pain of contradiction). Without experiencing them, we have no reason to think they exist. No reason, that is, before vision scientists began to provide evidence. Now evidence for subthreshold perception is so familiar that unconscious vision sounds perfectly natural (Dixon, 1981). Examples of preserved acuity without experience, as is found in patients with blindsight, has helped to seal the case (Weiskrantz, 1986). I predict that the idea of unconscious emotions will sound perfectly natural as more people recognize that processes very much like those underlying conscious emotions can go on without consciousness. The analogy to unconscious perception is especially apt, because emotions reside in perceptual systems of the brain, or so I shall argue hereafter.

### *The Neurofunctional Basis of Emotional Consciousness*

Is Emotional Consciousness and Consciousness of the Body

I have been arguing that emotions can exist without consciousness. Obviously, this is not meant to suggest that emotions are never conscious. For all I have said, they may be conscious most of the time. Any complete theory of emotion must explain emotional consciousness. What are we feeling when we experience a conscious emotion? How do emotions come to be felt? I address these questions in turn.

In earlier chapters, I have endorsed William James (1884) in presuming that emotional consciousness is consciousness of changes in bodily states. James argues for this by *Gedankenexperiment*. Imagine a conscious emotion, he says, then mentally subtract each bodily feeling. Imagine the feeling of terror without the felling of trembling, sweaty palms, tense muscles, contorted face, pounding heart, and shortened breadth. Introspectively, there is no remainder. I am satisfied by this argument, but every audience has a doubter.

Let me consider the doubts of someone who is impressed by what I called attitudinal emotions in chapter 8. In the case on nonattitudinal emotions, such as an intense panic brought on by seeing a snake, the body seems to be intimately involved. The conscious experience of panic is almost certainly a felt bodily change. But when we use the attitudinal locution "afraid *that,*" this does not always follow. One can be afraid that a court ruling will be overturned, without grimacing or trembling. The same can be said for many instances of emotions ascribed using the word "by" or "about." One can be angry about the state of the Union, or surprised by the latest polls, disgusted by abuses of power, or delighted about the recent election returns, all without any bodily symptoms.

One reply to the cases was already anticipated in chapters 4 and 8. I argued that when higher cognitive emotions such as jealousy occur without bodily symptoms, they are dispositional states. One can be jealous of one's lover without bodily symptoms, but not without the disposition to feel bodily symptoms. If seeing your lover in a compromising position with another person would not cause you to flush or cringe, you probably aren't jealous. When one uses an attitudinal emotion attribution to name a disposition, one is not referring to a conscious state. When that disposition is realized, the emotion enters consciousness through changes in the body, as the Jamesian theory predicts. You may *be* jealous for years but only *feel* jealous when the disposition wells up in your gut.

Other apparent counterexamples may be harder to defuse. Sometimes our attitudinal emotions seem both occurrent and conscious without having any bodily symptoms. Surprise affords an especially plausible font of examples. Imagine testifying, sincerely, that you were surprised by the latest polls. Perhaps you expected a very different outcome. When you read the numbers and express your surprise, you are not reporting a mere disposition to react; after all, you have just encountered the source of your surprise. Nevertheless, you may not feel your heart racing as you would if you were, say, surprised by an unexpected call reporting that you had won the lottery. Isn't this a case of a conscious emotion with no bodily symptoms?

At least two replies are available. First, it is an empirical question whether a person could experience surprise without bodily changes. The case may be impossible. It may be impossible to repress physiological changes when you encounter something unexpected. Second, "emotion" terms are sometimes used to refer to something other than emotions. Surprise is an emotion that occurs when one's expectations are violated. That does not mean that an emotion occurs every time one's expectations are violated. One may coolly judge that something was unexpected. We may have a use of "surprise" that extends to cases where we form a judgment about a core relational theme without the corresponding embodied appraisal. If you report cool surprise at the latest polls, this may be a way of saying you expected a different outcome. There is no strong intuition that "surprise" names an emotion in this context. Other emotion terms also have cool attitudinal uses in English. Several fixed figures of speech operate this way. We say "I'm afraid we have run out of white wine," "I'm sad to say I won't be able to attend the party," "I am mortified by his behavior," and "I'm happy to be here this evening." One might utter these clichés without any emotion.

Consider one more apparent counterexample. After a year of therapy, you come to believe that you are afraid of success. On one occasion, when you turn down an assignment that could lead to a promotion, you pause to reflect on your behavior and come to the conclusion that you are rejecting the opportunity out of fear. You don't feel any sweat on your palms or any increase in your heart rate, however. You are conscious of being afraid, but your body feels utterly unperturbed. Does this prove that emotions can be conscious without bodily symptoms?

One can respond to this objection by appealing to Block's access/phenomenal distinction. In this case, you may have access consciousness of fear without phenomenology. You know you are afraid, but you lack a qualitative experience of fear. I want to restrict the Jamesian analysis of emotions to phenomenal consciousness. It is a theory of emotional feelings, not self-attributed thoughts. A person in the situation described would say "I know I am afraid, but I do not feel afraid." The psychotherapy example provides no evidence for dissociation between phenomenally conscious fear and felt body states. I forecast that no evidence for such a dissociation will be forthcoming.

## A General Theory of Perceptual Consciousness

If conscious experience of emotions is really experience of bodily changes, then an explanation of how emotions become conscious may be subsumed under a general account of how perceptual states become phenomenally conscious (hereafter, just conscious). I believe that only perceptual states are capable of being conscious. I will not defend this claim here, but many would agree. Even conscious thoughts seem to be little more than conscious experiences of words and images resounding in our heads (Jackendoff, 1987). I also believe that all perceptual states become conscious in the same way. This is a controversial claim. Many researchers believe that different kinds of conscious experiences may have different explanations (e.g., Churchland, 1992; Flanagan, 1997; Wilkes, 1988). Their skepticism is fueled by the fact that there is no consciousness center in the brain (Dennett & Kinsbourne, 1992). There is no obvious difference between the brain states that are conscious and those that are not. Without any identifiable mark, we cannot be certain that every aspect of consciousness attains its phenomenal status in the same way. Instead, say the skeptics, we should analyze each aspect of experience separately, and strive for several theories of consciousness rather than one.

Consciousness could have a multifarious explanation, but I think that unity should be our working hypothesis. The reason for optimism is that different forms of consciousness have a tremendous amount in common. Here are four commonalities. First, as mentioned earlier, all conscious states can be reported on if we try, barring brain injury or other impediments. Second, all and only conscious states seem to candidates for entering episodic memory. If you have a memory of a specific event from the past, it will be a memory of an event that was experienced consciously. Third, all conscious states can be affected by attention. If you get distracted by one thing, you may lose your conscious awareness of another. And finally, all conscious states feel like something. The very fact that different states have phenomenology cries out for explanation. I conclude that we should be on the lookout for a unified theory. I also believe that the outline of such a theory is already available. I have defended such a theory elsewhere (Prinz, forthcoming b, and references therein). My goal here is not to repeat the full defense here, but to show how the theory that I favor can be extended to the case of emotion.

To find a unified theory of consciousness, I recommend the following strategy. We should begin by investigating the best understood sensory modality, vision. If we can arrive at a theory of how visual consciousness arises, we can then look to see whether other sense modalities obey the same principles. If they do, we will have a unified theory of consciousness. In the pages that follow, I will outline a theory of visual consciousness and then extend it to emotional consciousness.

The theory of consciousness I favor is built on the insights of Ray Jackendoff (1987). Jackendoff begins his analysis of consciousness by observing that sensory systems are hierarchically organized. Vision, most famously, can be roughly divided into three levels of processing: low, intermediate, and high. This organization was most influentially proposed by David Marr (1982), who is Jackendoff's primary source, but it has been elaborated within recent cognitive neuroscience. Low-level vision, associated with the primary visual cortex (V1), is concerned with local feature detection. Oriented lines and small patches of color are detected by cells with small receptive fields, without being integrated into a coherent whole. Intermediate-level vision, associated with extrastriate cortical areas (V2–V5), achieves integration. Here, lines come together to form contours, spots of color blend in context-sensitive ways, and motion and shading facilitate the perception of depth and dimension. High-level vision, associated with the inferior temporal cortex (TE, TEO), achieves viewpoint-invariant recognition. The very same object perceived at different orientations, in different positions of the visual field, and different distances, can cause the same cells in these regions to fire. High-level vision abstracts away from details, allowing us to see commonality across a range of objects and viewing conditions.

Of all these levels, Jackendoff observes that only the intermediate level corresponds with the contents of experience. Low-level vision is too piecemeal, and high-level vision is too abstract. Conscious vision delivers a world of bounded, three-dimensional objects, with coherent contours, contextually modulated colors, and highly specific locations and orientations in our visual surround. Jackendoff did not avail himself of neuroanatomical evidence when he developed his theory. He did not speculate about the location of intermediate-level vision in the brain. There is now very good evidence that the cells that carry the information that correlates best with the contents of consciousness reside in the extrastriate cortex (Koch & Braun, 1996). Damage to subregions in the extrastriate cortex selectively obliterate conscious awareness of visual features. Damage in higher visual brain areas spares visual experience, and disrupts recognition (Farah, 1990). Damage in lower areas results in blindness, but residual visual imagery has been reported (Seguin, 1886). All this supports Jackendoff's conjecture that visual consciousness arises in the intermediate level of processing.

Jackendoff goes on to argue that the intermediate level is also the locus of consciousness in other hierarchically organized perceptual systems. It is a unifying principle of consciousness. I think Jackendoff is right, but he is still missing a piece of the puzzle. The intermediate level is the location of consciousness, but mere activity in intermediate-level areas is not sufficient for consciousness. Bisiach (1992) draws this conclusion from studies of patients with visual neglect. Due to damage in centers of the brain associated with attention, neglect patients seem to lack conscious experience on the left side of their visual fields or the left side of visually presented objects. But, in some cases, they seem to achieve unconscious recognition of things presented on the left. If recognition is achieved, then they must be processing information all the way through the visual hierarchy, because recognition is achieved at the highest level. Bisiach concludes that Jackendoff's story is incomplete. Intermediate-level activity needs something more to become conscious.

I think the missing ingredient is attention. Attention is exactly what neglect patients are missing. When attention goes, phenomenal experience seems to go with it. This has been confirmed in people with healthy brains. Mack and Rock (1998) presented normal subjects with a visual task that requires a lot of attention, and then briefly flashed an unexpected object in the center of the visual field. Half of the subjects failed to experience the object. With no attention left to scan the visual scene, subjects become "inattentionally blind." So visual consciousness requires intermediate-level processing plus attention. I call this the AIR theory of consciousness, for *attended intermediate-level representations*.

The AIR theory is incomplete without an adequate account of attention. It might seem circular to define consciousness in terms of attention, because attention is often defined in terms of conscious awareness. Fortunately, other definitions of attention have been developed with psychology and cognitive neuroscience. I am partial to an analysis that has been proposed by Olshausen, Anderson, and van Essen (1994). They argue that attention is a process that modulates how information flows within the brain. When we attend, cells in one brain region are allowed to send signals to other brain regions. I suspect that perceptual attention (which can be focused on particular objects, ambiently spread across a perceptual field, or both) works by allowing information to flow between perceptual centers of the brain and working memory centers in lateral prefrontal cortex. In the case of vision, pathways to working memory primarily originate in high-level perceptual areas. The intermediate level manages to send information to working memory via the high-level areas. My suspicion is that working memory contains a temporary record of high-level visual representations together with a record of how those representations were derived from the intermediate level that came before. These two pieces of information allow the brain to recreate an intermediate-level representation by sending information back from working memory areas into the intermediate areas. If this is right, working memory does not contain a copy of intermediate representations, but it does contain instructions for reproducing such representations retroactively. These instructions are what Damasio (1989, 1994) calls dispositional representations. I surmise that attention is the process by which intermediate-level representations project forward into high-level perceptual processing areas in a way that leads to the formation of dispositional representations in working memory. If this is right, perception, attention, and working memory all coconspire in generating conscious experiences (compare Rees, 2001). The resulting theory is schematized in figure 9.1.

I do not mean to imply that consciousness arises in working memory. I think it arises in intermediate-level perceptual systems, when they "open the door" to working memory. This metaphor ultimately needs to be cashed out in neural terms. Some change in cellular activity makes the difference between activity remaining in perceptual regions and going on to working memory where dispositional representations can be formed. This change in cellular activity is the neural basis of consciousness. At the moment, we do not know exactly what the change consists in. Somehow, cells in perceptual areas are able to fire in a way that lets working memory areas take notice. If you want a Nobel prize, go figure out what that firing pattern is.

The AIR theory of consciousness seems to work for vision. I think it also works for other sensory modalities and, as I will argue presently, for emotion. The AIR theory finds further confirmation in its ability to account for each of the four common aspects of conscious states that I introduced earlier. It trivially accommodates the third commonality on my list. All conscious states can be affected by attention, because attention is the mechanism that brings states into consciousness. What about the remaining three points of comparison?

First consider the fact that all conscious states can be reported if we try. On the AIR theory, any state that becomes conscious sends a signal to working memory. It is very plausible that introspective verbal reports work by probing working memory. Working memory is a hub that allows information to transfer between the senses, and from senses to language production centers, which are located

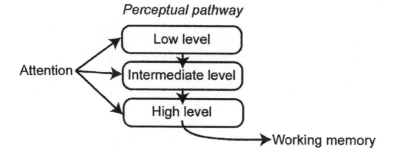

*Figure 9.1.*    The AIR theory of consciousness.

nearby. If consciousness arises when information is sent to working memory, then conscious states should be available for reporting when we try to report them.

The link between consciousness and working memory may also explain the link between consciousness and episodic memory. Time-sensitive fMRI techniques have been used to analyze episodic memory encoding. Buckner, Kelly, and Petersen (1999) found that brain regions associated with working memory activate *before* activations are seen in the medial posterior regions (around the hippocampus) associated with episodic memory. Their conclusion: episodic memories are encoded only after information is temporarily stored in working memory. If consciousness is the gateway to working memory, then it is no surprise that episodic memories are memories of conscious experiences.

The only remaining commonality on my list was that all conscious states feel like something; they are phenomenal. It turns out that the AIR theory cannot explain this fact. The AIR theory is a neurofunctional theory of consciousness (Prinz, 2001). It is functionalist because it says that a state becomes conscious only if it plays a particular functional role. Conscious states are states that send outputs to working memory. Consciousness arises due to an input/out dynamic involving working memory, attention, and perception. The AIR theory is *neuro*-functional, because it says that certain cellular activities may play in indispensable role in consciousness. Consciousness arises only when signals are sent to working memory as a consequence of yet-to-be-identified changes in cellular response. Neurofunctionism is a form of materialism. It characterizes consciousness in physical terms. All materialist theories leave what Joseph Levine (1993) calls an "explanatory gap." Why does this physical/functional process gives rise to consciousness? Couldn't the very same brain event generate a different kind of experience or no experience at all? On the face of it, materialist theories are jeopardized by their inability to answer such questions.

I cannot adequately address this worry here. The philosophical puzzles surrounding consciousness are challenging and would require a lengthy discussion.

I will only gesture at an answer. The AIR theory, like many other materialist theories, is an identity hypothesis. It says that phenomenal experiences *just are* AIRs. As an identify hypothesis, it explains a lot (the three common features of conscious states already discussed, for example). But it does not explain why certain physical states feel like something. Nor should it. Compare the hypothesis that water is $H_2O$. This explains why water is a liquid at room temperature and other such properties, but it does not explain why a particular chemical compound is water. The question "What is $H_2O$ water?" does not make any sense. It is like asking "Why are gnus wildebeests?" The only intelligible question is "What leads us to believe that $H_2O$ is water?" The answer is that we find it in the same places, and it explains various properties of water. Likewise, we can ask "What leads us to believe that AIRs are phenomenally conscious states?" The answer is about the same. We find them when we are conscious, and they explain various properties of conscious states.

I believe that the AIR theory accounts for the fact that all conscious states are phenomenally experienced, because it accounts for the other features that conscious states have in common. This is evidence for thinking that conscious states just are AIRs. The fact that AIRs are phenomenal is a brute fact. Like other identity claims, it does not need to be explained; it need only to be supported by the preponderance of evidence.

## The Emotion Processing Hierarchy

If emotional consciousness is to be explained by the AIR theory, it must first be established that emotional systems are hierarchically organized. So far, I have said nothing to support this claim. What would it mean to say that emotions are hierarchically organized? What could the levels possibly be?

Fortunately, we know where to look. If emotional consciousness is consciousness of bodily states, we should seek an emotion hierarchy in those regions of the brain associated with perception of the body. The body senses are not as well understood as vision. But cognitive neuroscientists have known about brain regions involved in processing information about the body for a long time. Some of the regions include brainstem structures (including reticular, periaqueductalm parabrachial nuclei in the dorsal pons and the nucleus of the solitary tract), primary somatosensory cortex, secondary somatosensory cortex, insula, and portions of cingulate cortex. Damasio (1999) conjectures that these regions are hierarchically organized. He hypothesizes two levels: first-order and second-order body representations. First-order body representations (associated with pons, somatosensory cortex, and insula) are presumed to play an autoregularoty role. Second-order representations rerepresent the first-order representations in order to provide integrated feedback, which can be modified through experience and exploited in guiding behavior. Damasio locates these maps in anterior cingulate cortex, but insular and second somatosensory cortex may also be involved. They receive inputs from primary somatosensory cortex, and are therefore able to represent patterns of bodily response (Augustine, 1996).

Damasio also conjectures that first- and second-order bodily representations form the basis of emotional consciousness. Consistent with this hypothesis, Critchley, Mathias, and Dolan (2001) obtained neuroimaging evidence that these regions show abnormal activity in patients with a neurological condition called pure autonomic failure. The symptoms of pure autonomic failure include both an impairment in perception of autonomic changes and diminished emotional experience. Critchley et al. conclude that their neuroimaging results are consistent with Damasio's hypothesis.

It is likely that different emotions occupy different patterns of activation within the anatomical structures I have mentioned. Different emotions may involve different regions within these structures. Disgust, for example, involves representations of the gut, while anger involves representations of the heart. Neuroscientists have not identified the specific neural response patterns for individual emotions, but available studies suggest that there are differences. Damasio et al. (2000) scanned the brains of individuals as they recalled experiences involving several different emotions, and they found that each emotion involved a different constellation of activity in brain regions associated with somatic response.

The distinction between first- and second-order body representations is suggestive. It is reminiscent of the distinction between low- and intermediate-level representations in vision. Second-order body representations, like intermediate-level visual states, integrate first-order body representations. Perhaps we can think of first-order body representations as representations of local changes in the body. One region may detect changes in visceral organs, another may detect changes in skeletal muscles, a third may detect changes in hormone levels, and so forth. It is reasonable to suppose that the brain regions that initially detect these changes operate in isolation from each other. It is also reasonable to suppose that each of these regions contains areas that are divided into subregions that detect local changes. The region that detects changes in visceral organs, for example, may have one subregion that is responsive to the intestines and another that is responsive to the heart. This can be compared to the small receptive fields in primary visual cortex. Higher regions may integrate these local changes; they may represent patterns of change across a range of organs, muscles, and chemicals. This can be compared to extrastriate visual regions that detect whole contours rather then isolated lines.

So far I have only mentioned two levels in the hierarchy of body experience. A third level may also exist. Recall that high-level visual processing plays a role in recognition. It abstracts away from the idiosyncrasies of specific vantage points. In body representation, the equivalent would be a level of processing that detected commonalities across the patterned bodily response represented at earlier levels of processing. Low-level systems detect local body changes, intermediate-level body systems detect patterns of body changes, and the hypothesized high-level systems abstract away from differences between patterns, treating a range of patterns as alike. If this body hierarchy exists, and is also an emotion hierarchy, we would expect this highest level to be the level at which emotion recognition is achieved. Is there any evidence for a high level?

Anecdotal evidence suggests an affirmative answer. Consider fear. As I have noted before, there are several different bodily states associated with fear. Some scary situations make us flee, and others make us freeze. There may be even greater variation than this. Depending on one's current bodily configuration and location, fleeing and freezing requires subtly different changes. According to my hypothesis, all of these differences would be captured at both the low and intermediate levels. Different bodily fear states would produce different activation in the brain regions that detect both local changes and patterned changes. Nevertheless, we recognize all these different states as instances of the same emotion; they are all fear. That recognitional capacity is best explained by postulating a high level of processing that treats disparate patterns as alike. This is the somatic equivalent of visual cells that are invariant across a range of vantage points.

If high-level emotion processing systems exist, we should be able to locate them anatomically. I offer two guesses as to where they might be. One possibility is that they reside in the ventromedial prefrontal cortex. This, recall, is the sector that Damasio associates with emotion-sensitive decision making. It is the region damaged in Phineas Gage and his contemporary counterparts. Damasio thinks that the ventromedial prefrontal cortex plays a role in reactivating emotions via top-down control in order to anticipate the affective costs and benefits of future actions. This function is consistent with a high-level recognition function. Consider the visual analogy again. In forming conscious visual images, we may use high-level visual representations to reactivate regions that are earlier in the visual hierarchy (Kosslyn, 1994). Likewise, emotions that are reactivated during reasoning are essentially emotional images. An image is just a state in a sensory system that has been generated from the top down rather than the bottom up. If portions of ventromedial prefrontal cortex participate in emotional image generation, then they are good candidates for comprising the high-level of processing in the emotion hierarchy.

Another region to consider is the rostral portion of the anterior cingulate cortex. Lane, Fink, Chan, and Dolan (1997) have implicated this region in what Lane calls reflexive emotional consciousness. In a neuroimaging study, Lane compares neuronal activity as subjects make a nonemotional judgment (indoors or outdoor) when viewing emotion eliciting images with neuronal activity as subjects focus on their emotions in order to report whether the experience was pleasant or unpleasant. When subjects were asked to report on their emotions, increased activation was seen in the rostral portion of the anterior cingulate cortex. This could be explained by assuming that the rostral anterior cingulate is important for recognition of our emotions. Perhaps subjects who are asked to report the valence of their emotions must first identify what emotions they are feeling, and that causes the rostral anterior cingulate to light up. If this interpretation is correct, then the rostral anterior cingulate is involved in high-level emotion processing. Unfortunately, Lane did not ask his subjects to name the specific emotions that they were experiencing, so we cannot be sure that recognition was taking place in his study. It is possible that the valence of an emotion can be determined without identifying that emotion. More studies are needed.

I said earlier that the cingulate cortex, the second somatosensory cortex, and the insula are possible sites of second-order body representations, which I equate with the intermediate level in the emotion hierarchy. The cingulate has been most extensively studied in this context, and I will focus my attention there. The cingulate cortex is a large structure with many subdivisions. If the rostral anterior cingulate cortex is part of high-level processing, then the intermediate level must reside elsewhere. One region of interest is the dorsal anterior cingulate (including Brodman area 24). As noted, Lane's group found activation in this region when subjects viewed emotionally charged pictures and films and when they recall emotional memories (Lane 2000; Lane et al., 1997).

Although much more research is needed, I think we can tentatively conclude that there is an emotion hierarchy extending from the pons and primary somatosensory cortex into the insula, secondary somatosensory cortex, and dorsal anterior cingulate cortex, and then into the rostral anterior cingulate and ventromedial prefrontal cortex (fig. 9.2). The AIR theory predicts that emotional consciousness arises at the intermediate level in this hierarchy. Secondary somatosensory and insular cortex have not been systematically studied in this context, but there are some suggestive findings. Both structures are active in many neuroimaging studies in which conscious emotions are induced. Insula damage can lead to the elimination of negative affect in pain (Berthier, Starkstein, & Leiguarda, 1988), and diminished activity in anterior insula is found in some patients with Huntington's disease who do not experience disgust (Phillips et al., 1997). There is even more direct evidence pertaining to dorsal anterior cingulate cortex. Lane et al. (1997) provide welcome confirmation of this prediction that this region is important to emotional consciousness. They found increased dorsal anterior cingulate activation in subjects who seem to be more aware of their emotions. They suspect that such people may have more intense emotional experiences. The site of increased activation, then, is a plausible locus of emotional consciousness. Lane concludes that dorsal anterior cingulate is the seat of "phenomenal awareness of the emotions." This aligns beautifully with the predictions of the AIR theory.

Further evidence for the role of the anterior cingulate cortex in emotional consciousness comes from studies of brain injuries. Damage to the anterior cingulate cortex is associated with a variety of emotional disturbances. In nonhuman mammals, anterior cingulate lesions can cause deficits in aggression, concern for others, pain aversion, avoidance learning, maternal behavior, and separation distress, as well as affectively modulated vocal and automomic response (see Vogt, Finch, & Olson, 1992, for review). In human beings, damage to the anterior cingulate can cause akinetic mutism. Patients with this condition suffer from a profound

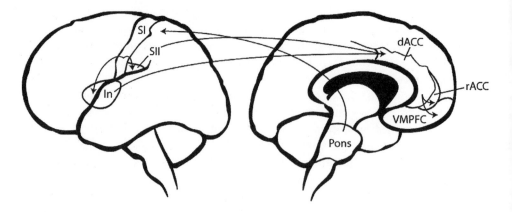

*Figure 9.2.*   Brain structures involved in the emotion hierarchy. SI, primary somatosensory cortex; SII, secondary somatosensory cortex; In, insula; dACC, dorsal anterior cingulate cortex; rACC, rostral anterior cingulate cortex; VMPFC, ventromedial prefrontal cortex.

lack of motivation despite a preserved capacity to perceive the world and understand language. They will not initiate actions, and they will hardly respond when spoken to. One patient who recovered from akinetic mutism reported that she felt that "nothing mattered" during the period of illness (Damasio & Van Hoesen, 1983, p. 98).

Testimony from victims of akinetic mutism is consistent with the conjecture that anterior cingulate is the locus of emotional consciousness. Mutism apparently involves a profound deficit in emotional experience. One can draw an analogy between mutism and apperceptive agnosia in vision. Apperceptive agnosia arises when areas within the intermediate-level visual system are damaged. Patients with this condition cannot recognize objects, nor can they copy pictures of objects. They seem to be incapable of perceiving shapes. Likewise, people suffering from akinetic mutism seem to be incapable of experiencing emotions.

The AIR theory also predicts that consciousness can be disrupted by damaging low-level perceptual areas. These areas feed crucial inputs to the intermediate level and make perception possible. In the case of vision, that prediction is borne out. Damage to the primary visual cortex, a center for early vision, results in blindness. In the case of emotions, damage to early processing centers seems to have a comparable affect. Damage to brainstem regions that register bodily states (as in some forms of paralysis) can indeed result in muted affect (see Damasio, 1999, for review).

To complete the analogy to vision, we should also consider cases where high-level processing centers are damaged. When this happens in the visual system, the result is associative agnosia. Like apperceptive agnosics, associative agnosics cannot recognize visually presented objects. But, unlike apperceptive agnosia, associative agnosics can successfully copy drawings of objects. This suggests that they are not blind to shape. They can discern contours, but they cannot make sense of them. They are blind to the meanings of shapes, not to the shapes themselves. Associative agnosia has an apparent analogue in the case of emotions. There is a condition called alexithymia, which is clinically defined as an inability to verbally express one's emotions (American Psychological Association, 1994). This makes it sound like a verbal disorder. In fact, it is more likely to be an inability to recognize emotions. People with alexithymia have difficulty saying how they are feeling, because they cannot recognize how they are feeling. This does not mean they lack emotions. People with alexithymia often report an unusual number of unexplained bodily ailments (Shipko, 1982). One explanation is that they are experiencing the body perturbations that comprise normal emotions but they fail to recognize those perturbations as emotions. Like associative agnosics, who experiences shapes without comprehension, alexithymics may experiences emotions without comprehension. The AIR theory offers an explanation. Alexithymia may result from a malfunction in high-level emotion centers.[3]

This constellation of disorders provides welcome support for the AIR theory of consciousness. If consciousness arises in the intermediate level, damage to early or intermediate-level centers should disrupt experience, and damage to high-level centers should impair recognition. Characteristic breakdowns in vision are consistent with these predictions, and preliminary evidence suggests that those breakdowns have analogues in emotion. The parallels are quite striking.

Defending the AIR theory for emotional consciousness requires one more issue, which I have yet to discuss. If the AIR theory is right, emotional consciousness also requires attention. There is plenty of good evidence that emotion affects attention (e.g., Öhman, Flykt, & Esteves, 2001) but little investigation into the affect of attention on emotion. Here, everyday experience will have to suffice. One plausible example was introduced earlier. Recall the fear-of-flying case. A plane phobic is distracted from a bout of terror while listing to a friend's story during an intercontinental flight. The story serves as an attentional lure. It demands focus and thereby distracts attention away from the emotional experience. Try this exercise. Next time you get angry, first focus on the anger to experience it fully, then take out a piece of paper and assign yourself a multidigit multiplication problem. See if the anger experience subsides as you perform the attention-demanding calculation. Often such attention effects are indirect. Experience of the emotion subsides because we stop thinking about the emotion *elicitor*. But direct cases are possible too. Consider moods, which often endure long after their

[3]Lane, Kaszniak, Ahern, & Schwartz (1997) offer a very different explanation of alexithymia. They describe it as the emotional equivalent of blindsight. They arrive at this conclusion because they suspect that alexithymics may have a residual emotional capacity, despite being poor at recognizing emotions. These symptoms are equally well explained by the assumption that alexithymia is an analogue of associate agnosia. The crucial test would be to find out whether emotions feel like anything to the alexithymic. The blindsight analogy predicts that they do not. I think that the prevalence of unexplained bodily complaints favors the associative agnosia analogy.

elicitors are gone. Moods can even lack elicitors entirely, as when they are chemically induced. We can briefly distract ourselves from the conscious experience of a mood (unless it is incredibly intense) by listening to a friend's stories, performing mathematical calculations, watching a movie, doing a crossword, and so on. These examples convince me that affective states are like visual states; if attention is focused elsewhere, they are not experienced consciously.

I think there is reason to be optimistic that the AIR theory is true of emotional consciousness. The evidence presented here is very preliminary, of course, but it warrants future research.

### What Is Consciousness For?

I have argued that emotions are sometimes conscious and sometimes unconscious. This raises a question. Why aren't emotions always unconscious? If they can do their job (detecting core relational themes) without consciousness, there seems to be no reason for them to be conscious. This is just a special case of a more general question: What function could consciousness possibly serve?

The AIR theory of consciousness points to a possible answer. If consciousness arises when information gets sent to working memory, then going to working memory may be the function of conscious states. Working memory is not just a temporary storage bin. It is the place where controlled reasoning and problem solving takes place. Controlled processes are the ones that orchestrate unrehearsed, context-sensitive responses. We can refer to such responses as "deliberate." Responses that are highly rehearsed can be performed without deliberation. They do not need working memory. That is why more familiar activities (walking, reading, eating) do not require full consciousness. Of course, we are conscious of the streets we walk on, the words we read, and the foods we eat, because each of these may carry novel information.

The link between consciousness and deliberate response also explains why the intermediate level is privileged. Low-level perceptual representations are not especially useful for deliberate response centers. Consider edge detectors in vision. Few deliberate actions or inferences pertain to isolated edges. This information does not need to get sent any further than the intermediate-level visual areas where edges assemble to form contours.[4] High-level representations contribute a bit more to deliberate response. The high level is often the level of recognition. If you run from an approaching bear you run because you have identified it as a bear and you know that bears are dangerous. But high-level representations are insufficient on their own. They abstract away from information that may be crucial for response selection. A high-level representation of a bear abstracts away from details of position and vantage point. It may help you to decide that you need to escape, but without position information, it will not help you decide an

---

[4]This is not to say that we cannot be conscious of edges. By narrowing the focus of attention on an edge, we can form an edge representation that iterates all the way up the visual hierarchy.

escape route. The intermediate level in vision is better suited for this purpose, because it represents objects from a particular point of view. The intermediate level is privileged because it is perspectival. It facilitates responses that depend on knowing our position in the world. The high level of visual perception tells us what sort of predicament we are in (e.g., what kinds of objects we are facing), and the intermediate level tells us how we are situated with respect to that predicament (e.g., whether objects are near or far). Since consciousness only arises at the intermediate level, we can conclude that the function of visual consciousness is to make ineliminably perspectival representations available to working memory structures that orchestrate deliberate response.[5]

The same lesson applies in the case of emotions. Low-level states in the emotion hierarchy register[6] bodily changes in isolation from each other. If one wants to use one's body to detect core relational themes, isolated responses offer little help. A rapidly racing heart could signal elation, terror, or rage. One has to be able to register the whole pattern to distinguish among these discrete emotions. Patterns are registered at the hypothesized intermediate level. The high level abstracts away from differences in patterns, treating flight and freezing as if they were the same. This level may be useful (it is valuable to know if you are afraid), but it is not sufficient on its own. In order to deliberate about an appropriate action, it is especially helpful to consider the response that our bodies have preselected for us. If I know that my body has put me into a freezing mode, I may elect to stay still rather than fleeing. The intermediate level is, once again, optimized for this purpose. Put a bit differently, the high level in the emotion hierarchy conveys information about one's predicament without conveying how one is situated with respect to that predicament. A high-level fear state indicates that one is facing physical danger, and an intermediate-level fear state indicates that the source of danger is related to one in a way that requires a particular kind of bodily response (e.g., small or large, near or far, moving or still, escapable or inescapable, etc.). Both levels represent physical danger (the core relational theme), but the intermediate level represents danger without abstracting away from the

---

[5]Readers familiar with Milner and Goodale (1995) may take issue with the story I am trying to tell. Milner and Goodale argue that visual consciousness and visually guided action are subserved by different brain systems—a ventral stream and a dorsal stream. The intermediate-level representations I have been talking about reside in the ventral stream. If the action-driving dorsal stream is unconscious, it may seem implausible to say that consciousness has the function of making information available for deliberate response. Certain deliberate responses (i.e., intentional visually guided actions) are apparently independent of consciousness. In response, I would argue that Milner and Goodale's results fail to demonstrate this last point. The unconscious dorsal stream receives inputs from the conscious ventral stream and from working memory centers that have access to ventral stream information. Therefore, even if visual consciousness is not located in the visually guided action system, that system may depend on conscious states when it guides actions that are under deliberate control. Milner and Goodale's work is consistent with this possibility, hence consistent with the story I've been trying to tell.

[6]Unlike higher level states in the emotion hierarchy, these low-level states might also be said to *represent* bodily changes, in addition to merely registering them.

# 10

---

# Is Getting Mad Like Seeing Red?

### *Emotion As Perception*

The mind is divided into different kinds of information-processing systems. There are perceptual systems that provide inputs, action and motor systems that provide output, and, perhaps, higher cognitive systems that engage in reasoning, planning, problem solving, and other mental operations that mediate between inputs and outputs when we move above the level of reflex response. One wants to know where emotions figure into this picture. One possibility is that emotions are sui generis. They may be a special class of states that cannot be reduced to perceptions, action commands, or higher cognitions. Another possibility is that they are complex states made up of parts that belong to each of these different systems. A third possibility is that they can be reduced to just one category. Perhaps they *are* perceptions, action commands, or higher cognitions. In this chapter, I want to explore the idea that emotions are perceptions.

The possibility that emotions are perceptions is interesting for a variety of reasons. If emotions reduce to perceptions and are not a sui generis class of mental entities, then the ontology of mental entities is smaller than some have presumed. If emotions are perceptions, then there are also epistemological consequences. Unlike a belief, it is peculiar to say that a perception is justified. If emotions are perceptions, then research on emotions can be informed by research in perceptual psychology. My account of emotional consciousness in chapter 9 was a case in point. Indeed, the thesis that emotions are perceptions has been implicit throughout the preceding chapters. It encapsulates much of what I have said. On the view that I have been defending, having an emotion is a way of perceiving one's place in the world. If it can be shown that emotions and perceptions are not alike, then some of the central claims of this book may be mistaken.

What would it mean to say that emotions are perceptions? To answer that, we must consider paradigm examples of perceptual states. These include states in our familiar sensory systems, such as vision, audition, and olfaction. If emotions are perceptions, then they must share essential features in common with seeing shapes, hearing sounds, and smelling fragrances. What, we must ask, makes sights, sounds, and smells count as perceptual?

As a first stab, one might try to exploit the definition of cognition offered in chapter 2. If cognitive states are ones that arise under top-down control, then perhaps perceptual states are ones that arise under bottom-up control. Roughly put, perceptions arise in us from outside of the brain. This is a good starting place. I think it is a necessary condition of a perceptual state that it consist of states that can be activated bottom-up. A mental state that could only be caused by act of voluntary mental effort would not count as perceptual. But bottom-up control cannot be the essence of the perceptual. First, many perceptual states can be generated by acts of voluntary mental effort. Mental images can be defined as perceptual states that are activated top-down. Second, it is possible that some nonperceptual states can be activated bottom-up. Certain compulsive thoughts may qualify. After decades of cultural indoctrination, an American patriot may internally mutter "God bless America" as a reflex response to seeing the flag. It is at least an open theoretical possibility that this thought is both nonperceptual and activated from the bottom up. The possibility of bottom-up activation is not sufficient for being perceptual.

I think that perceptual states can be defined as states in dedicated input systems (see Prinz [2002] for a longer defense of this definition). A dedicated input system is a mental system that has the function of receiving information from the body or the world via some priority class of transducers and internal representations. Dedicated input systems are perceptual modalities or senses. To count as perceptual, a mental state must inhabit a sense. Vision, audition, and olfaction are dedicated input systems. They each have their own neural pathways and proprietary representations. If emotions are literally perceptual, they must reside in such a system. This definition can help us determine whether alleged perceptual theories of emotion really merit that title.

Consider the theory advanced by de Sousa (1978, 1987). De Sousa claims that emotion can be usefully viewed as a form of perception, and he bases this claim on a number of parallels. For example, both perceptions and emotions can be felt, both are perspectival (one cannot entertain having an emotion without actually having it), and both can be hallucinatory (they can represent objects that are not really there). Parallels notwithstanding, de Sousa's explicit theory of the emotions does not turn out to be a perceptual theory. He defines emotions as "patterns of salience" that insinuate directions for inference and inquiry. He also says that emotions are learned by observing "paradigm scenarios," which are situations in which emotions are characteristically elicited. Emotions arise when we recognize current events as sufficiently similar to paradigm scenarios. Once a representation of a paradigm scenario is brought to mind, it draws our attention to features of a current situation and disposes us to draw certain inferences. Anger may arise when we recognize someone's behavior as offensive, and we may be moved to draw certain conclusions about that person's character.

I think de Sousa is right about paradigm scenarios. Such scenarios may count among the representations found in calibration files, and they play an important role in emotion elicitation. But de Sousa's theory fails to qualify as perceptual, because it does not implicate activity in a perceptual input system. His theory may seem to have a perceptual flavor because the notion of salience is associated with perception. When we visually attend to objects, for example, certain features are more salient than others. Salient features attract attention. But salience also has application in nonperceptual contexts. If I form the belief that Smith is a Republican, her attitudes toward fiscal policy, civil liberties, and social welfare may become more salient to me, and I may be inclined to draw certain inferences.

De Sousa explicitly denies that emotions are beliefs, and that may also suggest that emotion is a form of perception. De Sousa calls emotions modes of perceiving. But "mode of perceiving" is best interpreted as a metaphor on de Sousa's account. Emotions are interpretations of things without being explicit judgments. The same can be said of perceptual states. If I have yellow lenses in my sunglasses, I may see the world yellowly without judging that it is yellow. But many apparently nonperceptual states have this character too. A child might "see" her stuffed animals as living things. A mugger may "look at" passersby as victims, when deciding whom to assault. An artist may view a model as Venus or Adonis. These are forms of perception only in a nonliteral sense. It is no surprise then that de Sousa ends up concluding that emotions are not literally perceptions. They are merely analogous.

To find a literal perceptual theory, we must look elsewhere. Hume is sometimes credited with holding such a view. As I discussed in chapter 1, Hume (1739/1978) says emotions are second-order impressions. "Impressions" is often interpreted as Hume's term for perceptual states. A second-order impression is one that has been brought on by another impression or by an idea (ideas are just faint copies of impressions, for Hume). Emotions lack intrinsic meaning on Hume's account. They have meaning only in an extrinsic sense; they have characteristic causes and effects. Pride is a feeling that is caused by reflecting on our possessions or accomplishments, and it causes thoughts about the self.

It is not entirely clear why emotions should qualify as perceptual on Hume's account. What, other than stipulation, makes them count as impressions? Hume does not provide an especially clear answer to this question. He does not show that emotions qualify as states in dedicated input systems. Neither does he draw any compelling analogy between emotions and paradigm examples of perceptual states, such as sights, sounds, and smells. The fact that emotions can be phenomenally experienced is something they share in common with paradigm sensory states, but that is not evidence for the thesis that emotions are perceptual unless one provides the further argument that only perceptual states can be felt. No such argument can be found in Hume. Exegetically, it is probably best to abandon the assumption that Hume is defending a perceptual theory. The term "impression" should not be regarded as a synonym for perceptual state. Impressions are a motley category that includes two distinct types of states. These Hume calls impressions of sensation and impressions of reflection. The former may be identified with perceptual states, and the latter, which include emotions, make up an entirely distinct class.

The seeds of a truly perceptual theory can be found in Descartes (1649/1988). For Descartes, emotions are states of the soul that occur in response to movements of the "animal spirits" that flow through our bodies. He sometimes says they are "perceptions" of such bodily changes. But Descartes does not mean that emotions are states in perceptual systems. Instead, he regards emotions as pleasant or unpleasant feelings that draw out attention to some feature of the world and impel us to act in response. For example, he defines love as a state of the soul, caused by movement of the animal spirits, that incites one to join those objects that seem agreeable. Love seems to involve a wish (the wish to join another object) and an evaluation (the assessment of an object as agreeable). Neither of these components can be plausibly identified with a perceptual state. But by relating the emotions to changes in the body, Descartes helps plant the seeds for truly perceptual theories.

Those seeds are harvested by James and Lange. The James-Lange theory identifies emotions with feelings of bodily changes. The bodily changes in question are not movements of the animal spirits but perturbations in visceral organs and adjustments in skeletal muscles. This is clearly a perceptual theory. Emotions are states in the somatosensory system.

The embodied appraisal theory that I have been defending descends from the writings of James and Lange. It qualifies as perceptual for exactly the same reasons. Emotions are states within systems that are dedicated to detecting bodily changes. In my discussion of consciousness (chapter 9), I argued that the organization of the pathways that process emotions is comparable to the pathways in vision and other input systems. Emotions reside in a three-level hierarchy, where the intermediate level corresponds to conscious experience. I also argued that emotions are subject to characteristic breakdowns that parallel breakdowns found in the visual system. The emotion hierarchy can be regarded as a special subsystem within the broader somatosensory system.

This, however, is only half the story. The claim that emotions are perceptions falls trivially out of any somatic theory. Emotions reside in a dedicated input system. If my arguments for the bodily basis of emotions have been successful, the central thesis of this chapter has already been confirmed. There is, however, another dimension to that thesis. Perceptions can be defined in two ways. The first, which I have been discussing, has to do with their implementation. Perceptions must occur in perceptual systems. The second has to do with their informational properties. Perceptions pick up information in a distinctive way. Perceptions are states that are used to perceive things. Thus the question of whether emotions are perceptions has two parts. Are emotions perceptual states? And is having an emotion a way of perceiving something? The first question seems to have a trivial answer if somatic theories are right. The second question also seems trivial on one reading: according to somatic theories, emotions are ways of perceiving bodily changes. But the embodied appraisal theory raises a further question. I claim that emotions represent core relational themes. Changes in the body are the nominal contents of emotions, and core relational themes are their real contents. It is easy to see how emotions could be perceptions of their nominal contents on my view, but what about the real contents? Is there any sense in which we can say that core relational themes are perceived? I would like to defend a positive answer. Just as the visual system subdivides into hierarchical pathways for detecting color, form, motion, and position, the somatosensory system subdivides into pathways for detecting textures, shapes, temperature, injuries, and core relational themes.

On the face of it, this may sound very odd. How could core relational themes be just another feature that our senses pick up? Core relational themes appear to be extremely different from colors and textures. Ostensibly, it doesn't make sense to say that they can be perceived. I must address this worry. In fact, the perceptual theory of emotion comes under pressure from several directions. There are a number of apparent contrasts between emotion and perception. Some of these contrasts seem to show that emotions are not perceptual states, and some seem to show that emotions cannot be regarded as perceptions of core relational themes. I will examine these contrasts and argue that they are merely apparent. Emotions are perceptions, and they are used to perceive our relationship to the world.

### Apparent Contrasts

#### Unobservables

One knee-jerk response to the proposal that emotions are perceptions is to complain that core relational themes are not observable. They cannot be smelled or tasted or even touched (as the somatosensory theory of emotion seems to imply). If we literally perceive core relational themes, then core relational themes must be observable properties. This is not the case.

This objection has some intuitive pull, but it falls apart under the lens. To begin with, the objection gets nowhere without a theory of what it is for something to be observable. On one definition, an observable property is anything we can perceive with our senses. I am claiming that core relational themes can be perceived by our senses. If somatosensory systems contain states that represent core relational themes, then it follows that core relational themes are observable properties. To deny this without argument would beg the question. The objection requires another account of observable properties.

To escape this easy response, the objector might try to define observable properties as properties that be detected without inference. One has to do a lot of mental work before one can detect the presence of a demeaning offense, or a loss, or a danger. Perhaps these properties are not perceivable because they must be inferred. The problem with this reworked objection is that paradigm cases of perception require a lot of mental work too. On our best theories of vision, for example, multiple inferences are needed to go from the luminance arrays provided by the eyes to the three-dimensional structural descriptions provided by high-level vision. The fact that core relational themes are not detected without inference does not demonstrate that they are unobservable. (For more discussion see the section on indirectness.)

One might try to save the objection by claiming that observable properties must be out there to observe. There is a sense in which core relational themes are not out there. They depend on us. They are relational. Sadness is a representation of a loss, but something qualifies as a loss only if it is valued. A loss is always a loss *to me*. Perhaps perception only picks up properties that can actually inhere in external objects—properties that are nonrelational.

This restriction on observability will not sound plausible to anyone who has been immersed in the last thee hundred years of philosophical debates about perception. Many philosophers think we perceive secondary qualities. According to Locke (1690/1979), a secondary quality is a power that some external thing has to cause a mental state in us. Being red, for example, is analyzed as the property of having the power to cause a certain kind of experience in normal observers under normal viewing conditions. I do not think that emotions represent secondary qualities (see chapter 3), but secondary qualities show that paradigmatically observable properties can be relation. We can perceive powers to affect us.

Many other relational properties can be perceived as well. Consider the property of being about 10 feet away. This is an especially good example because there is nothing that being 10 feet away consistently looks like. As with emotions, perception of distance can involve a huge variety of viewing conditions. Different objects at that distance will engender radically different retinal arrays. These arrays may have nothing in common in virtue of which distance is perceived. The visual system detects distance using a variety of different tricks. Painters have known such tricks for ages. Overlapping objects, height in the visual field, saturation of hue, sharpness of line, binocular disparity, foreshortening, and linear perspective are among the clues that can convey information about distance.

Perceiving that an object is about 10 feet away involves the use of various other pieces of information. Likewise, perceiving an offense can involve the perception of an insult, a glare, an intrusion on personal space, a physical attack, and so on. Emotion systems cope with diversity by means of the body. The range of possible anger elicitors is unbounded, but every anger elicitor triggers a similar somatic response. As a result, situations that do not look alike may feel alike. The body serves as a common denominator uniting every offense. In this regard, the perception of offenses (and other core relational themes) may be even easier than the perception of distances.

I conclude that there is no obvious reason to deny that core relational themes are observable properties. Many observable properties require inferences to perceive, and many are relational. If core relational themes are represented by states in our perceptual systems, as I have maintained, then we should conclude that they are observable properties. We can feel the offensiveness of external events resonating through our flesh.

### Endurance

Another apparent contrast between emotions and perceptions is that emotions tend to outlast their precipitating conditions. When we encounter a red tomato, the visual experience of it does not endure past the encounter. When we avert our eyes, the redness disappears. Now consider what happens when someone insults us. The insult itself may last for a couple of seconds, but the anger lingers. It may linger for hours. If moods qualify as emotions (recall chapter 8), emotions can even last for months. Emotions have a curious independence from the conditions that bring them about.

I offer three replies. First, an insulting remark can haunt its victim. When we are insulted, we often repeat the insult over and over in our minds. When this happens, the precipitating event is recurrent. The original insult is short-lived, but its shadow remains in our imagination.

Second, the impression that anger outlasts its cause may depend on a failure to distinguish particular and formal objects. The particular object of an emotion is often brief. In the case of anger, the particular object may be an insulting utterance. The utterance may be brief, but the formal object is not. The formal object of anger is a demeaning offense. An offense is not an event; it is a property that events have in relation to us. Once an insulting remark has been uttered, it continues to have the property of being offensive. The remark continues to be an offense after it ends. Past events can be offensive to us in the present. This does not mean that lingering anger is a perception of the past. Like all perceptions, emotions represent current objects, events, and properties. Offensiveness resides in the present.

Third, even the particular object of anger can endure as long as the anger itself. When anger follows an insulting remark, it may be directed at the remark itself. One might get angry about a sequence of words. But it is more common to get angry at the person who uttered those words. Insults instigate anger, but anger latches onto the insulter. As long as the insulter exists, there is a particular object for anger. Anger can linger as long as we think about the person who caused it. It is wrong to say that emotions outlast their objects.

A persistent objector might be unsatisfied by these replies. There seem to be cases where lingering emotions have nothing to latch onto. Consider the case, mentioned in chapters 2 and 4, of the woman who gets angry at her spouse and then discovers that he did no wrong. The emotion may linger even though there has been no offense and no culprit. Such examples show that the temporal profile of an emotion can come unfettered from the situation that incites it and the property it represents. This appears to be an important difference between emotions and paradigm cases of perception.

This alleged difference is easy to dismiss. Paradigm perceptual representations can come unfettered from their causes too. Afterimages and hallucinations are possible examples. An image can remain imprinted on the retinae for a brief interval after a stimulus is removed. Imagine creatures whose visual systems work differently from ours. Whenever they see an object, their retinal images linger for several minutes. The object that caused a retinal image may move away, and another object may take its place, but the image remains, and the creature continues to perceive the original object. Emotions are a bit like this. When we detect a core relational theme, such as danger or offense, we continue to represent it for a period of time. Emotions may linger for a very good reason. They represent properties that bear on survival, and those properties are often difficult to detect. Recalcitrant false positives are an asset in a system designed for detecting core relational themes. The fact that many paradigm cases of perception are ephemeral does not prove that perceptual states must be ephemeral. If lingering retinal images conferred a survival advantage, retinal images would probably linger.

## Action

Emotions may also appear unlike paradigm cases of perceptual states because of their link to action. I have said out that emotions are motivating. They impel us to act. Being afraid can usher in an urge to flee, and being angry can usher in an urge to fight. In contrast, there is nothing very moving about seeing a red patch or hearing a tone. When paradigm cases of perception are motivating, it is usually in virtue of inciting an emotional response. Seeing a mangled body may impel us to shield our eyes, but the motivation operates under the reins of disgust. A person with an impaired capacity for disgust may see the very same body with no such reaction. This makes it look as if emotion systems are really output systems, not input systems, as the perceptual account would suggest.

As a first response, one might note that emotions are motives, not motivations. As I argued in chapter 8, emotions do not impel actions directly. They instigate the search for appropriate actions. They beg for action without demanding it. Thus emotions are not really output states. They are not action commands. They are, however, perceptions of the body's preparation for action. Their nominal contents are bodily states that enable us to behave in appropriate ways. In this sense, one might think of emotions in Gibsonian terms. Gibson (1979) says that in ordinary perception we perceive the actions afforded by the objects in our surround. We see that a chair affords sitting and a hammer affords wielding. Emotions are perceptions of affordances in this sense. By registering bodily changes, emotions allow us to literally perceive that situations afford a range of possible behavioral responses. Properly understood, the link between emotion and action supports the comparison to perception, rather than undermining it.

A second response to the action objection is also available. It must be noted that some paradigm instances of perception can have an impact on action. Smoke may cause the eyes to squint, and movement in one's peripheral visual field may cause one's head to turn. It has become fashionable to challenge the dichotomy between input and output systems, by showing that perception is bound up with various forms of motor response (e.g., Noë & O'Regan, 2001).[1]

These two responses to the action objection brush over a residual difference between emotions and paradigm perceptions. Emotions attain their relation to action, in part, from their valence markers. Embodied appraisals, the other component of emotions, are related to action in that they register bodily changes that enable action. Registering a bodily change is a perceptual activity in a straightforward sense. Valence markers are another story.[2] They do not register bodily states. Their content is best understood as imperative. It can be glossed by the instruction "More of this!" in the case of positive valence, or "Less of this!" in the case of negative valence. Valence markers are internal commands to sustain or eliminate a somatic state by selecting an appropriate action. Valence markers are not perceptual states. They are not states in our somatosensory systems. They can become decoupled from embodied appraisals, and they can be affixed to other kinds of mental states. I concede, then, that emotions contain a nonperceptual component.

This concession does not give up the game. It is still perfectly acceptable to say that emotions are perceptions, with the added qualification that they are valent perceptions. Not all valent perceptions are emotions. Other examples include itches, tickles, sumptuous tastes, and the sensory response to thick smoke. Emotions are more likely to instigate action than seeing a red patch or hearing an innocuous tone. But imagine seeing a blindingly bright red patch or hearing a loud jarring tone. Like emotions, these intense perceptions beg us to act. Perception can be motivating.

## Indirectness

The most glaring contrast between emotions and paradigm cases of perception is that emotional response is indirect. Emotions are reactions to perceptions or thoughts. They occur only after an emotionally relevant object has been encountered or considered. For example, when fear arises, it is usually a response to experiencing something dangerous. Fear may follow from hearing a loud noise, seeing a suspicious shadow, or thinking about an impeding economic crisis. This is why Hume said emotions are impressions of impressions. Paradigm cases of

---

[1]It is known that some neurons are involved in both perception and behavioral response. Most famously, mirror neurons in area F5 fire when one is observing a physical action and when one is performing the action, suggesting that they are involved in both inputs and outputs (Rizzolatti, Fadiga, Gallese, & Fogasi, 1996). We may discover neurons that behave like that in areas associated with emotion, such as the anterior cingulate. It is known that the cingulate is involved in both body perception and body regulation. Perhaps individual cells perform both tasks. Otherwise there may be small networks of interlinked input cells and output cells. Either way the connection between perceiving and acting is likely to be close.

[2]Interestingly, Gibson (1979, p. 137) suggests that the perception of affordances is evaluative; we see things as useful, inviting, repellent, and so on.

perception are not indirect. If you see a red patch, you do not need to have a prior perception or thought. Seeing a red patch is not a reaction to something other than the red patch. It is not mediated by intervening representational states other than those that occur earlier in visual processing.

This contrast seems to undermine the comparison between emotion and perception. Even if emotions are cloaked in somatosensory clothing, they *arise* under conditions that are extremely unlike standard perceptual states. The objection can be formulated by drawing a distinction between perceptual states and perceiving. Perceptual states comport with the definition I offered earlier. They are representations contained within perceptual input systems. Emotions are, if the embodied appraisal theory is right, perceptions in this sense. Not every perceptual state is attained through an act of perceiving. Perceiving involves a direct passage of information from sensory transducers. An experience of red caused by seeing a ripe tomato is both a perceptual state and the outcome of perceiving. The light reflected by the tomato is picked up by the retinae, passed through the optic nerve, and registered by the visual pathways within the brain. Contrast this with a mental image of a ripe tomato. An image is a perceptual state, but it is not generated by an act of perceiving. Mental images are perceptual in one sense but not another. Equating mental images with perceptions is misleading. Likewise for emotions. Emotions are not generated by direct transduction but are instead mediated by other internal sates. Emotions are not generated by acts of perceiving. Emotions are not perceptual in this sense.

This objection is not insuperable. The claim that emotions are indirect is partially true and partially false. Emotions generally arise as a consequence of some other mental state. That much is hard to deny. But when they arise, they are a direct response to changes in the body. Emotions are states in the somatosensory system. They follow directly upon patterned bodily changes. They are transduced by the early somatosensory detectors that register perturbations in bodily organs, muscles, and chemical levels. It is, therefore, false to say that emotions are not generated by acts of perceiving. They arise when we perceive our bodies. Emotions are perceptions in both senses of the term. They are perceptual states activated by perceiving. Hume's account is, strictly speaking, wrong. Emotions are not impressions of impressions; they are first-order impressions. In fact, emotions are first-order impressions in a double sense. They register features of the internal world—the world of our bodies. And they represent relational features of the external world—the core relational themes.

One might try to resuscitate the indirectness objection by contrasting the ways these two kinds of contents are perceived. Emotions register bodily changes directly, but their ability to represent core relational themes depends on the mediating contribution of prior mental states. Emotions are perceptions of bodily states, but they are not perceptions of core relational themes. They do not represent core relational themes by direct transduction.

To answer this rejoinder, consider some cases outside the arena of emotion. First, consider synesthesia. Some people regularly and consistently experience sensation in one sensory modality when another one is stimulated. For example, Cytowic (1993) describes the case of Michael Watson, who has shape experiences when he tastes things. One food may taste round and another may taste spiky. Or it might be more accurate to say he feels flavors. The spiky tactile experience represents one taste, and roundness represents another. The composer Michael Torke sees colors when he hears music (Berman, 1999). He experiences orange when he hears G sharp and blue when he hears D major. It makes intuitively good sense to say that his musically induced color experiences are perceptions. He sees the sounds.

Also consider prosthetic vision. Bach-y-Rita, Collins, Saunders, White, and Scadden (1999) developed a device that helps blind people "see" the world by converting live video image into tactile impressions on the person's back. Now imagine if a sighted person received extensive training with the device. We might imagine that the sighted person would form a visual image when the tactile array caused a shape impression. Her visual images might become so reliable and so automatic that she could navigate blindfolded using the device. If this were to happen, we might say that she could see the objects around her, even though her visual states were caused indirectly through touch.

These cases are exotic, but they show that one sense can be activated by another. More important, they allow us to test our intuitions about whether indirectness precludes perception. My intuition is that synesthetic and prostheically induced visual experiences are perceptions of the things that cause them to arise. They are perceptions of tones or shapes even if not direct perceptions. Indirectness does not seem to render these cases nonperceptual. One might try to push this point by considering what happens within a single modality. Every sense divides into multiple subsystems. In ordinary visual perception, for example, three-dimensional shape information has to be recovered from two-dimensional spectral patterns recorded from the retinae in early visual centers. High-level vision is, in this sense, indirect. It would be bizarre to conclude that we never perceive shapes. Indirectness is not the exception in perception but the rule. In the case of emotions, the only difference is that more than one sense modality is involved. This makes the case unusual, but indirectness as such seems to be a red herring.

What really matters, I submit, is not directness but receptivity. The senses are responsive to things. They can act automatically in a bottom-up fashion to pick up information available to the organism. And the contents of perception are determined (roughly) by those things that systematically initiate such a response. When Michael Torke experiences colors during a symphony, those colors are receptive in just this sense, and they are systematically triggered by certain sounds. That's why it seems appropriate to say that Torke is perceiving sound through color. The same is true for emotion. Suppose someone experiences fear after seeing a snake. The fear is a receptive response, systematically triggered by danger. No matter how indirect, it has the basic profile of a perception. Indeed, emotions have a better claim to being perceptual than cases of synethesia. In synethesia, the resulting sensory states arise without stimulation of the corresponding sense modality. Torke's visual states are triggered without the eyes. In emotion, the senses are stimulated. When a person sees the snake, the body changes, and those changes are picked up using somatosensory transducers.

In sum, emotions may be somewhat less direct that typical sights, sounds, and smells. Emotional responses generally depend on prior thoughts or perceptions. But this indirectness is perfectly compatible with the claim that emotion is a form of perception. Moreover, core relational themes count among the causes to which emotions are receptively and systematically linked. Such systematicity, rather than directness, is what really matters in perception. This supports the conclusion that emotions are perceptions of core relational themes.

## Modularity

Another contrast between emotion and paradigm cases of perception involves the level of interaction with higher cognition. Emotions are deeply and persistently influenced by activities in the most advanced parts of the mind. Emotions can be caused by careful and informed reflection. In addition, our repertoire of emotions is not genetically fixed. New emotions can emerge through a process of recalibration, which can involve the influence of judgments and beliefs (chapter 4). Emotions can also emerge or transform under the influence of culture (chapter 6). These facts are in tension with a widely received view of perception.

According to the received view, perceptual systems are modules. Fodor (1983) has developed the most influential account of modularity. He argues that modules have a number of distinctive properties, as follows.

1. Localized: modules are realized in dedicated neural architecture.
2. Subject to specific breakdowns: modules break in characteristic ways.
3. Mandatory: modules operate automatically.
4. Fast: modules generate outputs quickly.
5. Shallow: modules have relatively simple outputs.
6. Inaccessible: higher levels of processing have limited access to the representations within a module.
7. Informationally encapsulated: modules cannot be guided by information at higher levels of processing.
8. Ontogenetically determined: modules develop in a characteristic pace and sequence.
9. Domain specific: modules cope with a restricted class of inputs.

Some researchers have argued that perceptual systems are not modular in Fodor's sense (see, e.g., Churchland [1988] on vision and Bates [1994] on language). I have some sympathy with these critics (Prinz, forthcoming-a). But I do think Fodor's account captures something. Most of the features on his list are characteristic of most perceptual systems under many circumstances. I think it is useful to regard modularity as a cluster concept. Perceptual systems typically exhibit the preponderance of items 1–9. They approximate modules, in this Fodorian sense.

If emotions do not have the preponderance of these features, the analogy between emotion and perception will fail.

Emotional systems certainly exhibit some of the properties on Fodor's list. Emotions reside in dedicated neural pathways that can break down in character-istic ways (chapter 9). The outputs of emotional systems are shallow; they repre-sent patterned bodily changes, which can be detected without very complex pro-cessing. Emotion systems also appear to be relatively inaccessible; we do not have conscious access to the operations by which bodily changes are detected. One might resist the assertion that emotions are fast and mandatory. While some emotional responses fit this description (fear after hearing a shrill scream), others do not. Consider the phenomenon of gradually growing to love someone. This may be a tolerable exception. Many perceptual skills, such as learning to sex chickens by sight, also take time to cultivate. But once such a skill is acquired, it can be deployed with automatic speed. Likewise, once one has fallen in love, the visage of one's beloved can cause an immediate palpitation of the heart.

The remaining three criteria pose a greater challenge. On the face of it, emo-tions are not informationally encapsulated. They are guided by thoughts and by representations in other sensory modalities. Culturally informed beliefs and values can also influence the bodily states that underpin emotions. Emotions also seem to be ontogenetically plastic. Basic emotions may emerge in a fixed se-quence (Lewis, 2000), but nonbasic emotions can emerge at different times dur-ing the lifespan. Nonbasic emotions are often influenced by personal or cultural histories. Finally, there is a serious question about whether emotions are domain specific. An open-ended range of mental states can become triggers for an emo-tional response. Whereas vision responds to light hitting the retinae, emotions can respond to just about anything.

One might just dismiss such objections by rejecting Fodor's definition of modularity. As I have already indicated, his criteria may be overly restrictive. By Fodor's own admission, modularity may come in degrees. A system that fails to satisfy all of his criteria, or that satisfies them only to limited degree, might be classified as relatively modular nonetheless. Or, as I suggested earlier, we might think of modularity as a cluster concept and be content saying that emotions typically exhibit most items in the cluster.

These response strategies would be sufficient, but one can also face the objec-tions head-on. The alleged contrasts between emotion systems and Fodorian modules may evaporate on scrutiny. Consider, first, the contention that emotions are not domain specific. Emotions may appear to occur in response to an open-ended range of things, but there are two senses in which their inputs are quite re-stricted. First, emotions are always responses to patterned bodily changes, and second, emotions are always responses to core relational themes. One can think of bodily changes as proximal inputs and core relational themes as distal inputs. Just as vision is used to detect objects through light, emotions detect relational themes through the body.

The impression that emotions are not domain specific may derive from a failure to distinguish two kinds of pathways involved in emotion processing (see fig. 10.1). On the one hand, there are emotion *initiation pathways*. These lead from various mental states to patterned bodily changes. The amygdala may play a central role in the initiation pathway for fear, disgust, and sadness (Anderson & Phelps, 1998). The amygdala receives inputs from a variety of different brain regions and initiates a pattern of bodily outputs, which then give rise to these emotions. Other structures may play this role for other emotions. On the other hand, there are emotion response pathways. These pathways are where the actual emotions take place. They go from the body to brain centers that register bodily change. Inputs to the emotion initiation pathways can vary dramatically, and they can change through learning and experience. The amygdala, and related structures, is not domain specific. But the emotion response pathways are domain specific. They respond to bodily changes and core relational themes.

In response, one might first point out that modularity is consistent with some degree of plasticity. Fodor admits that ordinary perceptual systems may change their patterns of response over the course of development. For example, consider Gregory's (1966) suggestion that the Müller-Lyer illusion occurs only in cultures whose members see many sharp corners (see also Deregowski, 1974). If you live in a world with cubical buildings, straight lines with angular terminators will be perceived as closer or farther depending on the direction of the angles. If you've grown up with rounded corners, your visual system will not learn to draw this inference. The Müller-Lyer lines will appear equal in length. If you move from such a place to a world of Mies van der Rohe skyscrapers, your visual system will gradually adjust, and you will become vulnerable to the illusion. This shows that the visual system is not immutable and that changes can occur outside of a preprogrammed developmental sequence. Fodor does not see this as a challenge to the hypothesis that vision is modular. He admits that environment can impact vision but insists that such influences must be gradual. Likewise, one can claim that emotions change through gradual adjustments, as when culture drives us to develop new habits of the body. Such unscheduled changes in emotional response are broadly consistent with the kind of ontogenetic fixity that Fodor has in mind.

The objection from plasticity can also be answered by invoking the distinction between initiation and response pathways. The fact that some emotions do not emerge on a genetically fixed schedule is largely attributable to the plasticity of emotion initiation. Emotion initiation pathways house calibration files. Calibration files can be altered or acquired as a function of experience. This fosters the appearance of incredible ontogenetic variation in human emotional response, but the appearance misleads. Emotion response pathways may be comparatively stable and predictable over the course of development.

Similar considerations undermine the allegation that emotions are not informationally encapsulated. It is certainly true that higher cognitive states, including culturally informed judgments and values, can influence our emotions. Recall the case of acedia, experienced by those who grow tired from the monotony of religious practice. Don't such emotions demonstrate that emotions can be influ-

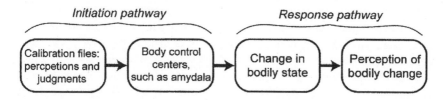

*Figure 10.1.* Emotion initiation and response pathways.

enced by higher cognition? Perhaps not. Emotions such as acedia are created by recalibrating previously existing emotions to a new class of eliciting conditions (e.g., going to church). Calibration files are part of the initiation pathway. Beliefs about the monotony of churchgoing need not directly interact with the embodied representation comprising the emotion itself. There may be no direct interaction between the information in calibration files and the emotions they calibrate. The calibration file causes a body response, and the body response causes the emotion. There is no need for direct talk between somatosensory areas of the brain and those areas that harbor evaluative judgments about social practices.

These considerations suggest that emotions *may* be informationally encapsulated. Is there any reason to think that they *are*? According to Fodor, informational encapsulation is evidenced by perceptual illusions. If a perceptual illusion persists even after we learn that it is an illusion, then it resides in a processing system that is not directly influenced by knowledge. The Müller-Lyer illusion is a case in point. The two lines continue to appear different in length even after we learn that they are the same. If perceptual systems could communicate directly with higher cognition, the Müller-Lyer illusion would disappear, or at least diminish, after measuring the lines.

Emotion systems are equally susceptible to persistent illusions. Consider, once more, the woman who continues to feel angry at her spouse despite the explicit and emphatic judgment that he is beyond reproach. Even people who are very well-adjusted can relate to this kind of case. Other recalcitrant emotions stem from psychiatric conditions. This is nowhere more clear than in the case of phobias. A person who is afraid of flying may know that planes are safer than cars but still feel mortal terror every time she boards a plane (Greenspan, 1988). Depression is another case in point. The depressive person may feel cripplingly sad while knowing that nothing terrible has happened. Consider, as well, the sadness that can result from reading a tragic novel that we know to be fictitious (see Walton, 1978). Or, better yet, consider sadness evoked by nonvocal music. In the hands of a good composer, a D-minor chord can send listeners into the abyss. Listeners know that there has been no loss, but the floodwaters of despair well up inside them. Panksepp (1995) has argued that some music causes sadness because it shares acoustic properties with the sound of infants' crying. As with the Müller-Lyer lines, however, understanding the illusion does not make the illusion go away.

Examples are easy to multiply. They strongly suggest that emotions are modular in the Fodorian sense. Once an emotion is triggered, judgments and other higher cognitive states are relatively ineffective in making it go away. Of course, judgments can exert some influence. Judgments can cause emotions, and judgment can change emotions. When a judgment causes an emotion, it is not directly interacting with the emotional response system. It is only triggering bodily changes that set the response in motion. Judgments may change emotions in the same way. They may trigger a change from one pattern of bodily responses to another. In both cases, the effects are indirect. The efficacy of our judgments is further delimited by a second fact. Calibration files can include perceptual triggers that operate at a fairly low level of processing. A person with a fear of flying may have a link between visual representations of airplanes and the amygdala. Because this link operates from within the visual system, judgments about the safety of air travel cannot preempt the fear response. In other words, initiation pathways may contain informationally encapsulated links between perceptual representations of emotion elicitors and the mechanisms that orchestrate bodily response. This makes emotions doubly impervious to direct higher cognitive control.

As Griffiths (1997) points out, the modularity of emotions offers a good explanation of their passivity. We do not seem to be in control of our emotions. They just happen to us. This common observation is etymologically enshrined in the term "passion." A comparable kind of passivity can be found in paradigm cases of perception. When we look at a ripe tomato, we cannot help but see red. No judgment or desire can block the path from retina to redness, just as no judgment or desire can block the path from body to affect. In both cases, passivity owes to modularity.

Some authors have argued that emotions are less passive than they may appear. Solomon (1976), for example, argues that emotions can be chosen. A similar theme appears in Aristotle (1985), who stresses emotional training. There is no conflict between the claim that emotions are passive and the claim that they can be controlled. Emotions are voluntary in a double sense. Thinking about something in the right way can certainly influence our emotions, and calibration files can be modified through education and experience. We exert control over emotions by choosing what to think about, and by cultivating calibration files. But emotions are also involuntary in a double sense. First, the thoughts and images contained in an established calibration file may set off emotions automatically. If one happens, by choice or accident, to activate a representation in a calibration file, an emotion will ensue. Second, once an emotion has been initiated, we cannot alter it by direct intervention. Initiation pathways and response pathways both operate without the luxury of control.

### Warrant

There is one more alleged contrast between emotion and paradigm cases of perception that I will consider. There used to be a consensus that emotions are irrational. As Alexander Pope (1733–34) put it, "What reason weaves, by passion is undone." Emotions are associated with our animal nature, the most primitive part of human psychology. Reason, in contrast, reflects the highest reaches of cognitive function and does its best to keep emotion in line. The Kants of the world argue that we should try to keep emotions in check, and the Rousseaus of the world want to unhinge the shackles of reason. Both positions buy into the same basic dichotomy. Now it is popular to argue that reason and emotion are inextricably bound (e.g., Damasio, 1994; de Sousa, 1987; Elster, 1996; Frank, 1988; Greenspan, 2000). Emotions, like higher cognitive states, can be perfectly rational.

One reason for the changing attitude comes from the observation that we often hold emotions up to normative standards. We regard emotions as appropriate or inappropriate, good or bad, noble or ignoble, or even justified or unjustified. A person who laughs at victims of adversity is open to censure. We might even call such an emotional response irrational. These normative standards are less frequently applied to paradigm cases of perception. Suppose Smith misperceives a mule as a horse. We do not say that Smith was irrational. We do not say she has done something inappropriate or complain that the perception was unjustified. Both perceptions and emotions have accuracy conditions. It is an error to visually represent a mule as a horse, and it is an error to fear something harmless. Fear represents danger, and harmless objects are not dangerous. But it can also be irrational to fear something, as when we fear foreigners simply because they are foreign. Normativity transcends accuracy, and it is more at home in the affective realm than in the realms of sight and touch (see Pitcher, 1965). Why this difference?

To begin, let us put emotions to one side and consider how normative assessment works in the context of arguments. Arguments can go wrong in two ways. They can rest on bad premises, or they can rest on bad inferences. When one normatively assesses an argument, one places blame or praise on its author. Blame or praise are appropriate only in contexts where a person has responsibility. For brevity's sake, we can steer clear of the vast literature on what responsibility consists in and keep things at an intuitive level. We blame a person who constructs an argument with bad premises or a bad inference; we say that person is responsible for these flaws. If the bad premise could have been avoided by reviewing information that was readily available to the arguer, then we may hold her blameworthy. We may even blame someone for relying on a true premise, if that premise has not been obtained through reliable means. When a premise lacks support, and its author is responsible for that fact, we can say it lacks *premise warrant*. Likewise, we may blame someone for drawing a bad inference, if the bad inference could have been avoided. An inference is bad if its conclusion has no tendency to follow from its premises. When an inference is bad, and its author is responsible for its faults, we say it lacks *inference warrant*.

These constructs carry over into the realm of emotions. We can think of emotions as conclusions to arguments. The mental representations used in the initiation pathway are like premises. They are the grounds on which the emotion is based. The calibration file is a mechanism that uses premises to trigger an emotional response. It specifies what kinds of information can serve as an emotion trigger. In that respect, it is like a collection of inference rules (e.g., *If you see a snake, experience fear*). The transition from a representation of an elicitor to an emotion can be regarded as an inference. It is a move from one group of meaningful mental states (representations of elicitors) to another (the emotion), and one can describe the former as reasons for the latter. Representations of elicitors trigger emotions precisely because emotions are more likely to be accurate when those eliciting conditions obtain. Fear is likely to be accurate (i.e., one is likely to be in danger) when one sees a snake. Therefore, the triggering process is not arbitrary. It is more like an inference.

The fact that emotions can be regarded as conclusions to arguments does not demonstrate that they are amenable to normative assessment. Normative assessment requires responsibility. There are at least two ways in which a person can be held responsible for her emotions. These correspond to premise warrant and inference warrant. Suppose Jones feels proud because she thinks she is prettier than Smith. In actuality Smith is better looking, and Jones simply failed to properly appreciate her beauty. Jones's smug delight is prefaced on a thought that is neither true nor adequately supported; it lacks premise warrant. Now suppose that physical attractiveness is not worthy of pride. Attractiveness is, to a certain extent, a function of our genetic makeup and the tastes of those around us. Neither of these things can be easily controlled by any individual. So attractiveness is, to a large degree, a happy accident, not an achievement. If pride is an emotion that is reserved for achievements, it is usually inappropriate to be proud of one's appearance. If Jones feels proud of her genetically determined looks, and she has access to information and skills that would allow her to banish looks from her calibration file, then she can be criticized for her emotion. Here, pride lacks inference warrant.

One might challenge this second example by arguing that pride must be applicable to attractiveness because it is reliably elicited by attractiveness. If the content of pride is determined by its causes, attractiveness is an appropriate cause. Generalizing the point, one might argue that an emotion can never be inappropriate when it occurs in response to something in a calibration file, because calibration files determine what emotions are about. This objection can be answered by appealing to a criterion of coherence. Let's imagine that pride operates under the control of a calibration file *most of whose contents* pertain to achievement. If that is the case, pride reliably detects achievement, and can qualify as an achievement representation. If that file includes *a few* elicitors that are not achievement based, it is incoherent. It includes elicitors that do not exhibit the property that pride reliably detects. If these illicit causes made their way into the calibration file as a result of our inattention—for example, if we cultivated a habit of being proud of our looks without noticing the incoherence—then we may be censured when they cause us to feel pride.

There are, in sum, two places for normativity to get a foothold in our emotional responses. We can be held responsible for having emotions based on bad premises or bad inferences, provided we are responsible for those premises and inferences. This connects to a pair of observations made earlier. Normative assessment of emotions is a function of the fact that emotions are partially under our control, and it is a function of the fact that emotions are indirect. This answers the question with which we began. Emotions differ from paradigm cases of perception precisely because of these two factors. If Smith mistakes a mule for a horse, and this is a consequence of how her visual system works under the operative viewing conditions, then she may escape blame. Her perceptual state is not based on any premises or inference rules over which she had control (she cannot control processes in early vision). Vision does not require an initiation pathway. It is not mediated, under ordinary conditions, by mental states outside the visual system—states for which a person might be held responsible.

These observations also show that the contrast between emotion and paradigm cases of perception will not hold under all circumstances. There are conditions under which visual judgments can be held to normative standards. If Smith chronically misperceives mules as horses and she has been assigned the task of identifying a particular mule, she may be obligated to improve her perceptual acuity. Alternatively, imagine that Smith misperceives a mule as a horse because she has taken a psychoactive drug. In either case, we may hold her accountable. This is just a way of pointing out that normative standards become applicable when a person has some control over her responses.

Conversely, there are cases in which people are not held responsible for their emotions. If someone experiences euphoria because of a chemical change that is caused by someone else, she may not be responsible for her reaction. Suppose Smith injects Jones with a drug that produces euphoria before showing her a documentary on forced labor camps in the former Soviet Union. If Jones chirps happily throughout the film, we will not blame her. Similar points may apply to emotions produced by facial feedback, phobias, or affective disorders.

I draw two interim conclusions. First, the contrast between emotions and paradigm perceptual states is not sharp. Both are amenable to normative assessment in some cases and not in others. Second, the normative assessment of an emotion generally arises because of features of its initiation pathway.

The second point suggests that emotions themselves may never be normatively assessable in their own right. Hume (1739/1978, II.iii.3) says, "a passion can never, in any sense, be call'd unreasonable, but when founded on a false supposition." In other words, the normative status of an emotion may derive entirely from the mental states that cause it. If an emotion is based on a mental state that is itself open to normative assessment, and that mental state is unwarranted, then the emotion may be unwarranted. If an emotion is caused by an item in a calibration file, and that item bears a questionable relation to the property that the emotion normally represents, then the emotion may be unwarranted. If we make sure that emotions are always caused by warranted premises and inferences, we can insulate them against normative censure.

The same point can be made by relocating the question of warrant to a different stage in the process of emotion elicitation. Let's assume it is inappropriate to laugh in the face of others' adversity (though note that Hobbes [1650/1994] thought this was exactly what laughter was for). Now consider someone who does this. That person may have a calibration file for amusement that contains representations of others' misfortune. It may be wrong, in some sense, to have such a file. But now ask, is it wrong to laugh in the face of adversity assuming such a calibration file is already in place? Put in this way, the answer may be negative. It is not wrong to feel amusement when one encounters something that matches the contents of your amusement file. Nor is it right. Once a calibration file has been set up, we cannot help but react to its contents. This is one source of emotional passivity. The response to items in our calibration files is automatic, and falls outside the jurisdiction of normative assessment. Viewed in this light, emotions are really arational.

The normative status of emotions is complicated by the fact that emotional response has both passive and active dimensions. Emotions tend to be more amenable to normative assessment than paradigm instances of perception, because their elicitation is more dependent on prior mental states and rules. Even so, there is always a sense in which emotional responses are beyond our control. There is a sense in which the most heinous passion is as innocent as seeing an afterimage.

I conclude that emotion is a form of perception. Having an emotion is literally perceiving our relationship to the world. Like perceptions, emotions can be inaccurate or even unjustified, in the ways I have described. But they can also be revelatory. They can deliver information that helps us assess how we are faring. They often allow us to pick up this information before we have made any pertinent judgments. A well-tuned calibration file can pick up subtle cues that send the body reeling. In many cases, we perceive these bodily perturbations before we have reflected on our situation. Emotions can even enter awareness before we have consciously accessed the subtle cues that triggered them. This is why we describe emotions as gut reactions. They are like bodily radar detectors that alert us to concerns. When we listen to our emotions, we are not being swayed by meaningless feelings. Nor are we hearing the cold dictates of complex judgments. We are using our bodies to perceive our position in the world.

# *Coda*
## Parting Ways

In chapter 1, I introduced two complementary problems for the emotion theorist. First, there was the problem of the parts. Every mental episode in which an emotion is experienced contains a number of different elements. We form thoughts, our bodies change, we become poised for action, our information-processing modes shift, and we experience conscious feelings. Some of these elements may be parts of the emotion; others may just be contingent concomitants. An emotion theorist must pick and choose. The second problem facing emotion theorists is the problem of plenty. When faced with all the different elements that could make up an emotion, one might adopt an encompassing strategy. Perhaps all of these elements count. Perhaps emotions are compounds built up of large a number of different parts. If one opts for this strategy, one has to explain how all these parts hang together. By way of conclusion, I want to review how the embodied appraisal theory handles these complementary problems.

There is a temptation to regard emotions as very complex. Each of the elements in an emotion episode seems to be essential to that emotion, and each of these elements seems to be a different kind of mental entity. Consequently, emotions seem to be assemblies of different kinds of mental entities. This conclusion can be dispelled by considering a parody. Suppose one wants to provide a theory of conscious visual states. What, one might ask, is a conscious red experience? In addressing this question, one might notice that there are many elements involved in conscious experiences of red. First, there is a physiological change, including, for example, a cellular response in the retinae. Then, there is the consciousness itself—the phenomenal feeling of redness. Experiences of red also seem to cause judgments; ordinary people cannot experience red without forming a thought, which would be expressed by saying "That's red!" In addition, there is likely to be an adjustment of attention (we focus on the red object) and an action tendency (we may be disposed to orient toward the red object, or reach for it). We may even call up memories of other red things.

To cope with such complexity, one might say that conscious red experiences have several parts. There is a feeling, a thought, an action tendency, an attention controller, and a memory trigger. One might try to identify mental entities (or neural correlates) corresponding to each of these things. When asked to point out which one is the red experience, one might point to the whole set of entities. Red experiences, one might say, have many components.

This complexity would be gratuitous. It would be better to say that a conscious red experience is a unitary mental entity that has several functions, properties, and effects. These entities feel like something, they carry information (that's red!), they arise under certain physiological conditions, they attract attention, they motivate action, they call up memories, and so forth. Many of these effects depend on the complicity of other mental states and operations, but we should not confuse the red experience with these. The red experience may have no parts.

A similar moral applies in the case of emotions. Let us look more carefully at the elements in an emotion episode. I have argued that bodily states are especially important to emotions (chapter 3). Following in the tradition of Descartes, James, Lange, and, more recently, Damasio, I believe that emotions are inner states that occur in response to bodily changes. That does not mean that bodily change is necessary for emotions. As James and Damasio pointed out, an emotion can arise when the brain areas associated with bodily change are active, even if no actual bodily change has taken place. Thus, bodily changes are standard causes, but not essential causes, of emotional states.

Bodily changes facilitate action. Blood flows when we are angry, because increased circulation enables aggressive response. But that does not mean that each emotion prepares us for a *specific* behavior (chapter 8). Nor does it mean that emotions *cause* us to act. Instead emotions enable a variety of behavioral responses. Emotions exert motivating force by means of valence markers. They goad us to select a response that is appropriate for perpetuating or ending the situations that induce them. The link between emotion and action is thus strong but indirect. Emotions compel us to act, but they are not action tendencies.

The relationship between emotions and feelings is more direct. When an emotion is felt, the feeling literally is the emotion. Feelings are brain states in perceptual systems. Emotions become conscious in just the way that other perceptual states become conscious (chapter 9). An emotional feeling is an embodied appraisal that is broadcasting to working memory, not an independent state that dangles beside the somatic appraisal. But this does not mean that I defend a feeling theory. First, emotions can also occur unconsciously. Second, all emotions carry information. They are never *mere* feelings.

This brings me to the thoughts that accompany our emotions. According to defenders of cognitive theories, emotions depend on propositional attitudes. These are construed as structured, concept-laden mental representations that are not identical to the somatic states associated with our emotions. I believe that some

emotions are caused by propositional attitudes, and that propositional attitudes can even play a role in determining the significance of our emotions (chapters 4 and 7). But I argued that emotions can occur without propositional atti-
tudes.Even our most advanced emotions can be triggered without any prior
judgment (chapter 4). At the same time, I argued that emotions may qualify as
thoughts in their own right. They represent core relational themes despite their
lack of propositional structure. They detect without describing (chapter 3). Emotions are not appraisals-plus-embodied-representations; they are embodied representations that qualify as appraisals. More succinctly, they are embodied
appraisals.

Let me turn, finally, to the changes in mental operations or processing modes
that accompany our emotions. I introduced this topic in chapter 1, and I will only
gesture at an account here. There is a large and growing literature exploring the
interactions between emotion and attention, memory, and styles of reasoning. Researchers have discovered that happiness tends to facilitate creative thinking
(Isen, Daubman, & Novicki, 1987). Fear increases risk estimates, and anger de-
creases risk estimates (Lerner & Keltner, 2000). Sadness promotes backward
thinking and draws attention to our own flaws (Alloy & Abrahamson, 1988). All
emotions seem to facilitate recall of prior events in which the same emotion was
experienced (Bower, 1981). Impressed by such findings, Oatley and Johnson-
Laird (1987) go so far as to identify certain emotions with changes in mental
operations—what they call modes of processing. I do not think this move is
required.

One can accommodate some of the experimental results by appealing to general features of how the mind works. For example, our ability to recall past
events in which we experienced the same emotions that we are experiencing in
the present can be explained by priming and the confirmation bias. Priming is a
global phenomenon in memory retrieval whereby present states facilitate recall of
related states. Present sorrows bring past sorrows to mind in much the way that
seeing a poodle would bring past poodle encounters to mind. The confirmation
bias is a general tendency to search for information that confirms what we already hold to be true. If one is in an angry state, one will look for evidence that
will justify and promote this state. That may involve recalling other episodes of
anger, which stand a chance of providing some precedent for one's current feelings. The confirmation bias also helps to explain attentional affects of emotions
and interactions with cognitive processing. Sadness may draw attention to flaws
and anger may draw attention to insults because these things tend to provide further evidence for thinking our emotions are appropriate. Fear may promote high
risk estimations, because those estimations can help sustain one's state of fear.
Sadness may promote analytic processing because analytic thought helps in the
identification of flaws. Happiness may promote creative thinking because creative
thinking leads to new discoveries that can stimulate further happiness.

Obviously this interpretation of the interaction between emotion and cognitive
operations needs much more development and support. The point I am trying to

make is that highly specific emotional effects on cognition could, in principle, be derived from general features of the mind. In support of the explanations I have offered, let me mention two intriguing experimental results. Research on the cognitive effects of happiness shows that happiness tends to promote successful problem solving. But some studies have gotten the opposite results. Happy people sometimes reason poorly. Isen (2000) proposes that the discrepancy derives from the fact that happy people excel at solving problems they find interesting. If you induce a happy state in a person, and then give her a boring problem, she will not apply much energy to it, and that will impair performance. This finding is hard to reconcile with the view that emotions simply are (or inevitably cause) specific modes of information processing. Instead, it seems that emotions cause us to use whatever processing modes promote their continuation. This interpretation predicts that emotions will not have their characteristic effects on mental operations when there is an independent reason for not sustaining an emotion. Some studies of emotional effects on memory support this prediction. Emotions normally facilitate retrieval of emotionally congruent memories. But the opposite happens in situations where people want to suppress their emotions. If you do not want to be elated, a happy state will actually facilitate recall of unhappy memories. The relation between emotions and information processing is not fixed. That relation is ordinarily influenced by default mechanisms and biases, such as priming and the confirmation bias, but it can be renegotiated to meet contextual demands. I conclude that we do not need to build anything into emotions (no special parts or mechanism) in order to explain how they interact with operations of the mind.

My more general conclusion is that emotions are relatively simple entities. They are comprised of just two parts: embodied appraisals and valence markers. But these two parts have considerable explanatory power. They are action-beckoning, body-registering, memory- and attention-facilitating thoughts that can be consciously experienced. This is a multicomponent theory, because emotions have two parts. But it is also a multifunction theory, because at least one of those parts can serve a variety of different roles. Embodied appraisals are thoughts and feelings. They register the body's preparations for action and prime congruent memories. In short, they do most of the things that theories of emotion have sought to explain. This provides an easy explanation of why the various features of emotions hang together. Emotions are not unstable assemblies of dissociable parts. They are not meanings, feelings, and action tendencies pasted together with mental glue. They are meaningful, feelable wholes that register action-enabling body changes.

Many researchers try to pack both too much and too little into emotions. They pack in too much by assuming that bodily changes, propositional attitudes, action dispositions, and feelings are essential parts or preconditions for emotions. I argued that all of these things are only contingently related to emotions. They are the causes and effects of emotions. Those causes and effects are certainly worthy of study, but they should not be mistaken for the emotions themselves. Researchers pack too much into emotions by assuming that simple mental entities cannot serve multiple functions. They underestimate the resources that are available to defenders of somatic theories. Even James failed to appreciate the rich resources nested in the perception of a racing heart. The embodied appraisal theory shows how to bundle a variety of different functions into a relatively simple package. The heart pounds with significance.

# References

Alloy, L., & Abrahamson, L. (1988). Depressive realism. In L. B. Alloy (Ed.), *Cognitive processes in depression* (pp. 441–485). New York: Guilford Press.

Amaral, D. G., Price, J. L., Pitkanen, A., & Carmichael, S. T. (1992). Anatomical organization of the primate amygdaloid complex. In J. Aggleton (Ed.), *The amygdala: Neurobiological aspects of emotion, memory, and mental dysfunction* (pp. 1–66). New York: Wiley-Liss.

American Psychiatric Association. (1994). *Diagnostic and statistical manual of mental disorders* (4th ed.). Washington, DC: Author.

Amorapanth, P., LeDoux, J. E., & Nader, K. (2000). Different lateral amygdala outputs mediate reactionand actions elicited by a fear-arousing stimulus. *Nature Neuroscience, 3,* 74–79.

Anderson, A. K., & Phelps, E.A. (1998). Intact recognition of vocal expressions of fear following bilateral lesions of the amygdala. *NeuroReport, 9,* 3607–3613.

Anisman, H., Zalcman, S., & Zacharko, R. (1993). The impact of stressors on immune and central neurotransmitter activity: Bidirectional communication. *Reviews in Neurosciences, 4,* 147–180.

Aristotle. (1961). *De anima.* (W. D. Ross, Trans.). Oxford: Clarendon Press.

Aristotle. (1984). *Rhetoric.* (W. R. Roberts, Trans.). In *The rhetoric and poetics of Aristole.* (E. P. J. Corbett, Ed.). New York: Modern Library.

Aristotle. (1985). *Nicomachean ethics.* (T. Irwin, Trans.). Indianapolis: Hackett.

Armon-Jones, C. (1986). The thesis of constructionism. In R. Harré (Ed.), *The social construction of emotions* (pp. 32–56). Oxford: Blackwell.

Armon-Jones, C. (1989). *Varieties of affect.* Toronto: University of Toronto Press.

Arnold, M. B. (1960). *Emotion and personality.* New York: Columbia University Press.

Arntz, A. (1993). Endorphins stimulate approach behavior, but do not reduce subjective fear: A pilot study. *Behaviour Research and Therapy, 31,* 403–405.

Augustine, J. R. (1996). Circuitry and functional aspects of the insular lobe in primate including humans. *Brain Research Reviews, 22,* 229–244.

Averill, J. R. (1980). A constructivist view of emotion. In R. Plutchik & H. Kellerman (Eds.), *Emotion: Theory, research and experience: Vol. 1. Theories of emotion* (pp. 305–339). New York: Academic Press.

Averill, J. R. (1985). The social construction of emotion: With special reference to love. In K. Gergen & K. Davis (Eds.), *The social construction of the person* (pp. 89–109). New York: Springer-Verlag.

Averill, J. R., & Boothroyd, P. (1977). On falling in love in conformance with the romantic ideal. *Motivation and Emotion, 3,* 235–247.

Bach-y-Rita, P., Collins, C. C., Saunders, F., White, B., & Scadden, L. (1969). Vision substitution by tactile image projection. *Nature, 221,* 963–964.

Barkow, J., Cosmides, L., & Tooby, J. (Eds.). (1992). *The adapted mind: Evolutionary psychology and the generation of culture.* New York: Oxford University Press.

Bartels, A., & Zeki, S. (2000). The neural basis of romantic love. *NeuroReport, 11,* 3829–3834.

Bates, E. (1994). Modularity, domain specificity and the development of language. *Discussions in Neuroscience, 10,* 136–149.

Bedford, E. (1957). Emotions. *Proceedings of the Artistotelian Society, 57,* 281–304.

Beirce, A. (1911/1999). *The devil's dictionary.* Oxford: Oxford University Press.

Benedict, R. (1946). *The chrysanthemum and the sword.* Boston: Houghton Mifflin.

Ben-Ze'ev, A. (2000). *The subtlety of emotions.* Cambridge: MIT Press.

Berlin, B., & P. Kay (1969). *Basic color terms: Their universality and evolution.* Berkeley: University of California Press.

Berman, G. (1999). *Synesthesia and the arts.* Cambridge: MIT Press.

Berridge, K. C. (1996). Food reward: Brain substrates of wanting and liking. *Neuroscience and Biobehavioral Reviews, 20,* 1–25.

Berridge, K. C. (1999). Pleasure, pain, desire, and dread: Hidden core processes of emotion. In D. Kahneman, E. Diener, & N. Schwarz (Eds.), *Well-being: The foundations of hedonic psychology* (pp. 525–557). New York: Russell Sage Foundation.

Berthier, M., Starkstein, S., & Leiguarda, R. (1988). Asymbolia for pain: A sensory-limbic disconnection syndrome. *Annals of Neurology, 24,* 41–49.

Bisiach, E. (1992). Understanding consciousness: Clues from unilateral neglect and related disorders. In A. D. Milner & M. D. Rugg (Eds.), *The neuropsychology of consciousness* (pp. 113–139). London: Academic Press.

Blair, R. (1995). A cognitive developmental approach to morality: Investigating the psychopath. *Cognition, 57,* 1–29.

Bless, H., Schwarz, N., & Kemmelmeier, M. (1996). Mood and stereotyping: The impact of moods on the use of general knowledge structures. *European Review of Social Psychology, 7,* 63–93.

Block, N. (1995). On a confusion about a function of consciousness. *Behavioral and Brain Sciences, 18,* 1995.

Boucher, J. D., & Carlson, O. E. (1980). Recognition of facial expression in three cultures. *Journal of Cross-Cultural Psychology, 11,* 263–280.

Bower, G. H. (1981). Mood and memory. *American Psychologist, 36,* 129–148.

Bowlby, J. (1973). *Attachment and loss: Vol. 2. Separation.* New York: Basic Books.

Boyd, R. (1989). What realism implies and what it does not. *Dialectica, 43,* 5–29.

Boyer, P. (2001). *Religion explained: The evolutionary origins of religious thought.* New York: Basic Books.

Briggs, J. L. (1970). *Never in anger: Portrait of an Eskimo family.* Cambridge: Harvard University Press.

Buckner, R. L., Kelley, W. M., & Petersen, S. E. (1999). Frontal cortex contributes to human memory formation. *Nature Neuroscience, 2,* 311–314.

Burge, T. (1986). Individualism and psychology. *Philosophical Review, 95,* 3–45.

Buss, D. M. (2000). *The dangerous passion.* New York: Free Press.

Buss, D. M., Larsen, R. J., & Westen, D. (1996). Sex differences in jealousy: Not gone, not forgotten, and not explained by alternative hypotheses. *Psychological Science, 7,* 373–375.

Buss, D. M., Larsen, R. J., Westen, D., & Semmelroth, J. (1992). Sex differences in jealousy: Evolution, physiology, and psychology. *Psychological Science. 3,* 251–255.

Buunk, B. P., Angleitner, A., Oubaid, V., & Buss, D. M. (1996). Sex differences in jealousy in evolutionary and cultural perspective: Tests from the Netherlands, Germany, and the United States. *Psychological Science, 7,* 359–363.

Cacioppo, J., Bernston, G., Larson, J., Poehlmann, K., & Ito, T. (2000). The psychophysiology of emotion. In M. Lewis & J. Haviland-Jones (Eds.), *Handbook of emotions* (2nd ed., pp. 173–191). New York: Guilford Press.

Camras, L. A. (1992). Basic emotions and expressive development. *Cognition and Emotion, 6,* 269–284.

Camras, L. A. (1994). Two aspects of emotional development: Expression and elicitation. In P. Ekman & R. J. Davidson (Eds.), *The nature of emotion: Fundamental questions* (pp. 347–352). New York: Oxford University Press.

Cannon, W. B. (1927). The James-Lange theory of emotion: A critical examination and an alternative theory. *American Journal of Psychology, 39,* 106–124.

Carroll, N. (1990). *The philosophy of horror, or paradoxes of the heart.* New York: Routledge.

Chagnon, N. A. (1968). *Yanomamö: The fierce people.* New York: Holt, Rinehart, and Winston.

Chevalier-Skolnikoff, S. (1973). Facial expression of emotion in nonhuman primates. In P. Ekman (Ed.), *Darwin and facial expression* (pp. 11–98). New York: Academic Press.

Chu, C. G. (1985). The changing concept of self in contemporary China. In A. J. Marsella, G. DeVos, & F. L. K. Hsu (Eds.), *Culture and self: Asian and Western perspectives* (pp. 252–277). New York: Tavistock.

Churchland, P. M. (1988). Perceptual plasticity and theoretical neutrality: A reply to Jerry Fodor. *Philosophy of Science, 55,* 167–187.

Churchland, P. S. (1992). Reduction and the neurobiological basis of consciousness. In A. J. Marcel & E. Bisiach (Eds.), *Consciousness in contemporary science* (pp. 273–304). Oxford: Clarendon Press.

Chwalisz, K., Diener, E., & Gallagher, D. (1988). Autonomic arousal feedback and emotional experience: Evidence from the spinal cord injured. *Journal of Personality and Social Psychology, 54,* 820–828.

Cloninger, C. R. (1994). Temperament and personality. *Current Opinion in Neurobiology, 4,* 266–273.

Clore, G. (1994a). Why emotions are never unconscious. In P. Ekman & R. J. Davidson (Eds.), *The nature of emotion: Fundamental questions* (pp. 285–290). New York: Oxford University Press.

Clore, G. (1994b). Why emotions require cognition. In P. Ekman & R. J. Davidson (Eds.), *The nature of emotion: Fundamental questions* (pp. 181–191). New York: Oxford University Press.

Cosmides, L. (1989). The logic of social exchange: Has natural selection shaped how humans reason? Studies with the Wason selection task. *Cognition, 31,* 187–276.

Cowie, F. (1998). *What's within? Nativism reconsidered.* New York: Oxford University Press.

Creighton, M. (1990). Revisiting shame and guilt cultures: A forty-year pilgrimage. *Ethos, 18,* 279–307.

Crespo, E. (1986). A regional variation: Emotions in Spain. In R. Harré (Ed.), *The social construction of emotions* (pp. 209–217). Oxford: Blackwell.

Critchley, H. D., Mathias, C. J., & Dolan, R. J. (2001). Neural correlates of first- and second-order representation of bodily states. *Nature Neuroscience, 4,* 207–212.

Cross-National Collaborative Group. (1992). The changing rate of major depression. *Journal of the American Medical Association, 268,* 3098–3115.

Cytowic, R. E. (1993). *The man who tasted shapes.* Cambridge: MIT Press.

Damasio, A. (1998). The somatic marker hypothesis and the possible functions of the prefrontal cortex. In A. Roberts, T. Robbins, & L. Weiskrantz (Eds.), *The prefrontal cortex: Executive and cognitive function* (pp. 36–50). Oxford: Oxford University Press.

Damasio, A., & Van Hoesen, G. W. (1983). Emotional disturbances associated with focal lesions of the limbic frontal lobe. In K. M. Heilman & P. Satz (Eds.), *Neuropsychology of human emotion* (pp. 85–110). New York: Guilford Press.

Damasio, A. R. (1989). Time-locked multiregional retroactivation: A systems-level proposal for the neural substrates of recall and recognition. *Cognition, 33,* 25–62.

Damasio, A. R. (1994). *Descartes' error: Emotion, reason and the human brain.* New York: Putnam.

Damasio, A. R. (1999). *The feeling of what happens: Body and emotion in the making of consciousness.* New York: Harcourt Brace.

Damasio, A. R., Grabowski, T. J., Bechara, A., Damasio, H., Ponto, L. L. B., Parvizi, J., & Hichwa, R. D. (2000). Subcortical and cortical brain activity during the feeling of self-generated emotions. *Nature Neuroscience, 3,* 1049–1056.

D'Andrade, R. G. (1992). Schemas and motivation. In R. G. D'Andrade & C. Strauss (Eds.), *Human motives and cultural models* (pp. 23–44*).* Cambridge, UK: Cambridge University Press.

Darwin, C. (1872/1998). *The expression of the emotions in man and animals* (P. Ekman, Ed.), (3rd ed.). New York: Oxford University Press.

Davidson R. J. (1992). Emotion and affective style: Hemispheric substrates. *Psychological Science, 3,* 39–43.

Davidson, R. J. (1994). On emotion, mood, and related affective constructs. In P. Ekman & R. J. Davidson (Eds.), *The nature of emotion: Fundamental questions* (pp. 51–55). Oxford: Oxford University Press.

Davidson, R. J., & Irwin, W. (1999). The functional neuroanatomy of emotion and affective style. *Trends in Cognitive Sciences, 3,* 11–21.

Davis, M. (1998). Are different parts of the extended amygdala involved in fear versus anxiety? *Biological Psychiatry, 44,* 1239–1247.

Davitz, J. (1969). *The language of emotion.* New York: Academic Press.

Dawkins, R. (1976). *The selfish gene.* Oxford: Oxford University Press.

Dennett, D., & Kinsbourne, M. (1992). Time and the observer: The where and when of consciousness in the brain. *Behavioral and Brain Sciences, 15,* 183–247.

Dennett, D.C. (1991). *Consciousness explained.* Boston: Little, Brown.

Deregowski, J. B. (1974). Illusion and culture. In R. Gregory & E. H. Gombrich (Eds.), *Illusion in nature and art* (pp. 160–191). New York: Scribner.

De Rivera, J. A. (1984). The structure of emotional relationships. *Review of Personality and Social Psychology, 5,* 116–145.

Descartes, René (1649/1988). *The passions of the soul.* In J. Cottingham, R. Stoothoff, & D. Murdoch (Trans. and Eds.), *Selected philosophical writings of René Descartes.* Cambridge, UK: Cambridge University Press.

De Sousa, R. (1978). The rationality of emotions. *Dialogue, 18,* 41–63.

De Sousa, R. (1987). *The rationality of emotions.* Cambridge: MIT Press.

D'Esposito, M., Postle, B. R., Ballard, D., & Lease, J. (1999). Maintenance versus manipulation of information held in working memory: An event-related fMRI study. *Brain and Cognition, 41,* 66–86.

DeSteno, D. A., & Salovey, P. (1996). Evolutionary origins of sex differences in jealousy? Questioning the "fitness" of the model. *Psychological Science, 7,* 367–372.

Devinsky, O., Morrell, M. J., & Vogt, B. A. (1995). Contributions of anterior cingulate cortex to behaviour. *Brain, 118,* 279–306.

De Waal, F. B. M. (1996). *Good natured: The origins of right and wrong in humans and other animals.* Cambridge: Harvard University Press.

Dick, L. (1995). "Pibloktoq" (Arctic hysteria): A construction of European–Inuit relations? *Arctic Anthropology, 32,* 1–42.

Diener, E., Sandvik, E., Seidlitz, L., & Diener, M. (1992). The relationship between income and subjective well-being: Relative or absolute? *Social Indicators Research, 28,* 253–281.

Diogenes Laertius (1925). *Lives of eminent philosophers* (R. D. Hicks, Trans.). New York: Loeb Classical Library.

Dion, K. L., & Dion, K. K. (1988). Romantic love: Individual and cultural perspectives. In R. J. Sternberg & M. L. Barnes (Eds.), *The psychology of love* (pp. 264–289). New Haven: Yale University Press.

Dixon, N. F. (1981). *Preconscious processing.* Chichester, UK: Wiley.

Doi, T. (1973). *The anatomy of dependence.* Tokyo: Kodansha International.

Dretske, F. (1981). *Knowledge and the flow of information.* Cambridge: MIT Press.

Dretske, F. (1986). Misrepresentation. In R. Bogdan (Ed.), *Belief: Form, content and function* (pp. 17–36). Oxford: Oxford University Press.

Dretske, F. (1988). *Explaining behavior.* Cambridge: MIT Press.

Dunning, D., & Story, A. L. (1991). Depression, realism, and the overconfidence effect: Are the sadder wiser when predicting future actions and events? *Journal of Personality and Social Psychology, 61,* 521–532.

Dupré, J. (2001). *Human nature and the limits of science.* Oxford: Oxford University Press.

Efran, J. S., & Spangler, T. J. (1979). Why grown-ups cry: A two-factor theory and evidence from *The Miracle Worker. Motivation and Emotion, 3,* 63–72.

Ekman, P. (1972). Universals and cultural differences in facial expressions of emotion. In J. Cole (Ed.), *Nebraska Symposium on Motivation, 1971* (vol. 19, pp. 207–283). Lincoln: University of Nebraska Press.

Ekman, P. (1977). Biological and cultural contributions to body and facial movement. In J. Blacking (Ed.), *Anthropology of the body* (pp. 34–84). London: Academic Press.

Ekman, P. (1992a). Are there basic emotions? A reply to Ortony and Turner. *Psychological Review, 99,* 550–553.

Ekman, P. (1992b). An argument for basic emotions. *Cognition and Emotion, 6,* 169–200.

Ekman, P. (1993). Facial expression and emotion. *American Psychologist, 48,* 384–392.

Ekman, P. (1994). Moods, emotions, and traits. In P. Ekman & R. J. Davidson (Eds.), *The nature of emotion: Fundamental questions* (pp. 56–58). New York: Oxford University Press.

Ekman, P. (1997). Should we call it expression or communication? *Innovations in Social Science Research, 10,* 333–344.

Ekman, P. (1999a). Basic emotions. In T. Dalgleish & T. Power (Eds.), *The handbook of cognition and emotion* (pp. 45–60). New York: Wiley.

Ekman, P. (1999b). Facial expressions. In T. Dalgleish & M. Power (Eds.), *Handbook of cognition and emotion.* New York: Wiley.

Ekman, P. (2003). *Emotions revealed: Recognizing faces and feelings to improve communication and emotional life.* New York: Times Books.

Ekman, P., & Friesen, W. V. (1971). Constants across cultures in the face and emotion. *Journal of Personality and Social Psychology, 17,* 124–129.

Ekman, P., & Friesen, W. V. (1986). A new pan-cultural facial expression of emotion. *Motivation and Emotion, 10,* 159–168.

Ekman, P., Sorenson, E. R., & Friesen, W. V. (1969). Pan-cultural elements in facial displays of emotions. *Science, 164,* 86–88.

Elliott, R., Friston, K. J., & Dolan, R. J. (2000). Dissociable neural responses in human reward systems. *Journal of Neuroscience, 20,* 6159–6165.

Ellsworth, P. C. (1994). William James and emotion: Is a century of fame worth a century of misunderstanding? *Psychological Review, 101,* 222–229.

Elster, J. (1996). Rationality and the emotions. *Economic Journal, 106,* 1386–1397.

Elster, J. (1999). *Alchemies of the mind: Rationality and the emotions.* Cambridge, UK: Cambridge University Press.

Emery, N. J., & Amaral, D. G. (2000). The role of the amygdala in primate social cognition. In R. D. Lane & L. Nadel (Eds.), *Cognitive neuroscience of emotion.* New York: Oxford University Press.

Eysenck, H. J. (1967). *The biological basis of personality.* Springfield, IL: Thomas.

Fanselow, M. S., & LeDoux, J. E. (1999). Why we think plasticity underlying Pavlovian fear conditioning occurs in the basolateral amygdala. *Neuron 23,* 229–232.

Farah, M. J. (1990). *Visual agnosia: Disorders of object recognition and what they tell us about normal vision.* Cambridge: MIT Press.

Feleky, A. M. (1914). The expression of the emotions. *Psychological Review, 21,* 33–41.

Fernández-Dols, J. M., & Ruiz-Belda, M. A. (1995). Are smiles a sign of happiness? Gold medal winners at the Olympic Games. *Journal of Personality and Social Psychology, 69,* 1113–1119.

Fessler, D. M. T. (1999). Toward an understanding of the universality of second order emotions. In A. L. Hinton (Ed.), *Biocultural approaches to the emotions* (pp. 75–116). Cambridge, UK: Cambridge University Press.

Finck, H. T. (1887). *Romantic love and personal beauty: Their development, causal relations, historic and national peculiarities.* London: Macmillan.

Fischman, M. W., & Foltin, R. W. (1992). Self-administration of cocaine by humans: A laboratory perspective. In G. R. Bock & J. Whelan (Eds.), *Cacaine: Scientific and social dimensions* (Vol. 166, pp. 165–180). Chichester, UK: Wiley.

Flanagan, O. (1997). Prospects for a unified theory of consciousness or, what dreams are made of. In N. Block, O. Flanagan, & G. Guzeldere (Eds.), *The nature of consciousness: Philosophical debates.* Cambridge: MIT Press.

Fodor, J. A. (1987). *Psychosemantics.* Cambridge: MIT Press.

Fodor, J. A. (1990). A theory of content, I and II. In *A theory of content and other essays* (pp. 51–136). Cambridge: MIT Press.

Fodor, J. A. (1983). *The modularity of mind.* Cambridge: MIT Press.

Fodor, J. A. (1998). *Concepts: Where cognitive science when wrong.* Oxford: Oxford University Press.

Frank, R. H. (1988). *Passions within reason: The strategic role of the emotions.* New York: Norton.

Freud, S. (1915/1984).The unconscious. In A. Richards (Ed.), *The Pelican Freud library: Vol. 11. On metapsychology: The theory of psychoanalysis* (pp. 159–222). Harmondsworth, UK: Penguin.

Freud, S. (1920/1922). *Beyond the pleasure principle.* (C. Hubback, Trans.). London: International Psycho-Analytical Press.

Fridlund, A. (1994). *Human facial expression. An evolutionary view.* San Diego, CA: Academic Press.

Friesen, W. V. (1972). Cultural differences in facial expressions in a social situation: An experimental test of the concept of display rules. (Doctoral dissertation, University of California, San Francisco, 1972).

Frijda, N. H. (1986). *The Emotions.* Cambridge, UK: Cambridge University Press.

Frijda, N. H. (1993). Moods, emotion episodes, and emotions. In M. Lewis & J. M. Haviland (Eds.), *Handbook of emotions* (pp. 381–404). New York: Guilford Press.

Frijda, N. H. (1994). Varieties of affect: Emotions and episodes, moods, and sentiments. In P. Ekman & R. J. Davidson (Eds.), *The nature of emotion: Fundamental questions* (pp. 56–58). Oxford: Oxford University Press.

Frijda, N. H., & Mesquita, B. (1994). The social roles and functions of emotions. In S. Kitayama & H. Markus (Eds.), *Emotions and culture: Empirical studies of mutual influence* (pp. 51–87). Washington, DC: American Psychological Association Press.

Frois-Wittman, J. (1930). The judgment of facial expression. *Journal of Experimental Psychology, 13,* 113–151.

Galati, D., Scherer, K. R., & Ricci-Bitti, P. E. (1997). Voluntary facial expression of emotion: Comparing congenitally blind with normally sighted encoders. *Journal of Personality and Social Psycholology, 73,* 1363–1379.

Geary, D. C., Rumsey, M., Bow-Thomas, C. C., & Hoard, M. (1995). Sexual jealousy as a facultative trait: Evidence from the pattern of sex differences in adults from China and the United States. *Ethology and Sociobiology, 16,* 355–384.

Geertz, C. (1973). *The interpretation of cultures: Selected essays.* New York: Basic Books.

Gibson, J. J. (1979). *The ecological approach to visual perception.* Boston: Houghton Mifflin.

Gigerenzer, G., & Hug, K. (1992). Reasoning about social contracts: Cheating and perspective change. *Cognition, 43,* 127–171.

Goldie, P. (2000). *The emotions.* New York: Oxford University Press.

Gordon, R. (1987). *The structure of emotions.* Cambridge, UK: Cambridge University Press.

Gray, J. A. (1982). *The neuropsychology of anxiety.* New York: Oxford University Press.

Gray, J. A. (1987). *The psychology of fear and stress* (2nd ed.). Cambridge, UK: Cambridge University Press.

Gray, J. A. (1991). The neuropsychology of temperament. In J. Strelau & A. Angleitner (Eds.), *Explorations in temperament* (pp. 105–128). New York: Plenum Press.

Greenspan, P. (1980). A case of mixed feelings: Ambivalence and the logic of emotion. In A. Rorty (Ed.), *Explaining emotions* (pp. 223–250). Berkeley: University of California Press.

Greenspan, P. (1988). *Emotions and reasons.* New York: Routledge.

Greenspan, P. (2000). Emotional strategies and rationality. *Ethics, 110,* 469–487.

Gregory, R. (1966). *Eye and brain: The psychology of seeing.* London: Weidenfeld and Nicholson.

Grice, H. P. (1957). Meaning. *Philosophical Review, 64,* 377–388.

Griffiths, P. E. (1989). Folk, functional, and neurochemical aspects of mood. *Philosophical Psychology, 2,* 17–30.

Griffiths, P. E. (1997). *What emotions really are.* Chicago: University of Chicago Press.

Griffiths, P. E. (2002). What is innateness? *Monist, 85,* 70–85.

Gross, J. J., Fredrickson, B. L., & Levenson, R. W. (1994). The psychophysiology of crying. *Psychophysiology, 31,* 460–468.

Hacking, I. (1999). *The social construction of what?* Cambridge: Harvard University Press.

Haidt, J., Koller, S., & Dias, M. (1993). Affect, culture, and morality, or is it wrong to eat your dog? *Journal of Personality and Social Psychology, 65,* 613–628.

Haidt, J., Rozin, P., McCauley, C. R., & Imada, S. (1997). Body, psyche and culture: The relationship between disgust and morality. *Psychology and Developing Societies, 9,* 107–131.

Hájek, A., & Philip, P. (2004). Desire beyond belief. *Australasian Journal of Philosophy, 8,* 77–92.

Hare, R. D. (1993). *Without conscience: The disturbing world of the psychopaths among us.* New York: Simon and Schuster

Harré, R. (1986). The social constructivist viewpoint. In R. Harré (Ed.), *The social construction of emotions* (pp. 2–14). Oxford: Blackwell.

Harris, C. H. (2000). Psychophysiological responses to imagined infidelity: The specific innate modular view of jealousy reconsidered. *Journal of Personality and Social Psychology, 78,* 1082–1091.

Harris, C. R., & Christenfeld, N. (1996). Jealousy and rational responses to infidelity across gender and culture. *Psychological Science, 7,* 378–379.

Hatfield, E. (1988). Passionate and companionate love. In R. J. Sternberg & M. L. Barnes (Eds.), *The psychology of love* (pp. 191–217). New Haven: Yale University Press.

Hauser, M. D. (2002). *Wild minds: What animals really think.* New York: Penguin.

Heelas, P. (1986). Emotion talk across cultures. In R. Harré (Ed.), *The social construction of emotions* (pp. 234–266). Oxford: Blackwell.

Heller, W., Nitschke, J. B., Etienne, M. A., & Miller, G. A. (1997). Patterns of regional brain activity differentiate types of anxiety. *Journal of Abnormal Psychology, 106,* 376–385.

Hill, K., & Hurtado, A. M. (1996). *Ache life history: The ecology and demography of a foraging people.* Chicago: Aldine Press.

Hobbes, Thomas. (1650/1994). Human nature, or, the fundamental elements of policie. In J. C. A. Gaskin (Ed.), *The elements of law, natural and politic.* New York: Oxford University Press.

Hohmann, G. W. (1966). Some effects of spinal cord lesions on experienced emotional feelings. *Psychophysiology, 3,* 143–156.

Holden, K. C., & Smock, P. J. (1991). The economic costs of marital dissolution: Why do women bear a disproportionate cost? *Annual Review of Sociology, 17,* 51–78.

Howell, S. (1981). Rules not words. In P. Heelas & A. Lock (Eds.), *Indigeneous psychologies* (pp. 134–144). London: Academic Press.

Hsu, F. L. K. (1975). *Iemoto: The heart of Japan.* New York: Wiley.

Hsu, F. L. K. (1981). *Americans and Chinese: Passage to difference.* Honolulu: University of Hawaii Press.

Hume, D. (1739/1978). *A treatise of human nature.* (P. H. Nidditch, Ed.). Oxford: Oxford University Press.

Hupka, R. B. (1991). The motive for the arousal of romantic jealousy: Its cultural origin. In P. Salovey (Ed.), *The psychology of jealousy and envy* (pp. 252–270). New York: Guilford Press.

Ikemoto, A., & Panksepp, J. (1999). The role of nucleus accumbens dopamine in motivated behavior: a unifying interpretation with special reference to reward-seeking. *Brain Research Reviews, 31,* 6–41.

Isen, A. M. (2000). Positive affect and decision making. In M. Lewis & J. Haviland-Jones (Eds.), *Handbook of emotion* (2nd ed., pp. 417–435). New York: Guilford.

Isen, A. M., Daubman, K. A., & Novicki, G. P. (1987). Positive affect facilitates creative problem solving. *Journal of Personality and Social Psychology, 52,* 1122–1131.

Izard, C. E. (1971). *The face of emotion.* New York: Appleton-Century-Crofts.

Izard, C. E. (1994). Answer—None: Cognition is one of four types of emotion activating systems. In P. Ekman & R. J. Davidson (Eds.), *The nature of emotion: Fundamental questions* (pp. 203–207). New York: Oxford University Press.

Jackendoff, R. (1987). *Consciousness and the computational mind.* Cambridge: MIT Press.

James, W. (1884). What is an emotion? *Mind, 9,* 188–205.

James, W. (1890). *The principles of psychology.* New York: Dover.

James, W. (1894). The physical basis of emotion. *Psychological Review, 1,* 516–529.

Jang, K. L., Livesley, W. J., Vernon, P. A., & Jackson, D. N. (1996). Heritability of personality disorder traits: A twin study. *Acta Psychiatrica Scandinavica, 94,* 438–444.

Johnson-Laird, P., & Oatley K. (2000). Cognitive and social construction in the emotions. In M. Lewis & J. Haviland-Jones (Eds.), *Handbook of emotions* (2nd ed. pp. 458–475). New York: Guilford Press.

Keil, F. C. (1989). *Concepts, kinds, and cognitive development.* Cambridge: MIT Press.

Kendler, K. S. (1993). Twin studies of psychiatric illness: Current status and future directions. *Archives of General Psychiatry, 50,* 905–915.

Kenny, A. (1963). *Action, emotion and will.* London: Routledge & Kegan Paul.

Kleinman, A. (1980). *Patients and healers in the context of culture.* Berkeley: University of California Press.

Kleinman, A. (1988). *Rethinking psychiatry: From cultural category to personal experience.* New York: Free Press.

Koch, C., & Braun, J. (1996). Towards the neuronal correlate of visual awareness. *Current Opinion in Neurobiology, 6,* 158–164.

Konner, M. (1976). Maternal care, infant behavior and development among the !Kung. In R. B. Lee & I. DeVore (Eds.), *Kalahari hunter-gatherers* (pp. 218–245). Cambridge: Harvard University Press.

Kosslyn, S. M. (1994). *Image and brain: The resolution of the imagery debate.* Cambridge: MIT Press.

Kraut, R. E., & Johnston, R. E. (1979). Social and emotional messages of smiling: An ethological approach. *Journal of Personality and Social Psychology, 37,* 1539–1553.

Kripke, S. A. (1980). *Naming and necessity.* Cambridge: Harvard University Press.

Kunst-Wilson W. R., & Zajonc, R. B. (1980). Affective discrimination of stimuli that can not be recognized. *Science, 207,* 557–558.

Lane, R. D. Kaszniak, A., Ahern, G., & Schwartz, G. (1997). Is alexithymia the emotional equivalent of blindsight? *Biological Psychiatry, 42,* 834–844.

Lane, R. D., Chua, P., & Dolan, R. (1999). Common effects of emotional valence, arousal and attention on neural activation during visual processing of pictures. *Neuropsychologia, 37,* 989–997.

Lane, R. D. (2000). Neural correlates of conscious emotional experience. In R. D. Lane & L. Nadel (Eds.), *Cognitive neuroscience of emotion* (pp. 345–370). New York: Oxford University Press.

Lane, R. D., Fink, G. R., Chau, P. M. L., & Dolan, R. J. (1997). Neural activation during selective attention to subjective emotional responses. *NeuroReport, 8,* 3969–3972.

Lang, P. J., Bradley, M. M., & Cuthbert, B. N. (1998). Emotion, motivation, and anxiety: Brain mechanisms and psychophysiology biological psychiatry. *Biological Psychology, 44,* 1274–1276.

Lange, C. G. (1885). *Om sindsbevaegelser: Et psyko-fysiologisk studie.* Copenhagen: Jacob Lunds. Reprinted in C. G. Lange & W. James (Eds.), I. A. Haupt (Trans.) *The emotions,* 1922, Baltimore: Williams and Wilkins.

Langfeld, H. S. (1918). Judgments of facial expression and suggestion. *Psychological Review, 25,* 488–494.

Larsen, R. J., & Diener, E. (1992). Problems and promises with the circumplex model of emotion. *Review of Personality and Social Psychology, 13,* 25–59.

Lazarus, R. S. (1984). On the primacy of cognition. *American Psychologist, 39,* 124–129.

Lazarus, R. S. (1991). *Emotion and adaptation.* New York: Oxford University Press.

Lazarus, R. S. (1994). The stable and the unstable in emotion. In P. Ekman & R. J. Davidson (Eds.), *The nature of emotion: Fundamental questions* (pp. 79–85). Oxford: Oxford University Press.

Lazarus, R. S. (1999). The cognition-emotion debate: A bit of history. In T. Dalgleish & M. Power (Eds.), *Handbook of cognition and emotion.* Chichester, UK: Wiley.

Lazarus, R. S., & Alfert, E. (1964). Short-circuiting of threat by experimentally altering cognitive appraisal. *Journal of Abnormal and Social Psychology, 69,* 195–205.

Lazarus, R. S., & Smith, C. (1993). Appraisal components, core relational themes, and the emotions. In N. Frijda (Ed.), *Appraisal and beyond* (pp. 233–270). Hillsdale, NJ: Erlbaum.

LeDoux, J. E. (1994). Emotional processing, but not emotions, can occur unconsciously. In P. Ekman & R. J. Davidson (Eds.), *The nature of emotion: Fundamental questions* (pp. 291–292). New York: Oxford University Press.

LeDoux, J. E. (1996). *The emotional brain.* New York: Simon and Schuster.

Leff, J. (1973). Culture and the differentiation of emotional states. *British Journal of Psychiatry, 123,* 299–306.

Lerner, J. S., & Keltner, D. (2000). Beyond valence: Toward a model of emotion-specific influences on judgment and choice. *Cognition and Emotion, 14,* 473–493.

Levenson, R. W., Ekman, P., & Friesen, W. V. (1990). Voluntary facial action generates emotion-specific autonomic nervous system activity. *Psychophysiology, 27,* 363–384.

Levine, J. (1993). On leaving out what it's like. In M. Davies & G. Humphreys (Eds.), *Consciousness: Psychological and philosophical essays* (pp. 121–136). Oxford: Blackwell.

Levy, R. I. (1973). *Tahitians: Mind and experience in the society islands.* Chicago: University of Chicago Press.

Levy, R. I. (1984). The emotion in comparative perspective. In K. R. Scherer & P. Ekman (Eds.), *Approaches to emotion* (pp. 397–412). Hillsdale, NJ: Erlbaum.

Lewis, C. S. (1936). *The allegory of love.* Oxford: Oxford University Press.

Lewis, D. (1988). Desire as belief. *Mind, 97,* 323–332.

Lewis, M. (2000). The emergence of human emotions. In M. Lewis & J. M. Haviland-Jones (Eds.), *Handbook of emotions* (2nd. ed., pp. 265–280). New York: Guilford Press.

Liberman, N., & Klar, Y. (1996). Hypothesis testing in Wason's selection task: Social exchange, cheating detection or task understanding. *Cognition, 58,* 127–156.

Liotti, M., Mayberg, H. S., Brannan, S. K., McGinnis, S., Jerabek, P., & Fox, P. T. (2000).

Differential limbic–cortical correlates of sadness and anxiety in healthy subjects: Implications for affective disorders. *Biological Psychiatry, 48,* 30–42.

Locke, J. (1690/1979). *An essay concerning human understanding* (P. H. Nidditch, Ed.). Oxford: Oxford University Press.

Lormand, E. (1985). Toward a theory of moods. *Philosophical Studies, 47,* 385–407.

Lucas, R. E., Diener, E., Grob, A., Suh, E. M., & Shao, L. (2000). Cross-cultural evidence for the fundamental features of extraversion. *Journal of Personality and Social Psychology, 79,* 452–468.

Lutz, C. (1988). *Unnatural emotions: Everyday sentiments on a Micronesian atoll and their challenge to Western theory.* Chicago: University of Chicago Press.

Luu, P., Collins, P., & Tucker, D. M. (2000). Mood, personality, and self-monitoring: Negative affect and emotionality in relation to frontal lobe mechanisms of error monitoring. *Journal of Experimental Psychology: General, 129,* 43–60.

Lyon, M. (1999). Emotion and embodiment: The respiratory mediation of bodily and social processes. In A. L. Hinton (Ed.), *Biocultural approaches to the emotions* (pp. 182–212). Cambridge, UK: Cambridge University Press.

Lyons, W. (1980). *Emotion.* Cambridge, UK: Cambridge University Press.

Mack, A., & Rock, I. (1998). *Inattentional blindness.* Cambridge: MIT Press.

MacLean, P. D. (1952). Some psychiatric implications of physiological studies of frontotemporal portion of limbic system (visceral brain). *Electroencephalography and Clinical Neurophysiology, 4,* 407–418.

MacLean, P. D. (1993). Cerebral evolution of emotion. In M. Lewis & J. M. Haviland (Eds.), *Handbook of emotions* (pp. 67–83). New York: Guilford Press.

MacLeod, C., & Mathews, A. (1991). Biased cognitive operations in anxiety: accessibility of information or assignment of processing priorities? *Behavioral Research and Therapy, 29,* 599–610.

Malt, B. C. (1994). Water is not $H_2O$. *Cognitive Psychology, 27,* 41–70.

Marañon, G. (1924). Contribution à l'étude de l'action émotive de l'adrenaline. *Revue Française d'Endocrinologie, 2,* 301–325.

Markus, H., & Kitayama, S. (1991). Culture and the self: implications for cognition, emotion, and motivation. *Psychological Review, 98,* 224–253.

Marr, D. (1982). *Vision: A computational investigation into the human representation and processing of visual information.* New York: Freeman.

Marrow, L. P., Overton, P. G., & Brian, P. F. (1999). A reevaluation of social defeat as an animal model of depression. *Journal of Psychopharmacology, 13,* 115–121.

Matsumoto, D. (1994). *People: Psychology from a cultural perspective.* Prospect Heights, IL: Waveland Press.

Matsumoto, D., Kudoh, T., Scherer, K., & Wallbott, H. (1988). Antecedents of and reactions to emotions in the United States and Japan. *Journal of Cross-Cultural Psychology, 19,* 267–286.

McDougall, W. (1908). *An introduction to social psychology.* London: Methuen.

McDowell, J. (1996). *Mind and world.* Cambridge: Harvard University Press.

Mead, M. (1928). *Coming of age in Samoa.* New York: William Morrow.

Meltzoff, A. N., & M. K. Moore. (1983). Newborn infants imitate adult facial gestures. *Child Development, 54,* 702–709.

Melzack, R., & Casey, K. L. (1968). Sensory, motivational, and central control determinants of pain: A new conceptual model. In D. Kenshalo (Ed.), *The skin sense* (pp. 223–243). Springfield, IL: Thomas.

Menon, U., & Shweder, R. A. (1994). Kali's tongue: Cultural psychology and the power of shame in Orissa, India. In S. Kitayama & H. Markus (Eds.), *Emotion and culture* (pp. 241–284). Washington, DC: American Psychological Association Press.

Meyer, G. J., & Shack, J. R. (1989). Structural convergence of mood and personality: Evidence for old and new directions. *Journal of Personality and Social Psychology, 57,* 691–706.

Millenson, J. R. (1967). *Principles of behavioral analysis.* New York: Macmillan.

Miller, R. S. (1996). *Embarrassment: Poise and peril in everyday life.* New York: Guilford Press.

Millikan, R. G. (1993). *White Queen psychology and other essays for Alice.* Cambridge: MIT Press.

Milner, A.D., & Goodale, M.A. (1995). *The visual brain in action.* Oxford: Oxford University Press.

Mineka, S., Davidson, M., Cook, M., & Keir, R. (1984). Observational conditioning of snake fear in rhesus monkeys. *Journal of Abnormal Psychology, 93,* 355–372.

Minsky, M. (1986). *The society of mind.* New York: Simon and Schuster.

Miyake, K., Campos, J., Kagan, J., & Bradshaw, D. L. (1986). Child development in Japan and the United States: Prospectives on cross-cultural comparisons. In H. Stevenson, H. Azuma, & K. Hakuta (Eds.), *Child development and education in Japan* (pp. 239–261). New York: Freeman.

Morris, D. (1994). *Bodytalk: The meaning of human gestures.* New York: Crown.

Morris, J. A., Öhman, A., & Dolan, R. J. (1999). A subcortical pathway to the right amygdala mediating "unseen" fear. *Proceedings of the National Academy of Science, 96,* 1680–1685.

Morsbach, H., & Tyler, W. J. (1986). A Japanese emotion, *Amae.* In R. Harré (Ed.), *The social construction of emotions* (pp. 289–307). Oxford: Blackwell.

Moscovitch, M. (1995) Confabulation. In D. Schacter (Ed.), *Memory distortion: How minds, brains, and societies reconstruct the past* (pp. 226–254). Cambridge: Harvard University Press.

Murphy, D., & Stich, S. (2000). Darwin in the madhouse: Evolutionary psychology and the classification of mental disorders. In P. Carruthers & A. Chamberlain (Eds.), *Evolution and the human mind* (pp. 62–92). Cambridge, UK: Cambridge University Press.

Nash, R. A. (1989). Cognitive theories of emotion. *Nous, 23,* 481–504.

Nasser, M. (1988). Culture and weight consciousness. *Journal of Psychosomatic Research, 32,* 573–577.

Nemeroff, C., & Rozin, P. (1992). Sympathetic magical beliefs and kosher dietary practice: The interaction of rules and feelings. *Ethos, 20,* 96–115.

Nesse, R., & G. Williams (1997). Are mental disorders diseases? In S. Baron-Cohen (Ed.), *The maladapted mind* (pp. 1–22). Hove, UK: Psychology Press.

Nesse, R. M. (1998). Emotional disorders in evolutionary perspective. *British Journal of Medical Psychology, 71,* 397–415.

Newman, P. L. (1965). *Knowing the Gururumba.* New York: Holt, Rinehart and Winston.

Nisbett, R., & D. Cohen. (1995). *The culture of honor: The psychology of violence in the south.* Boulder, CO: Westview Press.

Nisbett, R. E., & Wilson, T. D. (1977). Telling more than we can know: Verbal reports on mental processes. *Psychological Review, 84,* 231–259.

Noë, A., & O'Regan, J. K. (2001). A sensorimotor account of vision and visual consciousness. *Behavioral and Brain Sciences, 24,* 883–917.

Northoff, G., Richter, A., Gessner, M., Schlagenhauf, F., Stephan, K., Fell, J., Baumgart, F., Kaulisch, T., Kötter, R., Leschinger, A., Bargel, B., Witzel, T., Hinrichs, H.,

Bogerts, B., Scheich, H., & Heinze, H.-J. (2000). Functional dissociation between medial and lateral orbitofrontal cortical spatiotemporal activation in negative and positive emotions: A combined FMRI/MEG study. *Cerebral Cortex, 10,* 93–107.

Nussbaum, M. C. (2001). *Upheavals of thought: The intelligence of the emotions.* Cambridge, UK: Cambridge University Press.

Oatley, K., & Jenkins, J. M. (1996). *Understanding emotions.* Oxford: Blackwell.

Oatley, K., & Johnson-Laird, P. N. (1987) Towards a cognitive theory of emotions. *Cognition and Emotion, 1,* 29–50.

Öhman, A., Flykt, A., & Esteves, F. (2001). Emotion drives attention: Detecting the snake in the grass. *Journal of Experimental Psychology: General, 130,* 466–478.

Olshausen, B. A., Anderson, C. H., & van Essen, D. C. (1994). A neurobiological model of visual attention and invariant pattern recognition based task. *Journal of Neuroscience, 14,* 6171–6186.

Ortony, A., Clore, G. L., & Collins, A. (1988). *The cognitive structure of emotions.* Cambridge, UK: Cambridge University Press.

Ortony, A., & Turner, W. (1990). What's basic about basic emotions? *Psychological Review, 97,* 315–331.

Panksepp, J. (1995). The emotional sources of "chills" induced by music. *Music Perception, 13,* 171–207.

Panksepp, J. (2000). Emotions as natural kinds within the mammalian brain. In M. Lewis & J. Haviland-Jones (Eds.), *Handbook of emotions* (2nd. ed., pp. 137–156). New York: Guilford Press.

Panksepp, J., & Burgdorf, J. (2000). 50-kHz chirping (laughter?) in response to conditioned and unconditioned tickle-induced reward in rats: Effects of social housing and genetic variables. *Behavioural Brain Research, 115,* 25–38.

Paradiso, S., Johnson, D. L., Andreasen, N. C., O'Leary, D. S., Watkins, G. L., Boles Ponto, L. L., & Hichwa, R. D. (1999). Cerebral blood flow changes associated with attribution of emotional valence to pleasant, unpleasant, and neutral visual stimuli in a PET study of normal subjects. *American Journal of Psychiatry, 156,* 1618–1629.

Parkinson, B. (1995). *Ideas and realities of emotion.* London: Routledge.

Phillips, M. L., Young, A. W., Senior, C., Brammer, M., Andrew, C., Calder, A. J., Bullmore, E. T., Perrett, D. I., Rowland, D., Williams, S. C. R., Gray, J. A., & David, A. S. (1997). A specific neural substrate for perceiving facial expressions of disgust. *Nature, 389,* 495–498.

Pinker, S. (1994). *The language instinct: How the mind creates language.* New York: William Morrow.

Pinker, S. (1997). *How the mind works.* New York: Norton.

Pitcher, G. (1965). Emotion. *Mind, 74,* 324–346.

Ploghaus, A., Narain, C., Beckmann, C. F., Clare, S., Bantick, S., Wise, R., Matthews, P. M., Rawlins, J. N., & Tracey, I. (2001). Exacerbation of pain by anxiety is associated with activity in a hippocampal network. *Journal of Neuroscience, 21,* 9896–9903.

Plutchik, R. (1980). *Emotion: A psychoevolutionary synthesis.* New York: Harper and Row.

Plutchik, R. (1984). Emotions: A general psychoevolutionary theory. In K. Scherer & P. Ekman (Eds.), *Approaches to emotion* (pp. 197–220). Hillsdale, NJ: Erlbaum.

Plutchik, R. (2001). The nature of emotions. *American Scientist, 89,* 344–350.

Pope, A. (1733–1734/1997). *An essay on man* (F. Brady, Ed.). New York: Macmillan.

Price, J., Sloman, L., Gardner, R., Gilbert, P., & Rohde, P. (1994). The social competition hypothesis of depression. *British Journal of Psychiatry, 164,* 309–315.

Prinz, J. J. (2000). The duality of content. *Philosophical Studies, 100,* 1–34.

Prinz, J. J. (2001). Functionalism, dualism and the neural correlates of consciousness. In W. Bechtel, P. Mandik, J. Mundale, & R. Stufflebeam (Eds.), *Philosophy and the neurosciences: A reader.* Oxford: Blackwell.

Prinz, J. J. (2002). *Furnishing the mind: Concepts and their perceptual basis.* Cambridge: MIT Press.

Prinz, J. J. (2003a). Consciousness, computation, and emotion. In S. C. Moore & M. Oaksford (Eds.), *Emotional cognition: From brain to behaviour.* Amsterdam: John Benjamins.

Prinz, J. J. (2003b). Imitation and moral development. In S. Hurley & N. Chater (Eds.), *Perspectives on imitation: From cognitive neuroscience to social science.* Cambridge: MIT Press.

Prinz, J. J. (Forthcoming-a). Is the mind really modular? In R. Stainton (Ed.), *Debates in philosophy of psychology.* Oxford: Blackwell.

Prinz, J. J. (Forthcoming-b). A neurofunctional theory of consciousness. In A. Brook & K. Akins (Eds.), *Philosophy and neuroscience.*

Prinz, J. J. (In progress). *The emotional construction of morals.*

Provine, R. R. (2000). *Laughter: A scientific investigation.* New York: Viking Press.

Putnam, H. (1975). The meaning of "meaning." In *Philosophical Papers: Vol. 2. Mind, language and reality.* Cambridge, UK: Cambridge University Press.

Rainville, P., Carrier, B., Hofbauer, R. K., Bushnell, M. C., & Duncan, G. H. (1999). Dissociation of pain sensory and affective dimensions using hypnotic modulation. *Pain, 82,* 159–171.

Raleigh, M., McGuire, M., Brammer, G., Pollack, D., & Yuwiler, A. (1991). Serotonergic mechanisms promote dominance acquisition in adult male vervet monkeys. *Brain Research, 559,* 181–190.

Ralph, M. R. (1996). Circadian rhythms: Mammalian aspects. *Seminars in Cell and Developmental Biology, 7,* 821–830.

Read, K. (1967). Morality and the concept of the person among the Gahuku-Gama. In J. Middleton (Ed.), *Myth and cosmos* (pp. 185–230). New York: Natural History Press.

Rees, G. (2001). Neuroimaging of visual awareness in patients and normal subjects. *Current Opinion in Neurobiology, 11,* 150–156.

Reisenzein, R. (1983). The Schachter theory of emotion: Two decades later. *Psychological Bulletin, 94,* 239–264.

Reisenzein, R., Meyer, W.-U., & Schützwohl, A. (1995). James and the physical basis of emotion: A comment on Ellsworth. *Psychological Review, 102,* 757–761.

Reynolds, S. M., & Berridge, K. C. (2001). Fear and feeding in the nucleus accumbens shell: Rostrocaudal segregation of GABA-elicited defensive behavior versus eating behavior. *Journal of Neuroscience, 21,* 3261–3270

Rhudy, J. L., & Meagher, M. W. (2000). Fear and anxiety: Divergent effects on thermal pain thresholds in humans. *Pain, 84,* 65–75.

Rizzolatti, G., Fadiga, L., Gallese, V., & Fogassi, L. (1996). Premotor cortex and the recognition of motor actions. *Cognitive Brain Research, 3,* 131–141.

Roberts, R. C. (1988). What an emotion is: A sketch. *Philosophical Review, 97,* 183–209.

Robinson, J. (1983). Emotion, judgment, and desire. *Journal of Philosophy, 80,* 731–741.

Roethke, T. (1953). The waking. In *The waking: Poems 1933–1953.* Garden City, NY: Doubleday.

Rolls, E. T. (1999). *The brain and emotion.* Oxford: Oxford University Press.

Rorty, A. O. (1980). Introduction. In *Explaining emotions*. Berkeley: University of California Press.

Rosaldo, M. (1980). *Knowledge and passion*. Cambridge, UK: Cambridge University Press.

Rose, H., & Rose, S. (Eds.). (2000). *Alas poor Darwin: Arguments against evolutionary psychology*. New York: Vintage Books.

Roseman, I. J. (1984). Cognitive determinants of emotions: A structural theory. In P. Shaver (Ed.), *Review of Personality and Social Psychology* (Vol. 5, pp. 11–36). Beverly Hills: Sage Publications.

Roseman, I. J. (1994). Phenomenology, behaviors, and goals differentiate discrete emotions. *Journal of Personality and Social Psychology, 67*, 206–221.

Roseman, I. J., Spindel, M. S., & Jose, P. E. (1990). Appraisals of emotion-eliciting events: Testing a theory of discrete emotions. *Journal of Personality and Social Psychology, 59*, 899–915.

Rosenblatt, P. C., Walsh, R. P., & Jackson, D. A. (1976). *Grief and mourning in cross-cultural perspective*. New Haven: Human Relation Area Files Press.

Rosenthal, D. (1991). The independence of consciousness and sensory quality. In E. Villanueva (Ed.), *Consciousness: Philosophical issues* (Vol. 1, pp. 15–36). Atascadero, CA: Ridgeview.

Ross, L., Lepper, M. R., & Hubbard, M. (1975). Perseverance in self-perception and social perception: Biased attributional processes in the debriefing paradigm. *Journal of Personality and Social Psychology, 32*, 880–892.

Ross, L., & Nisbett, R.E. (1991). *The person and the situation*. New York: McGraw-Hill.

Rozin, P., Dow, S., Moscovitch, M., & Rajaram, S. (1998). What causes humans to begin and end a meal? A role for memory for what has been eaten, as evidenced by a study of multiple meal eating in amnesic patients. *Psychological Science, 9*, 392–396.

Rozin, P., Haidt, J., & McCauley, C. (1993). Disgust. In M. Lewis & J. Haviland (Eds.), *Handbook of emotions* (pp. 575–594). New York: Guilford Press.

Rozin, P., Markwith, M., & Stoess, C. (1997). Moralization: Becoming a vegetarian, the conversion of preferences into values and the recruitment of disgust. *Psychological Science, 8*, 67–73.

Rozin, P., Millman, L., & Nemeroff, C. (1986). Operation of the laws of sympathetic magic in disgust and other domains. *Journal of Personality and Social Psychology, 50*, 703–712.

Rozin, P., & Singh, L. (1999). The moralization of cigarette smoking in America. *Journal of Consumer Behavior, 8*, 321–337.

Russell, J. A. (1980). A circumplex model of affect. *Journal of Personality and Social Psychology, 39*, 1169–1178.

Russell, J. A. (1993). Forced-choice response format in the study of facial expression. *Motivation and Emotion, 17*, 41–51.

Russell, J. A. (1994). Is there universal recognition of emotion from facial expression? A review of cross-cultural studies. *Psychological Bulletin, 115*, 102–141.

Russell, J. A. (1995). Facial expressions of emotion: What lies beyond minimal universality. *Psychological Bulletin, 118*, 379–391.

Ryle, G. (1949). *The concept of mind*. Chicago: University of Chicago Press.

Sabini, J., Siepmann, M., Stein, J., & Meyerowitz, M. (2000). Who is embarrassed by what? *Cognition and Emotion, 14*, 213–240.

Sabini, J., & Silver, M. (1998). Emotions, responsibility, and character. In *Emotion, character, and responsibility*. Oxford: Oxford University Press.

Schachter, S., & Singer, C. (1962). Cognitive, social, and physiological determinants of emotional state. *Psychological Review, 69*, 379–399.

Schank, R., & Abelson, R. (1977). *Scripts, plans, goals and understanding*. Hillsdale, NJ: Erlbaum.

Scher, S., & Rauscher, F. (2002). *Evolutionary psychology: Alternative approaches*. Dordrecht: Kluwer.

Scherer, K. (1993). Studying the emotion-antecedent appraisal process: An expert system approach. *Cognition and Emotion, 7*, 325–356.

Scherer, K., Matsumoto, D., Wallbott, H., & Kudoh, T. (1988). Emotional experience in cultural context: A comparison between Europe, Japan, and the USA. In K. Scherer (Ed.), *Facets of emotion: Recent research* (pp. 5–30). Hillsdale, NJ: Erlbaum.

Scherer, K. R. (1984). On the nature and function of emotion: A component process approach. In K.R. Scherer & P. Ekman (Eds.), *Approaches to emotion* (pp. 293–317). Hillsdale, NJ: Erlbaum.

Scherer, K. R., & Wallbott, H. G. (1994). Evidence for universality and cultural variation of differential emotion response patterning. *Journal of Personality and Social Psychology, 66*, 310–328.

Seguin, E. G. (1886). A contribution to the pathology of hemianopsis of centeal origin (cortex-hemianopsia). *Journal of Nervous and Mental Diseases, 13*, 1–38.

Sellars, W. (1963). Philosophy and the scientific image of man. In *Science, perception and reality*. London: Routledge & Kegan Paul.

Shaver, P., Hazan, C., & Bradshaw, D. (1988). Love as attachment: The integration of three behavioral systems. In R. J. Sternberg & M. L. Barnes (Eds.), *The psychology of love* (pp. 68–99). New Haven: Yale University Press

Shin, L. M., Dougherty, D. D., Orr, S. P., Pitman, R. K., Lasko, M., Macklin, M. L., Alpert, N. M., Fischman, A. J., & Rauch, S. L. (2000). Activation of anterior paralimbic structures during guilt-related script-driven imagery. *Biological Psychiatry, 48*, 43–50.

Shipko, S. (1982). Alexithymia and somatization. *Psychotherepy and Psychosomatics, 37*, 193–201.

Simons R. C. (1996). *Boo! Culture, experience, and the startle reflex*. New York: Oxford University Press.

Simons, R. C., & Hughes, C. C. (1993). Culture-bound syndromes. In A. C. Gaw (Ed.), *Culture, ethnicity, and mental illness* (pp. 75–93). Washington, DC: American Psychiatric Press.

Singer, W., & Gray, C. M. (1995). Visual feature integration and the temporal correlation hypothesis. *Annual Review of Neuroscience, 18*, 555–586.

Sizer, L. (2000). Towards a computational theory of mood. *British Journal for the Philosophy of Science, 51*, 743–769.

Skinner, B. F. (1953). *Science and human behavior*. New York: Free Press.

Smith, C.A., & Ellsworth, P.C. (1985). Patterns of cognitive appraisal in emotion. *Journal of Personality and Social Psychology, 48*, 813–838.

Smith, C. A., & Lazarus, R. S. (1993). Appraisal components, core relational themes, and the emotions. *Cognition and Emotion, 7*, 233–269.

Smith, J. (1981). Self and experience in Maori culture. In P. Heelas & A. Lock (Eds.), *Indiginous psychologies* (pp. 145–159). London: Academic Press.

Solomon, R.C. (1976). *The passions*. New York: Doubleday.

Solomon, R. L. (1980). The opponent-process theory of acquired motivation. *American Psychologist, 35*, 691–712.

Sorenson, E. R. (1975). Culture and the expression of emotion. In T. R. Williams (Ed.), *Psychological anthropology* (pp. 361–372). Chicago: Aldine Press.

Spinoza, Benedict De. (1677/1994). *Ethics.* In *A Spinoza reader* (E. Curley, Trans. and Ed.). Princeton: Princeton University Press.

Stampe. E. (1987). The authority of desire. *Philosophical Review, 96,* 335–381.

Sroufe, L. A. (1984). The organization of emotional development. In K. Scherer & P. Ekman (Eds.), *Approaches to emotion* (pp. 109–128). Hillsdale, NJ: Erlbaum.

Stein, N. L., Trabasso, T., & Liwag, M. (1993). The representation and organization of emotional experience: Unfolding the emotion episode. In M. Lewis & J. M. Haviland (Eds.), *Handbook of emotions* (pp. 279–300). New York: Guilford Press.

Sternberg, R. J. (1986). A triangular theory of love. *Psychological Review, 93,* 119–135.

Stich, S. P. (1990). Rationality. In D. N. Osherson & E. E. Smith (Eds.), *Thinking: An invitation to cognitive science* (Vol. 3, pp. 173–198). Cambridge: MIT Press.

Stich, S.P., & Warfield, T. (1994). *Mental representation: A reader.* Oxford: Blackwell.

Strack, F., Martin, L. L., & Stepper, S. (1988). Inhibiting and facilitating conditions of facial expressions: A nonobtrusive test of the facial feedback hypothesis. *Journal of Personality and Social Psychology, 54,* 768–777.

Strahan, E., Spencer, S. J., & Zanna, M. P. (2002). Subliminal priming and persuasion: Striking while the iron is hot. *Journal of Experimental Social Psychology, 38,* 556–568.

Sullivan, P., Neale, M., & Kendler, K. (2000). Genetic epidemiology of major depression: Review and meta-analysis. *American Journal of Psychiatry, 157,* 1552–1562.

Sutton, S. K., & Davidson, R. J. (1997). Prefrontal brain asymmetry: A biological substrate of the behavioral approach and inhibition systems. *Psychological Science, 8,* 204–10

Tellegen, A., Lykken, D., Bouchard, T. J., Wilcox, K. J., Segal, N. J., & Rich, S. (1988). Personality similarity in twins reared apart and together. *Journal of Personality and Social Psychology, 54,* 1031–1039.

Thalberg, I. (1964). Emotion and thought. *American Philosophical Quarterly 1,* 45–55. (Selection reprinted in C. Calhoun & R. Solomon, *What is an emotion?* [pp. 291–304], 1970, New York: Oxford University Press.)

Tomkins, S. S. (1962). *Affect, imagery and consciousness.* New York: Springer.

Tomkins, S. S. (1979). Script theory: Differential magnification of affects. In H. E. Howe Jr., & R. A. Dienstbier (Eds.), *Nebraska Symposium on Motivation 1978* (Vol. 26, pp. 201–236). Lincoln: University of Nebraska Press.

Tooby, J., & Cosmides, L. (1990). The past explains the present: Emotion adaptations and the structure of ancestral environment. *Ethology and Sociobiology, 11,* 375–424.

Triandis, H.C. (1988). Collectivism vs. individualism: A reconceptualization of basic concept in cross-cultural psychology. In G. Verma & C. Bagley (Eds.), *Cross-cultural studies of personality, attitudes, and cognition* (pp. 60–95). London: Macmillan.

Trimble, J. E., Manson, S. M., Dinges, N. G., & Medicine, B. (1984). American Indian concepts of mental health: Reflections and directions. In P. B. Pedersen, N. Sartorius, & A. J. Marsella (Eds.), *Mental health services: The cross-cultural context* (pp. 199–220). Beverly Hills, CA: Sage.

Trivers, R.L. (1971). The evolution of reciprocal altruism. *Quarterly Review of Biology, 46,* 35–57.

Tully, T., & Quinn, W.G. (1985). Classical conditioning and retention in normal and mutant Drosophila melanogaster. *Journal of Comparative Physiology, A, 157,* 263–277.

Turnbull, C. M. (1972). *The mountain people.* New York: Simon and Schuster.

Updike, J. (1965). The Bulgarian poetess. In *The music school: Short stories* (pp. 211–231) New York: Knopf.

Valins, S. (1966). Cognitive effects of false heart-rate feedback. *Journal of Personality and Social Psychology, 4,* 400–408.

Vogt, B. A., Finch, D. M., & Olson, C. R. (1992). Functional heterogeneity in cingulate cortex: The anterior executive and posterior evaluative regions. *Cerebral Cortex, 2,* 435–443.

Wallace, J., & Sadella, E. (1966). Behavioral consequences of transgression: The effects of social recognition. *Journal of Experimental Research in Personality, 1,* 187–194.

Walton, K. (1978). Fearing fictions. *Journal of Philosophy, 75,* 5–27.

Warner, R. (1980). Enjoyment. *Philosophical Review, 89,* 507–526.

Watson, D., & Tellegen, A. (1985). Toward a consensual structure of mood. *Psychological Bullettin, 98,* 219–235.

Watson, J. B. (1919). *Psychology from the standpoint of a behaviorist.* Philadelphia: Lippincott.

Weiner, B. (1985). An attributional theory of achievement motivation and emotion. *Psychological Review, 92,* 548–573.

Weiskrantz, L. (1968). Emotion. In L. Weiskrantz (Ed.), *Analysis of behavioural change* (pp. 50–90). New York: Harper and Row.

Weiskrantz, L. (1986). *Blindsight: A case study and implications.* Oxford: Clarendon Press.

White, G. (1993). Emotions inside out: The anthropology of affect. In M. Lewis & J. M. Haviland (Eds.), *Handbook of emotions* (pp. 29–39). New York: Guilford.

Wierzbicka, A. (1999). *Emotions across languages and cultures: Diversity and universals.* Cambridge, UK: Cambridge University Press.

Wilkes, K. V. (1988).—, yishi, duh, um, and consciousness. In A. J. Marcel & E. Bisiach (Eds.), *Consciousness in contemporary science* (pp. 16–41). Oxford: Clarendon Press.

Williams, B. (1973). Morality and the emotions. In *Problems of the self.* Cambridge, UK: Cambridge University Press.

Wimmer, H., & Perner, J. (1983). Beliefs about beliefs: Representation and constraining function of wrong beliefs in young children's understanding of deception. *Cognition, 13,* 103–128.

Wollheim, R. (1999). *On the emotions.* New Haven: Yale University Press.

Wood, L. A. (1986). Loneliness. In R. Harré (Ed.), *The social construction of emotions* (pp. 184–208). Oxford: Blackwell.

Woodworth, R. S. (1918). *Dynamic psychology.* New York: Columbia University Press

Yap, P. M. (1965). Koro: A culture-bound depersonalization syndrome. *British Journal of Psychiatry, 3,* 43–50.

Yap P. M. (1974). *Comparative psychiatry: A theoretical framework.* Toronto: University of Toronto Press.

Young, A. M. J., Joseph, M. H., & Gray, J. A. (1993). Latent inhibition of conditioned dopamine release in rat nucleus accumbens. *Neuroscience, 54,* 5–9.

Zajonc, R. B. (1984). On the primacy of affect. *American Psychologist, 39,* 117–123.

Zajonc, R. B. (1994). Evidence for nonconscious emotions. In P. Ekman & R. J. Davidson (Eds.), *The nature of emotion: Fundamental questions* (pp. 293–297). New York: Oxford University Press.

Zajonc, R. B., Murphy, S. T., & Inglehart, M. (1989). Feeling and facial efference: Implications of the vascular theory of emotion. *Psychological Review, 96,* 395–416.

Zajonc, R. B., Murphy, S. T., & McIntosh, D. N. (1993). Brain temperature and subjective emotional experience. In M. Lewis & J. M. Haviland (Eds.), *Handbook of emotions* (pp. 209–220). New York: Guilford.

# Index

action tendencies, 7, 10, 11, 17, 193–194
affect programs, 17–18, 81–82, 84–86
akinetic mutism, 214–216
alexithymia, 217
Alloy, Lauren, 8, 243
*amae*, 131, 136, 140, 147
Amaral, David, 34, 115
amygdala, 34–35, 38–39, 107, 162, 234, 236
Anderson, Adam, 234
anger, 8, 13, 28–29, 71–72, 75, 112, 144
  actions associated with, 110–111, 193–194
  as a basic emotion, 87, 151
  cognitive effects of, 243
  content of, 15, 16, 227
  as culturally specific, 132–133, 137, 141
  as mood, 183
  in nonbasic emotions, 92, 93, 99, 145–147, 149
  physiology of, 73
  valence of, 168
animals, 33, 36, 74–75, 106–107, 114–115
anterior cingulate cortex, 170, 177, 212, 214–216
appraisals, 52, 77 (*see also* embodied appraisals)
  defined, 14
  molecular and molar, 15–16, 31
appraisal theory, dimensional, 14–17, 24–25, 30–33, 85–86, 91n. 6, 168 (*see also* cognitive theories)
Aristotle, 10–11, 193
Armon-Jones, Claire, 9, 26, 48, 133, 183
Arnold, Magda, 14, 17, 19
as-if loop, 6, 58, 72
attachment, 123–124, 145, 156
attended intermediate-level representations

(AIRs), 209–218 (*see also* consciousness)
attention, 8, 200–201, 209–210, 217, 243
attribution theory. *See* cognitive labeling theory
Averill, James, 132, 133, 136

Bach-y-Rita, Paul, 23
Bartels, Andreas, 96
basic emotions, 82, 86–97, 101–102, 144
  (*see also* nonbasic emotions)
  proposed lists of, 87, 150–156
  tests for, 88–90
Bates, Elizabeth, 232
Bedford, Erroll, 8, 27
behavioral activation and inhibition systems (BIS/BAS), 169–173
behavioral theories, 7
Benedict, Ruth, 141
Ben Ze'ev, Aaron, 19, 24
Berridge, Kent, 170, 195–196, 203
biological reductionism, 104–105, 114, 117, 129–130, 134
Bisiach, Edoardo, 209
blending. *See* nonbasic emotions
Bless, Herbert, 7
Block, Ned, 42, 203–204, 207
blushing, 125, 126, 156
bodily changes. *See also* embodied appraisals
  allegedly absent in emotions, 25, 94–95, 139, 180–181, 296
  as content of emotions, 58–60, 68–69, 212–214
  emotion specific, 72–74
  essential to emotions, 56–58
  present in emotions, 4–5, 163
  prototypes of, 72–73